$\sqrt{}$ $7.50
B&T

Forms
of
Tragedy

edited by

JAMES L. CALDERWOOD

HAROLD E. TOLIVER

university of california, irvine

Prentice-Hall, Inc.
englewood cliffs, new jersey

PRENTICE-HALL ENGLISH LITERATURE SERIES
Maynard Mack, *editor*

ISBN: 0-13-329250-9

Library of Congress Catalog Card Number: 79-181402

Printed in the United States of America

10   9   8   7   6   5   4   3   2   1

Prentice-Hall International, Inc., *London*
Prentice-Hall of Australia, Pty. Ltd., *Sydney*
Prentice-Hall of Canada, Ltd., *Toronto*
Prentice-Hall of India Private Limited, *New Delhi*
Prentice-Hall of Japan, Inc., *Tokyo*

Table
of
Contents

iii 59901

Preface

THIS ANTHOLOGY IS DESIGNED for college courses devoted either wholly or in part to the study of dramatic tragedy. It presents eight plays ranging from Sophocles to Jean Anouilh, selected for their literary distinction, not to provide comprehensive historical coverage: All ages may have venerated tragedy, but few have produced it. Indeed, some instructors will suspect that we have not produced it ourselves on all occasions in this text. Few selections of great tragedy would pass unchallenged. And appropriately so: As that Linnaeus of dramatic form, Polonius, implied with his plays "tragical-comical-historical-pastoral," no genre rests in a state of unsullied purity, neatly distinct. We have called this book *Forms of Tragedy* instead of *Tragedies* to suggest a certain flexibility and movement within—and even, in one or two instances, across the borders of—a literary province whose geography can never be exactly defined. That is not to say, however, that we are making a plea for generic permissiveness. At a time when the concept of tragedy is eroding under the windy uses to which the word itself is increasingly put, students need to work from, not toward, vagueness. Thus in the "Introduction to Tragedy" we have tried to negotiate between purity and permissiveness, suggesting that tragedy is somewhat freer than neoclassic prescriptions would imply and at the same time not so amorphous that it can become merely a catch-all category for plays that make students feel sad. The biographical notes attempt to set each play within the context of its author's literary career, and the headnotes make some preliminary connections between the form of tragedy and that of the individual play.

It goes without saying that the object of presenting plays under the heading of tragedy is not to qualify the student in the art of literary pigeonholing or to teach him in reading drama to hold individual plays up against generic paradigms and to check off criteria before admitting one to the inner sanctum of tragedy while banishing others to less hallowed precincts. Generic study is concerned with forms, not formulas—with dramatic categories sufficiently complex, capacious, and meaningful to do at least partial justice to the rich and elusive variety of individual plays. Though the student will discover that each play possesses its own distinctive integrity, he should also discover that its individuality is most readily apparent if it is first placed in the company of others of its kind and then distinguished from them.

JLC
HET
University of California, Irvine

Introduction to Tragedy

UNLIKE THE NAMES for some literary forms such as satire and novel, tragedy has both literary and popular meanings; and in the normal way of the world the popular meanings, which may be acquired with a small expenditure of intellectual capital, tend to drive the literary ones out of the marketplace. In newspapers and magazines the words "Tragedy Strikes" can caption stories about falling airplanes and rising taxes, disease, unease, death, divorce, tidal waves, broken bones or hopes, and lost kittens. Blessed with this sort of unlimited semantic stretch, tragedy becomes cursed also with attenuated significance: Meaning everything, it means nothing, or at best it merges into the indistinct conceptual haze of misfortune, adversity, and mischance. Though the word itself enjoys great currency, for too many people the concept has in effect ceased to exist.

TRAGEDY AND RITUAL

One way of restoring meaning to tragedy is by returning to early concepts of tragic form and their origins in ritual. In his *Poetics* (c. 330 B.C.) Aristotle says that tragedy arose not as a deliberate literary invention but as a gradual development from the "dithyramb"—a choric hymn in honor of the god Dionysus, who was sometimes called *dithyrambos* or, figuratively, "twice-born." Scholars differ about the precise connection between Dionysiac ritual and Greek tragedy, but one view suggests that the significance of the term *tragoidia* (from *tragon oide*, "song of goats") lies in the fact that the goat, traditionally associated with virility, was sacred to Dionysus and that Dionysiac ritual involved a symbolic *sparagmos* (dismemberment) of the god in which the goat as god-surrogate was torn apart and eaten. The purpose of such a rite may have been to foster communion with Dionysus, to enable his worshipers to absorb into themselves and hence to become one with the god (*entheos*), as in the Christian Eucharist.

Like the Babylonian Tammuz, the Phrygian Attis, and the Egyptian

1

Osiris (with whom the Greeks specifically identified him), Dionysus was a vegetation deity or life-spirit, a dying and reviving god whose cyclic rhythm paralleled the seasonal dying and reviving of life in nature; and since time was based on the seasons, he was also a year-daemon who enacted the annual death and rebirth of time. The sprouting of plants in the spring, especially the vine sacred to him, marked the god's birth or rebirth —the bursting forth of impulse and desire, the procreative marriage of god and earth mother—and was celebrated at the vernal equinox in Athens by a festival called the City Dionysia. After the harvest in the fall, the god died and vegetation faded as winter came on. Perhaps the god died *because* of the harvest, like the Phrygian vegetation god Lityerses, who was slain, it was thought, by the sickles of the reapers. At any rate the god's death was somehow the fault of the community and had to be atoned for. A *pharmakos* or scapegoat sacrifice—probably at first human and then later on animal—may have been chosen to serve as the community's "container" of sin and guilt, so that through his death or banishment the community was magically purged of wrongdoing, the god propitiated, and the slate of time wiped clean in preparation for the new year, the reborn god. Many modern scholars feel that the structure of tragedy derives from the cyclic rhythm of the dying and reviving god and that the tragic hero may be likened to both the god himself and the *pharmakos*.

Of specific features of the seasonal ritual little is known for certain, but its drunken orgiastic character bears small likeness to Greek tragedy in general. The ritual may have included an *agon*, or "contest," between the god and his enemies (life against death, light against darkness, summer against winter); a *pathos*, or scene-of-suffering, in which the god is slain, the *pharmakos* driven out, the king dismembered; a *threnos*, or "lamentation," for the dead god; an *anagnorisis*, or "discovery" and recognition of the dead god by his searching followers; and a *theophany*, or rebirth-resurrection of the god. The Greek historian Herodotus (484?–425? B.C.) said that Dionysiac rites in Greece resembled those honoring Isis and Osiris which he observed in Egypt, and central to these was a sacred drama in which worshipers re-enacted in a lakeside theater the story of Osiris' sufferings, death, and rebirth. In Egyptian mythology Osiris, son of sky and earth gods, was attacked and dismembered by his brother Set and his body scattered over the land like seed. After a long search his grieving sister-wife Isis found his fragmented body and with the help of the god Anubis and others sewed it together again, whereupon Osiris acquired eternal life as king of the underworld. Similarly, in Greek mythology, Dionysus Zagreus was caught and dismembered by the Titans and subsequently revivified by his grandmother Rhea. If the Egyptian myth gave rise to the ritual (or vice versa) of Osiris—if it served as a kind of script for the sacred drama witnessed by Herodotus—a similar development may have taken place in Greece, with the ritual drama gradually changing, losing some of its sacred character, and acquiring the features of Greek drama as we know it.

All of this is highly speculative of course, but it is curious that the death-search-discovery-resurrection sequence hypothesized of Greek and

Egyptian rituals is also apparent in what is called the *Quem Quaeritis* ("Whom do you seek") trope of the medieval Church liturgy, perhaps the earliest evidence of "drama" in Western culture after the Roman Church had itself outlawed drama around 700 A.D. An interpolation into the Introit or first phase of the Easter Mass, the *Quem Quaeritis* trope takes the form of a very brief ritual scene in which three women (actually priests) carrying spices with which to anoint the body of the crucified Jesus and "stepping delicately as though seeking something" approach the sepulchre (the altar in this case) where a priest playing an angel asks "Whom do you seek in the sepulchre, followers of Christ?" They reply that they are searching for the body of the crucified Christ. The angel informs them "He is risen!" And everyone rejoices.

From such an inauspicious matrix as this, English drama arose, passed through the stages of miracle and morality play, assimilated elements from native folk drama and festivals and later from classical drama, and finally flowered in Elizabethan tragedy and comedy. Similarly, between early Dionysiac ritual and mature Attic drama there were surely other transitional forms, perhaps one of which was a rural folk drama on the order of the English Mummer's Play featuring the death by combat and subsequent resurrection of a god-hero. Somewhere along the line the ritual of death-and-rebirth suffered a dismemberment of its own, the suffering and dying phase going to tragedy, the resurrection and sacred marriage to the earth mother going to comedy. (Aristotle says that comedy derived from the phallic songs, which presumably celebrated the restoration of the god's —and nature's—sexual potency.)

TRAGIC INEVITABILITY

From the seasonal ritual, then, tragedy would appear to inherit a pattern of action originally based on the waxing and waning of the sun daily and of vegetation annually, a pattern traditionally associated with the rise and fall of the turning wheel. Like the myth-ritual of vegetation deities, which dramatizes the quickening and weakening pulse of life in all things, the tragic pattern of rise and fall (maturing and wasting, flowering and withering, etc.) is an abstraction from the life process of man and organic nature, a foreshortening and intensifying of that process in the interests of significant form. In dramatic tragedy this rise and fall becomes what Aristotle called the *metabasis,* the change of fortune from prosperity to adversity, which as Chaucer's Monk reminds us dominated the medieval view of tragedy:

> *I wol biwaille in manere of tragedye*
> *The harm of hem that stoode in heigh degree,*
> *And fillen so that ther nas no remedye*
> *To bringe hem out of hir adversitee.*

As an abstraction from the life process, the rise and fall pattern is significant not as an illustration of life or an assertion about reality but as a structural principle shaping the tragic form, like the quest that shapes the form of most romances. Thus whereas the quest tends to bring forth the erratic episodic plots normally found in romance, the rise and fall pattern lends itself to plots following a strict sequence of action and reaction and hence exhibiting the sort of inevitability suggested by the phrase "what goes up must come down." Aristotle apparently had this in mind in his over-obvious insistence on the need for a beginning, middle, and end to the tragic plot; for if tragedy, as distinguished from epic, were to be a representation of a single unified action, then each phase of that actoin must issue logically and causally from its predecessor.

What this amounts to in actual practice is an evolution of action in which possibilities become narrowed into probabilities and finally into inevitabilities. Accident, coincidence, and sheer whimsy pop up everywhere in comedy because the comic form is not grounded in casuality. For the sake of the comic ending we will gladly suffer the miraculous reformations of an Oliver or a Duke Frederick in Shakespeare's *As You Like It* or the *deus ex machina* of a King's Officer in Moliere's *Tartuffe*. But gratuitous string-pulling in serious plays meets more resistance. A plot dealing in unmotivated suffering and undeserved death suggests, not tragedy, but a kind of inverted melodrama. Even in a tragic masterpiece like *King Lear* the sense of action being manipulated in the death of Cordelia left eighteenth-century audiences feeling that inevitability had given way to perversity and afflicted a number of would-be tragic dramatists with an itch to correct Shakespeare.

If the tragic plot makes the action of rise and fall seem inevitable, something in the hero's situation when he is at the zenith of good fortune must necessitate his fall. The seasonal god of myth and ritual was destined to fall simply because it is a condition of nature that the sun waxes and then wanes, that life flowers and then fades. One view of tragedy holds that an equally impersonal and usually external law must govern the tragic hero. Critics of this persuasion point to the gods and fates of Greek tragedy, to prophecies, wheels of fortune, family curses, astrological omens, and other indices of what Pope called "supernatural machinery." In modern works this machinery may be naturalized. If malevolent gods *above* nature seem outmoded, then nature herself may be malevolent to man. In Hemingway's *A Farewell to Arms* Lieutenant Henry likens mankind to a colony of ants trapped on a burning log. Other external causes of tragedy—external to the hero, that is—may be the hero's society, which is in some way or other corrupt (like Hamlet's Denmark or the Norway of Ibsen's plays), or unavoidable cultural influences such as the family (as in *Desire Under the Elms* and other O'Neill plays). The more the dramatist stresses causes outside the hero working on or through him, the further his hero descends toward the status of victim—from active agent to passive prey.

Many plays, however, do not exhibit this sort of determinism. King Lear is not impelled by any external agency to divide his kingdom, put his evil daughters in power, and banish Cordelia. Lear *acts* and the world reacts.

In a nontragic play like *Riders to the Sea* it is just the reverse, as Synge's heroine Maurya reacts to or suffers the deaths inflicted on her family by the sea. In *King Lear* the trigger of disaster is in man himself; in *Riders to the Sea* it is entirely outside man—in nature or in an abstract fatality somewhere behind the scenes that makes the sea its instrument. In *Lear* man is an active agent shaping his own destiny; in *Riders* he is a passive victim suffering a destiny imposed on him. In the former man's character participates in his fate, in the latter it has no meaningful bearing on his fate. Thus in *King Lear* we have tragedy; in *Riders to the Sea* a drama of pathos—moving, meaningful, but not tragic.

This does not mean that we can have tragedy only when a hero acts in perfect freedom of will, unaffected by outside influences. The cause of tragic action normally falls somewhere between the extremes of arbitrary fate and unlimited free will—in an indefinable territory where consciousness and compulsion collaborate. If the hero seems fated to act, his will ratifies his fate. If he seems to act freely, his act fashions a subsequent fate.

TRAGIC GUILT AND ACTION

With fate, free will, and suffering combining in tragedy, justice becomes a perennial issue for the dramatist, who generally stays within the extremes of totally deserved and totally undeserved punishment. The most influential formulation of the problem of justice in tragedy appears in Aristotle's *Poetics*. Having pointed out that the hero falls from prosperity into adversity—the tragic *metabasis*—Aristotle says that the act which precipitates this fall must be performed not as a deliberate evil but as a result of *hamartia*. Unfortunately, the meaning of *hamartia* is somewhat blurred. It is capable of being interpreted as a mere blunder, mistake, or error on the one hand and, on the other, as a moral or spiritual defect. As mere error, *hamartia* would imply a hero innocent of wrongdoing and hence unjustly punished; as a moral defect it would imply his guilt and the justice of his punishment. Neither position seems entirely satisfactory, as we shall see.

Hamartia is usually translated as "tragic flaw," and on the whole it has been taken to suggest some sort of moral failure on the hero's part. A major drawback to this notion of the flawed hero is that it implies a perfection of character apart from a single isolable shortcoming, on the analogy of a perfect vase with a single chip or crack. Tragic heroes, however, do not ordinarily fit this prescription. The assorted faults and frailties of the heroine in Strindberg's *Miss Julie,* of Raskolnikov in Dostoevski's *Crime and Punishment,* of Willie Loman in Miller's *Death of a Salesman* could be inventoried at impressive length. Even with heroes of a more heroic cut —Oedipus in *Oedipus Rex*, Shakespeare's Coriolanus, Milton's Samson— the idea of a single flaw is highly optimistic. Though normally higher in the chain of being than the rest of us, the tragic rero is still tethered to the human condition where vices and virtues are freely distributed.

Still, if most tragic heroes have their full quota of failings, some do not. The danger is that we shall set out on flaw-hunting expeditions through flawless territory, stalking about with high-powered Aristotelian weapons and bagging only a few undersized virtues. Given a critical permit, almost anyone will discover in himself a talent, sometimes bordering on genius, for detecting tragic flaws in unfortunate heroes. Not of course that there is any question about Macbeth's treasonous ambition or Medea's vindictiveness or Tamburlaine's compulsion to depopulate the earth. But it is not very persuasive to regard Prometheus' pity for mankind as a flaw of character or to discover in Antigone's decision to bury her brother's body a species of moral frailty. These are by no means unflawed, morally perfect characters, but the flaws they have do not cause or significantly contribute to the act from which their sufferings issue. And if we move still further along the moral spectrum, we come to characters like Eliot's Thomas Becket, Robert Bolt's Thomas More, Shaw's Saint Joan, and Christ in the Passion Play, at which point the search for operative moral flaws becomes an exercise in divination.

Unless we are to deny the high title of "goat-song" to works whose heroes are morally innocent sufferers, it would seem necessary to move beyond the notion of *hamartia* as a moral defect. Perhaps we can mark off a continuum of tragic guilt that ranges between two extremes, which we can call moral guilt and situational guilt. Moral guilt is the easier to identify since it can be incurred only when there are innocent alternatives to a given act. Macbeth, for instance, is morally guilty in murdering Duncan because an innocent alternative—not murdering Duncan—was available to him. For Orestes in Aeschylus' *Libation Bearers,* however, the alternative to murdering Clytemnestra is available only at the cost of disobeying the god Apollo and abandoning his duty to his father and king; and for Antigone in Sophocles' play of that title the alternative to burying Polynices involves betraying family honor and divine law. So too with Prometheus, Agamemnon in sacrificing Iphigenia, Socrates in Plato's *Apology,* Christ before Pilate, Cordelia in *King Lear,* Becket in *Murder in the Cathedral,* More in *A Man for All Seasons.* Each is caught between mutually exclusive imperatives: The laws of God and Caesar cannot both be honored at once, kings demand what conscience forbids, duty insists but love prohibits. In such situations any action entails a measure of guilt and leads to suffering.

At the opposite extreme from moral guilt, then, is situational guilt. Characters whose actions fall into this category are normally good men with whom we sympathize and whose sufferings we deplore while acknowledging their inevitability. Between the extreme points of moral and situational guilt lies an area in which situation conspires with moral failure in varying proportions to generate tragic sequences.

What is common to tragic heroes, this would suggest, is not that they act in either guilt or innocence, or that they act either with or without free will, but that they *act*—and suffer the consequences of acting. *Praxis,* Aristotle's term for dramatic action, seems an essential feature not only of the plot and presentation but of the tragic hero himself. Passive, uncommitted heroes whom the world acts upon—like the trapped characters in Maeterlinck's *The Intruder*—are not the stuff of which tragedy is made.

"Tragic guilt" thus includes but transcends both moral and situational guilt in that the hero is indicted for the "crime'" of action itself, whether good or bad. To say that action as such involves guilt probably puts something of a strain on the notion of guilt. What we mean is that a *significant* act—an act of commitment or assertion—is made oppressive by virtue of its preclusiveness, its incapacity to embrace more than a limited range of potential responses to a situation. That one commitment precludes others is of course a commonplace of human experience, giving rise to proverbs warning us of the dangers of putting all our eggs in one basket or reminding us that we cannot have our cake and eat it too. But tragedy is especially devoted to exploring the ways in which men suffer the consequences of preclusive acts. And a major consequence of such acts—one that makes the choice of action even more oppressive—is the fact that their preclusiveness reflects upon the actor. The hero's choice means that he performs *this* act and not another and hence that he becomes *this* and not another sort of character. So considered, tragic guilt centers in the inevitable reduction of freedom involved in any commitment to action, the reduction of human potential, the straitening of the self as it goes through the needle's eye of choice. (The ultimate implications of tragic guilt will be discussed a bit further on, when we come to the concept of *anagnorisis*.)

In tragedy, as A. C. Bradley has said, action issues from character; thus the tragic hero ought naturally to have a certain preclusiveness of character corresponding to the nature of the act he performs, even before he performs it. Like King Lear or Oedipus, he may be subject to an imperious whimsy leading to irrevocable acts and unexamined decisions. Often he has a form of intellectual tunnel-vision, like Camus' Caligula, who "sees nothing but his own idea," or Euripides' Pentheus, who is blind to the divinity in Dionysus. Clytemnestra, Faustus, Coriolanus, Phaedra, Ahab, Anouilh's Antigone—the obsessed hero runs the length and breadth of tragedy. Even when the hero acts deliberately, in full consciousness of conflicting values and imperatives, he is not the sort to seek compromises in an effort to do justice to both sides of an issue. It is in choruses, like those in *Agamemnon*, that we find worldly wisdom and a search for negotiable positions:

> *For Ruin is revealed the child*
> *Of not to be attempted actions . . .*
> *Measure is best.*

Measure, however, is not the goal of the tragic hero. He does not look for an Aristotelian golden mean but sets the issues in an *either/or* frame and commits himself irreversibly to one or the other. As Othello puts it:

> *Like to the Pontic Sea*
> *Whose icy current and compulsive course*
> *Ne'er feels retiring ebb, but keeps due on*
> *To the Propontic and the Hellespont,*
> *Even so my bloody thoughts, with violent pace,*
> *Shall ne'er look back, ne'er ebb to humble love,*

> *Till that a capable and wide revenge*
> *Swallow them up.*

So Oedipus keeps a compulsive course in his search for Laius' killer,
Racine's Phaedra in her love for Hippolytus, Ephraim Cabot (*Desire Under
the Elms*) in his devotion to the rocky land.

At one extreme, where the hero is in danger of not measuring up to
tragic status, we have the insentient character who acts impulsively because
he cannot perceive alternatives or consequences: Giovanni, for instance, in
Ford's *'Tis Pity She's a Whore,* whose incestuous passions defy all obstacles;
or Goethe's Egmont, whose blind naiveté hurries him to entrapment; or
Marlowe's Tamburlaine and Jonson's Sejanus, whose egoism and brutality
simply override all moral issues. At the other extreme, where the hero is
in danger of not "measuring down" to tragic stature, we find the profoundly
sentient character whose awareness of the complexities of his situation requires a prolonged preparation for action, as in the cases of Hamlet and
Eliot's Thomas Becket.

Thus the gradually constricting scope of the tragic plot as it moves from
the possible, to the probable, to the inevitable, has its interior counterpart
in the character of the tragic hero, so that both plot and character empha-
size the preclusiveness and irreversibility of tragic action. In addition to
the unyielding character of the hero, the irreversibility of his commitment
is usually reinforced by some kind of outside constraint. This may take the
form of the curse that cannot be revoked (for instance Theseus' invocation
to Poseidon to destroy Hippolytus), the legal sentence (Oedipus' doom of
death or banishment for Laius' killer), the pact or vow (Faustus' pact with
the devils, Othello's "sacred vow" of vengeance), or the authoritarian
decree (Lear's decision to divide his kingdom, Bernarda Alba's establish-
ment of an eight-year period of mourning).

But whatever the reason, whether from sense of duty, allegiance to
principle, rigidity of will, or sheer intransigence, the hero sticks to his
commitment. "Break what break will!" Oedipus cries as the truth grows
imminent. "I have sworn," Lear says of his banishing Cordelia, "I am
firm!" Macbeth is no less resolute in his weariness:

> *I am in blood*
> *Stepped in so far that, should I wade no more,*
> *Returning were as tedious as go o'er.*

And Camus' Caligula echoes Macbeth: "No, there's no return. I must go
on and on, until the consummation." The hero's initial act sets him on
rails, and in suffering the world's reaction he "bears it out even to the edge
of doom." That does not mean that he remains oblivious to the claims of
the world or to his own failures; but it does mean that he must retain the
dignity of his position under attack, that he must make some assertion of
self, register some impulse of resistance as the world closes in on him.
Were he merely to collapse, like Shakespeare's King John, or to recant
piously, like some heroes of morality plays, he would be something other
than a tragic character.

SUFFERING AND ACTION

This brings us to the second phase of tragedy, which Aristotle calls
pathos, "suffering." Although suffering may be suffering however it is generated, we need to distinguish pathetic from tragic suffering on the basis
of their different causes. For suffering to be tragic, we have suggested, it
must not simply descend on the hero from nowhere, like the safe that falls
on a pedestrian, but develop, rather, as a consequence of his own action.
Desdemona suffers and dies not because of her actions but because of
Othello's, and Duncan is destroyed by Macbeth, not himself. Cassandra in
Agamemnon, Oedipus' children in *Oedipus Rex,* Job and Abraham in the
Biblical tales, Ophelia in *Hamlet,* Oswald in Ibsen's *Ghosts,* Laura Wing-
field in Williams' *The Glass Menagerie,* the pathetic heroes in Stoppard's
Rosencrantz and Guildenstern Are Dead—all these are characters primarily
acted upon rather than acting, recipients of unexpected and inexplicable
suffering.

If we call this kind of suffering pathetic instead of tragic, we are not
saying that it is somehow inferior to tragic suffering but only that it is
different in terms of its cause, nature, and meaning. Tragic heroes are not
born, as it were, but self-made. They may begin as victims of pathetic
suffering but then graduate to tragic status by acting. Racine's Phaedra,
for instance, is initially pictured as the victim of a family curse, literally
dying of the disease of love inflicted on her by Venus. But she does not let
the disease remain an affliction from the outside; she accepts it, making it
an instrument of her own will by declaring her feelings to Hippolytus and
later by accusing him to Theseus. Similarly, Hamlet is at first the victim
of a situation not of his own making, Othello the victim of Iago's malignity,
and Macbeth the victim of the witches' prophecies and his wife's instiga-
tions. But for these heroes suffering is not final. they transform it into a
matrix of subsequent action. Refusing to remain victims, they make victims of others.

Since it is unusual to find an entirely passive character in drama, it
is normally not so much *whether* he acts as how *significantly* he acts that
determines the tragic or nontragic nature of a character's suffering. What
constitutes an act of tragic significance is not easily defined in a way that
will apply to all tragic heroes. Perhaps we could say that it is an act of
engagement, commitment, or assertion in which the character of the hero
is concentrated or summed up, his self defined, his values, aspirations, and
impulses for good and evil condensed and clarified. On this view the child
who chases a ball into the street and is struck by a car acts, but not with
tragic significance. The airplane pilot who misreads his altimeter or mis-
judges the height of a peak suffers from errors of eyesight, not, like tragic
heroes, from failures of vision. We spoke earlier of Maurya, the heroine of
Synge's *Riders to the Sea,* who in suffering the deaths of her family never
acts, only reacts. Her last son, however, does act; he sets out for Galway
across the water to sell some horses at the fair, disregarding pleas that he

remain. Thus he comes nearer than Maurya to being a tragic character. But as his sister says, "It's the life of a young man to be going on the sea." What we witness is not an act of tragic significance in which the self is summoned into realization but an act of routine courage, of a man going stolidly about his daily and dangerous business.

For the most part so far, we have been stressing the hero's role as the radical individual who becomes increasingly isolated from his society through an uncompromising commitment to a course of action or because a single act has set him apart from others. Most tragic heroes do move toward isolation, usually in the form of death or banishment, and even before they reach this point they have become alienated from their normal world. Thus Christ, abandoned by his disciples and denied by Peter, cries out on the cross, "My God, why has Thou forsaken me?" Prometheus staked to his rock, Oedipus blinded, Faustus awaiting the devils, Lear on his "wheel of fire," Samson eyeless in Gaza, Halvard Solness falling from his scaffolding (*The Master Builder*), Lavinia Mannon in her shuttered house (*Mourning Becomes Electra*)—all present images of the isolated individual suffering for having asserted his will and values in the teeth of accepted norms, of having aspired like Icarus beyond the range of ordinary men. The mythic analogues to this aspect of the tragic hero are various self-assertive but suffering gods on the order of Prometheus, Dionysus, and Lucifer. Like them, the hero is a paradoxical figure. He is greater than us in his power for good and evil, goes beyond us in his drive for fulfillment and in the magnitude of the claims he makes for self or principle. But what is greater in him puts him in greater jeopardy than we to loss, to suffering, to death.

The self-deifying impulse in the tragic hero is usually crystalized in his social or political station; he is a king, general, nobleman—or if none of these, if merely, say, a father or an architect, he is nevertheless the leader or focal point of the world of the play. This initial connection between hero and his society is attenuated as his fortunes alter for the worse, but it is rarely broken because as he loses political or social power the hero often gains a form of medicinal power, becoming in some way a sacrificial figure. The Greek term for this, for the scapegoat, is *pharmakos,* a man or animal in which society's guilts and ills are magically deposited and whose destruction therefore restores society to health. The year-daemon—Attis, Osiris, Dionysus—begins his life in purity, grows old and bloated with the sins of the community as the year proceeds, and finally is slain as a pollution, thereby restoring time and society to a state of innocence. The limited political power that Christ might have exercized over the Jews was sacrificed to the much greater spiritual power He possessed as *pharmakos,* the divine scapegoat carrying off man's sins. Behind a number of tragic heroes we can see in varying degrees of clarity the paradoxical figure of the divine scapegoat. Oedipus is both the godlike deliverer of Thebes from the curse of the Sphinx *and* the incestuous murderer whose banishment is required for the city to be freed from the plague. Macbeth begins in glory, buying golden opinions from everyone as the queller of rebellions, but then becomes the very source of Scotland's contamination, the tyrant grown old in sin whose head must be carried in on the point of Macduff's pike before "the time is free." It is a comment on modern domestic tragedy that Willie Loman, whose name implies his unheroic stature, cannot aspire to godlike status but only to the level of *pharmakos* when he seeks through one last sale, of his insured life, to carry off the economic and social ills that have burdened his family.

The paradox of the *pharmakos* is that he is valuable to society precisely to the extent that he is contaminated. When Oedipus stands revealed as the murderer of Laius, he becomes laden with sin—but, because of that, with virtue too, since he now has the power to carry off the plague. From this standpoint the hero appears as the gutter of society's guilt, sin, corruption. It is not impossible, however, to regard him as the chalice that contains society's most sacred virtues. The saint, no less than the great sinner, may have an element of the *pharmakos* about him. If he does not miraculously take upon himself the sins of the world, from a more worldly standpoint he may, by suffering or death, relieve others from the burden of self-reproach, the oppressive consciousness of not measuring up to the unattainable ideal that he embodies. Merely by existing, the saint demands too much and hence becomes, like Joan of Arc in Shaw's play, "insufferable" to ordinary men. So Job's friends take a certain consolation from regarding his sufferings as the punishment of sin; anyone so afflicted must be guilty. Lowering Job may not elevate them much, but it normalizes their shortcomings and purges them by redefinition. Nobody kills saints without first killing off their claims to saintliness and redefining them as sinners, heretics, or imposters. And as with other *pharmakos* figures, the way down is the way up; pollution is transformed into spiritual power, debasement into sanctity. So it is with some tragic heroes. "They told me I was everything," Lear says, " 'tis a lie, I am not ague-proof." In the storm Lear must cast off along with his clothes his claims to majesty, reaching the rock bottom of the human condition before finding an order of recovery. Samson must play the role of muscular clown before the Philistines to earn the strength that topples the pillars. Oedipus must become a wandering pariah before he is spiritually transfigured in *Oedipus at Colonus*.

ANAGNORISIS

This raises the question of what emerges from tragic suffering. The hero acts, he suffers, and then what? The earliest relevant answer, given by Aeschylus, may still be the best: "Through suffering—wisdom." Aristotle says nothing about the nature of tragic wisdom—for him *anagnorisis* means recognition or discovery, the hero's realization of what he has done, and its virtue seems to lie in the fact that it arouses pity and fear in the audience. The German philosopher Hegel is more explicit. For him the end of a tragedy is marked by a recognition of cosmic justice. In his view the tragic hero is always a victim of what we have called earlier situational guilt: He has chosen one kind of "right" at the expense of others that have equal claims on him. The result of this choice is an imbalance in what

Hegel calls the Ethical Substance, an abstract Platonic entity which is the sum and source of all specific "rights'" or "goods." However, with the suffering and death of the offending agent, the hero, this imbalance is stabilized again. Out of the hero's sufferings, then, comes his awareness of the role he has unwittingly played in the grand scheme of things and his acknowledgement of the justice of a death that heals the breach he created in the Ethical Substance. Everything, it would appear, is ultimately for the best in this best of all possible tragic worlds.

Not, however, for Hegel's young competitor Schopenhauer. What we really see at the end of a tragedy, Schopenhauer claims, is not the triumph of justice but of evil, the triumph of a malign cosmic will that frustrates and inexorably destroys even the well-endowed and apparently powerful among us. Amid defeat and general chaos, all we and the tragic hero can achieve is a sense of tragic resignation, a stoical acceptance of the worst that can happen—an attitude very much like that recommended by medieval plays featuring the falls of noble men.

These two positions—the one involving a sense of reconciliation verging on optimism, the other a sense of resignation verging on despair—are useful not because they define the tragic vision but because they define its limits, the points at which tragedy begins to turn into something else: the melodrama of triumph, where at the end the hero's gains cancel out his losses, and at the other extreme the melodrama of disaster, where his losses cancel out his gains. At the upper limit, close to the drama of triumph, we find works like Aeschylus' *Eumenides,* Sophocles' *Electra,* Chaucer's *Troilus and Criseyde*, Milton's *Samson Agonistes,* Shaw's *Saint Joan,* and Eliot's *The Family Reunion.* Near the lower limit, where we approach (and in some cases reach) the literature of disaster and despair, we find works like Euripides' *Hecuba* and *The Trojan Women,* Shakespeare's *Troilus and Cressida,* Hardy's *Tess of the D'Urbervilles* and *Jude the Obscure,* Gorki's *The Lower Depths,* O'Neill's *The Iceman Cometh,* Ionesco's *The Chairs,* and Pinter's *The Dumbwaiter.*

The melodrama of triumph sees man only winning, that of disaster man only losing; but in the divided focus of the tragic vision victory and defeat become interinvolved. The hero's loss of material prosperity, power, or status in the eyes of others coalesces with his suffering and culminates in his death. But out of suffering and despite death something is gained—perception, insight, understanding, perhaps even wisdom—for which we can use Aristotle's term *anagnorisis.* To the victim of disaster in real life—the man stricken with a fatal disease, the mother whose child drowns, all those who die by accident and suffer by chance—suffering is an end in itself, a point beyond which there is nothing. Questions like "Where did I go wrong—or right?" and "What did I prove and was it worth it?" are unanswerable. All that remains is the blank inscrutable fact that what has happened has indeed happened. If *form* consists in a meaningful relation between parts, then disaster, which exhibits no relation between self and suffering, is at bottom formless, chaotic, disordered.

The tragic *anagnorisis,* on the other hand, is essentially a recognition of form, a discovery of how self, action, and suffering have cooperated to shape the experience of the hero. Thus we normally find the hero near the end of his play looking back on a point of change, a crucial decision, a fatal act that led through a series of consequences to the present moment, and seeing also how the present, carried by the momentum of time and action, drives on to a determined future—how, as Faustus says, "The stars move still, time runs, the clock will strike." According to the seventeenth-century philosopher Thomas Hobbes, "Hell is truth seen too late." The sight of it causes Oedipus to blind himself, Lady Macbeth to lapse into an endless ritual of purification, and Anouilh's Antigone to cry "Creon was right. It is terrible to die!"

If tragic truths are often appalling, the act of perceiving them is an achievement of mind and spirit in which the hero transcends both self and suffering. In a sense he breaks out of the limited role of a character locked into the plot of his play and achieves a vision *of* the play as a whole and of his role in it that is analogous to that of the playwright himself. From his new perspective the identity he felt he possessed is seen as an illusion, and he now recognizes his fallen self, as in Macbeth's—

> *My way of life*
> *Is fallen into the sear, the yellow leaf;*
> *And that which should accompany old age,*
> *As honor, love, obedience, troops of friends,*
> *I must not look to have—but in their stead*
> *Curses, not loud but deep, mouth-honor, breath*
> *Which the poor heart would fain deny, and dare not.*

Macbeth's bleak realization of how what he might have been has dwindled into what he now is underscores the preclusiveness of the tragic act as it reflects on the self. The hero's decision to act, to go a certain route, not only precludes other potential acts but contributes to the formation of a self that precludes others: He *is* what he has done. Thus to some extent the hero, as he realizes the form his life has taken, mourns the potential selves that have been lost to him. At the end of Camus' *Caligula* the hero addresses his image in a mirror, saying "I've stretched out my hands . . . but it's always you I find, you only, confronting me, and I've come to hate you. I have chosen a wrong path, a path that leads to nothing." Even Caligula's search for unlimited freedom has created, not an all-encompassing self, but an entirely limited and repellant identity—"you only." So Marlowe's Faustus laments the value he might have enjoyed: "For vain pleasure of twenty-four years hath Faustus lost eternal joy and felicity." And even Coriolanus, one of the least sentient of Shakespeare's tragic heroes, seeks in dying to transcend the degraded self he has become and recapture his heroic identity of earlier days.

Suffering for the tragic hero, then, however painful, is not merely a crushing defeat but an incitement to knowledge, awareness, vision. Even Prometheus, whose name means the "fore-thinker" and who knew in advance all that was to follow, continues to reassess and explore the issues involved in his tragedy, dominating his suffering not only through sustained defiance and courage but through repeated acts of understanding. Job,

too, though an innocent victim, acts like a tragic hero in making suffering an avenue to self-awareness. He does not simply cave in, on the one hand, nor automatically trumpet his innocence, on the other, but strives to master his experience through a re-examination of self, faith, and the mystery of justice.

The range and profundity of the *anagnorisis* will of course vary from hero to hero, but for *anagnorisis* to occur at all the hero must be endowed with a certain degree of vision and understanding. In this regard Willie Loman's status as a tragic hero is seriously in doubt, since he goes to his death with all his illusions about winning friends and influencing people still intact, unable really to see his sons Biff and Happy or, more damaging, even himself. As Biff says after his death, "He never knew who he was." At the other extreme, King Lear undergoes a sustained *anagnorisis* in which he graduates from a foolish, egoistic, willful old man who "hath ever but slenderly known himself" to one shot through with humility, compassion, and self-knowledge. Macbeth does not undergo a transformation of character like that of Lear, but as he perceives the inevitability of what lies before him he refuses to exchange the role of tragic hero for that of pathetic victim. Unlike a lesser man, he accepts responsibility for his fate, facing the withering knowledge of what he has become without shifting his guilt to fortune, the witches, or his wife. "The unexamined life," Socrates said, "is not worth living." For some tragic heroes, even the examined life may not seem worth living—but examine it they nevertheless do. As the concept of *anagnorisis* implies, tragic heroes, though they usually die, do not die blindly.

Biographical Note

SOPHOCLES

SOPHOCLES (496?–406 B.C.) was born in an Athenian suburb, Colonus, where his father Sophillus was a prosperous tradesman. Reputed to have been handsome, athletic, and well-liked, he played the leading role in his earliest plays but later gave up acting because of a weak voice. He married twice and had three children, one of whom (Iophon) later became a tragic dramatist also. In contrast to the good fortune that seems to have attended both his private life and his public career as playwright (he was supposed to have won first or second prize at the dramatic contests in Athens twenty-four times) his own plays are distinguished by a severe and grimly ironic tragic vision. Of the more than 100 plays he is said to have written, only seven have survived entire —*Ajax, Antigone, Electra, Oedipus at Colonus, Oedipus Rex, Philoctetes,* and *Trachiniae*—and an eighth, the satyr play *Ichneutae,* has survived in large part. Sophocles' contributions to the tragic theater include the addition of a third actor (one actor and a chorus originally presented the play; then Aeschylus added a second actor and Sophocles a third, who played various roles), the expansion of the chorus from twelve to fifteen members, and the use of painted scenery.

Oedipus Tyrannos

sophocles

In front of the palace of OEDIPUS *at Thebes. Near the altar stands the* PRIEST *with a large crowd of supplicants.*

[*Enter* OEDIPUS.]

OEDIPUS My children, why do you crowd and wait at my altars?
    Olive branches . . . and wreathes of sacred flowers—
    Why do you bring these, my people of Thebes? Your streets
    Are heavy with incense, solemn with prayers for healing,
    And when I heard your voices, I would not let   5
    My messengers tell me what you said. I came
    To be your messenger myself, Oedipus, whose name
    Is greatest known and greatest feared.
    (*to* PRIEST) Will you tell me, then? You have dignity enough
    To speak for them all—is it fear that makes you kneel   10
    Before me, or do you need my help? I am ready,
    Whatever you ask will be done . . . Come, I am not cold
    Or dead to feeling—I will have pity on you.
PRIEST King Oedipus, our master in Thebes, if you will look
    At your altars, and at the ages of those who kneel there,   15
    You will see children, too small to fly far from home;
    You will see old men, slow with the years they carry,
    And priests—I am a priest of Zeus; and you will see
    The finest warriors you have; the rest of your people
    Kneel, praying, in the open city, in the temples   20
    Of Athene, and in the shrine where we keep a flame
    Always alive and the ash whispers the future.
    Look about you. The whole city drowns
    And cannot lift its hand from the storm of death

* Sophocles, *Oedipus Rex*, trans. by Kenneth Cavander, published by Chandler Publishing Company, San Francisco.

In which it sinks: the green corn withers   25
In the fields, cattle die in the meadows.
Our wives weep in agony, and never give birth!
Apollo brings his fire like a drover and herds us
Into death, and nature is at war with herself.
Thebes is sick, every house deserted, and the blind   30
Prison of the dead grows rich with mourning
And our dying cries.
Eternal powers control our lives, and we do not
Think you are their equal; yet we pray to you, as your children,
Believing that you, more than any man, may direct   35
Events, and come to terms with the powers beyond us.
When the savage riddle of the Sphinx enslaved
Thebes, you came to set us free. We
Were powerless, we could not tell you how to answer her.
And now they say, and it is believed, that you   40
Were close to God when you raised our city from the dead.
Oedipus, we pray to your power, which can overcome
Sufferings we do not understand; guard us
From this evil. In heaven and earth there must
Be some answer to our prayer, and you may know it.   45
You have struggled once with the powers above us and been
Victorious; we trust that strength and believe your words.
Oedipus, you are the royal glory of Thebes—
Give us life; Oedipus—think. Because
You overpowered the evil in the Sphinx   50
We call you saviour still. Must we remember
Your reign for the greatness in which you began, and the sorrow
In which you ended? The country is sick, and you
Must heal us. You were once our luck, our fortune, the augury
Of good we looked for in the world outside. Fulfil   55
That augury now. You are king of Thebes, but consider:
Which is it better to rule—a kingdom? Or a desert?
What is a castle or a ship if there are
No men to give it life? Emptiness! Nothing!
OEDIPUS My children, I know your sorrows, I know why   60
You have come, and what you ask of me. I see
The pain of sickness in you all, and yet in all
That sickness, who is so sick as I? Each
Of you has one sorrow, his grief is his own—
But I must feel for my country, for myself,   65
And for you. That is why you did not find me
Deaf or indifferent to your prayers. No,
I have spent many tears, and in my thoughts
Travelled long journeys. And then I saw
That we could be saved in one way only;   70
I took that way and sent Creon, my brother-
In-law, to the Oracle of Apollo; there

The god will tell him how I can save the city—
The price may be an act of sacrifice, or perhaps
A vow, a prayer, will be enough ... But the days   75
Run on and the measure of time keeps pace with them
And I begin to fear. What is he doing?
I did not think he would stay so long—he should not
Stay so long ... But when he comes I will do
Whatever the god commands; if I disobeyed   80
It would be a sin.
PRIEST   Heaven listened then;
This messenger says that Creon is returning.
OEDIPUS My lord Apollo, let his news be the shining sun
That answers our prayers and guides us out of death!
PRIEST I can see him now ... the news must be good.   85
Look, there is a crown of bay thick with flowers
Covering his hair.
OEDIPUS   At last we shall know the truth.
If I shout, he will hear me ... Creon!
My brother, son of Menoeceus, Lord of Thebes,
What answer does Apollo send to us? Do you bring   90
An answer?

[*Enter* CREON.]

CREON Our danger is gone. This load of sorrow
Will be lifted if we follow the way
Where Apollo points.
OEDIPUS   What does this mean? I expected
Hope, or fear, but your answer gives me neither.
CREON I am ready to tell you my message now, if you wish;   95
But they can hear us, and if we go inside . . .
OEDIPUS Tell me now and let them hear! I must not think
Of myself; I grieve only when my people suffer.
CREON Then this is what I was told at Delphi:
Our land is tainted. We carry the guilt in our midst.   100
A foul disease, which will not be healed unless
We drive it out and deny it life.
OEDIPUS   But how
Shall we be clean? How did this happen to us?
CREON The crime of murder is followed by a storm.
Banish the murder and you banish the storm, kill   105
Again and you kill the storm.
OEDIPUS   But Apollo means
One man—who is this man?
CREON   My lord,
There was once a king of Thebes; he was our master
Before you came to rule our broken city.
OEDIPUS I have heard of him ... I never saw your king.   110

CREON Now that he is dead your mission from the god
    Is clear: take vengeance on his murderers!
OEDIPUS But where are they now? The crime is old,
    And time is stubborn with its secrets. How
    Can you ask me to find these men?
CREON   The god said   115
    You must search in Thebes; what is hunted can
    Be caught, only what we ignore escapes.
OEDIPUS Where was the murder? Was Laius killed in the city?
    Or did this happen in another country?
CREON   He was travelling
    To Delphi, he said. But he never returned to the palace   120
    He left that day.
OEDIPUS   Did no one see this?
    A messenger? The guard who watched his journey? You could
    Have questioned them.
CREON They were all killed, except
    One. He ran home in terror, and could only
    Repeat one thing.
OEDIPUS   What did he repeat?   125
    Once we have learnt one thing, we may learn the rest.
    This hope is the beginning of other hopes.
CREON He said they met some robbers who killed the king.
    He talked of an army, too strong for the servants of Laius.   130
OEDIPUS Robbers would not dare to kill a king—unless
    They had bribes. They must have had bribes from the city!
CREON We suspected that, but with Laius dead
    We were defenceless against our troubles.
OEDIPUS   Were
    Your troubles so great that they prevented you
    From knowing the truth? Your king had been murdered . . . !   135
CREON   But the Sphinx
    Had a riddle to which there was no answer, and we thought
    Of our closest sorrows. We had no time for other
    Mysteries.
OEDIPUS   But I will begin again, and make your mysteries   140
    Plain. Apollo was right, and you were right,
    To turn my thoughts to the king who died. Now
    You will see the measure of my power; I come to defend you.
    Avenging your country and the god Apollo.
    (*aside*) If I can drive out this corruption and make the city   145
    Whole, I shall do more than save my people,
    Who are my friends, but still my subjects—I shall save
    Myself. For the knife that murdered Laius may yet
    Drink from my heart, and the debt I pay to him
    Lies to my own credit.   150
    My children, quickly, leave this altar and take
    Your branches. I will have the people of Thebes assembled

To hear that I shall do all the god commands.
And in the end we shall see my fortune smiling
From heaven, or my fall.

[*Exit* OEDIPUS.]

PRIEST Let us go, my sons; our king has given the order   155
    We came to hear. May Apollo, who sent this answer
    From his oracle, come to lay our sickness
    To rest, and give us life.

[*Exeunt* PRIEST, CREON, *and some of the elders.*]

[*Enter* CHORUS.]

CHORUS From golden Delphi Apollo replies to Thebes   160
    And the words of heaven send a warning.
    As a lyre is strung and tightened, so we
    Are tightened by fear.
    As a lyre trembles, so we tremble at the touch of fear.
    Apollo, god of healing, god of newness,
    We fear you, and the commands you send to humble us.   165
    Do you ask a new submission? Or is your command
    The same as we hear in every wind, and every season, and
        every year?
    Only the child of golden hope, whose voice
    Will never die, only the spirit of truth can tell us.   170
    First in my prayers is the goddess Athene, the daughter of Zeus;
    Second, her sister Artemis, who is queen in Thebes,
    For she sits at our country's heart, pure and honoured,
    In a temple like the sun. And third in our prayer
    Is Phoebus Apollo, whose arm reaches over all the world.
    Come three times to drive our wrongs before you!   175
    If ever in the past, when evil and blindness
    Rose like a wave, when grief was burning in our city,
    If ever you banished that grief,
    Come now to help us.

    There is no numbering our sorrows;   180
    The whole country is sick, and mortal will and human mind
    Are no weapons to defend us.
    The great earth whom we call our mother
    Is barren and dead; women weep in the pain of childbirth
    But they fall sick and die.   185
    Look, can you see the dying go following each other,
    Gliding like gentle birds, quicker
    Then the restless flash of fire that will never sleep,
    The dying on their flight to the shore

Where evening sits like a goddess?   190
The city of the dying goes countless away
And the children of life fall to the earth,
The toys of death,
With no pity and no remembering tears.

In the rest of our city wives and mothers   195
Stand grey at the altars,
Which tell us of a certainty resisting the seas of doubt;
They weep, pray, plead for release
From the harsh revenge which heaven brings.
A cry for healing rises and burns above the still crowd   200
That mourns in the city.
Send us strength that will look kindly on us,
Golden daughter of Zeus.
Ares, the god of war, confronts us, bitter in his cruelty,
And his shout burns like fire;   205
But his war is fought with no armour, and Ares
Carries no shield, for he brings his conflict
Into the moment of our birth and death.
Oh turn him flying down the winds, turn him
Back and dash him from our country   210
Into the wide chambers where Amphitrite sleeps,
Or to the lonely cliffs of Thrace where the seas
Allow no guests. For Ares comes to finish
The deadly work left undone by the night.
Zeus, you are the lord of lightning, lord of fire,   215
Destroy him with your thunder, crush our enemy!

Lord Apollo, god in the sun, we pray for your light;
Strike with your golden spears and your hands of fire,
Strike to protect us.
We pray for Artemis to bring her chaste fires,   220
Which we see her carry like a shining torch across
The mountains where the wolf runs.
I call you, the god with the golden crown,
Born in our country, Bacchus,
With the fire of wine in your cheek,   225
And the voice of wine in your shout,
Come with your pine branch burning, and your Maenads
Following the light, the fire of heaven's madness
In their eyes, come to guard us against the treacherous power
Who goes to war with justice and the harmony of heaven!   230

[*Enter* OEDIPUS.]

OEDIPUS You have told me of your need. Are you content
        To hear me speak, obey my words, and work

To humour the sickness? . . . Then you will thrust away
The weight with which you struggle, and fulfill
Your need. I am a stranger to this story,   235
And to the crime; I have no signs to guide me,
And so if I am to trap this murderer, my hunt
Must follow every hope. I am speaking, then,
To every citizen of Thebes, and I shall not
Exempt myself, although I am a citizen only   240
In name, and not in blood.
Whoever knows the murderer of Laius, son
Of Labdacus, must make his knowledge mine.
It is the king's command! And if he is afraid,
Or thinks he will escape, I say to him, "Speak!   245
You will go into exile, but you will go unharmed—
Banishment is all you have to fear."
Or if you know the assassin comes from another
Country, you must not be silent. I shall pay
The value of your knowledge, and your reward   250
Will be more than gratitude.
But if I find only silence, if you are afraid
To betray a friend or reveal yourself, and lock
The truth away, listen, this is my decree:
This murderer, no matter who he is, is banished   255
From the country where my power and my throne
Are supreme. No one must shelter him or speak to him;
When you pray to heaven, he must not pray with you;
When you sacrifice, drive him away, do not
Give him holy water, beat him from your doors!   260
He carries the taint of corruption with him—for so
The god Apollo has revealed to me . . . You see
How I serve the god and revenge the king who died!
I curse that murderer; if he is alone, I curse him!
If he shares his guilt with others, I curse him! May   265
His evil heart beat out its years in sorrow,
Throughout his life may he breathe the air of death!
If I give him shelter, knowing who
He is, and let him feel the warmth of my fire,
I ask this punishment for myself.   270
This must de done! In every word I speak
I command obedience, and so does the god Apollo,
And so does your country, which a barren sickness
And an angry heaven drag to death. But even
If it is not a god that comes to punish you   275
It would be shame to leave your land impure.
Your king was killed—he was a royal and noble
Man; hunt his murderer down!
I live in Laius' palace, my queen was once
The queen of Laius, and if his line had prospered   280

His children would have shared my love.
But now time has struck his head to earth
And in revenge I will fight for him as I
Would fight for my own father. My search will never
End until I take in chains the murderer   285
Of Laius, son of Labdacus. I pray heaven
That those who will not help me may watch the soil
They have ploughed crumble and turn black, let them see
Their women barren, let them be destroyed by the fury
That scourges us, but may it rage more cruelly!   290
And for all the Thebans who will obey me gladly
I ask the strength of justice, and the power of heaven.
So we shall live in peace; so we shall be healed.
CHORUS Your curse menaces me, my lord, if I lie.
    I swear I did not kill him, nor can I tell   295
    Who did. Apollo sent the reply, and Apollo
    Should find the murderer.
OEDIPUS   Yes, we believe
    It is Apollo's task—but we cannot make
    The gods our slaves; we must act for ourselves.
CHORUS   Our next
    Hope then, must be . . .
OEDIPUS   And every hope   300
    You have. When I search, nothing escapes.
CHORUS We know a lord who sees as clearly as the lord
    Apollo—Teiresias; we could ask Teiresias, my king,
    And be given the truth.
OEDIPUS   Creon told me, and his advice
    Did not lie idle for want of action. I have sent   305
    Two servants . . . It is strange they are not here.
CHORUS And there are the old rumours—but they tell us
    nothing . . .
OEDIPUS What do these rumours say? I must know
    Everything.
CHORUS   They say some travellers killed him.
OEDIPUS I have heard that too. But the man who saw those
    travellers   310
    Was never seen himself.
CHORUS   The murderer will leave our country;
    There is a part of every man that is ruled
    By fear, and when he hears you curse . . .
OEDIPUS   A sentence
    Holds no terror for the man who is not afraid
    To kill.
CHORUS But now he will be convicted. Look,   315
    They are leading your priest to you; Teiresias comes.
    When he speaks, it is the voice of heaven
    That we hear.

[*Enter* TEIRESIAS, *guided by a boy*.]

OEDIPUS   Teiresias, all things lie
   In your power, for you have harnessed all
   Knowledge and all mysteries; you know what heaven   320
   Hides, and what runs in the earth below, and you
   Must know, though you cannot see, the sickness with which
   Our country struggles. Defend us, my lord, and save us—
   We shall find no other defence or safety.
   For Apollo—and yet you must have heard the message—   325
   Apollo, whom we asked in our doubt, promised release—
   But on one condition: that we find the murderers
   Of Laius, and banish them, or repay the murder.
   Teiresias, the singing birds will tell you of the future,
   You have many ways of knowing the truth. Do not grudge   330
   Your knowledge, but save yourself and your city, save me,
   For murder defiles us all. Think of us
   As your prisoners, whose lives belong to you!
   To have the power and use that power for good
   Is work to bring you honour.
TEIRESIAS   When truth cannot help   335
   The man who knows, then it brings terror. I knew
   That truth, but I stifled it. I should not have come.
OEDIPUS What is it? You come as sadly as despair.
TEIRESIAS Send me away, I tell you! Then it will be easy
   For you to play the king, and I the priest.   340
OEDIPUS This is no reply. You cannot love Thebes—your own
   Country, Teiresias—if you hide what the gods tell you.
TEIRESIAS I see your words guiding you on the wrong
   Path; I pray for my own escape.
OEDIPUS   Teiresias!
   You do not turn away if you know the truth; we all   345
   Come like slaves to a king with our prayers to you.
TEIRESIAS But you come without the truth, and I can never
   Reveal my own sorrows, lest they become
   Yours.
OEDIPUS You cannot? Then you know and will not tell us!   350
   Instead, you plan treason and the city's death.
TEIRESIAS I mean to protect us both from pain. You search
   And probe, and it is all wasted. I will not tell you!
OEDIPUS You demon! You soul of evil! You would goad
   A thing of stone to fury. Will you never speak?   355
   Can you feel, can you suffer? Answer me, and end this!
TEIRESIAS You see wrong in my mood, you call me evil—blind
   To the mood that settles in you and rages there.
OEDIPUS Rages! Yes, that is what your words
   Have done, when they shout your contempt for Thebes.   360
TEIRESIAS The truth will come; my silence cannot hide it.

OEDIPUS And what must come is what you must tell me.

TEIRESIAS I can tell you no more, and on this answer let
    Your fury caper like a beast.

OEDIPUS It is
    A fury that will never leave me. Listen, I know   365
    What you are. I see now that you conspired to plan
    This murder, and you committed it—all but the stroke
    That killed him. If you had eyes, I would have said
    The crime was yours alone.

TEIRESIAS   Oedipus, I warn you!   370
    Obey your own decree and the oath you swore.
    Never from this day speak to me, or to these nobles;
    You are our corruption, the unholiness in our land.

OEDIPUS How you must despise me to flaunt your scorn like this.
    Thinking you will escape. How?

TEIRESIAS   I have escaped.
    I carry the truth; it is my child, and guards me.   375

OEDIPUS Truth! Who taught you? Heaven never taught you!

TEIRESIAS You taught me; you forced me to the point of speech.

OEDIPUS Repeat your words, I do not remember this speech.

TEIRESIAS You did not understand? Or do you try to trap me?

OEDIPUS I know nothing! Repeat your truth!   380

TEIRESIAS I said, you are the murderer you are searching for.

OEDIPUS Again you attack me, but I will not forgive you again!

TEIRESIAS Shall I say more to make your anger sprawl?

OEDIPUS All you have breath for—it will all be useless.

TEIRESIAS Then . . . you live with your dearest one in burning
    Shame, and do not know it; nor can you see   385
    The evil that surrounds you.

OEDIPUS Do you think
    You will always smile in freedom if you talk like this?

TEIRESIAS If truth can give strength, I will.

OEDIPUS   It can—
    But not to you; you have no truth. Your senses   390
    Have died in you—ears: deaf! eyes: blind!

TEIRESIAS Yes, be bitter, mock at me, poor Oedipus.
    Soon they will all mock as bitterly as you.

OEDIPUS You live in perpetual night; you cannot harm
    Me, nor anyone who moves in the light.

TEIRESIAS   Your downfall   395
    Will come, but I will not be the cause. Apollo
    Is a great power; he watches over the end.

OEDIPUS Did you or Creon plan this?

TEIRESIAS   Creon is not
    Your enemy; you carry your enemy with you—in your soul.

OEDIPUS We have wealth and power, the mind reaches higher,
    grows,   400
    Breaks its own fetters, our lives are great and envied,

And the world rewards us—with spitefulness and hate!
Consider my power—I did not come begging, the city
Laid its submission in my hands as a gift.
Yet, for this power, Creon, my trusted, my first   405
Friend, goes like a thief behind my back,
Tries to exile me, and sends this wizard,
This patcher of threadbare stories, this cunning peddler
Of the future, with no eyes except   410
For money, and certainly no eyes for mysteries.
Tell me, tell me, when did you ever foretell the truth?
When the Sphinx howled her mockeries and riddles
Why could you find no answer to free the city?
Her question was too hard for the simple man,
The humble man; only heaven's wisdom could find   415
A reply. But you found none! Neither your birds
Above you, nor the secret voice of your inspiration
Sent you knowledge—then we saw what you were!
But I came, ignorant Oedipus, and silenced her,
And my only weapon was in my mind and my will;   420
I had no omens to teach me. And this is the man
You would usurp! You think, when Creon is king
You will sit close to the throne; but I think
Your plans to drive the accursed away will return
To defeat you, and to defeat their architect.   425
You are old, Teiresias, or else your prophetic wisdom
Would have been your death.

CHORUS   Your majesty, what he has said
And your reply—they were both born in anger.
We do not need this wildness; we ask the best
Fulfilment of Apollo's commands. This must be the search.   430

TEIRESIAS [*to* OEDIPUS] You flourish your power; but you must give
    me the right
To make my reply, and that will have equal power.
I have not lived to be your servant, but Apollo's;
Nor am I found in the list of those whom Creon
Protects. You call me blind, you jeer at me—   435
I say your sight is not clear enough to see
Who shares your palace, nor the rooms in which you walk,
Nor the sorrow about you. Do you know who gave you birth?
You are the enemy of the dead, and of the living,
And do not know it. The curse is a two-edged sword,   440
From your mother, from your father; the curse will hunt you,
Like a destruction, from your country. Now
You have sight, but then you will go in blindness;
When you know the truth of your wedding night
All the world will bear your crying to rest,   445
Every hill a Cithaeron to echo you.
You thought that night was peace, like a gentle harbour—

But there was no harbour for that voyage, only grief.
Evil crowds upon you; you do not see
How it will level you with your children and reveal   450
Yourself as you truly are. Howl your abuse
At Creon and at me ... All men must suffer,
Oedipus, but none will find suffering more terrible
Than you.

OEDIPUS   Must I bear this? Must I be silent?
Die! Go to your death! Leave my palace now!   455
Get away from me!

TEIRESIAS Yet you called me here, or I would not have come.

OEDIPUS If I had known you would talk in the raving language
Of a madman, I would never have sent for you.

TEIRESIAS I am no more than you see. You see a madman,   460
The parents who gave you life saw a prophet.

OEDIPUS My parents? Wait! Who were my parents?

TEIRESIAS Today will be your parent, and your murderer.

OEDIPUS Always riddles, always lies and riddles!

TEIRESIAS You were best at solving riddles, were you not?   465

OEDIPUS When you think of my greatness, it inspires your mockery.

TEIRESIAS That greatness has conspired to be your traitor.

OEDIPUS I saved this country, I care for nothing else.

TEIRESIAS Then I shall go ... (*to his guide*) Boy, lead me away.

OEDIPUS Yes, lead him ... You come and trouble me—you are
nothing   470
But hindrance to my plans. Go, and I shall be safe.

TEIRESIAS I came to speak, and I shall not leave until I speak.
I need not cower at your frown, you cannot
Harm me. This man for whom you search,   475
Whom you threaten, and to the people call "the murderer
Of Laius," this man is here, a stranger, a foreigner;
But he will see his Theban blood, though he will not
Have any joy at the discovery.
He will be blind—though now he sees; a beggar—
Though now he is rich, and he will go feeling   480
Strange ground before him with a stick.
He is a father to children—then he will
Be called their brother; he is his mother's son—
Then he will be called her husband, then
He will be called his father's murderer.   485
Consider this when you walk between your palace walls;
If you find I have been false to you, then say
That all my prophetic wisdom is a lie.

[*Exeunt all but the* CHORUS.]

CHORUS In the rock at Delphi there is a cave
Which is the mouth of heaven; now   490

The cave warns us of one man, whose hands are red
With murder, and whose actions
Break the unspoken laws that shackle us.
Time tells him now to escape,
Faster than the jostling horses of the storm,   495
For Apollo, the son of Zeus, leaps down on him,
Armed with lightning, dressed in fire,
And the terrible avengers follow where he goes,
The Furies who never mistake and are never cheated.
From the snow of Parnassus over Delphi the message   500
Gleamed and came shining to Thebes.
We must all hunt the murderer
Who hides from justice. Like a lonely bull
He crosses and crosses our country, through the harsh forests,
The hollows of the mountains, and the rocks.   505
Sadly thinking and alone,
Sadly trying to escape
The words that came from Delphi, the heart of the world.
But their wings are always beating in his head.

The wisdom of the priest sets fear, fear, beating in our blood;   510
Truth or lies, nothing comforts, nothing denies.
The world is built out of our beliefs,
And when we lose those beliefs in doubt,
Our world is destroyed, and the present and the past
Vanish into night.   515
We must have proof, a certainty that we can touch
And feel, before we turn against Oedipus.
The land is peopled with rumours and whispers—
They cannot make us avenge King Laius,
Whose death is guarded by such mystery.   520

All that men may do is watched and remembered
By Zeus, and by Apollo. But they are gods;
Can any man, even the prophet, the priest,
Can even he know more than us?
And if he can, who will be judge of him, and say he lied   525
Or spoke the truth.
Yet wisdom may come to us, not the wisdom that sees
How the world is ruled, but the wisdom that guides
The modest life. In this alone we may excel.
But the proof must be clear and certain,   530
Before I can accuse Oedipus.
Remember that the Sphinx came flying
To meet him, evil beyond our comprehension,
And we saw his wisdom then, we knew and felt
The goodness of his heart towards our country.   535
Thoughts cannot be guilty traitors to such a man.

[*Enter* CREON.]

CREON Lords of Thebes, this message has called me here
　　　In terror . . . These crimes of which our king accuses me—
　　　No one would dare to think of them! If he
　　　Believes I could wrong him, or even speak of wrong,　　　540
　　　At such a time, when we are in such sorrow,
　　　Let me die! I have no wish to live out my years
　　　If I must live them suspected and despised.
　　　I will not bear this slander, which is no trifle
　　　To forget, but the greatest injury—the name　　　545
　　　Of traitor. The people will call me that, even
　　　You will call me that!
CHORUS　　　　　　　　His fury mastered him;
　　　Perhaps he did not mean the charge.
CREON　　　　　　　　　　　　He said
　　　To you all—you all heard—that the priest
　　　Had been told to lie, and that I had planned the answer?　　　550
CHORUS He said that, but I know he did not mean it.
CREON　　　　　　　　　　　　　And when he
　　　Accused me, he seemed master of his thoughts, and there was
　　　Reason in his voice?
CHORUS　　　　　　　I cannot remember,
　　　I do not observe my king so closely . . . But here
　　　He comes from the palace himself to meet you.

[*Enter* OEDIPUS.]

OEDIPUS So,　　　555
　　　My citizen, you have come to your king? Your eyes have great
　　　Courage—they can look on my palace out of a murderer's
　　　Face, a robber's face! Yes, I know you;
　　　You blaze, you thief of power . . . In heaven's name
　　　Tell me: when you planned to kill me, did you think I had　　　560
　　　Become a coward or a fool? Did you think I would not
　　　Notice your treason stalking me? Or were you sure
　　　That if I knew, I would not dare defence?
　　　See your insane attempt! You try to capture
　　　Power, which must be hunted with armies and gold;　　　565
　　　But no one will follow you, no one will make
　　　You rich!
CREON　　　Wait! You have accused, but you must not judge
　　　Until you have heard my defence; I can reply.
OEDIPUS You talk with the fangs of cleverness; but how
　　　Can I understand? I understand only　　　570
　　　That you are my enemy, and dangerous.
CREON There is one thing I must say; hear it first.
OEDIPUS One thing you must not say: "I am innocent."

CREON You are stubborn, Oedipus, your will is too hard;
    It is nothing to treasure, and you are wrong to think it is. 575
OEDIPUS Treason, crimes against a brother, will not
    Escape justice: you are wrong to think they will.
CREON I do not quarrel with your talk of justice.
    But tell me how I have harmed you: what is my crime?
OEDIPUS Did you persuade me—perhaps you did not—to send for 580
    The priest whom we used to worship for his wisdom?
CREON And I still have faith in that advice.
OEDIPUS   How long
    Is it since Laius . . .
CREON   What has Laius to do
    With this? I do not see . . .
OEDIPUS   Since he was hidden
    From the living sun, since he was attacked and killed? 585
CREON The years are old and the time is long since then.
OEDIPUS Was Teiresias already a priest and prophet then?
CREON As wise as now, and no less honoured and obeyed.
OEDIPUS But at the time he did not mention me?
CREON I did not hear him . . .
OEDIPUS   But surely you tried to find 590
    The murderer?
CREON   We searched, of course, we could discover
    Nothing.
OEDIPUS   If I was guilty, why did Teiresias
    Not accuse me then? He must have known, for he is wise.
CREON I do not know. If I cannot know the truth 595
    I would rather be silent.
OEDIPUS   But there is one truth
    You will confess to; none knows it better . . . ?
CREON What is that? I shall deny nothing . . .
OEDIPUS That only by some insidious plan of yours
    Could Teiresias ever say I murdered Laius!
CREON If he says that, I cannot unsay it for him; 600
    But give me an answer in return for mine.
OEDIPUS Question till you have no questions left;
    You cannot prove me a murderer.
CREON   Now,
    You have married my sister?
OEDIPUS   I do not deny it; the truth
    Was in your question.
CREON   You and she rule 605
    This country, you are equal?
OEDIPUS   If she has a wish
    I grant it all to her.
CREON   And am I not
    Considered equal to you both?
OEDIPUS   Yes, there your friendship

Shows the face of evil it concealed.
CREON No, reason to yourself as I have reasoned.   610
   First, imagine two ways of ruling, each
   Bringing equal power. With one of these fear
   Never leaves you, but with the other you sleep
   Calm in the night. Who do you think
   Would not choose the second? I feel no ambition   615
   To be the king, when I have the power of a king.
   For I have my place in the world, I know it, and will not
   Overreach myself. Now, you give me all
   I wish, and no fear comes with the gift;
   But if I were king myself, much more would be forced   620
   Upon me. Why should I love the throne better
   Than a throne's power and a throne's majesty
   Without the terrors of a throne? Now,
   I may smile to all, and all will bow to me;
   Those who need you petition me,   625
   For I am their hopes of success. Is this such a worthless
   Life that I should exchange it for yours? Treason
   Is for those who cannot value what they have.
   I have never had longing thoughts about your power,
   Nor would I help a man who had. Send   630
   To Delphi, make a test of me, ask the god
   Whether my message was true, and if you find
   I have plotted with your priest, then you may kill me—
   I will be your authority, I will assent
   When you decree my death. But do not accuse me   635
   Yet, when you know nothing. You wrong your friends
   To think them enemies, as much as you do wrong
   To take enemies for friends. Think, be sure!
   You banish life from your body—and life you love
   Most dearly—by banishing a good friend.   640
   Time will set this knowledge safely in your heart;
   Time alone shows the goodness in a man—
   One day is enough to tell you all his evil.
CHORUS My king, a cautious man would listen; beware
   Of being convinced too quickly. Suddenness is not safety.   645
OEDIPUS When the attack is quick and sudden, and the plot
   Runs in the darkness, my thoughts must be sudden
   In reply. If I wait, sitting in silence,
   He will have done his work, and I lost
   My chance to begin.
CREON   Your decision then! Will you   650
   Banish me?
OEDIPUS   No, not banishment; I
   Will have your life! You must teach men the rewards
   That I keep for the envious and the cruel.
CREON Will you not listen to persuasion and the truth?   655

OEDIPUS You will never persuade me that you speak the truth.

CREON No, I can see you are blind to truth.

OEDIPUS   I see
  Enough to guard my life.

CREON   My life is as precious
  To me.

OEDIPUS   But you are a traitor!

CREON You know nothing!

OEDIPUS Yet the king must rule.

CREON   Not when the king is evil.

OEDIPUS My city! My city!   660

CREON It is my city too, do not forget that!

CHORUS Stop, my lords! Look, here is Jocasta coming to you
  From the palace, at the moment when she may help you
  To bring this quarrel to rest.

[*Enter* JOCASTA.]

JOCASTA My lords, it is pitiful to hear your senseless voices   665
  Shouting and wrangling. Have you no shame? Our country
  Is sick, and you go bustling about your private
  Quarrels. My king, you must go inside, and you,
  Creon, go to the palace. At this time
  We have no troubles except the plague; all   670
  Others are pretence.

CREON   My sister, your sovereign, Oedipus,
  Condemns me cruelly in his efforts to be just.
  He will banish me, or murder me; in both he does wrong.

OEDIPUS No, I have found a traitor, my queen, who plots
  Against my life.

CREON   Never let me breathe   675
  In freedom again, let me die under your curse,
  If I am guilty of those crimes!

JOCASTA   Oh, Oedipus,
  Believe him. Believe him for the sake of those words
  That heaven witnessed; you have a duty to that oath,
  And to me, and to your people.   680

CHORUS Obey her, my lord, I beg you; do not be harsh,
  Be wise.

OEDIPUS   Must I be ruled by you?

CHORUS Creon was always wise and faithful in the past; his oath
      was great
  And you must respect it.

OEDIPUS You know what you are asking?

CHORUS   I know.   685

OEDIPUS Tell me, what do you advise?

CHORUS He is your friend—that is a truth
  As simple as the light of day;

But only confused and uncertain rumours call him traitor;
No cause to rob him of his honour.   690
OEDIPUS But listen, in asking this, you ask
  For my banishment, or for my death.
CHORUS No! By the sun who is prince of the sky!
  If that was ever my intention,
  I pray for death, without friends on earth   695
  Without love in heaven,
  Death in pain and misery.
  Now, now, when the decaying earth eats our lives
  Away, will you add your quarrels to all
  That we already suffer?   700
OEDIPUS Let him go then; I shall die, I do not care;
  I shall be driven into banishment and disgrace.
  I do this for love and pity of you. For him, I feel none;
  Wherever he goes, he cannot escape my hatred.
CREON For you submission is a torment—you do not hide it.   705
  And when you force your way against the world
  You crush us all beneath you. Such natures
  Find their own company most terrible to bear.
  It is their punishment.
OEDIPUS Leave my sight, then! Leave me to myself!   710
CREON I shall leave you. In all the time you knew me,
  You never understood me . . . They see my innocence.

[*Exit* CREON.]

CHORUS My queen, take our king to the palace now.
JOCASTA I must know what has happened.
CHORUS Doubt and suspicion. Oedipus spoke without thinking;   715
  He was unjust, and Creon cannot bear injustice.
JOCASTA Both were to blame?
CHORUS   Yes.
JOCASTA   What was said?
CHORUS The country is weary with sickness already;
  I am content, content to go no further
  And let the evil rest.   720
OEDIPUS You see what you have done, you good,
  Good adviser? My temper was a spear
  And you have turned the edge and blunted it.
CHORUS Your majesty, I have repeated many times—
  But I tell you again;   725
  I would have been robbed of all my senses,
  Emptied of all my reason,
  If I caused your death.
  You came like the wind we pray for in danger,
  When the storm was conquering us with sorrows,   730
  And carried our country into safety. Again

You may bring a spirit to guide us.
JOCASTA But I still do not know why you were quarrelling, my
    king,
    And I must know, for they talked of your death.
OEDIPUS   Jocasta,
    You may command me when even my people may not,   735
    And I let Creon go. But he had conspired
    Against me . . .
JOCASTA   Treason! Is this true? Can you prove it?
OEDIPUS He says I am Laius' murderer.
JOCASTA   How
    Can he know? Has he always known, or has someone told him?
OEDIPUS He sent that priest Teiresias, the wicked Teiresias.   740
    Creon's lips do not commit themselves to words!
JOCASTA Then set all this talk aside and listen. I
    Will teach you that no priest, no holy magic
    Can know your future or your destiny. And my proof
    Is as short as the stroke of a knife. Once, an oracle   745
    Came to Laius—I will not say it was from
    Apollo—but from Apollo's priests. It told him
    He was destined to be murdered by the son that I
    Would bear to him. But Laius, so they say,
    Was murdered by robbers from another country at a place   750
    Where three roads meet. A son was born
    To us, but lived no more than three days. Yes,
    Laius pinned his ankles together and sent him
    Away to die on a distant, lonely mountain.
    Once he was there, no power could make him a murderer,   755
    Nor make Laius die at the hands of his son—
    And he feared that above anything in the world.
    You see how you may rely upon priests and their talk
    Of the future. Never notice them! When god wishes
    The truth discovered, he will easily work his will.   760
OEDIPUS As I listened, my queen, my thoughts went reaching out
    And touched on memories that make me shudder . . .
JOCASTA What memories? You stare as if you were trapped.
OEDIPUS You said—I heard you say—that Laius' blood
    Was spilt at a place where three roads meet.   765
JOCASTA We were all told that, and no one has denied it.
OEDIPUS And where is the place where this happened?
JOCASTA   The country
    Is called Phocis; the road splits, to Delphi
    And to Daulia.
OEDIPUS   When did all this happen?
JOCASTA The city was given the news a little before   770
    You became king of Thebes.
OEDIPUS   God,
    What do you hold prepared for me?

JOCASTA   Oedipus!
   What made you frown when I talked of your becoming king?
OEDIPUS Do not ask me yet . . . Laius—what was he like?
   His appearance, his age, describe them to me.   775
JOCASTA He was tall, his hair beginning to be flecked with a down
   Of white; he was built like you . . .
OEDIPUS Stop! You torture me!
   I have hurled myself blindly against unthinking
   Fury and destruction!
JOCASTA   How? I cannot bear
   To watch you, my lord.
OEDIPUS   So little hope is frightening.   780
   Listen, Teiresias the priest was not blind!
   But one more answer, one more, will be better proof.
JOCASTA I dare not answer; but if my answers help you,
   Ask.
OEDIPUS When he left Thebes, was he alone,
   Or did he have a company of men at arms   785
   So that all could recognize he was a king?
JOCASTA No, five were all the travellers, and one
   Was a herald. A single chariot carried Laius . . .
OEDIPUS Yes! Now I see the truth . . . Who told you this?
JOCASTA A servant, the only man who returned alive.   790
OEDIPUS Is he still in the palace with us?
JOCASTA No, after
   He escaped, and found that you were king, and Laius
   Dead, he imlored me by my duty to a suppliant
   To send him away. To the country, he said, herding
   Sheep on the hillsides, where he could never see   795
   The city he had left . . . And I let him go; he was
   A good servant, deserving more than this
   Small favour.
OEDIPUS He must be found at once;
   Can this be done?
JOCASTA Yes, but why do you want him?
OEDIPUS My queen, as I look into myself I begin to fear;   800
   I had no right to say those things, and so
   I must see this man.
JOCASTA   He will come. But I
   Expect to be told your sorrows, my king, when they weigh
   So heavily.
OEDIPUS   And I will not refuse you, Jocasta.
   I have come to face such thoughts, and who should hear   805
   Of them before you? I walk among
   Great menaces.
   My father is king of Corinth—Polybus; my mother—
   Merope from Doris. In Corinth I was called
   Their prince, their greatest noble, until   810

This happened to me—it was strange, yet not
So strange as to deserve my thoughts so much.
A man, stuffed with wine at a feast, called out
To me as he drank. He said I was a son only
In the imagination if my father. Anger 815
And pain would not let me rest that day; the next
I went to my parents and questioned them. They answered
The drunkard harshly for his insulting story,
And for their sakes I was glad he lied. Yet I always
Felt the wound, and the story spread in whispers. 820
At last I went to Delphi—my parents did not know—
But Apollo thought me unworthy of an answer
To that question. Instead he foretold many trials,
Many dangers, many sorrows. I was to be
My mother's husband, I was to murder my own 825
Father, my children would carry the guilt and none
Would dare look on them. When I heard this
I ran from my home and afterwards knew the land
Only by the stars that stood above it.
Never must I see the shame of that evil prophecy 830
Acted out by me in Corinth. I travelled
Until I came to this place where you say your king
Was killed . . . My wife, this is the truth . . . I will tell you . . .
My journey brought me to the meeting of three roads;
And there a herald, and an old man who rode 835
A chariot drawn by mares, came toward me . . .
Jocasta, the rider was like the man you described!
He and the herald, who went in front, tried
To force me out of their path. In a rage I struck
The one who touched me, the servant at the wheel. 840
The old man watched me, and waited till I was passing;
Then from the chariot he aimed at the crown of my head
With the twin prongs of his goad. It was a costly
Action! Slashing with my stick I cut at him
And my blow tumbled him backwards out of the chariot— 845
Then I killed them all! If this man I met may be said
To resemble Laius, to be, perhaps, Laius,
I stand condemned to more sorrow than any man,
More cursed by an evil power than any man.
No one in Thebes, no stranger, may shelter me 850
Or speak to me; they must hunt me from their doors.
And I, it was I, who cursed myself, cursed myself!
And the dead king's pillow is fouled by the touch
Of my murdering hands. Is the evil in my soul?
Is my whole nature tainted? Must I go into exile, 855
Never see my people again, nor turn home
And set foot in Corinth?—for if I do, I must wed
My mother, and kill my father—Polybus, who gave me

Life and youth. Can you see this happen, and then
Deny that a cruel power has come to torture me?   860
No! You heavens, you pure light and holiness!
Let me die before that day, hide me before
I feel that black corruption in my soul!
CHORUS My king, this is a frightening story. But hope,
Until you hear from the man who saw what happened.   865
OEDIPUS Yes, that is all the hope I have. Oedipus
Waits for one man, and he is a shepherd.
JOCASTA What makes you so eager for him to come?
OEDIPUS I reason like this. We may find that his story
Matches yours. Then I shall be as free   870
As if this had never happened.
JOCASTA   Was there anything in what
I said that could have such power?
OEDIPUS   You said
He told you robbers murdered Laius. If he still
Says "robbers" and not "a robber," I am innocent.
One man cannot be taken for many.   875
But if he says a murderer, alone,
The guilt comes to rest on me.
JOCASTA But we all
Heard him say "robbers"; that is certain. He cannot
Unsay it. I am not alone, for the whole city heard.
But even if he swerves a little from his old account,   880
That will not prove you Laius' murderer,
Not in truth, not in justice. For Apollo said
He was to be killed by a son that was born to me . . .
And yet my son, poor child, could not have killed him.
For he died first . . . but that shows the deceit   885
Of prophecies. They beckon at you, but I
Would fix my eyes ahead, and never look at them!
OEDIPUS You are right. Nevertheless send someone
To bring me that servant; do not forget.
JOCASTA   Yes,
I will send now. Let us go to the palace;   890
I would do nothing that could harm or anger you.

[*Exeunt all but the* CHORUS.]

CHORUS All actions must beware of the powers beyond us, and
each word
Must speak our fear of heaven. I pray
That I may live every hour in obedience.
The laws that hold us in subjection   895
Have always stood beyond our reach, conceived
In the high air of heaven. Olympus

Was their sire, and no woman on earth
Gave them life. They are laws
That will never be lured to sleep in the arms of oblivion,   900
And in their strength heaven is great and cannot grow old.
Yet man desires to be more than man, to rule
His world for himself.
This desire, blown to immensity
On the rich empty food of its ambition,   905
Out of place, out of time,
Clambers to the crown of the rock, and stands there,
Tottering; then comes the steepling plunge down to earth,
To the earth where we are caged and mastered.
But this desire may work for good   910
When it fights to save a country, and I pray
That heaven will not weaken it then.
For then it comes like a god to be our warrior
And we shall never turn it back.

Justice holds the balance of all things,   915
And we must fear her.
Do not despise the frontiers in which we must live,
Do not cross them, do not talk of them,
But how before the places where the gods are throned.
Time will come with cruel vengeance on the man   920
Who disobeys; that is the punishment
For those who are proud and are more than men—
They are humbled.
If a man grows rich in defiance of this law,
If his actions trespass on a world that he should fear,   925
If he reaches after mysteries that no man should know,
No prayer can plead for him when the sword of heaven is
    raised.
If he were to glory in success
All worship would fall dumb.

Delphi is the heart of the world and holds its secrets;   930
The temple of Zeus, and Olympia, command our prayers;
But we shall never believe again
Until the truth of this murder is known.
Let us be sure of our beliefs, give us proof.
Zeus, you may do your will: do not forget that you are
    immortal,
                                                                  935
Your empire cannot die; hear our prayers.
For the oracle given to Laius in the years of the long past
Is dying and forgotten, wiped from the memory,
Apollo's glory turns to shadows,
And all divinity to ruin.   940

[*Enter* JOCASTA.]

JOCASTA My lords, I have been summoned by my thoughts
  To the temples of the gods, and I have brought
  These garlands and this incense for an offering.
  Oedipus is like a lonely bird among
  The terrors that flock about his mind. He forgets   945
  His wisdom, and no longer thinks the past will guide him
  When he tries to foresee the future. Instead, he is
  The slave of any word that talks of fear.
  I try to reach him, to make him see that there is hope,
  But it is useless; I have failed. And so I turn   950
  To you, Apollo, nearest to us in Thebes,
  A suppliant with prayers and gifts. Resolve this doubt
  By sending the truth. He is the guide and master
  Of our ship. What shall we do when even he
  Is struck into bewilderment?   955

[*Enter* MESSENGER.]

MESSENGER I do not know this country. Will you show me the
  palace
  Of King Oedipus? I must find King Oedipus . . .
  Do you know where he is?
CHORUS   This is his palace, sir.
  He is inside, and you see his queen before you.
MESSENGER Heaven give her and all she loves riches   960
  And happiness if she is the queen of such a king.
JOCASTA I return your greeting. You have spoken well and deserve
  Well wishing. But what do you want with Oedipus?
  Or do you bring a message for us?
MESSENGER   A message
  Of good, for your palace and your husband, my queen.
JOCASTA   What
  is it? Who sent you here?   965
MESSENGER I come from Corinth.
  My story may be quickly told. You will be glad, of course,
  For the news is glad, and yet . . . yet you may grieve.
JOCASTA Well, what is this story with a double meaning?
MESSENGER The people of Corinth—it was already announced
  There—will make Oedipus their king.
JOCASTA   But why?   970
  Your king is Polybus. He is wise, revered . . .
MESSENGER But no longer our king. Death hugs him to the earth.
JOCASTA Is this true? Polybus is dead?
MESSENGER By my hopes of living out my years, it is true.
JOCASTA Servant, go, tell this to your master. Run!   975

[*Exit* SERVANT.]

Where are the prophecies of heaven now? Always
Oedipus dreaded to kill this man, and hid
From him. But look, Polybus has been murdered
By the careless touch of time, and not by Oedipus.

[*Enter* OEDIPUS.]

OEDIPUS Dear Jocasta, dear wife, why have you called me   980
    Here from the palace?
JOCASTA   This man brings a message;
    Listen, and then ask yourself what comes
    Of the oracles from heaven that used to frighten us.
OEDIPUS Who is this man? What has he to say to me?
JOCASTA He comes from Corinth, and his message is the death   985
    Of Polybus. You will never see Polybus again!
OEDIPUS You said that, stranger? Let me hear you say that plainly.
MESSENGER Since you force me to give that part of my message first,
    I repeat, he walks among the dead.
OEDIPUS   A plot?
    Or did sickness conspire to kill him?
MESSENGER   A small   990
    Touch on the balance sends old lives to sleep.
OEDIPUS So, my poor father, sickness murdered you.
MESSENGER And many years had measured out his life.
OEDIPUS Oh look, look, who would listen to Apollo
    Talking in his shrine at Delphi, or notice birds   995
    That clamour to the air? They were the signs
    That told me—and I believed—that I would kill
    My father. But now he has the grave to protect him,
    While I stand here, and I never touched a sword . . .
    Unless he died of longing to see me—   1000
    Then perhaps he died because of me. No!
    Polybus lies in darkness, and all those prophecies
    Lie with him, chained and powerless.
JOCASTA I told you long ago how it would happen . . .
OEDIPUS Yes, but I was led astray by fears.   1005
JOCASTA Then think no more of them; forget them all.
OEDIPUS Not all. The marriage with my mother—I think of it.
JOCASTA But is there anything a man need fear, if he knows
    That chance is supreme throughout the world, and he cannot
    See what is to come? Give way to the power   1010
    Of events and live as they allow! It is best.
    Do not fear this marriage with your mother. Many
    Men have dreams, and in those dreams they wed
    Their mothers. Life is easiest, if you do not try

To oppose these things that seem to threaten us.   1015
OEDIPUS You are right, and I would agree with all
    You say, if my mother were not alive. And though
    You are right, I must fear. She is alive.
JOCASTA Think of your father, and his grave.
    There is a light to guide you.
OEDIPUS   It does guide me!   1020
    I know he . . . But she is alive and I am afraid.
MESSENGER You are afraid of a woman, my lord?
OEDIPUS   Yes,
    Merope—Polybus was her husband.
MESSENGER How can you be afraid of her?
OEDIPUS   A prophecy warned me
    To beware of sorrow . . .
MESSENGER   Can you speak of it, or are you   1025
    Forbidden to talk of these things to others?
OEDIPUS   No,
    I am not forbidden. The Oracle at Delphi
    Has told me my destiny—to be my mother's husband
    And my father's murderer. And so I left
    Corinth, many years ago and many   1030
    Miles behind me. The world has rewarded me richly,
    And yet all those riches are less than the sight
    Of a parent's face.
MESSENGER   And you went into exile because
    You feared this marriage?
OEDIPUS   And to save myself from becoming
    My father's murderer.
MESSENGER   Then, my king,   1035
    I ought to have freed you from that fear since I
    Wished to be thought your friend.
OEDIPUS   Your reward
    Will be measured by my gratitude.
MESSENGER I had hoped for reward
    When you returned as king of your palace in Corinth.
OEDIPUS I must never go where my parents are.
MESSENGER   My son,   1040
    You do not know what you say; I see you do not.
OEDIPUS How, sir? Tell me quickly.
MESSENGER   . . . If you live in exile
    Because of Polybus and Merope.
OEDIPUS   Yes, and I live
    In fear that Apollo will prove he spoke the truth.
MESSENGER And it is from your parents that the guilt is to come?   1045
OEDIPUS Yes, stranger, the fear never leaves my side.
MESSENGER You have no cause to be afraid—do you know that?
OEDIPUS No cause? But they were my parents—that is the cause!

MESSENGER No cause, because they were not your parents,
    Oedipus.
OEDIPUS What do you mean? Polybus was not my father?   1050
MESSENGER As much as I, and yet no more than I am.
OEDIPUS How could my father be no more than nothing?
MESSENGER But Polybus did not give you life, nor did I.
OEDIPUS Then why did he call me son?
MESSENGER   Listen, you were
    A gift that he took from my hands.
OEDIPUS   A child   1055
    Given him by a stranger? But he loved me
    Dearly.
MESSENGER He had no children, and so consented.
OEDIPUS So you gave me to ... Had you bought me for your slave?
    Where did you find me?
MESSENGER   You were lying beneath the trees
    In a glade upon Cithaeron.
OEDIPUS   What were you doing on Cithaeron?
MESSENGER My flocks were grazing in the mountains;   1060
    I was guarding them.
OEDIPUS   Guarding your flocks—you were
    A shepherd, a servant!
MESSENGER It was in that service that I saved
    Your life, my child.
OEDIPUS   Why? Was I hurt or sick
    When you took me home?
MESSENGER   Your ankles will be my witness
    That you would not have lived.
OEDIPUS Why do you talk   1065
    Of that? The pain is forgotten!
MESSENGER   Your feet were pierced
    And clamped together. I set you free.
OEDIPUS   The child
    In the cradle had a scar—I still carry
    The shame of it.
MESSENGER   You were named in remembrance
    Of that scar.
OEDIPUS In heaven's name, who did this?   1070
    My mother? My father?
MESSENGER   I do not know. The man
    Who gave you to me knows more of the truth.
OEDIPUS But you said you found me! Then it was not true ...
    You had me from someone else?
MESSENGER   Yes, another
    Shepherd gave me the child.
OEDIPUS   Who? Can you   1075
    Describe him?

MESSENGER   They said he was a servant of Laius.
OEDIPUS Laius, who was once king of Thebes?
MESSENGER   Yes,
    This man was one of his shepherds.
OEDIPUS   Is he still
    Alive; could I see him?
MESSENGER   Your people here
    Will know that best.
OEDIPUS Do any of you,   1080
    My friends, know the shepherd he means? Has he
    Been seen in the fields, or in the palace? Tell me,
    Now! It is time these things were known!
CHORUS   I think
    He must be the man you were searching for, the one
    Who left the palace after Laius was killed.   1085
    But Jocasta will know as well as I.
OEDIPUS My wife, you remember the man we sent for a little
    Time ago? Is he the one this person means?
JOCASTA Perhaps . . . But why should he . . . Think nothing of this!
    Do not idle with memories and stories . . .   1090
OEDIPUS No, I have been given these signs, and I must
    Follow them, until I know who gave me birth.
JOCASTA No! Give up this search! I am tortured and sick
    Enough. By the love of heaven, if you value life . . .
OEDIPUS Courage! You are still a queen, though I discover   1095
    That I am three times three generations a slave.
JOCASTA No, listen to me, I implore you! You must stop!
OEDIPUS I cannot listen when you tell me to ignore the truth.
JOCASTA But I know the truth, and I only ask you to save
    Yourself.
OEDIPUS I have always hated that way to safety!   1100
JOCASTA But evil lies in wait for you . . . Oh, do not let him
    Find the truth!
OEDIPUS Bring this shepherd to me,
    And let her gloat over the riches of her ancestry.
JOCASTA My poor child! Those are the only words
    I shall ever have for you . . . I can speak no others!   1105

[*Exit* JOCASTA.]

CHORUS What is the torment that drives your queen so wildly
    Into the palace, Oedipus? Her silence threatens
    A storm. I fear some wrong . . .
OEDIPUS   Let the storm
    Come if it will. I must know my birth,
    I must know it, however humble. Perhaps she,   1110
    For she is a queen, and proud, is ashamed
    That I was born so meanly. But I consider

Myself a child of Fortune, and while she brings me
Gifts, I shall not lack honour. For she has given me
Life itself; and my cousins, the months, have marked me   1115
Small and great as they marched by. Such
Is my ancestry, and I shall be none other—
And I will know my birth!
CHORUS There are signs
Of what is to come, and we may read them,
Casting our thoughts into the future,   1120
And drawing in new knowledge.
For we have seen how the world goes
And we have seen the laws it obeys.
Cithaeron, mountain of Oedipus, the moon
Will not rise in tomorrow's evening sky   1125
Before our king calls you his true father,
His only nurse and mother—and then
You will have your greatest glory.
You will be honoured with dances and choirs
For your gentle kindness to our king—Hail   1130
To the god Apollo! May he be content
With all our words.

Pan walks among the mountains, and one
Of the immortal nymphs could have lain with him;
Who was the goddess who became your mother, Oedipus?   1135
Or was she the wife of Apollo, for he loves
The wild meadows and the long grass.
Or was it the prince of Cyllene, Hermes?
Or, Bacchus, whose palace is the mountain top?
Did he take you as a gift from the nymphs of Helicon,   1140
With whom he plays through all his immortal years?
OEDIPUS I never knew the shepherd or encountered him,
My people, but the man I see there must be
The one we have been seeking. His age answers
My riddle for me; it holds as many years   1145
As our messenger's. And now I see that those
Who lead him are my servants. But you have known him
Before, you can tell me whether I am right.
CHORUS Yes, we recognise him—the most faithful
Of Laius' shepherds.
OEDIPUS And you, Corinthian,   1150
You must tell me first. Is this the man you mean?
MESSENGER It is; you see him there.

[*Enter* SHEPHERD.]

OEDIPUS   You, sir, come to me,
Look me in the eyes, and answer all my questions!

 Did you once serve Laius?
SHEPHERD   Yes, and I was born
 In his palace; I was not brought from another country . . . 1155
OEDIPUS Your life? How were you employed?
SHEPHERD   Most
 Of my life I watched his flocks.
OEDIPUS   And where
 Was their pasture? They had a favourite meadow?
SHEPHERD Sometimes Cithaeron, sometimes the places near.
OEDIPUS Do you recognise this man? Did you see him on Cithaeron? 1160
SHEPHERD Why should anyone go there? Whom do you mean?
OEDIPUS Here! Standing beside me. Have you ever met him?
SHEPHERD I do not think so . . . My memory is not quick.
MESSENGER We should not wonder at this, your majesty;
 But I shall remind him of all he has forgotten.   1165
 I know that he remembers when for three
 Whole years I used to meet him near Cithaeron,
 Six months, from each spring to the rising of the Bear;
 I had a single flock and he had two.
 Then, in the winters, I would take my sheep to their pens 1170
 While he went to the fields of Laius . . . Did this happen?
 Have I told it as it happened, or have I not?
SHEPHERD The time is long since then . . . yes, it is the truth.
MESSENGER Good; now, tell me: you know the child you gave
  me . . . ?
SHEPHERD What is happening? What do these questions mean? 1175
MESSENGER Here is the child, my friend, who was so little then.
SHEPHERD Damnation seize you! Can you not keep your secret?
OEDIPUS Wait, Shepherd! Do not find fault; as I listened
 I found more fault in you than in him.
SHEPHERD   What
 Have I done wrong, most mighty king?
OEDIPUS   You will not 1180
 Admit the truth about that child.
SHEPHERD   He wastes
 His time. He talks, but it is all lies.
OEDIPUS When it would please me, you will not speak; but you will
 When I make you cry for mercy . . .
SHEPHERD   No, my king,
 I am an old man—do not hurt me!   1185
OEDIPUS [*to guards*] Take his arms and tie them quickly!
SHEPHERD   But why,
 Poor child? What more do you want to know?
OEDIPUS   You gave
 The boy to this Corinthian?
SHEPHERD   Yes, I did . . .
 And I should have prayed for death that day.

OEDIPUS Your prayer will be answered now if you lie to me!   1190
SHEPHERD But you will surely kill me if I tell the truth.
OEDIPUS He will drive my patience to exhaustion!
SHEPHERD   No!
    I told you now, I did give him the child.
OEDIPUS Where did it come from? Your home? Another's?
SHEPHERD It was not mine, it was given to me.
OEDIPUS   By someone   1195
    In the city? . . . I want to know the house!
SHEPHERD   By all that is holy,
    No more, your majesty, no more questions!
OEDIPUS   You die
    If I have to ask again!
SHEPHERD   The child was born
    In the palace of King Laius.
OEDIPUS   By one of his slaves?
    Or was it a son of his own blood?
SHEPHERD   My king,   1200
    How shall I tell a story of such horror?
OEDIPUS And how shall I hear it? And yet I must, must hear.
SHEPHERD The child was called his son. But your queen in the
    palace
May tell you the truth of that most surely.
OEDIPUS Jocasta gave you the child?
SHEPHERD   Yes, my king.   1205
OEDIPUS Why? What were you to do?
SHEPHERD   I was to destroy him.
OEDIPUS The poor mother asked that?
SHEPHERD   She was afraid.
    A terrible prophecy . . .
OEDIPUS   What?
SHEPHERD There was a story
    That he would kill his parents.
OEDIPUS   Why did you give
    The child away to this stranger?
SHEPHERD   I pitied it.   1210
    My lord, and I thought he would take it to the far land
Where he lived. But he saved its life only for
Great sorrows. For if you are the man he says,
You must know your birth was watched by evil powers.
OEDIPUS All that was foretold will be made true! Light,   1215
    Now turn black and die; I must not look on you!
See, this is what I am; son of parents
I should not have known, I lived with those
I should not have touched, and murdered those
A man must not kill!

[*Exit* OEDIPUS.]

CHORUS Every man who has ever lived   1220
    Is numbered with the dead; they fought with the world
    For happiness, yet all they won
    Was a shadow that slipped away to die.
    And you, Oedipus, are all those men. I think of the power
    Which carried you to such victories and such misery   1225
    And I know there is no joy or triumph in the world.

    Oedipus aimed beyond the reach of man
    And fixed with his arrowing mind
    Perfection and rich happiness.
    The Sphinx's talons were sharp with evil, she spoke in the
        mysteries   1230
    Of eternal riddles, and he came to destroy her,
    To overcome death, to be a citadel
    Of strength in our country.
    He was called our king, and was
    The greatest noble in great Thebes.   1235
    And now his story ends in agony.
    Death and madness hunt him,
    Destruction and sorrow haunt him.
    Now his life turns and brings the reward of his
        greatness . . .
    Glorious Oedipus, son, and then father,   1240
    In the same chamber, in the same silent room,
    Son and father in the same destruction;
    Your marriage was the harvesting of wrong.
    How could it hold you where your father lay,
    And bear you in such silence for such an end?   1245

    Child of Laius, I wish, I wish I had never known you,
    For now there is only mourning, sorrow flowing
    From our lips.
    And yet we must not forget the truth;
    If we were given hope and life, it was your work.   1250

[*Enter* SERVANT.]

SERVANT My lords of Thebes, on whom rest all the honours
    Of our country, when you hear what has happened,
    When you witness it, how will you bear your grief
    In silence? Weep, if you have ever loved
    The royal house of Thebes. For I do not think   1255
    The great streams of the Phasis or the Ister
    Could ever wash these walls to purity. But all

The crimes they hide must glare out to the light,
Crimes deliberate and considered. The sorrows
We choose ourselves bring the fiercest pain!   1260
CHORUS We have seen great wrongs already, and they were
     frightening.
Do you bring new disasters?
SERVANT   I bring a message
That I may tell, and you may hear, in a few
Swift words. Jocasta is dead.
CHORUS Then she died in grief. What caused her death?   1265
SERVANT It was her own will. Of that terrible act
The worst must remain untold, for I did not watch it.
Yet you will hear what happened to our poor queen
As far as memory guides me. When she went
Into the domed hall of the palace, whirled   1270
On the torrent of her grief, she ran straight
To her marriage chamber, both hands clutched at her hair,
Tearing like claws. Inside, she crashed shut the door
And shrieked the name Laius, Laius who died
So long ago. She talked to herself of the son   1275
She once bore, and of Laius murdered by that son;
Of the mother who was left a widow, and became
Wife and mother again in shame and sorrow.
She wept for her marriage, in which her husband gave
To her a husband, and her children, children.   1280
How her death followed I cannot tell you . . .
We heard a shout, and now Oedipus blazed
And thundered through the door. I could not see
How her sorrow ended, because he was there,
Circling in great mad strides, and we watched   1285
Him. He went round begging to each
Of us; he asked for a sword, he asked to go
To his wife who was more than a wife, to his mother in whom
His birth and his children's birth, like two harvests
From the same field, had been sown and gathered. His grief   1290
Was a raging madness, and some power must have guided
     him—
It was none of us who were standing there. He gave
A cry full of fear and anguish, then, as if
A ghost was leading him, he leaped against the double
Doors of Jocasta's room. The hinges tilted   1295
Full out of their sockets, and shattered inside
The chamber—and there we saw his wife, hanging
By her throat in the grip of a tall rope. And when
He saw her, he shrieked like a wounded beast, wrenched loose
The knot that held her, and laid her on the ground.   1300
What followed was terrible to watch. He ripped

The gold-worked brooches from her robes—she wore them
As jewels—and raised them above his head. Then he plunged
them
Deep into the sockets of his eyes, shouting
That he would never look upon the wrongs   1305
He had committed and had suffered. Now
In his blackness he must see such shapes as he deserved
And never look on those he loved. Repeating
This like a chant, he lifted his hands and stabbed
His eyes, again and again. We saw his eyeballs   1310
Fill with tears of blood that dyed his cheeks,
And a red stream pouring from his veins, dark
As the blood of life, thick as storming hail.
Yes, this is a storm that has broken, a storm
That holds the queen and the king in its embrace.   1315
They were rich and fortunate, and they were so
As we should wish to be. Now, in one day,
See how we must mourn them. The blind rush
To death, the shame, all the evils that we
Have names for—they have escaped none!   1320
CHORUS Has our poor king found ease for his sorrow yet?
SERVANT He shouts at us to open the doors and show
    To all Thebes the murderer of his father
    And his mother's . . . his words are blasphemous,
    I dare not speak them . . . He will be driven from Thebes,   1325
    Will not stay beneath this curse that he called upon
    Himself. Yet he needs help and a guide. No one
    Could bear that agony . . . But he comes himself to show you;
    The great doors of the palace open, and what you will see
    Will turn you away in horror—yet will ask for pity.   1330

[*Enter* OEDIPUS.]

CHORUS This suffering turns a face of terror to the world.
    There is no story told, no knowledge born
    That tells of greater sorrow.
    Madness came striding upon you, Oedipus,
    The black, annihilating power that broods   1335
    And waits in the hand of time . . .
    I cannot look!
    We have much to ask and learn and see.
    But you blind us with an icy sword of terror.
OEDIPUS Where will you send this wreckage and despair of man?   1340
    Where will my voice be heard, like the wind drifting emptily
    On the air. Oh you powers, why do you drive me on?
CHORUS They drive you to the place of horror,
    That only the blind may see,
    And only the dead hear of.   1345

OEDIPUS Here in my cloud of darkness there is no escape,
 A cloud, thick in my soul, and there it dumbly clings;
 That cloud is my own spirit
 That now wins its fiercest battle and turns back
 To trample me . . . The memory of evil can tear   1350
 Like goads of molten fire, and go deep.
 Infinity could not be so deep.
CHORUS More than mortal in your acts of evil.
 More than mortal in your suffering, Oedipus.
OEDIPUS You are my last friend, my only help; you have 1355
 Waited for me, and will care for the eyeless body
 Of Oedipus. I know you are there . . . I know . . .
 Through this darkness I can hear your voice.
CHORUS Oedipus, all that you do
 Makes us draw back in fear. How could you take 1360
 Such vivid vengeance on your eyes? What power lashed you on?
OEDIPUS Apollo, my lords, Apollo sent this evil on me.
 I was the murderer; I struck the blow. Why should I
 Keep my sight? If I had eyes, what could delight them?
CHORUS It is so; it is as you say.   1365
OEDIPUS No, I can look on nothing . . .
 And I can love nothing—for love has lost
 Its sweetness, I can hear no voice—for words
 Are sour with hate . . . Take stones and beat me
 From your country. I am the living curse, the source 1370
 Of sickness and death!
CHORUS Your own mind, reaching after the secrets
 Of the gods, condemned you to your fate.
 If only you had never come to Thebes . . .
OEDIPUS But when my feet were ground by iron teeth 1375
 That bolted me in the meadow grass,
 A man set me free and ransomed me from death.
 May hell curse him for that murderous kindness!
 I should have died then
 And never drawn this sorrow on those I love 1380
 And on myself . . .
CHORUS Our prayers echo yours.
OEDIPUS Nor killed my father
 Nor led my mother to the room where she gave me life.
 But now the gods desert me, for I am 1385
 Born of impurity, and my blood
 Mingles with those who gave me birth.
 If evil can grow with time to be a giant
 That masters and usurps our world,
 That evil lords its way through Oedipus. 1390
CHORUS How can we say that you have acted wisely?
 Is death not better than a life in blindness?
OEDIPUS Do not teach me that this punishment is wrong—

I will have no advisers to tell me it is wrong!
Why choke my breath and go among the dead   1395
If I keep my eyes? For there I know I could not
Look upon my father or my poor mother . . .
My crimes have been too great for such a death.
Or should I love my sight because it let me
See my children? No, for then I would   1400
Remember who their father was. My eyes
Would never let me love them, nor my city,
Nor my towers, nor the sacred images
Of gods. I was the noblest lord in Thebes,
But I have stripped myself of Thebes, and become   1405
The owner of all miseries. For I commanded
My people to drive out the unclean thing, the man
Heaven had shown to be impure in the house
Of Laius.
I found such corruption in me—could I see   1410
My people and not turn blind for shame? . . .
My ears are a spring, and send a river
Of sound through me; if I could have dammed that river
I would have made my poor body into a bolted prison
In which there would be neither light nor sound.   1415
Peace can only come if we shut the mind
Away from the sorrow in the world outside.
Cithaeron, why did you let me live? Why
Did you not kill me as I lay there? I would
Have been forgotten, and never revealed the secret   1420
Of my birth. Polybus, Corinth, the palace
They told me was my father's, you watched over
My youth, but beneath that youth's nobility lay
Corruption—you see it in my acts, in my blood!
There are three roads, a hidden valley, trees,   1425
And a narrow place where the roads meet—they
Drink my blood, the blood I draw from my father—
Do they remember me, do they remember what I did?
Do they know what next I did? . . . The room, the marriage
Room—it was there I was given life, and now   1430
It is there I give the same life to my children.
The blood of brothers, fathers, sons, the race
Of daughters, wives, mothers, all the blackest
Shame a man may commit . . . But I must not name
Such ugly crimes. Oh, you heavens, take me   1435
From the world and hide me, drown me in oceans
Where I can be seen no more! Come, do not fear
To touch a single unhappy man. Yes, a man,
No more. Be brave, for my sufferings can fall to no one
But myself to bear!
CHORUS Oedipus, Creon came   1440

While you were praying; he brings advice and help.
You can protect us no more, and we turn to him.
OEDIPUS What can I say to Creon? I have given him
    No cause to trust me or to listen. In all I said
    Before, he has seen that I was wrong.   1445

[*Enter* CREON *with* ANTIGONE *and* ISMENE.]

CREON I have not come scorning or insulting you, Oedipus,
    For those wrongs. (*To servants*) Have you no shame before
    Your countrymen? At least show reverence to the sun's
    Flame that sends us life, and do not let
    This curse lie open to disfigure heaven.   1450
    Neither earth, nor the pure falling rain, nor light
    May come near it. Take him to the palace now!
    When evil grows in the family, only the family
    May hear of it and look without pollution.
OEDIPUS Creon, I thought . . . but now you have struck those fears   1455
    Away—you will be a gentle king.
    But I ask one thing, and I ask it to help you,
    Not myself, for I am hated by powers too strong
    For us.
CREON What do you ask so eagerly?
OEDIPUS Banish me from the country now. I must go   1460
    Where no one can see or welcome me again.
CREON I would have done so, Oedipus, but first
    I must know from Apollo what he commands.
OEDIPUS But we have heard all his answer—destroy the
    Parricide, the unholiness, destroy me!   1465
CREON So it was said . . . And yet we are in such danger;
    It is better to hear what we must do.
OEDIPUS   Why need you
    Go to Delphi for my poor body?
CREON Delphi will never deceive us; you know it speaks
    The truth.
OEDIPUS   But Creon, I command you! . . . I will kneel   1470
    And pray to you . . . Bury my queen as you wish
    In her royal tomb; she is your sister and
    And it is her right. But as for myself, I
    Must never think of entering my father's city
    Again, so long as its people live. Let me   1475
    Have no home but the mountains, where the hill
    They call Cithaeron, my Cithaeron, stands.
    There my mother and my father, while
    They lived, decreed I should have my grave.
    My death will be a gift from them, for they   1480
    Have destroyed me . . . And yet I know that sickness
    Cannot break in and take my life, nothing

May touch me. I am sure of this, for each moment
Is a death, and I am kept alive only
For the final punishment . . . But let it go, 1485
Let it go, I do not care what is done with me.
Creon, my sons will ask nothing more from you;
They are men, wherever they go they will take what they need
From life. But pity my two daughters, who will have
No love. All that was owned by me, they shared, 1490
And when I banqueted, they were always beside me.
You must become their father . . . But let me touch them
And talk to them of our sorrows. Come, my lord,
Come, my noble kinsman, let me feel them
In my arms and believe they are as much my own 1495
As when I saw . . . I cannot think . . . Their weeping,
Their dear voices are near. Creon has pited me
And given me my children. Is this true?
CREON I sent for them; I know what joy they would give you
And how you loved them once. Yes, it is true. 1500
OEDIPUS May heaven bless your life, and may the power
Watching us, guard you more safely on the throne
Than me, My children, where are you? Come near, come
To my hands; they are your brother's hands and they
Went searching out and took your father's seeing 1505
Eyes to darkness. I did not know my children,
And did not ask, but now the world may see
That I gave you life from the source that gave me mine.
Why is there no light? I cannot see you! . . . And tears
Come when I think of the years you will have to live 1510
In a cruel world. In the city they will shun you,
Fear your presence; when they feast and dance in the streets
You will not be allowed to watch, and they
Will send you weeping home. And when you come
To the years of marriage, children, who will there be 1515
So careless of his pride as to accept the shame
That glares on my birth and on yours? "Your father
Killed his father!" "Your father gave life where he
Was given life, you are children where he was once
A child." That will be your humiliation! 1520
And who will wed you?
No one, my daughters, there will be no one, and I see
You must pine to death in lonely childlessness.
Creon, you are their father, you alone.
For they have lost their parents. Do not let them go 1525
Into beggary and solitude—their blood is yours.
I have nothing, but do not afflict them with
My poverty. Have pity on them. See, so young
And robbed of all except your kindliness.
Touch me once, my lord, and give your consent.

My children, I would have said much to comfort
And advise you—but how could you understand?
But pray, you must pray to live as the world allows
And find a better life than the father whom you follow.
CREON No more now. Go inside the palace.   1530
OEDIPUS It is hard, but I must obey.
CREON   All things are healed
    By time.
OEDIPUS But Creon, I demand one thing before
    I go.
CREON   What do you demand?
OEDIPUS   Banishment!
CREON Only heaven can answer your prayer. When Apollo . . .
OEDIPUS But Apollo can only detest me.   1535
CREON Then your prayer will be
    The sooner heard.
OEDIPUS   You mean what you say?
CREON   I cannot
    Promise, when I see nothing certain.
OEDIPUS   Now!
                              Exile me now!
CREON Go then, and leave your children.
OEDIPUS You must not take them from me!
CREON   You give   1545
    Commands as if you were king. You must remember
    Your rule is over, and it could not save your life.
CHORUS Men of Thebes, look at the king who ruled
    Your country; there is Oedipus.
    He knew how to answer the mystery   1550
    Of evil in the Sphinx, and was our greatest lord.
    We saw him move the world with his will, and we envied him.
    But look, the storm destroys him, the sea
    Has come to defeat him.
    Remember that death alone can end all suffering;   1555
    Go towards death, and ask for no greater
    Happiness than a life
    In which there has been no anger and no pain.

Biographical Note

SHAKESPEARE

WILLIAM SHAKESPEARE (1564–1616) was born in the rural town of Stratford-on-Avon, the eldest son of John Shakespeare, a well-to-do glover, and his wife Mary Arden, who came from a prosperous farming family. Little is known of his early life except that he probably attended the excellent Stratford grammar school and at the age of eighteen married Anne Hathaway, with whom he had three children. About ten years later, around 1590, he was in London writing poems and plays and acting in one of the two major theatrical companies of the time, the Lord Chamberlain's Company. During the next twenty years he wrote two long narrative poems *(Venus and Adonis* and *The Rape of Lucrece)*, 154 sonnets, and some 37 plays. His income as an actor, playwright, and, most of all, a shareholder in the Globe Theater enabled him to retire around 1610 to Stratford. His plays were collected after his death by his long-time friends and acting colleagues, Heminges and Condell, and published in what is called the First Folio of 1623, where they are grouped as tragedies, comedies, and histories.

Shakespeare's literary career is usually divided into three phases, the first (from about 1590 to 1600) dominated by comedy e.g., *Love's Labour's Lost, A Midsummer Night's Dream, Much Ado About Nothing, As You Like It, Twelfth Night;* the second (from about 1600 to 1608) dominated by tragedy—e.g., *Hamlet, Othello, King Lear, Macbeth;* and the third (from about 1608 to 1613) dominated by a form of comedy heavily indebted to romance—e.g., *A Winter's Tale* and *The Tempest.*

The Tragedy of Macbeth

william shakespeare

CHARACTERS

DUNCAN *King of Scotland*
MALCOLM ⎫ *his sons*
DONALBAIN ⎭
MACBETH ⎫
BANQUO ⎪
MACDUFF ⎪
LENNOX ⎪ *noblemen of Scotland*
ROSS ⎬
MENTEITH ⎪
ANGUS ⎪
CAITHNESS ⎭
FLEANCE *son to* BANQUO
SIWARD *Earl of Northumberland*
YOUNG SIWARD *his son*
SEYTON *an officer attending on* MACBETH
BOY *son to* MACDUFF
A CAPTAIN
AN ENGLISH DOCTOR

A SCOTTISH DOCTOR
A PORTER
AN OLD MAN
THREE MURDERERS
LADY MACBETH
LADY MACDUFF
A GENTLEWOMAN *attending on* LADY MACBETH
THE WEIRD SISTERS
HECATE
THE GHOST OF BANQUO
APPARITIONS
LORDS
OFFICERS
SOLDIERS
MESSENGERS
ATTENDANTS

SCENE: *Scotland and England.*

ACT I

SCENE I. *Thunder and lightning. Enter three* WITCHES.

1. WITCH. When shall we three meet again?
    In thunder, lightning, or in rain?
2. WITCH. When the hurlyburly's done,
    When the battle's lost and won.
3. WITCH. That will be ere the set of sun.
1. WITCH. Where the place?
2. WITCH.   Upon the heath.
3. WITCH. There to meet with Macbeth.

5

1. WITCH. I come, Graymalkin!
2. WITCH. Paddock calls.
3. WITCH.   Anon!
ALL. Fair is foul, and foul is fair.   10
    Hover through the fog and filthy air.
Exeunt.

SCENE II. *Alarum within. Enter* KING [DUNCAN], MALCOLM, DONAL-
BAIN, LENNOX, *with* ATTENDANTS, *meeting a bleeding* CAPTAIN.

KING. What bloody man is that? He can report,
    As seemeth by his plight, of the revolt
    The newest state.
MALCOLM.   This is the sergeant
    Who like a good and hardy soldier fought
    'Gainst my captivity. Hail, brave friend!   5
    Say to the King the knowledge of the broil
    As thou didst leave it.
CAPTAIN.   Doubtful is stood,
    As two spent swimmers that do cling together
    And choke their art. The merciless Macdonwald
    (Worthy to be a rebel, for to that   10
    The multiplying villainies of nature
    Do swarm upon him) from the Western Isles
    Of kerns and gallowglasses is supplied;
    And Fortune, on his damned quarrel smiling,
    Showed like a rebel's whore. But all's too weak: 15
    For brave Macbeth (well he deserves that name),
    Disdaining Fortune, with his brandished steel,
    Which smoked with bloody execution,
    Like valor's minion carved out his passage
    Till he faced the slave;   20
    Which ne'er shook hands nor bade farewell to him
    Till he unseamed him from the nave to the chops
    And fixed his head upon our battlements.
KING. O valiant cousin! worthy gentleman!
CAPTAIN. As whence the sun 'gins his reflection   25
    Shipwracking storms and direful thunders break,
    So from that spring whence comfort seemed to come
    Discomfort swells. Mark, King of Scotland, mark.
    No sooner justice had, with valor armed,
    Compelled these skipping kerns to trust their heels   30
    But the Norweyan lord, surveying vantage,

I.i.8–9 *Graymalkin, Paddock:* little gray cat   22 *nave:* navel.
    and toad (spirits serving the witches).   31 *surveying vantage:* perceiving an op-
I.ii.13 *kerns and gallowglasses:* two kinds   portunity.
    of Irish soldiers.

With furbished arms and new supplies of men,
Began a fresh assault.
KING.   Dismayed not this
Our captains, Macbeth and Banquo?
CAPTAIN.   Yes,
As sparrows eagles, or the hare the lion.   35
If I say sooth, I must report they were
As cannons overcharged with double cracks,
So they doubly redoubled strokes upon the foe.
Except they meant to bathe in reeking wounds,
Or memorize another Golgotha,   40
I cannot tell—
But I am faint; my gashes cry for help.
KING. So well thy words become thee as thy wounds,
They smack of honor both. Go get him surgeons.

[*Exit* CAPTAIN, *attended.*]

Enter Ross *and* ANGUS.

Who comes here?
MALCOLM. The worthy Thane of Ross.   45
LENNOX. What a haste looks through his eyes! So should he look
That seems to speak things strange.
ROSS.   God save the King!
KING. Whence cam'st thou, worthy Thane?
ROSS.   From Fife, great King,
Where the Norweyan banners flout the sky
And fan our people cold.   50
Norway himself, with terrible numbers,
Assisted by that most disloyal traitor
The Thane of Cawdor, began a dismal conflict,
Till that Bellona's bridegroom, lapped in proof,
Confronted him with self-comparisons,   55
Point against point, rebellious arm 'gainst arm,
Curbing his lavish spirit: and to conclude,
The victory fell on us.
KING.   Great happiness!
ROSS.   That now
Sweno, the Norways' king, craves composition;
Nor would we deign him burial of his men   60
Till he disbursed, at Saint Colme's Inch,
Ten thousand dollars to our general use.
KING. No more that Thane of Cawdor shall deceive

37 *cracks:* explosive charges.
39 *Except:* unless.
54 *Bellona's bridegroom:* i.e., Macbeth, as

bridegroom of the goddess of war;
proof: armor.

Our bosom interest. Go pronounce his present death
And with his former title greet Macbeth.   65
Ross. I'll see it done.
KING. What he hath lost, noble Macbeth hath won.
Exeunt.

SCENE III. *Thunder. Enter the three* WITCHES.

1. WITCH. Where hast thou been, sister?
2. WITCH. Killing swine.
3. WITCH. Sister, where thou?
1. WITCH. A sailor's wife had chestnuts in her lap
   And mounched and mounched and mounched. "Give me,"
      quoth I.   5
   "Aroint thee, witch!" the rumpfed ronyon cries.
   Her husband's to Aleppo gone, master o' the Tiger:
   But in a sieve I'll thither sail
   And, like a rat without a tail,
   I'll do, I'll do, and I'll do.   10
2. WITCH. I'll give thee a wind.
1. WITCH. Th' art kind.
3. WITCH. And I another.
1. WITCH. I myself have all the other,
   And the very ports they blow,   15
   All the quarters that they know
   I' th' shipman's card.
   I'll drain him dry as hay.
   Sleep shall neither night nor day
   Hang upon his penthouse lid.   20
   He shall live a man forbid.
   Weary sev'nights, nine times nine,
   Shall he dwindle, peak, and pine.
   Though his bark cannot be lost,
   Yet it shall be tempest-tost.   25
   Look what I have.
2. WITCH. Show me, show me.
1. WITCH. Here I have a pilot's thumb,
   Wracked as homeward he did come.
Drum within.
3. WITCH. A drum, a drum!   30
   Macbeth doth come.
ALL. The weird sisters, hand in hand,
   Posters of the sea and land,
   Thus do go about, about,   34

I.iii.6 *Aroint:* be gone.   20 *penthouse lid:* eyelid.
17 *card:* compass.   33 *Posters:* swift riders.

Thrice to thine, and thrice to mine,
And thrice again, to make up nine.
Peace! The charm's wound up.

Enter MACBETH *and* BANQUO.

MACBETH. So foul and fair a day I have not seen.
BANQUO. How far is't called to Forres? What are these,
    So withered and so wild in their attire   40
    That look not like the inhabitants o' the earth
    And yet are on't? Live you, or are you aught
    That man may question? You seem to understand me,
    By each at once her choppy finger laying
    Upon her skinny lips. You should be women,   45
    And yet your beards forbid me to interpret
    That you are so.
MACBETH. Speak, if you can. What are you?
1. WITCH. All hail, Macbeth! Hail to thee, Thane of Glamis!
2. WITCH. All hail, Macbeth! Hail to thee, Thane of Cawdor!
3. WITCH. All hail, Macbeth, that shalt be King hereafter!   50
BANQUO. Good sir, why do you start and seem to fear
    Things that do sound so fair? I' the name of truth,
    Are ye fantastical, or that indeed
    Which outwardly ye show? My noble partner
    You greet with present grace and great prediction   55
    Of noble having and of royal hope,
    That he seems rapt withal. To me you speak not.
    If you can look into the seeds of time
    And say which grain will grow and which will not,
    Speak then to me, who neither beg nor fear   60
    Your favors nor your hate.
1. WITCH. Hail!
2. WITCH. Hail!
3. WITCH. Hail!
1. WITCH. Lesser than Macbeth, and greater.   65
2. WITCH. Not so happy, yet much happier.
3. WITCH. Thou shalt get kings, though thou be none.
    So all hail, Macbeth and Banquo!
1. WITCH. Banquo and Macbeth, all hail!
MACBETH. Stay, you imperfect speakers, tell me more: 70
    By Sinel's death I know I am Thane of Glamis,
    But how of Cawdor? The Thane of Cawdor lives,
    A prosperous gentleman; and to be King
    Stands not within the prospect of belief,
    No more than to be Cawdor. Say from whence   75

39 *Forres:* town near Inverness.   71 *Sinel:* Macbeth's father.
53 *fantastical:* imaginary.

You owe this strange intelligence, or why
Upon this blasted heath you stop our way
With such prophetic greeting. Speak, I charge you.

WITCHES *vanish.*

BANQUO. The earth hath bubbles as the water has,
    And these are of them, Whither are they vanished?   80
MACBETH. Into the air, and what seemed corporal melted
    As breath into the wind. Would they had stayed.
BANQUO. Were such things here as we do speak about?
    Or have we eaten on the insane root
    That takes the reason prisoner?   85
MACBETH. Your children shall be kings.
BANQUO.   You shall be King.
MACBETH. And Thane of Cawdor too. Went it not so?
BANQUO. To the selfsame tune and words. Who's here?

Enter Ross *and* ANGUS.

ROSS. The King hath happily received, Macbeth,
    The news of thy success; and when he reads   90
    Thy personal venture in the rebels' fight,
    His wonders and his praises do contend
    Which should be thine or his. Silenced with that,
    In viewing o'er the rest o' the selfsame day,
    He finds thee in the stout Norweyan ranks,   95
    Nothing afeard of what thyself didst make—
    Strange images of death. As thick as hail
    Came post with post, and everyone did bear
    Thy praises in his kingdom's great defense
    And poured them down before him.
ANGUS.   We are sent   100
    To give thee from our royal master thanks;
    Only to herald thee into his sight,
    Not pay thee.
ROSS. And for an earnest of a greater honor,
    He bade me, from him, call thee Thane of Cawdor;   105
    In which addition, hail, most worthy Thane,
    For it is thine.
BANQUO.   What, can the devil speak true?
MACBETH. The Thane of Cawdor lives. Why do you dress me
    In borrowed robes?
ANGUS.   Who was the Thane lives yet,
    But under heavy judgment bears that life   110
    Which he deserves to lose. Whether he was combined

84 *insane:* causing insanity.   106 *addition:* honor.
90 *reads:* thinks about.   109 *Who:* he who.

With those of Norway, or did line the rebel
With hidden help and vantage, or that with both
He labored in his country's wrack, I know not;
But treasons capital, confessed and proved,   115
Have overthrown him.
MACBETH.   [*aside*] Glamis, and Thane of Cawdor—
The greatest is behind! [*to* Ross *and* ANGUS] Thanks for your
pains.
[*aside to* BANQUO] Do you not hope your children shall be
kings,
When those that gave the Thane of Cawdor to me
Promised no less to them?
BANQUO.   [*to* MACBETH] That, trusted home,   120
Might yet enkindle you unto the crown,
Besides the Thane of Cawdor. But 'tis strange:
And oftentimes, to win us to our harm,
The instruments of darkness tell us truths,   124
Win us with honest trifles to betray's
In deepest consequence.—
Cousins, a word, I pray you.
MACBETH. [*aside*] Two truths are told,
As happy prologues to the swelling act
Of the imperial theme.—I thank you, gentlemen.—   129
[*aside*] This supernatural soliciting
Cannot be ill, cannot be good. If ill,
Why hath it given me earnest of success,
Commencing in a truth? I am Thane of Cawdor.
If good, why do I yield to that suggestion
Whose horrid image doth unfix my hair   135
And make my seated heart knock at my ribs
Against the use of nature? Present fears
Are less than horrible imaginings.
My thought, whose murder yet is but fantastical,
Shakes so my single state of man that function   140
Is smothered in surmise and nothing is
But what is not.
BANQUO.   Look how our partner's rapt.
MACBETH. [*aside*] If chance will have me King, why chance may
crown me
Without my stir.
BANQUO.   New honors come upon him
Like our strange garments, cleave not to their mould   145
But with the aid of use.
MACBETH.   [*aside*] Come what come may,
Time and the hour runs through the roughest day.

112 *line:* aid (literally, stuff).   120 *home:* completely.
117 *behind:* beyond, in the distance or   137 *use:* normal functioning.
future.   140 *function:* normal activity.

BANQUO. Worthy Macbeth, we stay upon your leisure.
MACBETH. Give me your favor. My dull brain was wrought
    With things forgotten. Kind gentlemen, your pains   150
    Are regist'red where every day I turn
    The leaf to read them. Let us toward the King.
    [*aside to* BANQUO] Think upon what hath chanced, and at
        more time,
    The interim having weighed it, let us speak
    Our free hearts each to other.
BANQUO.   Very gladly.   155
MACBETH. Till then, enough—Come, friends.
Exeunt.

SCENE IV. *Flourish. Enter* KING [DUNCAN], LENNOX, MALCOLM,
    DONALBAIN, *and* ATTENDANTS.

KING. Is execution done on Cawdor? Are not
    Those in commission yet returned?
MALCOLM.   My liege,
    They are not yet come back. But I have spoke
    With one that saw him die; who did report
    That very frankly he confessed his treasons,   5
    Implored your Highness' pardon, and set forth
    A deep repentance. Nothing in his life
    Became him like the leaving it. He died
    As one that had been studied in his death
    To throw away the dearest thing he owed   10
    As 'twere a careless trifle.
KING.   There's no art
    To find the mind's construction in the face.
    He was a gentleman on whom I built
    An absolute trust.

Enter MACBETH, BANQUO, ROSS, *and* ANGUS.

                        O worthiest cousin,   15
    The sin of my ingratitude even now
    Was heavy on me. Thou art so far before
    That swiftest wing of recompense is slow
    To overtake thee. Would thou hadst less deserved,
    That the proportion both of thanks and payment
    Might have been mine! Only I have left to say,   20
    More is thy due than more than all can pay.
MACBETH. The service and the loyalty I owe,

154 *free:* open, honest.   9 *studied:* schooled.
I.iv.2 *Those in commission:* those assigned   10 *owed:* owned.
    to execute Cawdor.   16 *before:* ahead.

In doing it pays itself. Your Highness' part
Is to receive our duties, and our duties
Are to your throne and state children and servants,   25
Which do but what they should by doing everything
Safe toward your love and honor.
KING.   Welcome hither.
I have begun to plant thee and will labor
To make thee full of growing. Noble Banquo,
That hast no less deserved nor must be known   30
No less to have done so, let me enfold thee
And hold thee to my heart.
BANQUO.   There if I grow,
The harvest is your own.
KING.   My plenteous joys,
Wanton in fullness, seek to hide themselves
In drops of sorrow. Sons, kinsmen, thanes,   35
And you whose places are the nearest, know
We will establish our estate upon
Our eldest, Malcolm, whom we name hereafter
The Prince of Cumberland; which honor must
Not unaccompanied invest him only,   40
But signs of nobleness, like stars, shall shine
On all deservers. From hence to Inverness,
And bind us further to you.
MACBETH. The rest is labor which is not used for you.
I'll be myself the harbinger, and make joyful   45
The hearing of my wife with your approach;
So, humbly take my leave.
KING.   My worthy Cawdor!
MACBETH. [*aside*] The Prince of Cumberland—that is a step
On which I must fall down or else o'erleap,
For in my way it lies. Stars, hide your fires;   50
Let not light see my black and deep desires.
The eye wink at the hand; yet let that be
Which the eye fears, when it is done, to see.   *Exit.*
KING. True, worthy Banquo: he is full so valiant,
And in his commendations I am fed;   55
It is a banquet to me. Let's after him,
Whose care is gone before to bid us welcome.
It is a peerless kinsman.
Flourish. Exeunt.

SCENE V. *Enter* MACBETH'S WIFE, *alone, with a letter.*

LADY. [*reads*] "They met me in the day of success; and I have
learned by the perfect'st report they have more in them than
mortal knowledge. When I burned in desire to question them

further, they made themselves air, into which they vanished.
Whiles I stood rapt in the wonder of it, came missives from   5
the King, who all-hailed me Thane of Cawdor, by which title,
before, these weird sisters saluted me, and referred me to the
coming on of time with 'Hail, King that shalt be!' This have
I thought good to deliver thee, my dearest partner of greatness,
that thou mightst not lose the dues of rejoicing by being ig-   10
norant of what greatness is promised thee. Lay it to thy heart,
and farewell."
Glamis thou art, and Cawdor, and shalt be
What thou art promised. Yet do I fear thy nature.
It is too full o' th' milk of human kindness
To catch the nearest way. Thou wouldst be great,   15
Art not without ambition, but without
The illness should attend it. What thou wouldst highly,
That wouldst thou holily; wouldst not play false,
And yet wouldst wrongly win. Thou'dst have, great Glamis,   20
That which cries "Thus thou must do" if thou have it;
And that which rather thou dost fear to do
Than wishest should be undone. Hie thee hither,
That I may pour my spirits in thine ear
And chastise with the valor of my tongue
All that impedes thee from the golden round   25
Which fate and metaphysical aid doth seem
To have thee crowned withal.

Enter MESSENGER.

                      What is your tidings?
MESSENGER. The King comes here tonight.
LADY.   Thou'rt mad to say it!
Is not thy master with him? who, were't so,   30
Would have informed for preparation.
MESSENGER. So please you, it is true. Our Thane is coming.
One of my fellows had the speed of him,
Who, almost dead for breath, had scarcely more
Than would make up his message.   35
LADY.   Give him tending;
He brings great news.

Exit MESSENGER.

            The raven himself is hoarse

I.v.20–23 *Thou'dst ... undone:* You desire the crown, which can be gotten only by murder; and, moreover, you desire the murder of Duncan, too, your hesitance in the matter arising not from moral scruples but only from cowardice.
26 *round:* crown.

That croaks the fatal entrance of Duncan
Under my battlements. Come, you spirits
That tend on mortal thoughts, unsex me here,
And fill me from the crown to the toe top-full   40
Of direst cruelty. Make thick my blood;
Stop up th' access and passage to remorse,
That no compunctious visitings of nature
Shake my fell purpose nor keep peace between
Th' effect and it. Come to my woman's breasts   45
And take my milk for gall, you murd'ring ministers,
Wherever in your sightless substances
You wait on nature's mischief. Come, thick night,
And pall thee in the dunnest smoke of hell,
That my keen knife see not the wound it makes,   50
Nor heaven peep through the blanket of the dark
To cry "Hold, hold!"

Enter MACBETH.

                        Great Glamis! worthy Cawdor!
Greater than both, by the all-hail hereafter!
Thy letters have transported me beyond   55
This ignorant present, and I feel now
The future in the instant.
MACBETH.   My dearest love,
Duncan comes here tonight.
LADY.   And when goes hence?
MACBETH. Tomorrow, as he purposes.
LADY.   O, never
Shall sun that morrow see!
Your face, my Thane, is as a book where men   60
May read strange matters. To beguile the time,
Look like the time; bear welcome in your eye,
Your hand, your tongue; look like th' innocent flower,
But be the serpent under't. He that's coming
Must be provided for; and you shall put   65
This night's great business into my dispatch,
Which shall to all our nights and days to come
Give solely sovereign sway and masterdom.
MACBETH. We will speak further.
LADY.   Only look up clear.
To alter favor ever is to fear.   70
Leave all the rest to me.
Exeunt.

47 *sightless:* invisible.   69 *look up clear:* appear undisturbed.
48 *wait on:* assist.   70 *favor:* color, i.e., to blanch.

SCENE VI. *Hautboys and torches. Enter* KING [DUNCAN], MALCOLM, DONALBAIN, BANQUO, LENNOX, MACDUFF, ROSS, ANGUS, *and* ATTENDANTS.

KING. This castle hath a pleasant seat. The air
    Nimbly and sweetly recommends itself
    Unto our gentle senses.
BANQUO.   This guest of summer,
    The temple-haunting martlet, does approve
    By his loved mansionry that the heaven's breath   5
    Smells wooingly here. No jutty, frieze,
    Buttress, nor coign of vantage, but this bird
    Hath made his pendent bed and procreant cradle.
    Where they most breed and haunt, I have observed
    The air is delicate.

Enter LADY [MACBETH].

KING.   See, see, our honored hostess!   10
    The love that follows us sometime is our trouble,
    Which still we thank as love. Herein I teach you
    How you shall bid God 'ield us for your pains
    And thank us for your trouble.
LADY.   All our service
    In every point twice done, and then done double,   15
    Were poor and single business to contend
    Against those honors deep and broad wherewith
    Your Majesty loads our house. For those of old,
    And the late dignities heaped up to them,
    We rest your hermits.
KING.   Where's the Thane of Cawdor?   20
    We coursed him at the heels and had a purpose
    To be his purveyor; but he rides well,
    And his great love, sharp as his spur, hath holp him
    To his home before us. Fair and noble hostess,
    We are your guest tonight.
LADY.   Your servants ever   25
    Have theirs, themselves, and what is theirs, in compt,
    To make their audit at your Highness' pleasure,
    Still to return your own.
KING.   Give me your hand.
    Conduct me to mine host: we love him highly
    And shall continue our graces towards him.   30
    By your leave, hostess.
Exeunt.

I.vi *Hautboys:* oboes.   12 *which:* though.
11 *our trouble:* troublesome.   13 *bid:* pray; *'ield us:* reward me.

SCENE VII. *Hautboys. Torches. Enter a* SEWER, *and divers* SERVANTS
with dishes and service over the stage. Then enter MACBETH.

MACBETH. If it were done when 'tis done, then 'twere well
　　It were done quickly. If the assassination
　　Could trammel up the consequence, and catch
　　With his surcease success, that but this blow
　　Might be the be-all and the end-all here,　　　　　　　　　5
　　But here, upon this bank and shoal of time,
　　We'd jump the life to come. But in these cases
　　We still have judgment here, that we but teach
　　Bloody instructions, which, being taught, return
　　To plague the inventor. This even-handed justice　　　10
　　Commends the ingredients of our poisoned chalice
　　To our own lips. He's here in double trust:
　　First, as I am his kinsman and his subject,
　　Strong both against the deed; then, as his host,
　　Who should against his murderer shut the door,　　　15
　　Not bear the knife myself. Besides, this Duncan
　　Hath borne his faculties so meek, hath been
　　So clear in his great office, that his virtues
　　Will plead like angels, trumpet-tongued, against
　　The deep damnation of his taking-off;　　　　　　　　20
　　And pity, like a naked newborn babe
　　Striding the blast, or heaven's cherubin horsed
　　Upon the sightless couriers of the air,
　　Shall blow the horrid deed in every eye
　　That tears shall drown the wind. I have no spur　　25
　　To prick the sides of my intent, but only
　　Vaulting ambition, which o'erleaps itself
　　And falls on the other—

Enter LADY [MACBETH].

　　　　　　　　　　　How now? What news?
LADY. He has almost supped. Why have you left the chamber?
MACBETH. Hath he asked for me?
LADY.　　　　　　　　　Know you not he has?　　　　30
MACBETH. We will proceed no further in this business.
　　He hath honored me of late, and I have bought
　　Golden opinions from all sorts of people,
　　Which would be worn now in their newest gloss,
　　Not cast aside so soon.
LADY.　　　　　　　　Was the hope drunk　　　　　35

I. vii *Sewer:* chief servant.　　　　17 *faculties:* prerogatives as king.
1 *done:* over, finished.　　　　　18 *clear:* guiltless, unstained.
7 *jump:* risk.　　　　　　　　　23 *sightless couriers:* i.e., the winds.

Wherein you dressed yourself? Hath it slept since?
And wakes it now to look so green and pale
At what it did so freely? From this time
Such I account thy love. Art thou afeard
To be the same in thine own act and valor   40
As thou art in desire? Wouldst thou have that
Which thou esteem'st the ornament of life,
And live a coward in thine own esteem?
Letting "I dare not" wait upon "I would,"
Like the poor cat i' the adage.

MACBETH.   Prithee, peace!   45
I dare do all that may become a man;
Who dares do more is none.

LADY.   What beast was't then
That made you break this enterprise to me?
When you durst do it, then you were a man;
And to be more than what you were, you would   50
Be so much more the man. Nor time, nor place,
Did then adhere, and yet you would make both.
They have made themselves, and that their fitness now
Does unmake you. I have given suck, and know
How tender 'tis to love the babe that milks me: 55
I would, while it was smiling in my face,
Have plucked my nipple from his boneless gums
And dashed the brains out, had I so sworn as you
Have done to this.

MACBETH.   If we should fail?

LADY.   We fail?
But screw your courage to the sticking place   60
And we'll not fail. When Duncan is asleep
(Whereto the rather shall his day's hard journey
Soundly invite him) his two chamberlains
Will I with wine and wassail so convince
That memory, the warder of the brain,   65
Shall be a fume, and the receipt of reason
A limbeck only. When in swinish sleep
Their drenched natures lie as in a death,
What cannot you and I perform upon
The unguarded Duncan? what not put upon   70
His spongy officers, who shall bear the guilt
Of our great quell?

MACBETH.   Bring forth men-children only;
For thy undaunted mettle should compose

---

45 *the adage:* "The cat would eat fish, but
would not wet her feet."
52 *adhere:* seem suitable.
53 *that their:* that very.

60 *But:* only.
67 *limbeck:* alembic, the cap of a still.
74 *received:* accepted as true.

Nothing but males. Will it not be received,
When we have marked with blood those sleepy two 75
Of his own chamber and used their very daggers,
That they have done't?
LADY.   Who dares receive it other,
As we shall make our griefs and clamor roar
Upon his death?
MACBETH.   I am settled and bend up
Each corporal agent to this terrible feat. 80
Away, and mock the time with fairest show;
False face must hide what the false heart doth know.
Exeunt.

ACT II

SCENE I. *Enter* BANQUO, *and* FLEANCE *with a torch before him.*

BANQO. How goes the night, boy?
FLEANCE. The moon is down; I have not heard the clock.
BANQUO. And she goes down at twelve.
FLEANCE.   I take't, 'tis later, sir.
BANQUO. Hold, take my sword. There's husbandry in heaven;
Their candles are all out. Take thee that too. 5
A heavy summons lies like lead upon me,
And yet I would not sleep. Merciful powers,
Restrain in me the cursed thoughts that nature
Gives way to in repose.

Enter MACBETH, *and a* SERVANT *with a torch.*

                    Give me my sword!
Who's there? 10
MACBETH. A friend.
BANQUO. What, sir, not yet at rest? The King's abed.
He hath been in unusual pleasure and
Sent forth great largess to your offices.
This diamond he greets your wife withal 15
By the name of most kind hostess, and shut up
In measureless content.
MACBETH.   Being unprepared,
Our will became the servant to defect,
Which else should free have wrought.
BANQUO.   All's well.

II.i.4 *husbandry:* thrift.
 5 *that:* probably his dagger.
 6 *summons:* i.e., to sleep.
14 *offices:* servants' quarters.

17–19 *Being ... wrought:* Being unprepared,
 our will to receive the king generously
 could not be carried out.

I dreamt last night of the three weird sisters.   20
To you they have showed some truth.
MACBETH.   I think not of them.
  Yet when we can entreat an hour to serve,
  We would spend it in some words upon that business,
  If you would grant the time.
BANQUO.   At your kind'st leisure.
MACBETH. If you shall cleave to my consent, when 'tis,   25
  It shall make honor for you.
BANQUO.   So I lose none
  In seeking to augment it, but still keep
  My bosom franchised and allegiance clear,
  I shall be counseled.
MACBETH.   Good repose the while.   29
BANQUO. Thanks, sir. The like to you.

Exeunt BANQUO [*and* FLEANCE].

MACBETH. Go bid thy mistress, when my drink is ready,
  She strike upon the bell. Get thee to bed.   *exit* [SERVANT].
  Is this a dagger which I see before me,
  The handle toward my hand? Come, let me clutch thee!
  I have thee not, and yet I see thee still.   35
  Art thou not, fatal vision, sensible
  To feeling as to sight? or art thou but
  A dagger of the mind, a false creation
  Proceeding from the heat-oppressed brain?
  I see thee yet, in form as palpable   40
  As this which now I draw.
  Thou marshall'st me the way that I was going,
  And such an instrument I was to use.
  Mine eyes are made the fools o' the other senses,
  Or else worth all the rest. I see thee still,   45
  And on thy blade and dudgeon gouts of blood,
  Which was not so before. There's no such thing.
  It is the bloody business which informs
  Thus to mine eyes. Now o'er the one half-world
  Nature seems dead, and wicked dreams abuse   50
  The curtained sleep. Witchcraft celebrates
  Pale Hecate's offerings; and withered murder,
  Alarumed by his sentinel, the wolf,
  Whose howl's his watch, thus with his stealthy pace,
  With Tarquin's ravishing strides, towards his design   55

25 *cleave ... when 'tis:* side with me at the   52 *Hecate's offerings:* rituals of Hecate,
  right time.   goddess of witchcraft.
46 *dudgeon:* handle.   55 *Tarquin:* Roman tyrant who raped
48–49 *informs Thus:* falsely communicates.   Lucrece.

Moves like a ghost. Thou sure and firm-set earth,
Hear not my steps which way they walk, for fear
The very stones prate of my where-about
And take the present horror from the time,
Which now suits with it. Whiles I threat, he lives;   60
Words to the heat of deeds too cold breath gives. *A bell rings.*
I go, and it is done: the bell invites me.
Hear it not, Duncan, for it is a knell
That summons thee to heaven, or to hell.   *exit.*

SCENE II. *Enter* LADY [MACBETH].

LADY. That which hath made them drunk hath made me bold;
    What hath quenched them hath given me fire. Hark! Peace!
    It was the owl that shrieked, the fatal bellman
    Which gives the stern'st good night. He is about it.
    The doors are open, and the surfeited grooms   5
    Do mock their charge with snores. I have drugged their possets,
    That death and nature do contend about them
    Whether they live or die.
MACBTH. [*within*] Who's there? What, ho?
LADY. Alack, I am afraid they have awaked,
    And 'tis not done! The attempt, and not the deed,   10
    Confounds us. Hark! I laid their daggers ready—
    He could not miss 'em. Had he not resembled
    My father as he slept, I had done't.

Enter MACBETH.

                                My husband!
MACBETH. I have done the deed. Didst thou not hear a noise?
LADY. I heard the owl scream and the crickets cry.   15
    Did not you speak?
MACBETH.   When?
LADY.   Now.
MACBETH.   As I descended?
LADY. Ay.
MACBETH. Hark!
            Who lies i' the second chamber?
LADY. Donalbain.
MACBETH. This is a sorry sight. [*Looking at his hands.*]   20
LADY. A foolish thought, to say a sorry sight.
MACBETH. There's one did laugh in's sleep, and one cried
    "Murder!"

II.ii.3 *fatal bellman:* who rang outside the   crimes.
  cells of condemned men the night be-   6 *possets:* nightcaps of ale and warm milk.
  fore execution to remind them of their

That they did wake each other. I stood and heard them.
But they did say their prayers and addressed them
Again to sleep.
LADY.   There are two lodged together.   25
MACBETH. One cried "God bless us!" and "Amen!" the other,
As they had seen me with these hangman's hands,
List'ning their fear. I could not say "Amen!"
When they did say "God bless us!"
LADY.   Consider it not so deeply.
MACBETH. But wherefore could not I pronounce "Amen"?   30
I had most need of blessing, and "Amen"
Stuck in my throat.
LADY.   These deeds must not be thought
After these ways; so, it will make us mad.
MACBETH. Methought I heard a voice cry "Sleep no more!
Macbeth does murder sleep"—the innocent sleep,   35
Sleep that knits up the raveled sleave of care,
The death of each day's life, sore labor's bath,
Balm of hurt minds, great nature's second course,
Chief nourisher in life's feast.
LADY.   What do you mean?
MACBETH. Still it cried "Sleep no more!" to all the house;   40
"Glamis hath murdered Sleep, and therefore Cawdor
Shall sleep no more, Macbeth shall sleep no more."
LADY. Who was it that thus cried? Why, worthy Thane,
You do unbend your noble strength to think
So brainsickly of things. Go, get some water   45
And wash this filthy witness from your hand.
Why did you bring these daggers from the place?
They must lie there: go, carry them, and smear
The sleepy grooms with blood.
MACBETH.   I'll go no more.
I am afraid to think what I have done;   50
Look on't again I dare not.
LADY.   Infirm of purpose!
Give me the daggers. The sleeping, and the dead,
Are but as pictures. 'Tis the eye of childhood
That fears a painted devil. If he do bleed,
I'll gild the faces of the grooms withal,   55
For it must seem their guilt.

Exit. Knocking within.

MACBETH.   Whence is that knocking?
How is't with me when every noise appalls me?

---

36 *raveled sleave:* tangled skein.   38 *second course:* sleep as an after-dinner
                                             nap.

What hands are here? Ha! they pluck out mine eyes.
Will all great Neptune's ocean wash this blood
Clean from my hand? No, this my hand will rather   60
The multitudinous seas incarnadine,
Making the green one red.

Enter LADY [MACBETH].

LADY. My hands are of your color, but I shame
      To wear a heart so white. (*Knock.*) I hear a knocking
      At the south entry. Retire we to our chamber.   65
      A little water clears us of this deed.
      How easy is it then! Your constancy
      Hath left you unattended. (*Knock.*) Hark! more knocking.
      Get on your nightgown, lest occasion call us
      And show us to be watchers. Be not lost   70
      So poorly in your thoughts.
MACBETH. To know my deed, 'twere best not know myself. (*Knock.*)
      Wake Duncan with thy knocking! I would thou couldst.
Exeunt.

SCENE III. *Enter a* PORTER. *Knocking within.*

PORTER. Here's a knocking indeed! If a man were porter of hell
      gate, he should have old turning the key. (*Knock.*) Knock,
      knock, knock. Who's there, i' the name of Beelzebub? Here's
      a farmer that hanged himself on the expectation of plenty.
      Come in time! Have napkins enow about you; here you'll   5
      sweat for't. (*Knock.*) Knock, knock. Who's there, in the other
      devil's name? Faith, here's an equivocator, that could swear in
      both the scales against either scale; who committed treason
      enough for God's sake, yet could not equivocate to heaven. O
      come in, equivocator. (*Knock.*) Knock, knock, knock. Who's   10
      there? Faith, here's an English tailor come hither for stealing
      out of a French hose. Come in, tailor. Here you may roast your
      goose. (*Knock.*) Knock, knock. Never at quiet! What are you?—
      But this place is too cold for hell. I'll devil-porter it no further.
      I had thought to have let in some of all professions that go   15
      the primrose way to the everlasting bonfire. (*Knock.*) Anon,
      anon! [*Opens the gate.*] I pray you remember the porter.

Enter MACDUFF *and* LENNOX.

67–68 *Your constancy ... unattended:* Your
  resolution has abandoned you.
II.iii.3 *old:* frequent.
  4 *a farmer ... plenty:* who, having hoarded
  crops, killed himself when it became

apparent that a plentiful harvest, which
would lower prices, was forthcoming.
13 *goose:* pressing iron; also venereal disorder; also whore.

MACDUFF. Was it so late, friend, ere you went to bed,
 That you do lie so late?
PORTER. Faith, sir, we were carousing till the second cock; and   20
 drink, sir, is a great provoker of three things.
MACDUFF. What three things does drink especially provoke?
PORTER. Marry, sir, nose-painting, sleep, and urine. Lechery, sir, it
 provokes, and unprovokes: it provokes the desire, but it takes
 away the performance. Therefore much drink may be said to 25
 be an equivocator with lechery: it makes him, and it mars
 him; it sets him on, and it takes him off; it persuades him,
 and disheartens him; makes him stand to, and not stand to;
 in conclusion, equivocates him in a sleep, and giving him the
 lie, leaves him.   30
MACDUFF. I believe drink gave thee the lie last night.
PORTER. That it did, sir, i' the very throat on me; but I requited
 him for his lie; and, I think, being too strong for him, though
 he took up my legs sometime, yet I made a shift to cast him.
MACDUFF. Is thy master stirring?   35

Enter MACBETH.

 Our knocking has awaked him: here he comes.
LENNOX. Good morrow, noble sir.
MACBETH.   Good morrow, both.
MACDUFF. Is the King stirring, worthy Thane?
MACBETH.   Not yet.
MACDUFF. He did command me to call timely on him;
 I have almost slipped the hour.
MACBETH.   I'll bring you to him.   40
MACDUFF. I know this is a joyful trouble to you;
 But yet 'tis one.
MACBETH.   The labor we delight in physics pain.
 This is the door.
MACDUFF.   I'll make so bold to call,
 For 'tis my limited service. [*Exit.*]
LENNOX. Goes the King hence today?
MACBETH.   He does; he did appoint so. 45
LENNOX. The night has been unruly. Where we lay,
 Our chimneys were blown down; and, as they say,
 Lamentings heard i' the air, strange screams of death,
 And prophesying, with accents terrible,
 Of dire combustion and confused events   50
 New hatched to the woeful time. The obscure bird
 Clamored the livelong night. Some say the earth

20 *second cock:* 3 A.M.   42 *physics:* eliminates.
34 *made a shift:* managed; *cast:* throw (as 44 *limited:* appointed.
 a wrestler), throw up (as a drinker), 51 *bird:* owl.
 urinate.

Was feverous and did shake.
MACBETH.   'Twas a rough night.
LENNOX. My young remembrance cannot parallel
    A fellow to it.   55

Enter MACDUFF.

MACDUFF. O horror, horror, horror! Tongue nor heart
    Cannot conceive nor name thee!
MACBETH and LENNOX.   What's the matter?
MACDUFF. Confusion now hath made his masterpiece:
    Most sacrilegious murder hath broke ope
    The Lord's anointed temple and stole thence   60
    The life o' the building!
MACBETH.   What is't you say—the life?
LENNOX. Mean you his Majesty?
MACDUFF. Approach the chamber and destroy your sight
    With a new Gorgon. Do not bid me speak—
    See, and then speak yourselves.

Exeunt MACBETH *and* LENNOX.

                      Awake, awake!   65
    Ring the alarum bell! Murder and treason!
    Banquo and Donalbain! Malcolm, awake!
    Shake off this downy sleep, death's counterfeit,
    And look on death itself. Up, up, and see
    The great doom's image. Malcolm! Banquo!
    As from your graves rise up and walk like sprites   70
    To countenance this horror. Ring the bell! *Bell rings.*

Enter LADY [MACBETH].

LADY. What's the business,
    That such a hideous trumpet calls to parley
    The sleepers of the house? Speak, speak!
MACDUFF.   O gentle lady,   75
    'Tis not for you to hear what I can speak:
    The repetition in a woman's ear
    Would murder as it fell.

Enter BANQUO.

                O Banquo, Banquo!
    Our royal master's murdered!
LADY.   Woe, alas!

70 *great doom's image:* likeness of the day   72 *countenance:* look upon and look like.
   of judgment.

What, in our house?

BANQUO.   Too cruel anywhere.
   Dear Duff, I prithee contradict thyself
   And say it is not so.

Enter MACBETH, LENNOX, *and* ROSS.

MACBETH. Had I but died an hour before this chance,
   I had lived a blessed time; for from this instant
   There's nothing serious in mortality: 85
   All is but toys. Renown and grace is dead,
   The wine of life is drawn, and the mere lees
   Is left this vault to brag of.

Enter MALCOLM *and* DONALBAIN.

DONALBAIN. What is amiss?
MACBETH.   You are, and do not know't.
   The spring, the head, the fountain of your blood   90
   Is stopped, the very source of it is stopped.
MACDUFF. Your royal father's murdered.
MALCOLM.   O' by whom?
LENNOX. Those of his chamber, as it seemed, had done't.
   Their hands and faces were all badged with blood;
   So were their daggers, which unwiped we found   95
   Upon their pillows. They stared and were distracted.
   No man's life was to be trusted with them.
MACBETH. O, yet I do repent me of my fury
   That I did kill them.
MACDUFF.   Wherefore did you so?
MACBETH. Who can be wise, amazed, temp'rate and furious,   100
   Loyal and neutral, in a moment? No man.
   The expedition of my violent love
   Outrun the pauser, reason. Here lay Duncan,
   His silver skin laced with his golden blood;
   And his gashed stabs looked like a breach in nature   105
   For ruin's wasteful entrance: there, the murderers,
   Steeped in the colors of their trade, their daggers
   Unmannerly breeched with gore. Who could refrain
   That had a heart to love, and in that heart
   Courage to make's love known?
LADY.   Help me hence, ho!   110
MACDUFF. Look to the lady.
MALCOLM.   [*aside to* DONALBAIN] Why do we hold
      our tongues,
   That most may claim this argument for ours?

85 *serious in mortality:* worth taking seri-   102 *expedition:* speed.
   ously in life.   103 *pauser:* retarder.
86 *toys:* trifles.   111 *Look:* tend.

DONALBAIN. [*to* MALCOLM] What should be spoken here,
    Where our fate, hid in an auger hole,
    May rush and seize us? Let's away: 115
    Our tears are not yet brewed.
MALCOLM. [*to* DONALBAIN] Nor our strong sorrow
    Upon the foot of motion.
BANQUO.   Look to the lady
[LADY MACBETH *is carried out.*]
    And when we have our naked frailties hid,
    That suffer in exposure, let us meet   120
    And question this most bloody piece of work,
    To know it further. Fears and scruples shake us.
    In the great hand of God I stand, and thence
    Against the undivulged pretense I fight
    Of treasonous malice.
MACDUFF.   And so do I.   125
ALL.   So all.
MACBETH. Let's briefly put on manly readiness
    And meet i' the hall together.
ALL.   Well contented.

Exeunt [*all but* MALCOLM *and* DONALBAIN].

MALCOLM. What will you do? Let's not consort with them.
    To show an unfelt sorrow is an office
    Which the false man does easy. I'll to England.   130
DONALBAIN. To Ireland I. Our separated fortune
    Shall keep us both the safer. Where we are,
    There's daggers in men's smiles; the near in blood,
    The nearer bloody.
MALCOLM.   This murderous shaft that's shot
    Hath not yet lighted, and our safest way   135
    Is to avoid the aim. Therefore to horse,
    And let us not be dainty of leave-taking
    But shift away. There's warrant in that theft
    Which steals itself when there's no mercy left.
Exeunt.

SCENE IV. *Enter* ROSS *with an* OLD MAN.

OLD MAN. Threescore and ten I can remember well;
    Within the volume of which time I have seen
    Hours dreadful and things strange, but this sore night
    Hath trifled former knowings.
ROSS.   Ha, good father,

115 *auger:* i.e., a small (hole).   124 *undivulged pretense:* secret designs.
118 *Upon the foot of motion:* begun.   II.iv.7 *traveling lamp:* the sun.
121 *question:* discuss.

Thou seest the heavens, as troubled with man's act,   5
Threatens his bloody stage. By the clock 'tis day,
And yet dark night strangles the traveling lamp.
Is't night's predominance or the day's shame
That darkness does the face of earth entomb
When living light should kiss it?
OLD MAN.   'Tis unnatural,   10
Even like the deed that's done. On Tuesday last
A falcon, towering in her pride of place,
Was by a mousing owl hawked at and killed.
ROSS. And Duncan's horses (a thing most strange and certain),
Beauteous and swift, the minions of their race,   15
Turned wild in nature, broke their stalls, flung out,
Contending 'gainst obedience, as they would make
War with mankind.
OLD MAN. 'Tis said they eat each other.
ROSS. They did so, to the amazement of mine eyes
That looked upon't.

Enter MACDUFF.

                         Here comes the good Macduff.   20
How goes the world, sir, now?
MACDUFF.   Why, see you not?
ROSS. Is't known who did this more than bloody deed?
MACDUFF. Those that Macbeth hath slain.
ROSS.   Alas the day,
What good could they pretend?
MACDUFF.   They were suborned.
Malcolm and Donalbain, the King's two sons,   25
Are stol'n away and fled, which puts upon them
Suspicion of the deed.
ROSS.   'Gainst nature still.
Thriftless ambition, that will raven up
Thine own live's means! Then 'tis most like
The sovereignty will fall upon Macbeth.   30
MACDUFF. He is already named, and gone to Scone
To be invested.
ROSS.   Where is Duncan's body?
MACDUFF. Carried to Colmekill,
The sacred storehouse of his predecessors
And guardian of their bones.
ROSS.   Will you to Scone?   35
MACDUFF. No, cousin, I'll to Fife.
ROSS.   Well, I will thither
MACDUFF. Well, may you see things well done there—Adieu—

24 *pretend:* expect.   28 *raven up:* eat up.

Lest our old robes sit easier than our new!
Ross. Farewell, father.
OLD MAN. God's benison go with you, and with those   40
    That would make good of bad, and friends of foes.
Exeunt omnes.

ACT III

SCENE I. *Enter* BANQUO.

BANQUO. Thou hast it now—King, Cawdor, Glamis, all,
    As the weird women promised; and I fear
    Thou play'dst most foully for't. Yet it was said
    It should not stand in thy posterity.
    But that myself should be the root and father   5
    Of many kings. If there come truth from them,
    (As upon thee, Macbeth, their speeches shine)
    Why, by the verities on thee made good,
    May they not be my oracles as well
    And set me up in hope? But hush, no more!   10

Sennet sounded. Enter MACBETH *as King,* LADY [MACBETH], LEN-
NOX, ROSS, LORDS, *and* ATTENDANTS.

MACBETH. Here's our chief guest.
LADY.   If he had been forgotten,
    It had been as a gap in our great feast,
    And all-thing unbecoming.
MACBETH. Tonight we hold a solemn supper, sir,
    And I'll request your presence.
BANQUO.   Let your Highness   15
    Command upon me, to the which my duties
    Are with a most indissoluble tie
    Forever knit.
MACBETH Ride you this afternoon?
BANQUO. Ay, my good lord.
MACBETH. We should have else desired your good advice,   20
    Which still hath been both grave and prosperous,
    In this day's council; but we'll take tomorrow.
    Is't far you ride?
BANQUO. As far, my lord, as will fill up the time
    'Twixt this and supper. Go not my horse the better,   25
    I must become a borrower of the night
    For a dark hour or twain.
MACBETH.   Fail not our feast.

40 *benison:* blessing.   14 *solemn:* formal.
III.i.13 *all-thing:* entirely.

BANQUO. My lord, I will not.
MACBETH. We hear our bloody cousins are bestowed
        In England and in Ireland, not confessing   30
        Their cruel parricide, filling their hearers
        With strange invention. But of that tomorrow,
        When therewithal we shall have cause of state
        Craving us jointly. Hie you to horse. Adieu,
        Till you return at night. Goes Fleance with you?   35
BANQUO. Ay, my good lord. Our time does call upon's.
MACBETH. I wish your horses swift and sure of foot,
        And so I do commend you to their backs.
Farewell.   *Exit* BANQUO.
        Let every man be master of his time   40
        Till seven at night. To make society
        The sweeter welcome, we will keep ourself
        Till supper time alone. While then, God be with you!

                            Exeunt LORDS [*and others*].

        Sirrah, a word with you. Attend those men
        Our pleasure?   45
SERVANT. They are, my lord, without the palace gate.
MACBETH. Bring them before us.

Exit SERVANT.

        To be thus is nothing, but to be safely thus—
        Our fears in Banquo stick deep,
        And in his royalty of nature reigns that   50
        Which would be feared. 'Tis much he dares;
        And to that dauntless temper of his mind
        He hath a wisdom that doth guide his valor
        To act in safety. There is none but he
        Whose being I do fear; and under him   55
        My genius is rebuked, as it is said
        Mark Antony's was by Caesar. He chid the sisters
        When first they put the name of King upon me,
        And bade them speak to him. Then, prophetlike,
        They hailed him father to a line of kings.   60
        Upon my head they placed a fruitless crown
        And put a barren sceptre in my gripe,
        Thence to be wrenched with an unlineal hand,
        No son of mine succeeding. If't be so,
        For Banquo's issue have I filed my mind;   65

---

44 *Sirrah:* term used to address inferiors.   65 *issue:* offspring; *filed:* defiled probably,
49 *in:* concerning.   but perhaps also sharpened and ex-
56 *genius is rebuked:* spirit is put down.   acerbated.

For them the gracious Duncan have I murdered;
Put rancors in the vessel of my peace,
Only for them, and mine eternal jewel
Given to the common enemy of man
To make them kings—the seed of Banquo kings!   70
Rather than so, come, Fate, into the list,
And champion me to th' utterance! Who's there?

Enter SERVANT *and two* MURDERERS.

Now go to the door and stay there till we call.   *Exit* SERVANT.
Was it not yesterday we spoke together?
MURDERERS. It was, so please your Highness.
MACBETH.   Well then, now   75
Have you considered of my speeches? Know
That it was he in the times past which held you
So under fortune, which you thought had been
Our innocent self. This I made good to you
In our last conference, passed in probation with you   80
How you were borne in hand, how crossed, the instruments,
Who wrought with them, and all things else that might
To half a soul and to a notion crazed
Say "Thus did Banquo."
1. MURDERER.   You made it known to us.
MACBETH. I did so, and went further, which is now   85
Our point of second meeting. Do you find
Your patience so predominant in your nature
That you can let this go? Are you so gospeled
To pray for this good man and for his issue
Whose heavy hand hath bowed you to the grave   90
And beggared yours forever?
1. MURDERER.   We are men, my liege.
MACBETH. Ay, in the catalogue ye go for men,
As hounds and greyhounds, mongrels, spaniels, curs,
Shoughs, water-rugs, and demiwolves are clept
All by the name of dogs. The valued file   95
Distinguishes the swift, the slow, the subtle,
The housekeeper, the hunter, every one
According to the gift which bounteous nature
Hath in him closed, whereby he does receive
Particular addition, from the bill   100

---

68 *eternal jewel:* immortal soul.
72 *champion:* combat; *utterance:* uttermost
point (death).
80 *passed in probation with:* proved to.
81 *borne in hand:* duped along; *crossed:*
frustrated.

88 *gospeled:* subdued by gospel teachings
such as "Love thy enemies."
94 *shoughs:* shaggy-haired lapdogs.
95 *valued file:* list of ratings.
100 *Particular addition:* special distinction;
from: contrary to.

That writes them all alike; and so of men.
Now, if you have a station in the file,
Not in the worst rank of manhood, say't;
And I will put that business in your bosoms
Whose execution takes your enemy off,   105
Grapples you to the heart and love of us,
Who wear our health but sickly in his life,
Which in his death were perfect.
2. MURDERER.   I am one, my liege,
Whom the vile blows and buffets of the world
Have so incensed that I am reckless what   110
I do to spite the world.
1. MURDERER.   And I another,
So weary with disasters, tugged with fortune,
That I would set my life on any chance
To mend it or be rid on't.
MACBETH.   Both of you
Know Banquo was your enemy.   115
MURDERERS.   True, my lord.
MACBETH. So is he mine, and in such bloody distance
That every minute of his being thrusts
Against my near'st of life; and though I could
With barefaced power sweep him from my sight
And bid my will avouch it, yet I must not,   120
For certain friends that are both his and mine,
Whose loves I may not drop, but wail his fall
Who I myself struck down. And thence it is
That I to your assistance do make love,
Masking the business from the common eye   125
For sundry weighty reasons.
2. MURDERER.   We shall, my lord,
Perform what you command us.
1. MURDERER.   Though our lives—
MACBETH. Your spirits shine through you. Within this hour at most
I will advise you where to plant yourselves,
Acquaint you with the perfect spy o' the time,   130
The moment on't, for't must be done tonight
And something from the palace (always thought
That I require a clearness); and with him,
To leave no rubs nor botches in the work,
Fleance his son, that keeps him company,   135
Whose absence is no less material to me
Than is his father's, must embrace the fate
Of that dark hour. Resolve yourselves apart;

113 *set:* risk.
116 *distance:* disagreement.
120 *avouch:* justify.

132 *always thought:* constantly keeping in
    mind.
134 *rubs:* imperfections.

I'll come to you anon.
MURDERERS.   We are resolved, my lord.
MACBETH. I'll call upon you straight. Abide within.   140

[*Exeunt* MURDERERS.]

    It is concluded. Banquo, thy soul's flight,
    If it find heaven, must find it out tonight.
Exeunt.

SCENE II. *Enter* MACBETH's LADY *and a* SERVANT.

LADY. Is Banquo gone from court?
SERVANT. Ay, madam, but returns again tonight.
LADY. Say to the King I would attend his leisure
    For a few words.
SERVANT.   Madam, I will.   [*Exit.*]
LADY.   Nought's had, all's spent,
    Where our desire is got without content.   5
    'Tis safer to be that which we destroy
    Than by destruction dwell in doubtful joy.

Enter MACBETH.

    How now, my lord? Why do you keep alone,
    Of sorriest fancies your companions making,
    Using those thoughts which should indeed have died   10
    With them they think on? Things without all remedy
    Should be without regard. What's done is done.
MACBETH. We have scorched the snake, not killed it.
    She'll close and be herself, whilst our poor malice
    Remains in danger of her former tooth.   15
    But let the frame of things disjoint, both the worlds suffer,
    Ere we will eat our meal in fear, and sleep
    In the affliction of these terrible dreams
    That shake us nightly. Better be with the dead,
    Whom we, to gain our peace, have sent to peace,   20
    Than on the torture of the mind to lie
    In restless ecstasy. Duncan is in his grave;
    After life's fitful fever he sleeps well.
    Treason has done his worst: nor steel nor poison,
    Malice domestic, foreign levy, nothing,   25
    Can touch him further.
LADY.   Come on,

III.ii.16 *disjoint:* break apart; *both the*   21 *torture:* torturing rack.
   worlds: heaven and earth.   22 *ecstasy:* fever, madness.

Gentle my lord, sleek o'er your rugged looks;
Be bright and jovial among your guests tonight.
MACBETH. So shall I, love; and so, I pray, be you.
    Let your remembrance apply to Banquo;   30
    Present him eminence both with eye and tongue:
    Unsafe the while, that we must lave
    Our honors in these flattering streams
    And make our faces vizards to our hearts,
    Disguising what they are.
LADY.   You must leave this.   35
MACBETH. O, full of scorpions is my mind, dear wife!
    Thou know'st that Banquo, and his Fleance, lives.
LADY. But in them Nature's copy's not eterne.
MACBETH. There's comfort yet; they are assailable.
    Then be thou jocund. Ere the bat hath flown   40
    His cloistered flight, ere to black Hecate's summons
    The shard-born beetle with his drowsy hums
    Hath rung night's yawning peal, there shall be done
    A deed of dreadful note.
LADY.   What's to be done?
MACBETH. Be innocent of the knowledge, dearest chuck,   45
    Till thou applaud the deed. Come, seeling night,
    Scarf up the tender eye of pitiful day,
    And with thy bloody and invisible hand
    Cancel and tear to pieces that great bond
    Which keeps me pale. Light thickens, and the crow   50
    Makes wing to the rooky wood.
    Good things of day begin to droop and drowse,
    Whiles night's black agents to their preys do rouse.
    Thou marvell'st at my words, but hold thee still;
    Things bad begun make strong themselves by ill.   55
    So prithee go with me.
Exeunt.

SCENE III. *Enter three* MURDERERS.

1. MURDERER. But who did bid thee join with us?
3. MURDERER.   Macbeth.
2. MURDERER. He needs not our mistrust, since he delivers
    Our offices and what we have to do
    To the direction just.

---

31 *Present him eminence:* treat him defer-
   entially.
34 *vizards:* masks.
38 *copy:* copyhold, lease.
42 *shard-born:* dung-engendered.
46 *seeling:* stiching together (as a hawk's

eyelids were stitched to make him
tractable).
49 *bond:* Banquo's lease on life.
III.iii.2–4 *He . . . just:* We need not mistrust this man since he repeats our
instructions from Macbeth exactly.

1. MURDERER.   Then stand with us.
   The west yet glimmers with some streaks of day.   5
   Now spurs the lated traveler apace
   To gain the timely inn, and near approaches
   The subject of our watch.
3. MURDERER.   Hark, I hear horses.
BANQUO. *(within)* Give us a light there, ho!
2. MURDERER.   Then 'tis he: the rest
   That are within the note of expectation   10
   Already are i' the court.
1. MURDERER.   His horses go about.
3. MURDERER. Almost a mile; but he does usually,
   So all men do, from hence to the palace gate
   Make it their walk.

Enter BANQUO, *and* FLEANCE, *with a torch.*

2. MURDERER.   A light, a light!
3. MURDERER.   'Tis he.
1. MURDERER. Stand to't.   15
BANQUO.   It will be rain tonight.
1. MURDERER. Let it come down!
BANQUO. O, treachery! Fly, good Fleance, fly, fly, fly!
   Thou mayst revenge—O slave!

[*Dies.* FLEANCE *escapes.*]

3. MURDERER. Who did strike out the light?
1. MURDERER.   Was't not the way?
3. MURDERER. There's but one down: the son is fled.   20
2. MURDERER. We have lost best half of our affair.
1. MURDERER. Well, let's away, and say how much is done.
Exeunt.

SCENE IV. *A Banquet prepared. Enter* MACBETH, LADY [MACBETH],
   ROSS, LENNOX, LORDS, *and* ATTENDANTS.

MACBETH. You know your own degrees—sit down:
   At first and last, the hearty welcome.
LORDS.   Thanks to your Majesty.
MACBETH. Ourself will mingle with society
   And play the humble host.   5
   Our hostess keeps her state, but in best time
   We will require her welcome.

---

10 *within the note of expectation:* i.e., on
   the guest list.

LADY. Pronounce it for me, sir, to all our friends,
　　For my heart speaks they are welcome.

Enter FIRST MURDERER, *to the door.*

MACBETH. See, they encounter thee with their hearts' thanks.   10
　　Both sides are even. Here I'll sit i' the midst.
　　Be large in mirth; anon we'll drink a measure
　　The table round. [*Goes to door.*]
　　There's blood upon thy face.
MURDERER.   'Tis Banquo's then.
MACBETH. 'Tis better thee without than he within.   15
　　Is he dispatched?
MURDERER.   My lord, his throat is cut:
　　That I did for him.
MACBETH.   Thou art the best o' th' cutthroats.
　　Yet he's good that did the like for Fleance:
　　If thou didst it, thou art the nonpareil.
MURDERER. Most royal sir, Fleance is scaped.   20
MACBETH. [*aside*] Then comes my fit again. I had else been perfect—
　　Whole as the marble, founded as the rock,
　　As broad and general as the casing air.
　　But now I am cabined, cribbed, confined, bound in
　　To saucy doubts and fears.—But Banquo's safe?   25
MURDERER. Ay, my good lord. Safe in a ditch he bides,
　　With twenty trenched gashes on his head,
　　The least a death to nature.
MACBETH.   Thanks for that.—
　　[*aside*] There the grown serpent lies; the worm that's fled
　　Hath nature that in time will venom breed,   30
　　No teeth for the present.—Get thee gone. Tomorrow
　　We'll hear ourselves again.

Exit MURDERER.

LADY.   My royal lord,
　　You do not give the cheer. The feast is sold
　　That is not often vouched, while 'tis a-making,
　　'Tis given with welcome. To feed were best at home;   35
　　From thence, the sauce to meat is ceremony:
　　Meeting were bare without it.

Enter the GHOST OF BANQUO *and sits in* MACBETH'S *place.*

III.iv.23 *casing:* encasing, enclosing.   34 *vouched:* authenticated by cordial speech.
29 *worm:* serpent.   35 *To feed:* merely to eat.
33 *sold:* not given freely.   36 *From thence:* away from home.

MACBETH.   Sweet remembrancer!
    Now good digestion wait on appetite,
    And health on both!
LENNOX.   May't please your Highness sit.
MACBETH. Here had we now our country's honor roofed   40
    Were the graced person of our Banquo present—
    Who may I rather challenge for unkindness
    Than pity for mischance!
ROSS.   His absence, sir,
    Lays blame upon his promise. Please't your Highness
    To grace us with your royal company?   45
MACBETH. The table's full.
LENNOX.   Here is a place reserved, sir.
MACBETH. Where?
LENNOX. Here, my good lord. What is't that moves your Highness?
MACBETH. Which of you have done this?
LORDS.   What, my good lord?
MACBETH. Thou canst not say I did it; never shake   50
    Thy gory locks at me.
ROSS. Gentlemen, rise. His Highness is not well.
LADY. Sit, worthy friends. My lord is often thus,
    And hath been from his youth. Pray you keep seat.
    The fit is momentary; upon a thought   55
    He will again be well. If much you note him,
    You shall offend him and extend his passion.
    Feed, and regard him not.—Are you a man?
MACBETH. Ay, and a bold one, that dare look on that
    Which might appall the devil.
LADY.   O proper stuff!   60
    This is the very painting of your fear.
    This is the air-drawn dagger which you said
    Led you to Duncan. O, these flaws and starts,
    Impostors to true fear, would well become
    A woman's story at a winter's fire,   65
    Authorized by her grandam. Shame itself!
    Why do you make such faces? When all's done,
    You look but on a stool.
MACBETH.   Prithee see there!
    Behold! Look! Lo!—How say you?
    Why, what care I? If thou canst nod, speak too.   70
    If charnel houses and our graves must send
    Those that we bury back, our monuments
    Shall be the maws of kites.

[*Exit* GHOST.]

40 *our country's honor roofed:* all Scot-   72 *our monuments:* our only graves.
   land's honored men under one roof.   73 *maws of kites:* bellies of birds of prey.
62 *air-drawn:* carried on the air.

LADY.   What, quite unmanned in folly?
MACBETH. If I stand here, I saw him.
LADY.   Fie, for shame!
MACBETH. Blood hath been shed ere now, i' the olden time,   75
    Ere humane statute purged the gentle weal;
    Ay, and since too, murders have been performed
    Too terrible for the ear. The time has been
    That, when the brains were out, the man would die,
    And there an end. But now they rise again,   80
    With twenty mortal murders on their crowns,
    And push us from our stools. This is more strange
    Than such a murder is.
LADY.   My worthy lord,
    Your noble friends do lack you.
MACBETH.   I do forget.
    Do not muse at me, my most worthy friends;   85
    I have a strange infirmity, which is nothing
    To those that know me. Come, love and health to all!
    Then I'll sit down. Give me some wine, fill full.

Enter GHOST.

    I drink to the general joy o' the whole table,
    And to our dear friend Banquo, whom we miss.   90
    Would he were here! To all, and him, we thirst,
    And all to all.
LORDS.   Our duties, and the pledge.
MACRETH. Avaunt, and quit my sight! Let the earth hide thee!
    Thy bones are marrowless, thy blood is cold;
    Thou hast no speculation in those eyes   95
    Which thou dost glare with!
LADY.   Think of this, good peers,
    But as a thing of custom. 'Tis no other.
    Only it spoils the pleasure of the time.
MACBETH. What man dare, I dare.
    Approach thou like the rugged Russian bear,   100
    The armed rhinoceros, or the Hyrcan tiger;
    Take any shape but that, and my firm nerves
    Shall never tremble. Or be alive again
    And dare me to the desert with thy sword.
    If trembling I inhabit then, protest me   105
    The baby of a girl. Hence, horrible shadow!
    Unreal mock'ry, hence!

[*Exit* GHOST.]

                Why, so—Being gone,

76 *purged the gentle weal:* civilized society.

I am a man again. Pray you sit still.
LADY. You have displaced the mirth, broke the good meeting,
 With most admired disorder.
MACBETH.   Can such things be,   110
 And overcome us like a summer's cloud
 Without our special wonder? You make me strange
 Even to the disposition that I owe,
 When now I think you can behold such sights
 And keep the natural ruby of your cheeks   115
 When mine is blanched with fear.
ROSS.   What sights, my lord?
LADY. I pray you speak not; he grows worse and worse.
 Question enrages him. At once, good night.
 Stand not upon the order of your going,
 But go at once.
LENNOX.   Good night and better health   120
 Attend his Majesty.
LADY.   A kind good night to all.

Exeunt LORDS.

MACBETH. It will have blood, they say: blood will have blood.
 Stones have been known to move and trees to speak;
 Augures and understood relations have
 By maggot-pies and choughs and rooks brought forth   125
 The secret'st man of blood. What is the night?
LADY. Almost at odds with morning, which is which.
MACBETH. How say'st thou, that Macduff denies his person
 At our great bidding?
LADY.   Did you send to him, sir?
MACBETH. I hear it by the way; but I will send.   130
 There's not a one of them but in his house
 I keep a servant fee'd. I will tomorrow
 (And betimes I will) to the weird sisters.
 More shall they speak, for now I am bent to know
 By the worst means the worst. For mine own good   135
 All causes shall give way. I am in blood
 Stepped in so far that, should I wade no more,
 Returning were as tedious as go o'er.
 Strange things I have in head, that will to hand,
 Which must be acted ere they may be scanned.   140
LADY. You lack the season of all natures, sleep.
MACBETH. Come, we'll to sleep. My strange and self-abuse

109 *admired:* dumbfounding.
111 *overcome:* happen to.
112–113 *make me . . . owe:* usurp my role as
 a brave man.

124 *Augures:* auguries; *understood rela-*
 tions: omens (often contained in birds'
 cries) properly interpreted.
133 *betimes:* quickly.

Is the initiate fear that wants hard use.
We are yet but young in deed.
Exeunt.

SCENE V. *Thunder. Enter the three* WITCHES, *meeting* HECATE.

1. WITCH. Why, how now, Hecate! You look angerly.
HECATE. Have I not reason, beldams as you are,
    Saucy and overbold? How did you dare
    To trade and traffic with Macbeth
    In riddles and affairs of death;   5
    And I, the mistress of your charms,
    The close contriver of all harms,
    Was never called to bear my part
    Or show the glory of our art?
    And, which is worse, all you have done   10
    Hath been but for a wayward son,
    Spiteful and wrathful, who, as others do,
    Loves for his own ends, not for you.
    But make amends now: get you gone
    And at the pit of Acheron   15
    Meet me i' the morning. Thither he
    Will come to know his destiny.
    Your vessels and your spells provide,
    Your charms and everything beside.
    I am for the air. This night I'll spend   20
    Unto a dismal and a fatal end.
    Great business must be wrought ere noon.
    Upon the corner of the moon
    There hangs a vap'rous drop profound;
    I'll catch it ere it come to ground;   25
    And that, distilled by magic sleights,
    Shall raise such artificial sprites
    As by the strength of their illusion
    Shall draw him on to his confusion.
    He shall spurn fate, scorn death, and bear   30
    His hopes 'bove wisdom, grace, and fear;
    And you all know security
    Is mortals' chiefest enemy.   *Music and a song.*
    Hark! I am called. My little spirit, see,
    Sits in a foggy cloud and stays for me.   *[Exit.]* 35
[*Sing within* "Come away, come away," *etc.*]

136 *All causes ... way:* all else must take
    second place.
142 *self-abuse:* self-imposed delusion.
143 *initiate fear:* the fearfulness of the in-
    experienced.

III.v.2 *beldams:* old hags.
  7 *close:* secret.
15 *Acheron:* river in Hell (here, Hell it-
    self).

1. WITCH. Come, let's make haste: she'll soon be back again. *Exeunt.*

SCENE VI. *Enter* LENNOX *and another* LORD.

LENNOX. My former speeches have but hit your thoughts,
    Which can interpret farther. Only I say
    Things have been strangely borne. The gracious Duncan
    Was pitied of Macbeth. Marry, he was dead!
    And the right valiant Banquo walked too late,   5
    Whom you may say (if't please you) Fleance killed,
    For Fleance fled. Men must not walk too late.
    Who cannot want the thought how monstrous
    It was for Malcom and for Donalbain
    To kill their gracious father? Damned fact,   10
    How it did grieve Macbeth! Did he not straight,
    In pious rage, the two delinquents tear
    That were the slaves of drink and thralls of sleep?
    Was not that nobly done? Ay, and wisely too,
    For 'twould have angered any heart alive   15
    To hear the men deny 't. So that I say
    He has borne all things well. And I do think
    That, had he Duncan's sons under his key
    (As, an't please heaven, he shall not) they should find
    What 'twere to kill a father. So should Fleance.   20
    But peace! for from broad words, and 'cause he failed
    His presence at the tyrant's feast, I hear
    Macduff lives in disgrace. Sir, can you tell
    Where he bestows himself?
LORD.   The son of Duncan,
    From whom this tyrant holds the due of birth,   25
    Lives in the English court and is received
    Of the most pious Edward with such grace
    That the malevolence of fortune nothing
    Takes from his high respect. Thither Macduff
    Is gone to pray the holy King upon his aid   30
    To wake Northumberland and war-like Siward;
    That by the help of these (with Him above
    To ratify the work) we may again
    Give to our tables meat, sleep to our nights,
    Free from our feasts and banquets bloody knives,   35
    Do faithful homage and receive free honors—
    All which we pine for now. And this report
    Hath so exasperate the King that he

27 *artificial sprites:* spirits produced by
  magic.
III.vi.1 *hit:* matched.
  3 *borne:* managed.

8 *cannot want the thought:* can help
  thinking.
21 *broad:* plain, open.
30 *upon:* for.

    Prepares for some attempt of war.
LENNOX.   Sent he to Macduff?
LORD. He did; and with an absolute "Sir, not I,"   40
    The cloudy messenger turns me his back
    And hums, as who should say, "You'll rue the time
    That clogs me with this answer."
LENNOX.   And that well might
    Advise him to a caution, t' hold what distance
    His wisdom can provide. Some holy angel   45
    Fly to the court of England and unfold
    His message ere he come, that a swift blessing
    May soon return to this our suffering country
    Under a hand accursed!
LORD.   I'll send my prayers with him. *Exeunt.*

ACT IV

SCENE I. *Thunder. Enter the three* WITCHES.

1. WITCH. Thrice the brinded cat hath mewed.
2. WITCH. Thrice, and once the hedgepig whined.
3. WITCH. Harpier cries.—'Tis time, 'tis time!
1. WITCH. Round about the cauldron go;
    In the poisoned entrails throw.   5
    Toad, that under cold stone
    Days and nights has thirty-one
    Swelt'red venom, sleeping got,
    Boil thou first i' the charmed pot.
ALL. Double, double, toil and trouble,   10
    Fire burn, and cauldron bubble.
2. WITCH. Fillet of a fenny snake,
    In the cauldron boil and bake;
    Eye of newt, and toe of frog,
    Wool of bat, and tongue of dog,   15
    Adder's fork, and blindworm's sting,
    Lizard's leg, and howlet's wing—
    For a charm of pow'rful trouble
    Like a hell broth boil and bubble.
ALL. Double, double, toil and trouble,   20
    Fire burn, and cauldron bubble.
3. WITCH. Scale of dragon, tooth of wolf,
    Witch's mummy, maw and gulf
    Of the ravined salt-sea shark,

IV.i.1 *brinded:* striped.   to be poisonous.
 3 *Harpier:* the third witch's spirit.   23 *mummy:* medicine made from a mum-
12 *fenny:* fen-like.   my, or flesh of a mummy.
16 *blindworm:* slow-worm, mistakenly thought

Root of hemlock digged i' the dark,   25
Liver of blaspheming Jew,
Gall of goat, and slips of yew
Slivered in the moon's eclipse,
Nose of Turk, and Tartar's lips,
Finger of birth-strangled babe   30
Ditch-delivered by a drab
Make the gruel thick and slab.
Add thereto a tiger's chaudron
For the ingredients of our cauldron.
ALL. Double, double, toil and trouble,   35
Fire burn, and cauldron bubble.
2. WITCH. Cool it with a baboon's blood,
Then the charm is firm and good.

Enter HECATE *and the other three* WITCHES.

HECATE. O, well done! I commend your pains,
And everyone shall share i' the gains.   40
And now about the cauldron sing
Like elves and fairies in a ring,
Enchanting all that you put in.

Music and a song, "Black spirits," etc.
[*Exeunt* HECATE *and singers.*]

2. WITCH. By the pricking of my thumbs,
Something wicked this way comes.   45
Open locks,
Whoever knocks!

Enter MACBETH.

MACBETH. How now, you secret, black, and midnight hags,
What is't you do?
ALL.   A deed without a name.
MACBETH. I conjure you by that which you profess,   50
Howe'er you come to know it, answer me.
Though you untie the winds and let them fight
Against the churches, though the yesty waves
Confound and swallow navigation up,
Though bladed corn be lodged and trees blown down,   55
Though castles topple on their warders' heads,
Though palaces and pyramids do slope
Their heads to their foundations, though the treasure

31 *drab:* whore.   50 *that . . . profess:* i.e., black magic.
33 *chaudron:* entrails.

Of nature's germens tumble all together
Even till destruction sicken, answer me   60
To what I ask you.
1. WITCH.   Speak.
2. WITCH.   Demand.
3. WITCH.   We'll answer.
1. WITCH. Say if th' hadst rather hear it from our mouths
Or from our masters'.
MACBETH.   Call 'em. Let me see 'em.
1. WITCH. Pour in sow's blood that hath eaten
Her nine farrow; grease that's sweaten   65
From the murderer's gibbet throw
Into the flame.
ALL.   Come, high or low,
Thyself and office deftly show!

Thunder. FIRST APPARITION, *an armed Head.*

MACBETH. Tell me, thou unknown power—
1. WITCH. He knows thy thought:
Hear his speech, but say thou nought.   70
1. APPARITION. Macbeth, Macbeth, Macbeth, beware Macduff!
Beware of the Thane of Fife! Dismiss me.—Enough.
                                   He descends.
MACBETH. Whate'er thou art, for thy good caution thanks:
1. WITCH. He will not be commanded. Here's another,   75
More potent than the first.

Thunder. SECOND APPARITION, *a bloody Child.*

2. APPARITION. Macbeth, Macbeth, Macbeth—
MACBETH. Had I three ears, I'd hear thee.
2. APPARITION. Be bloody, bold, and resolute! Laugh to scorn
The power of man, for none of woman born   80
Shall harm Macbeth.   *Descends.*
MACBETH. Then live, Macduff—what need I fear of thee?
But yet I'll make assurance double sure
And take a bond of fate. Thou shalt not live;
That I may tell pale-hearted fear it lies   85
And sleep in spite of thunder.

Thunder. THIRD APPARITION, *a Child crowned, with a tree in his*
    hand.

                         What is this
That rises like the issue of a king

---

59 *nature's germens:* seeds of life.   88 *round:* crown.
68 *office:* special powers.

And wears upon his baby brow the round
And top of sovereignty?
ALL.   Listen, but speak not to't.
3. APPARITION. Be lion-mettled, proud, and take no care   90
  Who chafes, who frets, or where conspirers are!
  Macbeth shall never vanquished be until
  Great Birnam Wood to high Dunsinane Hill
  Shall come against him.   *Descends.*
MACBETH.   That will never be.
  Who can impress the forest, bid the tree   95
  Unfix his earth-bound root? Sweet bodements, good!
  Rebellious dead rise never till the Wood
  Of Birnam rise, and our high-placed Macbeth
  Shall live the lease of nature, pay his breath
  To time and mortal custom. Yet my heart   100
  Throbs to know one thing. Tell me, if your art
  Can tell so much: Shall Banquo's issue ever
  Reign in this kingdom?
ALL.   Seek to know no more.
MACBETH. I will be satisfied. Deny me this,
  And an eternal curse fall in you! Let me know.
  Why sinks that cauldron? and what noise is this? *Hautboys.*   105
1. WITCH. Show!
2. WITCH. Show!
3. WITCH. Show!
ALL. Show his eyes, and grieve his heart!   110
  Come like shadows, so depart!

A show of eight KINGS *and* BANQUO'S GHOST, [*the last* KING] *with
  a glass in his hand.*

MACBETH. Thou art too like the spirit of Banquo. Down!
  Thy crown does sear mine eyeballs. And thy hair,
  Thou other gold-bound brow, is like the first.
  A third is like the former. Filthy hags,   115
  Why do you show me this? A fourth? Start, eyes!
  What, will the line stretch out to the crack of doom?
  Another yet? A seventh? I'll see no more.
  And yet the eighth appears, who bears a glass
  Which shows me many more; and some I see   120
  That twofold balls and treble sceptres carry.
  Horrible sight! Now I see 'tis true;
  For the blood-boltered Banquo smiles upon me

95 *impress:* draft into military service.
99 *lease of nature:* natural lifespan.
100 *mortal custom:* natural death.
121 *twofold...sceptres:* insignia of England and Scotland, united when King

James V of Scotland became, in 1603,
King James I of England Banquo was
supposed to be an ancestor of James.
123 *blood-boltered:* blood-coated.

1. WITCH. Ay, sir, all this is so. But why   125
    Stands Macbeth thus amazedly?
    Come, sisters, cheer we up his sprites
    And show the best of our delights.
    I'll charm the air to give a sound
    While you perform your antic round,   130
    That this great king may kindly say
    Our duties did his welcome pay.

Music. The WITCHES *dance and vanish.*

MACBETH. Where are they? Gone? Let this pernicious hour
    Stand aye accursed in the calendar!
    Come in, without there!   135

Enter LENNOX.

LENNOX.   What's your Grace's will?
MACBETH. Saw you the weird sisters?
LENNOX.   No, my lord.
MACBETH. Came they not by you?
LENNOX.   No indeed, my lord.
MACBETH. Infected be the air whereon they ride,
    And dammed all those that trust them! I did hear
    The galloping of horse. Who was't came by?   140
LENNOX. 'Tis two or three, my lord, that bring you word
    Macduff is fled to England.
MACBETH. Fled to England?
LENNOX. Ay, my good lord.
MACBETH. [*aside*] Time, thou anticipat'st my dread exploits.
    The flighty purpose never is o'ertook   145
    Unless the deed go with it. From this moment
    The very firstlings of my heart shall be
    The firstlings of my hand. And even now,
    To crown my thoughts with acts, be it thought and done:
    The castle of Macduff I will surprise,   150
    Seize upon Fife, give to the edge o' the sword
    His wife, his babes, and all unfortunate souls
    That trace him in his line. No boasting like a fool;
    This deed I'll do before this purpose cool.
    But no more sights!—Where are these gentlemen?   155
    Come, bring me where they are.   *Exeunt.*

SCENE II. *Enter* MACDUFF'S WIFE, *her* SON, *and* ROSS.

WIFE. What had he done to make him fly the land?

130 *antic round:* fantastic circular dance.   IV.ii.9 *wants...touch:* lacks natural pro-
144 *anticipat'st:* forestall'st.   tectiveness.
145 *flighty:* hastening.

Ross. You must have patience, madam.
WIFE.   He had none.
   His flight was madness. When our actions do not,
   Our fears do make us traitors.
Ross.   You know not
   Whether it was his wisdom or his fear.   5
WIFE. Wisdom? To leave his wife, to leave his babes,
   His mansion and his titles in a place
   From whence himself does fly? He loves us not,
   He wants the natural touch. For the poor wren,
   The most diminutive of birds, will fight,   10
   Her young ones in her nest, against the owl.
   All is the fear and nothing is the love;
   As little is the wisdom, where the flight
   So runs against all reason.
Ross.   My dearest coz,
   I pray you school yourself. But for your husband,   15
   He is noble, wise, judicious, and best knows
   The fits o' the season. I dare not speak much further,
   But cruel are the times when we are traitors
   And do not know ourselves; when we hold rumor
   From what we fear, yet know not what we fear   20
   But float upon a wild and violent sea
   Each way and none. I take my leave of you.
   Shall not be long but I'll be here again.
   Things at the worst will cease, or else climb upward
   To what they were before.—My pretty cousin,   25
   Blessing upon you!
WIFE. Fathered he is, and yet he's fatherless.
Ross. I am so much a fool, should I stay longer
   It would be my disgrace and your discomfort.
   I take my leave at once.   *[Exit.]*
WIFE.   Sirrah, your father's dead;   30
   And what will you do now? How will you live?
SON. As birds do, mother.
WIFE.   What, with worms and flies?
SON. With what I get, I mean; and so do they.
WIFE. Poor bird! thou'dst never fear the net nor lime,
   The pitfall nor the gin.   35
SON. Why should I, mother? Poor birds they are not set for.
   My father is not dead for all your saying.
WIFE. Yes, he is dead. How wilt thou do for a father?
SON. Nay, how will you do for a husband?
WIFE. Why, I can buy me twenty at any market,   40

14 *coz:* cousin.
15 *school:* learn restraint.
19 *know ourselves:* know that we are
  traitors.

29 *It would ... discomfort:* i.e., he would
  weep.
34 *lime:* birdlime.
35 *gin:* trap.

SON. Then you'll buy 'em to sell again.
WIFE. Thou speak'st with all thy wit; and yet, i' faith,
    With wit enough for thee.
SON. Was my father a traitor, mother?
WIFE. Ay, that he was!   45
SON.. What is a traitor?
WIFE. Why, one that swears and lies.
SON. And be all traitors that do so?
WIFE. Everyone that does so is a traitor and must be hanged.
SON. And must they all be hanged that swear and lie?   50
WIFE. Everyone.
SON. Who must hang them?
WIFE. Why, the honest men.
SON. Then the liars and swearers are fools, for there are liars and
    swearers enow to beat the honest men and hang up them.   55
WIFE. Now God help thee, poor monkey! But how wilt thou do for
    a father?
SON. If he were dead, you'ld weep for him. If you would not, it
    were a good sign that I should quickly have a new father.
WIFE. Poor prattler, how thou talk'st!   60

Enter a MESSENGER.

MESSENGER. Bless you, fair dame! I am not to you known,
    Though in your state of honor I am perfect.
    I doubt some danger does approach you nearly.
    If you will take a homely man's advice,
    Be not found here. Hence with your little ones!   65
    To fright you thus methinks I am too savage;
    To do worse to you were fell cruelty,
    Which is too nigh your person. Heaven preserve you!
    I dare abide no longer.   *Exit.*
WIFE.   Whither should I fly?   70
    I have done no harm. But I remember now
    I am in this earthly world, where to do harm
    Is often laudable, to do good sometime
    Accounted dangerous folly. Why then, alas,
    Do I put up that womanly defense   75
    To say I have done no harm?

Enter MURDERERS.

                             What are these faces?
MURDERER. Where is your husband?
WIFE. I hope in no place so unsanctified

41 *sell:* sell them out, betray.   69 *doubt:* fear.
68 *in your ... perfect:* I know your high
   rank.

Where such as thou mayst find him.   80
MURDERER.   He's a traitor.
SON. Thou liest, thou shag-eared villain!
MURDERER.   What, you egg! [*Stabs him*]
    Young fry of treachery!
SON.   He has killed me, mother.   85
    Run away, I pray you! [*Dies.*]

Exit [LADY MACDUFF], *crying* "Murder!" [*pursued by* MURDERERS].

SCENE III. *Enter* MALCOLM *and* MACDUFF.

MALCOLM. Let us seek out some desolate shade, and there
    Weep our sad bosoms empty.
MACDUFF.   Let us rather
    Hold fast the mortal sword, and like good men,
    Bestride our downfall'n birthdom. Each new morn
    New widows howl, new orphans cry, new sorrows   5
    Strike heaven on the face, that it resounds
    As if it felt with Scotland and yelled out
    Like syllable of dolor.
MALCOLM. What I believe, I'll wail;
    What know, believe; and what I can redress,
    As I shall find the time to friend, I will.   10
    What you have spoke, it may be so perchance.
    This tyrant, whose sole name blisters our tongues,
    Was once thought honest; you have loved him well;
    He hath not touched you yet. I am young; but something
    You may deserve of him through me, and wisdom   15
    To offer up a weak, poor, innocent lamb
    T' appease an angry god.
MACDUFF.   I am not treacherous.
MALCOLM. But Macbeth is.
    A good and virtuous nature may recoil
    In an imperial charge. But I shall crave your pardon.   20
    That which you are, my thoughts cannot transpose:
    Angels are bright still though the brightest fell;
    Though all things foul would wear the brows of grace,
    Yet grace must still look so.
MACDUFF.   I have lost my hopes.
MALCOLM. Perchance even there where I did find my doubts.   25
    Why in that rawness left you wife and child,

IV.iii.8 *Like syllable:* with comparable sounds.
14–15 *but ... me:* but you may be rewarded by him for betraying me.
15 *wisdom:* it would be smart.

19 *recoil:* give way.
20 *In an imperial charge:* before a king's command.
22 *the brightest:* Lucifer.
26 *rawness:* vulnerable state.

Those precious motives, those strong knots of love,
Without leave-taking? I pray you,
Let not my jealousies be your dishonors,
But mine own safeties. You may be rightly just   30
Whatever I shall think.
MACDUFF.   Bleed, bleed, poor country!
Great tyranny, lay thou thy basis sure,
For goodness dare not check thee, wear thou thy wrongs,
The title is affeered! Fare thee well, lord.
I would not be the villain that thou think'st   35
For the whole space that's in the tyrant's grasp
And the rich East to boot.
MALCOLM.   Be not offended.
I speak not as in absolute fear of you.
I think our country sinks beneath the yoke.
It weeps, it bleeds, and each new day a gash   40
Is added to her wounds. I think withal
There would be hands uplifted in my right;
And here from gracious England have I offer
Of goodly thousands. But, for all this,
When I shall tread upon the tyrant's head   45
Or wear it on my sword, yet my poor country
Shall have more vices than it had before,
More suffer, and more sundry ways than ever,
By him that shall succeed.
MACDUFF.   What should he be?
MALCOLM. It is myself I mean, in whom I know   50
All the particulars of vice so grafted
That, when they shall be opened, black Macbeth
Will seem as pure as snow, and the poor state
Esteem him as a lamb, being compared
With my confineless harms.
MACDUFF.   Not in the legions   55
Of horrid hell can come a devil more damned
In evils to top Macbeth.
MALCOLM.   I grant him bloody,
Luxurious, avaricious, false, deceitful,
Sudden, malicious, smacking of every sin
That has a name. But there's no bottom, none,   60
In my voluptuousness. Your wives, your daughters,
Your matrons, and your maids could not fill up
The cistern of my lust; and my desire
All continent impediments would o'erbear

26 *rawness:* vulnerable state.   51 *particulars:* various aspects.
29 *jealousies:* suspicions.   58 *Luxurious:* lecherous.
34 *affeered:* confirmed.   64 *continent:* chaste and restraining.
38 *absolute:* total.

That did oppose my will. Better Macbeth   65
  Than such an one to reign.
MACDUFF.   Boundless intemperance
  In nature is a tyranny. It hath been
  The untimely emptying of the happy throne
  And fall of many kings. But fear not yet
  To take upon you what is yours. You may   70
  Convey your pleasures in a spacious plenty
  And yet seem cold—the time you may so hoodwink.
  We have willing dames enough. There cannot be
  That vulture in you to devour so many
  As will to greatness dedicate themselves,   75
  Finding it so inclined.
MALCOLM.   With this there grows
  In my most ill-composed affection such
  A stanchless avarice that, were I King
  I should cut off the nobles for their lands,
  Desire his jewels, and this other's house,   80
  And my more-having would be as a sauce
  To make me hunger more, that I should forge
  Quarrels unjust against the good and loyal,
  Destroying them for wealth.
MACDUFF.   This avarice
  Sticks deeper, grows with more pernicious root   85
  Than summer-seeming lust, and it hath been
  The sword of our slain kings. Yet do not fear.
  Scotland hath foisons to fill up your will
  Of your mere own. All these are portable,
  With other graces weighed.   90
MALCOLM. But I have none. The king-becoming graces,
  As justice, verity, temp'rance, stableness,
  Bounty, perseverance, mercy, lowliness.
  Devotion, patience, courage, fortitude,
  I have no relish of them, but abound   95
  In the division of each several crime,
  Acting it many ways. Nay, had I power, I should
  Pour the sweet milk of concord into hell,
  Uproar the universal peace, confound
  All unity on earth.
MACDUFF.   O Scotland, Scotland!   100
MALCOLM. If such a one be fit to govern, speak.
  I am as I have spoken.
MACDUFF.   Fit to govern?
  No, not to live! O nation miserable,

---

77 *ill-composed affection:* disordered will.   89 *mere own:* own property; *portable:*
87 *sword:* killer.   bearable.
88 *foisons:* plenty.   96 *In the division of:* in every part of.

With an untitled tyrant bloody-sceptred,
When shalt thou see thy wholesome days again,   105
Since that the truest issue of thy throne
By his own interdiction stands accursed
And does blaspheme his breed? Thy royal father
Was a most sainted king; the queen that bore thee,
Oft'ner upon her knees than on her feet,   110
Died every day she lived. Fare thee well.
These evils thou repeat'st upon thyself
Hath banished me from Scotland. O my breast,
Thy hope ends here!
MALCOLM.   Macduff, this noble passion,
Child of integrity, hath from my soul   115
Wiped the black scruples, reconciled my thoughts
To thy good truth and honor. Devilish Macbeth
By many of these trains hath sought to win me
Into his power; and modest wisdom plucks me
From overcredulous haste; but God above   120
Deal between thee and me, for even now
I put myself to thy direction and
Unspeak mine own detraction, here adjure
The taints and blames I laid upon myself
For strangers to my nature. I am yet   125
Unknown to woman, never was forsworn,
Scarcely have coveted what was mine own,
At no time broke my faith, would not betray
The devil to his fellow, and delight
No less in truth than life. My first false speaking   130
Was this upon myself. What I am truly,
Is thine and my poor country's to command;
Whither indeed, before thy here-approach,
Old Siward with ten thousand warlike men   134
Already at a point was setting forth.
Now we'll together; and the chance of goodness
Be like our warranted quarrel! Why are you silent?
MACDUFF. Such welcome and unwelcome things at once
'Tis hard to reconcile.

Enter a DOCTOR.

MALCOLM. Well, more anon. Comes the King forth, I pray you?   140
DOCTOR. Ay, sir. There are a crew of wretched souls
That stay his cure. Their malady convinces

---

107 *interdiction:* prohibition.   135 *at a point:* armed and ready.
111 *Died:* renounced worldly life.   136 *goodness:* success.
118 *trains:* devices.   137 *warranted:* justified.
131 *upon:* against.   142 *convinces:* defeats.

The great assay of art; but at his touch,
Such sanctity hath heaven given his hand,
They presently amend.
MALCOLM.   I thank you, doctor.   145

Exit [DOCTOR].

MACDUFF. What's the disease he means?
MALCOLM.   'Tis called the evil.
A most miraculous work in this good King,
Which often since my here-remain in England
I have seen him do: how he solicits heaven
Himself best knows, but strangely visited people,   150
All swol'n and ulcerous, pitiful to the eye,
The mere despair of surgery, he cures,
Hanging a golden stamp about their necks,
Put on with holy prayers; and 'tis spoken,   154
To the succeeding royalty he leaves
The healing benediction. With this strange virtue,
He hath a heavenly gift of prophecy,
And sundry blessings hang about his throne
That speak him full of grace.

Enter Ross.

MACDUFF.   See who comes here.
MALCOLM. My countryman; but yet I know him not.   160
MACDUFF. My ever gentle cousin, welcome hither.
MALCOLM. I know him now. Good God, betimes remove
    The means that makes us strangers!
ROSS.   Sir, amen.
MACDUFF. Stands Scotland where it did?
ROSS.   Alas, poor country,
    Almost afraid to know itself. It cannot   165
    Be called our mother but our grave, where nothing
    But who knows nothing is once seen to smile;
    Where sighs and groans, and shrieks that rent the air,
    Are made, not marked; where violent sorrow seems
    A modern ecstasy. The dead man's knell   170
    Is there scarce asked for who, and good men's lives
    Expire before the flowers in their caps,
    Dying or ere they sicken.
MACDUFF.   O' relation

143 *assay of art:* efforts of medical science.
146 *evil:* king's evil (scrofula).
150 *visited:* afflicted.
152 *mere:* total.
162 *betimes:* hastily.

167 *who:* the man who.
169 *marked:* noticed.
170 *modern ecstasy:* ordinary emotion.
173 *or ere:* before.

Too nice, and yet too true!
MALCOLM.   What's the newest grief
Ross. That of an hour's age doth hiss the speaker;   175
    Each minute teems a new one.
MACDUFF.   How does my wife?
Ross. Why, well.
MACDUFF.   And all my children?
Ross.   Well too.
MACDUFF. The tyrant has not battered at their peace?
Ross. No, they were well at peace when I did leave 'em.
MACDUFF. Be not a niggard of your speech. How goes't?   180
Ross. When I came hither to transport the tidings
    Which I have heavily borne, there ran a rumor
    Of many worthy fellows that were out,
    Which was to my belief witnessed the rather
    For that I saw the tyrant's power afoot.   185
    Now is the time of help. Your eye in Scotland
    Would create soldiers, make our women fight
    To doff their dire distresses.
MALCOLM.   Be't their comfort
    We are coming thither. Gracious England hath
    Lent us good Siward and ten thousand men,   190
    An older and a better soldier none
    That Christendom gives out.
Ross.   Would I could answer
    This comfort with the like. But I have words
    That would be howled out in the desert air,
    Where hearing should not latch them.
MACDUFF.   What concern they,   195
    The general cause or is it a fee-grief
    Due to some single breast?
Ross.   No mind that's honest
    But in it shares some woe, though the main part
    Pertains to you alone.
MACDUFF.   If it be mine,
    Keep it not from me, quickly let me have it.   200
Ross. Let not your ears despise my tongue forever,
    Which shall possess them with the heaviest sound
    That ever yet they heard.
MACDUFF.   Humh! I guess at it.
Ross. Your castle is surprised, your wife and babes
    Savagely slaughtered. To relate the manner   205

173–74 *relation Too nice:* account too detailed and exact.
176 *teems:* brings forth.
183 *out:* in arms.
184 *witnessed:* affirmed.

195 *latch:* catch.
196 *fee-grief:* private grief.
197 *honest:* honorable.
204 *surprised:* suddenly attacked.

Were, on the quarry of these murdered deer,
To add the death of you.
MALCOLM.   Merciful heaven!
What, man! Ne'er pull your hat upon your brows.
Give sorrow words. The grief that does not speak
Whispers the o'erfraught heart and bids it break.   210
MACDUFF. My children too?
ROSS.   Wife, children, servants, all
That could be found.
MACDUFF. And I must be from thence?
My wife killed too?
ROSS.   I have said.
MALCOLM.   Be comforted.
Let's make us med'cines of our great revenge
To cure this deadly grief.   215
MACDUFF. He has no children. All my pretty ones?
Did you say all? O hell-kite! All?
What, all my pretty chickens and their dam
At one fell swoop?
MALCOLM. Dispute it like a man.
MACDUFF.   I shall do so;   220
But I must also feel it as a man.
I cannot but remember such things were
That were most precious to me. Did heaven look on
And would not take their part? Sinful Macduff,
They were all struck for thee! Naught that I am,   225
Not for their own demerits but for mine
Fell slaughter on their souls. Heaven rest them now!
MALCOLM. Be this the whetstone of your sword. Let grief
Convert to anger; blunt not the heart, enrage it.
MACDUFF. O, I could play the woman with mine eyes   230
And braggart with my tongue. But, gentle heavens,
Cut short all intermission. Front to front
Bring thou this fiend of Scotland and myself.
Within my sword's length set him. If he scape,
Heaven forgive him too!   235
MALCOLM.   This time goes manly.
Come, go we to the King. Our power is ready;
Our lack is nothing but our leave. Macbeth
Is ripe for shaking, and the powers above
Put on their instruments. Receive what cheer you may.
The night is long that never finds the day.   *Exeunt.*   240

---

206 *quarry:* heap of slaughtered animals.
220 *Dispute:* fight against.
225 *Naught:* wicked.

232 *intermission:* postponement;
     Front: face.
239 *Put on:* advance; *instruments:* agents.

ACT V

Scene I. *Enter a* Doctor *of Physic and a* Waiting Gentlewoman.

Doctor. I have two nights watched with you, but can perceive no
truth in your report. When was it she last walked?

Gentlewoman. Since his Majesty went into the field I have seen
her rise from her bed, throw her nightgown upon her, unlock
her closet, take forth paper, fold it, write upon't, read it, after-   5
wards seal it, and again return to bed; yet all this while in a
most fast sleep.

Doctor. A great perturbation in nature, to receive at once the
benefit of sleep and do the effects of watching! In this slumb'ry
agitation, besides her walking and other actual performances,   10
what (at any time) have you heard her say?

Gentlewoman. That, sir, which I will not report after her.

Doctor. You may to me, and 'tis most meet you should.

Gentlewoman. Neither to you nor anyone, having no witness to
confirm my speech.   15

Enter Lady [Macbeth], *with a taper.*

Lo you, here she comes! This is her very guise, and, upon my
life, fast asleep! Observe her; stand close.

Doctor. How came she by that light?

Gentlewoman. Why, it stood by her.   20
She has light by her continually.
'Tis her command.

Doctor. You see her eyes are open.

Gentlewoman. Ay, but their sense are shut.

Doctor. What is it she does now?   25
Look how she rubs her hands.

Gentlewoman. It is an accustomed action with her, to seem thus
washing her hands. I have known her continue in this a
quarter of an hour.

Lady. Yet here's a spot.   30

Doctor. Hark, she speaks. I will set down what comes from her,
satisfy my remembrance the more strongly.

Lady. Out, damned spot! Out, I say! One—two—why then 'tis time
to do't. Hell is murky. Fie, my lord, fie! a soldier and afeard?
What need we fear who knows it, when none can call our   35
power to accompt? Yet who would have thought the old man
to have had so much blood in him?

Doctor. Do you mark that?

Lady. The Thane of Fife had a wife. Where is she now? What,
will these hands ne'er be clean? No more o' that, my lord, no   40
more o' that! You mar all with this starting.

DOCTOR. Go to, go to! You have known what you should not.
GENTLEWOMAN. She has spoke what she should not, I am sure of
    that. Heaven knows what she has known.
LADY. Here's the smell of the blood still. All the perfumes of   45
    Arabia will not sweeten this little hand. Oh, oh, oh!
DOCTOR. What a sigh is there! The heart is sorely charged.
GENTLEWOMAN. I would not have such a heart in my bosom for
    the dignity of the whole body.
DOCTOR. Well, well, well.   50
GENTLEWOMAN. Pray God it be, sir.
DOCTOR. This disease is beyond my practice. Yet I have known
    those which have walked in their sleep who have died holily
    in their beds.
LADY. Wash your hands, put on your nightgown, look not so pale!   55
    I tell you yet again, Banquo's buried. He cannot come out
    on's grave.
DOCTOR. Even so?
LADY. To bed, to bed! There's knocking at the gate. Come, come,
    come, come, give me your hand! What's done cannot be un-   60
    done. To bed, to bed, to bed!   *Exit.*
DOCTOR. Will she go now to bed?
GENTLEWOMAN. Directly.
DOCTOR. Foul whisp'rings are abroad. Unnatural deeds
    Do breed unnatural troubles. Infected minds   65
    To their deaf pillows will discharge their secrets.
    More needs she the divine than the physician.
    God, God forgive us all! Look after her;
    Remove from her the means of all annoyance,
    And still keep eyes upon her. So good night.   70
    My mind she has mated, and amazed my sight.
    I think, but dare not speak.
GENTLEWOMAN.   Good night, good doctor. *Exeunt.*

SCENE II. *Drum and Colors. Enter* MENTEITH, CAITHNESS, ANGUS,
    LENNOX, *and* SOLDIERS.

MENTEITH. The English pow'r is near, led on by Malcolm,
    His uncle Siward, and the good Macduff.
    Revenges burn in them; for their dear causes
    Would to the bleeding and the grim alarm
    Excite the mortified man.
ANGUS.   Near Birnam Wood   5
    Shall we well meet them; that way are they coming.
CAITHNESS. Who knows if Donalbain be with his brother?

V.i.62 *starting:* shying.   102 *mated:* bewildered.
100 *annoyance:* physical harm.   V.ii.5 *mortified:* dead.

LENNOX. For certain, sir, he is not. I have a file
  Of all the gentry. There is Siward's son
  And many unrough youths that even now   10
  Protest their first of manhood.
MENTEITH.   What does the tyrant?
CAITHNESS. Great Dunsinane he strongly fortifies.
  Some say he's mad; others, that lesser hate him,
  Do call it valiant fury; but for certain
  He cannot buckle his distempered cause   15
  Within the belt of rule.
ANGUS.   Now does he feel
  His secret murders sticking on his hands.
  Now minutely revolts upbraid his faith-breach.
  Those he commands move only in command,
  Nothing in love. Now does he feel his title   20
  Hang loose about him, like a giant's robe
  Upon a dwarfish thief.
MENTEITH.   Who then shall blame
  His pestered senses to recoil and start,
  When all that is within him does condemn
  Itself for being there?
CAITHNESS.   Well, march we on   25
  To give obedience where 'tis truly owed.
  Meet we the med'cine of the sickly weal;
  And with him pour we in our country's purge
  Each drop of us.
LENNOX.   Or so much as it needs
  To dew the sovereign flower and drown the weeds.   30
  Make we our march towards Birnam.   *Exeunt, marching.*

SCENE III. *Enter* MACBETH, DOCTOR, *and* ATTENDANTS.

MACBETH. Bring me no more reports. Let them fly all!
  Till Birnam Wood remove to Dunsinane,
  I cannot taint with fear. What's the boy Malcolm?
  Was he not born of woman? The spirits that know
  All mortal consequences have pronounced me thus: 5
  "Fear not, Macbeth. No man that's born of woman
  Shall e'er have power upon thee." Then fly, false thanes,
  And mingle with the English epicures.
  The mind I sway by and the heart I bear
  Shall never sag with doubt nor shake with fear.   10

Enter SERVANT.

18 *minutely:* every minute; *revolts:* defec-
tors.
27 *med'cine:* i.e., Malcolm; *weal:* country.

V.iii.14 *prick ... fear:* draw   blood   and
  smear it over your pallor.
15 *patch:* dolt.

The devil damn thee black, thou cream-faced loon!
   Where got'st thou that goose look?
SERVANT. There is ten thousand—
MACBETH.   Geese, villain?
SERVANT.   Soldiers, sir,
MACBETH. Go prick thy face and overred thy fear,
   Thou lily-livered boy. What soldiers, patch?   15
   Death of thy soul; those linen cheeks of thine
   Are counsellors to fear. What soldiers, whey-face?
SERVANT. The English force, so please you.
MACBETH. Take thy face hence.

[*Exit* SERVANT.]

                           Seyton!—I am sick at heart,
When I behold—Seyton, I say—This push   20
Will cheer me ever, or disseat me now.
I have lived long enough. My way of life
Is fall'n into the sear, the yellow leaf,
And that which should accompany old age,
As honor, love, obedience, troops of friends,   25
I must not look to have; but, in their stead,
Curses not loud but deep, mouth-honor, breath,
Which the poor heart would fain deny, and dare not.
Seyton!

Enter SEYTON.

SEYTON. What's your gracious pleasure?
MACBETH.   What news more?   30
SEYTON. All is confirmed, my lord, which was reported.
MACBETH. I'll fight till from my bones my flesh be hacked.
   Give me my armor.
SEYTON.   'Tis not needed yet.
MACBETH. I'll put it on.
   Send out more horses, skirr the country round,   35
   Hang those that talk of fear. Give me mine armor.
   How does your patient, doctor?
DOCTOR.   Not so sick, my lord,
   As she is troubled with thick-coming fancies
   That keep her from her rest.
MACBETH.   Cure her of that!
   Canst thou not minister to a mind diseased,   40
   Pluck from the memory a rooted sorrow,
   Raze out the written troubles of the brain,
   And with some sweet oblivious antidote

35 *skirr:* scour.   47 *physic:* medicine.

Cleanse the stuffed bosom of that perilous stuff
Which weighs upon the heart?
DOCTOR.   Therein the patient   45
    Must minister to himself.
MACBETH. Throw physic to the dogs, I'll none of it!
    Come, put mine armor on. Give me my staff.
    Seyton, send out.—Doctor, the thanes fly from me.—
    Come, sir, dispatch.—If thou couldst, doctor, cast   50
    The water of my land, find her disease,
    And purge it to a sound and pristine health,
    I would applaud thee to the very echo,
    That should applaud again.—Pull't off, I say.—
    What rhubarb, senna, or what purgative drug   55
    Would scour these English hence? Hear'st thou of them?
DOCTOR. Ay, my good lord. Your royal preparation
    Makes us hear something.
MACBETH.   Bring it after me!
    I will not be afraid of death and bane
    Till Birnam Forest come to Dunsinane.   60

[*Exeunt all but the* DOCTOR.]

DOCTOR. Were I from Dunsinane away and clear,
    Profit again should hardly draw me here.   *Exit.*

SCENE IV. *Drum and colors. Enter* MALCOLM, SIWARD, MACDUFF,
    SIWARD'S SON, MENTEITH, CAITHNESS, ANGUS, [LENNOX, ROSS,] *and*
    SOLDIERS, *marching.*

MALCOLM. Cousins, I hope the days are near at hand
    That chambers will be safe.
MENTEITH.   We doubt it nothing.
SIWARD. What wood is this before us?
MENTEITH.   The Wood of Birnam.
MALCOLM. Let every soldier hew him down a bough
    And bear't before him. Thereby shall we shadow   5
    The numbers of our host and make discovery
    Err in report of us.
SOLDIERS.   It shall be done.
SIWARD. We learn no other but the confident tyrant
    Keeps still in Dunsinane and will endure
    Our setting down before't.
MALCOLM.   'Tis his main hope,   10
    For where there is advantage to be given
    Both more and less have given him the revolt,

50 *dispatch:* hurry.   V.iv.2 *chambers:* sleeping rooms.
50–51 *cast . . . water:* analyze the urine.   12 *more and less:* nobles and commoners.

And none serve with him but constrained things
Whose hearts are absent too.
MACDUFF.   Let our just censures
  Attend the true event, and put we on   15
  Industrious soldiership.
SIWARD.   The time approaches
  That will with due decision make us know
  What we shall say we have and what we owe.
  Thoughts speculative their unsure hopes relate,
  But certain issue strokes must arbitrate—   20
  Towards which advance the war.

Exeunt, marching.

SCENE V. *Enter* MACBETH, SEYTON, *and* SOLDIERS, *with drum and colors.*

MACBETH. Hang out our banners on the outward walls.
  The cry is still, "They come!" Our castle's strength
  Will laugh a siege to scorn. Here let them lie
  Till famine and ague eat them up.
  Were they not forced with those that should be ours,   5
  We might have met them dareful, beard to beard,
  And beat them backward home.

A cry within of women.

                        What is that noise?
SEYTON. It is the cry of women, my good lord.
MACBETH. I have almost forgot the taste of fears.
  The time has been my senses would have cooled   10
  To hear a night-shriek, and my fell of hair
  Would at a dismal treatise rouse and stir
  As life were in't. I have supped full with horrors.
  Direness, familiar to my slaughterous thoughts,
  Cannot once start me.

[*Enter* SEYTON.]

               Wherefore was that cry?   15
SEYTON. The Queen, my lord, is dead.
MACBETH. She should have died hereafter;
  There would have been a time for such a word.
  Tomorrow, and tomorrow, and tomorrow

15 *Attend...event:* await the outcome. V.v.5 *forced:* reinforced.
19 *Thoughts...relate:* guesses as to the 11 *fell:* pelt.
future merely reflect our hopes.

Creeps in this petty pace from day to day,   20
To the last syllable of recorded time;
And all our yesterdays have lighted fools
The way to dusty death. Out, out, brief candle!
Life's but a walking shadow, a poor player   25
That struts and frets his hour upon the stage
And then is heard no more. It is a tale
Told by an idiot, full of sound and fury,
Signifying nothing.

Enter a MESSENGER.

Thou com'st to use thy tongue: thy story quickly!
MESSENGER. Gracious my lord,   30
   I should report that which I say I saw,
   But know not how to do't.
MACBETH.   Well, say, sir.
MESSENGER. As I did stand my watch upon the hill,
   I looked toward Birnam, and anon methought
   The wood began to move.
MACBETH.   Liar and slave!   35
MESSENGER. Let me endure your wrath if't be not so.
   Within this three mile may you see it coming.
   I say, a moving grove.
MACBETH.   If thou speak'st false,
   Upon the next tree shall thou hang alive
   Till famine cling thee. If thy speech be sooth,   40
   I care not if thou dost for me as much.
   I pull in resolution, and begin
   To doubt the equivocation of the fiend,
   That lies like truth. "Fear not, till Birnam Wood
   Do come to Dunsinane!" and now a wood   45
   Comes toward Dunsinane. Arm, arm, and out!
   If this which he avouches does appear,
   There is nor flying hence nor tarrying here.
   I 'gin to be aweary of the sun,
   And wish the estate o' the world were now undone.   50
   Ring the alarum bell! Blow wind, come wrack,
   At least we'll die with harness on our back.   *Exeunt.*

SCENE VI. *Drum and colors. Enter* MALCOLM, SIWARD, MACDUFF,
and their ARMY, *with boughs.*

MALCOLM. Now near enough. Your leavy screens throw down

40 *cling:* shrivel; *sooth:* true.   V.vi.4 *battle:* battalion.
42 *pull in:* rein in.

And show like those you are. You, worthy uncle,
Shall with my cousin, your right noble son,
Lead our first battle. Worthy Macduff and we
Shall take upon's what else remains to do,   5
According to our order.
SIWARD.   Fare you well.
Do we but find the tyrant's power tonight,
Let us be beaten if we cannot fight.
MACDUFF. Make all our trumpets speak, give them all breath,
Those clamorous harbingers of blood and death.   10

Exeunt. Alarums continued.

SCENE VII. *Enter* MACBETH.

MACBETH. They have tied me to a stake. I cannot fly,
But bearlike I must fight the course. What's he
That was not born of woman? Such a one
Am I to fear, or none.

Enter YOUNG SIWARD.

YOUNG SIWARD. What is thy name?
MACBETH.   Thou'lt be afraid to hear it.   5
YOUNG SIWARD. No, though thou call'st thyself a hotter name
Than any is in hell.
MACBETH.   My name's Macbeth.
YOUNG SIWARD. The devil himself could not pronounce a title
More hateful to mine ear.
MACBETH.   No, nor more fearful.
YOUNG SIWARD. Thou liest, abhorred tyrant! With my sword   10
I'll prove the lie thou speak'st.

Fight, and YOUNG SIWARD *slain.*

MACBETH. Thou wast born of woman.
But swords I smile at, weapons laugh to scorn,
Brandished by man that's of a woman born.   *Exit.*

Alarums. Enter MACDUFF.

MACDUFF. That way the noise is. Tyrant, show thy face!
If thou beest slain and with no stroke of mine,   15
My wife and children's ghosts will haunt me still.

6 *order:* plans.   V.vii.1 *stake:* to which bears were chained
                                        to be baited by dogs.

I cannot strike at wretched kerns, whose arms
Are hired to bear their staves. Either thou, Macbeth,
Or else my sword with an unbattered edge
I sheathe again undeeded. There thou shouldst be: 20
By this great clatter one of greatest note
Seems bruited. Let me find him, Fortune,
And more I beg not!   *Exit. Alarums.*

Enter MALCOLM *and* SIWARD.

SIWARD. This way, my lord. The castle's gently rend'red:
    The tyrant's people on both sides do fight,   25
    The noble thanes do bravely in the war,
    The day almost itself professes yours
    And little is to do.
MALCOLM.   We have met with foes
    That strike beside us.
SIWARD.   Enter, sir, the castle.   *Exeunt. Alarum.*

SCENE VIII. *Enter* MACBETH.

MACBETH. Why should I play the Roman fool and die
    On mine own sword? Whiles I see lives, the gashes
    Do better upon them.

Enter MACDUFF.

MACDUFF.   Turn, hellhound, turn!
MACBETH. Of all men else I have avoided thee.
    But get thee back! My soul is too much charged   5
    With blood of thine already.
MACDUFF.   I have no words;
    My voice is in my sword, thou bloodier villain
    Than terms can give thee out!

Fight. Alarum.

MACBETH. Thou losest labor.
    As easy mayst thou the intrenchant air
    With thy keen sword impress as make me bleed.   10
    Let fall thy blade on vulnerable crests.
    I bear a charmed life, which must not yield
    To one of woman born.
MACDUFF.   Despair thy charm,

17 *kerns:* ordinary foot soldiers.   22 *bruited:* announced.
18 *staves:* spears.   24 *rend'red:* surrendered.

And let the angel whom thou still hast served
Tell thee, Macduff was from his mother's womb   15
Untimely ripped.
MACBETH. Accursed be that tongue that tells me so,
    For it hath cowed my better part of man!
    And be these juggling fiends no more believed,
    That palter with us in a double sense,   20
    That keep the word of promise to our ear
    And break it to our hope. I'll not fight with thee.
MACDUFF. Then yield thee, coward,
    And live to be the show and gaze o' the time.
    We'll have thee, as our rarer monsters are,   25
    Painted upon a pole, and underwrit
    "Here may you see the tyrant."
MACBETH.   I will not yield,
    To kiss the ground before young Malcolm's feet
    And to be baited with the rabble's curse.
    Though Birnam Wood be come to Dunsinane,   30
    And thou opposed, being of no woman born,
    Yet I will try the last. Before my body
    I throw my warlike shield. Lay on, Macduff,
    And damned be him that first cries "Hold, enough!"

Exeunt fighting. Alarums. [Re-enter fighting, and MACBETH *slain.
Exit* MACDUFF.] *Retreat and flourish. Enter, with drum and
colors,* MALCOLM, SIWARD, ROSS, THANES, *and* SOLDIERS.

MALCOLM. I would the friends we miss were safe arrived.   35
SIWARD. Some must go off; and yet, by these I see,
    So great a day as this is cheaply bought.
MALCOLM. Macduff is missing, and your noble son.
ROSS. Your son, my lord, has paid a soldier's debt.
    He only lived but till he was a man,   40
    The which no sooner had his prowess confirmed
    In the unshrinking station where he fought
    But like a man he died.
SIWARD.   Then he is dead?
ROSS. Ay, and brought off the field. Your cause of sorrow
    Must not be measured by his worth, for then   45
    It hath no end.
SIWARD.   Had he his hurts before?
ROSS. Ay, on the front.
SIWARD.   Why then, God's soldier be he.
    Had I as many sons as I have hairs,
    I would not wish them to a fairer death.
    And so his knell is knolled.

V.viii.20 *palter:* quibble.   36 *go off:* die.

MALCOLM.   He's worth more sorrow,   50
    And that I'll spend for him.
SIWARD.   He's worth no more.
    They say he parted well and paid his score,
    And so, God be with him. Here comes newer comfort.

Enter MACDUFF, *with* MACBETH's *head.*

MACDUFF. Hail, King, for so thou art. Behold where stands
    The usurper's cursed head. The time is free   55
    I see thee compassed with thy kingdom's pearl,
    That speak my salutation in their minds,
    Whose voices I desire aloud with mine—
    Hail, King of Scotland!
ALL.   Hail, King of Scotland!

Flourish.

MALCOLM. We shall not spend a large expense of time   60
    Before we reckon with your several loves
    And make us even with you. My Thanes and kinsmen,
    Henceforth be Earls, the first that ever Scotland
    In such an honor named. What's more to do
    Which would be planted newly with the time—   65
    As calling home our exiled friends abroad
    That fled the snares of watchful tyranny,
    Producing forth the cruel ministers
    Of this dead butcher and his fiend-like queen,
    Who (as 'tis thought) by self and violent hands   70
    Took off her life—this, and what needful else
    That calls upon us, by the grace of Grace
    We will perform in measure, time, and place.
    So thanks to all at once and to each one,
    Whom we invite to see us crowned at Scone.   75

56 *compassed:* surrounded.   73 *in measure:* in the proper manner.

Biographical Note

RACINE

The son of a lawyer, JEAN RACINE (1639–1699) spent his early years at the Jansenist seminary at Port-Royal, near Paris, where he received a rigorous Catholic upbringing and a solid grounding in classical studies. On moving to the Collège d'Harcourt to study philosophy he became attracted to the theater, wrote three plays (all rejected by theatrical companies) and a few poems, and somewhat scandalized his devout relatives by his literary libertinism. They sent him off to the province of Languedoc in hopes that his uncle, the vicar-general of the diocese, might assist him into the ministry. Two years later, in 1663, he returned to Paris and resumed writing. A congratulatory "Ode on the King's Convalescence" brought him a gift of six hundred liras from Louis XIV, and not long thereafter his play *The Thebaide,* inspired by the Oedipus plays of Sophocles, was accepted by Molière and presented by his company at the Palais-Royal. The performance was badly received, as was that of his next play, *Alexander the Great,* whereupon Racine broke with Molière and went over to a rival company. During the next ten years or so Racine set his Jansenist background vigorously behind him, enjoying the high life of Paris and the favors of various actresses and writing a series of great tragedies (including *Andromache, Berenice, Mithridates,* and *Iphigenia*) and his only comedy, *The Pleaders,* a spoof of lawyers. In 1677 however, after *Phaedra* had been jeered by his enemies, Racine quit the theater, married the wealthy Catherine de Romanet, and settled down to a life of scholarship and piety. In 1689 and 1691 he wrote two final plays, *Esther* and *Athaliah,* based on Biblical subjects.

Phaedra

jean racine

CHARACTERS

THESEUS *king of Athens, son of Aegeus*
PHAEDRA *wife of* THESEUS, *daughter of Minos and of Pasiphae*
HIPPOLYTUS *son of* THESEUS *and of Antiope, queen of the Amazons*
ARICIA *a princess of the royal house of Athens*

OENONE *nurse and confidant of* PHAEDRA
THERAMENES *tutor and friend of* THESEUS
ISMENE *confidant of* ARICIA
PANOPE *a lady in the court of* PHAEDRA
GUARDS

ACT I

THE SCENE *is at Troezen, a city in the Peloponnesus.*

[HIPPOLYTUS *and* THERAMENES *enter.*]

HIPPOLYTUS. My mind is made up. I am leaving, Theramenes,
    And ending my stay in gracious Troezen,
    For shaken as I am by dreadful doubts,
    I begin to feel shame at my idleness.
    Six months and more my father has been away,   5
    And yet I do not know the fate of one so dear to me;
    I do not even know what regions may be hiding him.
THERAMENES. And in what regions, my lord, would you then search?
    Already, in answer to your just fears,
    I have sailed the two seas that surround Corinth;   10
    I have asked for Theseus of the people on those shores
    Where one sees Acheron lose itself among the dead;

* *From Phaedra by Jean Racine, trans. by Wesley Goddard, published by Chandler Publishing Company, San Francisco. Copyright © 1951 by Chandler Publishing Company. Reprinted by permission.*

I.10 *the two seas:* the Ionian and the Aegean seas.
12 *Acheron:* a river flowing from Epirus, a country of northwestern Greece, into Hades.

I have visited Elis and, leaving Taenarus,
Have gone on to the sea where Icarus fell.
With what new hope, in what happy place,   15
Do you expect to find the trace of his steps?
Who knows, indeed, if the King your father
Wants the secret of his absence learned?
While we, along with you, fear for his life,
He may be quietly hiding his newest loves,   20
Waiting, that some deluded loving girl . . .
HIPPOLYTUS. Theramenes, stop, and show respect for Theseus.
Long since recovered from his youthful ways,
He is now held back by no unworthy obstacle;
And with his inconstancy ended by his own vows,   25
Phaedra for long has feared no rivals.
    In short, by searching for him, I will follow duty,
And I will flee this place which I dare see no more.
THERAMENES. Since when, my lord, do you fear the sight
Of this peaceful place, so dear to your childhood,   30
And which I have seen that you prefer
To the pompous tumult of Athens and the court?
What danger, or rather what pain, sends you away?
HIPPOLYTUS. Those happy times are gone. All has changed
Since the gods have sent here to these shores   35
The daughter of Minos and Pasiphae.
THERAMENES. I understand. I know the cause of your suffering.
Phaedra here distresses you and hurts your sight:
A dangerous stepmother, who showed her true self
By sending you to exile when first she saw you.   40
But her hate, which once enveloped you,
Either has vanished or is now much weakened.
    Besides, what risks can you be made to face
By a dying woman, by one who wants to die?
Phaedra, struck by an ill of which she will not speak,   45
Weary of herself and of the very day,
Can she form plots against you?
HIPPOLYTUS. Her empty hate is not what I fear.
Hippolytus, in leaving, flees another enemy.
I flee, I will admit it, that young Aricia,   50
Descendant of a fatal line conspiring against us.
THERAMENES. What! Do you yourself, my lord, persecute her?

13 *Elis:* a country of ancient Greece, on the western shore of the Peloponnesus; *Taenarus:* southernmost tip of the Peloponnesus.

14 *Icarus:* the son of Daedalus; he fell in the Aegean, having escaped from the labyrinth of Crete by the use of wings insecurely fastened on with wax, which melted in the sun.

20 *his newest loves:* Theseus had already seduced Antiope, Ariadne, Phaedra, Helen, and Peribea.

36 *daughter of Minos and Pasiphae:* this early mention of Pasiphae, famous because of her unnatural love for a bull, establishes the hereditary taint in Phaedra's character.

Did ever this sweet sister of the cruel Pallantides
Have a hand in the schemes of her treacherous brothers?
Must you now hate her innocent charms?   55
HIPPOLYTUS. If I hated her, I would not flee.
THERAMENES [*after a pause*]. My lord, may I be allowed to inter-
pret your flight?
Could it be you are no more that proud Hippolytus,
Implacable enemy of the laws of love
And of the yoke that Theseus has so often worn?   60
Is Venus, so long disdained by your pride,
Trying in this to justify Theseus,
And by putting you on a level with other men
Has she forced you to burn incense on her altars?
Would you be in love, my lord?   65
HIPPOLYTUS. Friend, what are you saying?
You who have known my thoughts since I first took breath,
Can you ask me to disavow in shame
The feelings of a heart so proud, so disdainful?
Small wonder that an Amazon mother should give   70
With her milk this pride which seems to astound you.
Indeed, with years and growing knowledge of myself,
I came to approve of what I saw in me.
Attached to me by a sincere devotion,
You would tell me then the story of my father.   75
You know how my heart, attentive to your voice,
Warmed to hear the tale of his noble exploits,
When you painted for me this fearless hero
Consoling the mortals upon the absence of Alcides—
The monsters destroyed and the brigands punished,   80
Procrustes, Cercyon, and Sciron, and Sinis,
And the scattered bones of the giant of Epidaurus,
And Crete smoking with the blood of the Minotaur.
But then you told of less glorious deeds:
His faith offered everywhere and everywhere received,   85
Helen stolen from her parents in Sparta,
Salamis a witness to the tears of Peribea;

53 *Pallantides:* the fifty brothers of Aricia (reduced to six by Racine) who were killed by their cousin Theseus, with whom they were rivals for the throne of Athens.
70 *Amazon mother:* Antiope, Hippolytus' mother by an earlier marriage of Theseus, had been queen of the Amazons, a warlike nation of women.
79 *Alcides:* another name for Hercules.
81 *Procrustes, etc.:* all Greek brigands, famous for their methods of torture, who were killed by Theseus.
82 *Epidaurus:* a town on the Aegean coast,

the home of another of Theseus' victims.
83 *Minotaur:* a monster—half man, half bull—shut up in the labyrinth of Crete, living off human sacrifices until killed by Theseus. The Minotaur was born of the union between Pasiphae and a bull and was thus the half-brother of Phaedra.
86 *Helen:* abducted by Theseus, later the wife of Menelaus, and eventually the cause of the Trojan War.
87 *Peribea:* abandoned by Theseus and later married to the king of Salamis.

So many more, whose names have escaped him,
Too credulous hearts that his love has deceived:
Ariadne telling the rocks of her abandonment,   90
Phaedra, too, abducted, but to a happier end.
   You know how, regretting to hear this talk,
I often pressed you to shorten your account;
Happy, had I been able to erase from memory   95
This shameful half of so fine a tale!
   Would I, in my turn, see myself bound by love?
And would the gods have so degraded me?
Unmanly sighs are all the more contemptible
Without the great deeds which can excuse the King;
For no monsters subdued by me as yet   100
Have given me the right to be as frail as he.
   Yet even had my resistance been softened,
Would I have chosen Aricia to be my conqueror?
Would not my wandering senses remember
The eternal obstacle which lies between us?   105
My father rejects her, and by severest laws
He forbids any heirs be given to her brothers,
For he fears an offspring of this guilty stock.
With their sister he wants to bury their name,
And never for her will wedding fires be lit   110
While yet she lives and still is in his care.
Should I espouse her rights against an angry father?
Shall I make a show of such temerity
And like a fool embark upon an insane love . . .
THERAMENES. My lord, though one's final hour be known above,   115
Still heaven ignores the reasons that guide our acts.
Theseus opens your eyes while wishing to close them,
And his hate, fanning in you a rebellious love,
Lends to his enemy one grace she did not have.
   So why be afraid of a love that is pure?   120
If its promise is sweet, do you not dare to taste it,
Or will you always maintain such a timorous scruple?
Do you fear being lost in the path of Hercules?
What hearts has Venus not been known to master?
And where would you be, you who are fighting the goddess,   125
If Antiope, like you, opposed to her laws,
Had not burned with a chaste love for Theseus?
   But what do you gain by affecting this proud talk?
Admit it; you are changed. And for some days
One sees you less often, arrogant and alone,   130
Now making a chariot fly along the shore,

90 *Ariadne:* Phaedra's sister, abandoned by Theseus on the Island of Naxos.
91 *happier end:* because Phaedra, at least, was legitimately married to Theseus.

123 *Hercules:* Hercules was also noted as a woman-chaser.
126 *Antiope:* the mother of Hippolytus.

Now, wise in the art invented by Neptune,
Making docile a courser till then unbroken.
Today the forests echo less often to our cries.
Charged with an inner fire, your eyes are heavy.   135
There can be no doubt: you are in love, you burn;
You are dying from an ill which you would hide.
Has Aricia cast a spell and been able to please you?
HIPPOLYTUS. Theramenes, I am leaving and will search for my
  father.
THERAMENES. Will you see Phaedra before you go, my lord?   140
HIPPOLYTUS. Such is my plan. You may tell her of it.

[*Exit* THERAMENES.]

Let us see her, since thus my duty orders.

[*He sees* OENONE *entering.*]

    But what new distress troubles her dear Oenone?
OENONE. Alas, my lord, what trouble can equal mine?
    The Queen has nearly reached her fated end,   145
    And though I watch both night and day,
    She dies in my arms of an ill that she conceals.
    Some eternal disorder reigns within her soul.
    Her uneasy grief takes her from her bed;
    She wants to see the day; yet her deep sadness   150
    Commands me ever to let her be alone . . .
        She comes
HIPPOLYTUS. It is enough. I will leave her here
    And will not show to her a hateful face.

[*Exit* HIPPOLYTUS *as* PHAEDRA *enters.*]

PHAEDRA. Let us go no farther. Let us stop, dear Oenone.   155
    I can hold up no more. My strength abandons me.
    My eyes are blinded by the light I see again,
    And my trembling knees give way beneath me. [*She sits.*]
    Alas!
OENONE. Almighty gods, may our tears appease you!   160
PHAEDRA. How these vain jewels, how these veils weigh upon me!
    What meddling hand, in making all these knots,
    Has thus arranged my hair upon my brow?
    Everything overwhelms me and hurts me and conspires to
        hurt me.
OENONE. Thus one sees how her wishes overrule one another!   165

132 *Neptune:* though god of the sea, he   Greeks.
  also was responsible for introducing   158 [*She sits*]: the only stage direction
  the horse and horsemanship to the   given by Racine in the entire play.

You yourself, condemning your unjust resolve,
Urged on our hands to adorn you;
You yourself, remembering your earlier strength,
Wanted to show yourself and to see again the light.
You see it, Madam; and, ready now to hide,   170
You hate the day that you came out to find.

PHAEDRA [*looking toward the sun*].
Noble and brilliant father of a woeful family,
You whose daughter my mother was proud to be,
Who blush in shame at the trouble you see me in,
Sun, I come to look on you for one last time.   175

OENONE. What! You will not give up this cruel desire?
Shall I always see you, renouncing life,
Make dismal preparations for your death?

PHAEDRA. Oh, gods! That I might be seated in the forest shade,
That I might, through a cloud of noble dust,   180
Follow with my eye a chariot coursing down the field!

OENONE. What, Madam?

PHAEDRA. I am mad. Where am I, and what have I said?
Where have I let wander my wishes—and my mind?
I have lost it; the gods have robbed me of its use.   185
Oenone, the blush of shame covers my face;
I let you see too well my miseries,
And my eyes, despite me, fill with tears.

OENONE. Ah, if you must blush, blush for the silence
Which but aggravates the violence of your hurt.   190
Refusing all our aid, deaf to all our words,
Do you, without pity, want to end your days?
What madness cuts them short in the middle of their run?
What spell or what poison has dried up their source?
    Three times have the shadows darkened the heavens   195
Since sleep last entered upon your eyes;
And three times the day has chased away dark night
Since your body has languished without food.
By what frightful purpose are you tempted?
By what right do you lay hands upon yourself?   200
You offend the gods, the authors of your life;
You betray the husband to whom your promise binds you;
You betray, in the end, your own unhappy children,
Whom you thrust beneath a yoke of iron.
Consider that the same day will rob them of their mother   205
And give hope to the foreign woman's son,
To that implacable enemy of you and of your blood,
The son whom an Amazon has borne,
That Hippolytus . . .

PHAEDRA. Oh, gods!   210

175 *Sun:* Phaedra's mother, Pasiphae, was
    the daughter of Apollo, the sun god.

OENONE. This reproach touches you.
PHAEDRA. Wretch, what name did your mouth utter?
OENONE. Well, your anger burst forth with good reason.
　　I like to see you tremble at this baleful name.
　　Live then. May love and duty bring you back to life.　　215
　　Live. Do not let the son of a Scythian,
　　Crushing your children beneath a hateful power,
　　Command the finest blood of Greece and of the gods.
　　But do not delay. Each moment brings you nearer death.
　　Build up at once your weakened strength,　　220
While still the torch of life endures
　　And, though nearly out, can yet be lit again.
PHAEDRA. I have made it burn too long, in guilt.
OENONE. What, do you feel torn by some remorse?
　　What crime has brought about such torment?　　225
　　Can your hands be stained by innocent blood?
PHAEDRA. Thanks be to heaven, my hands bear no guilt.
　　If only my heart were as innocent as they!
OENONE. What awful project, then, have you begotten
　　That your heart should still be struck with terror?　　230
PHAEDRA. I have said enough. Spare me the rest.
　　I die, to save myself so painful a confession.
OENONE. Die, then, and keep your inhuman silence;
　　But seek another hand to close your eyes.
　　Though you have but a park of life within you,　　235
　　My soul will be the first to go among the dead.
　　A thousand open roads lead always down,
　　And my just bitterness will find the shortest way.
　　　Cruel one, when has my devotion proved untrue?
　　Do you recall that my arms held you at your birth?　　240
　　For you I left all—my native land, my children.
　　Is this the way to repay my loyalty?
PHAEDRA. What fruit do you want from so much argument?
　　You would tremble with horror should I break my silence.
OENONE. And what could you tell me that would equal　　245
　　The horror of seeing you expire before my eyes?
PHAEDRA. When you know my crime and the fate which crushes me,
　　I shall die nonetheless, but I shall die more guilty yet.
OENONE. [kneeling]. Madam, in the name of the tears I have shed
　　for you,
　　By your knees which I clasp to my heart,　　250
　　Free my mind of this dreadful doubt.
PHAEDRA. You wish it. Rise.

---

216 *Scythion:* i.e., an Amazon, Scythia be-
　　ing an area north of the Caspian Sea
　　inhabited by the Amazons.
218 *of Greece and of the gods:* Phaedra's

sons have Theseus as a father and
both Apollo and Jupiter as ultimate
ancestors.

OENONE. Speak. I listen to your words.
    PHAEDRA. Heaven, what shall I say, and where do I begin?
OENONE. Offend me no more with these vain fears.   255
PHAEDRA. This is the fatal anger of Venus, and her hate!
    To what madness my mother was driven by love!
OENONE. Forget the past, Madam, and may to all posterity
    An eternal silence hide this memory.
PHAEDRA. Ariadne, my sister, wounded too by such love,   260
    You died on the shores where you were abandoned.
OENONE. What are you doing, Madam? And what torment
    Stirs you against all your family today?
PHAEDRA. Since Venus wishes it, of this piteous line
    I perish the last, the most wretched of all.   265
OENONE. Are you in love?
PHAEDRA. I know love in all its fury.
OENONE. For whom?
PHAEDRA. You are about to hear the ultimate horror.
    I love ... At this fatal name I tremble, I quake.   270
    I love ...
OENONE. Whom?
PHAEDRA. You know the son of the Amazon,
    That prince whom so long I myself have oppressed?
OENONE. Hippolytus! Great gods!   275
PHAEDRA. It is you who have named him.
OENONE. Merciful heaven! My blood freezes in my veins.
    The despair and crime that befall a cursed race!
    That fated voyage that led to this unhappy strand!
    Did you need to come here to this dangerous shore?   280
PHAEDRA. My ill comes from further back. No sooner
    Was I engaged by law to the son of Aegeus,
    Than my repose, my happiness, seemed assured.
    Then Athens showed me my proud enemy;
    I saw him, I blushed, I paled at his sight.   285
    A new emotion troubled my lost soul.
    My eyes no longer saw; I could not speak;
    I felt my whole body both burning and benumbed.
       In all this I saw Venus and her fearful fires,
    Inevitable torments of the family she pursues—   290
    Torments I thought I could avoid by vows:
    I built a temple to her and adorned it with care;
    I surrounded myself with victims of sacrifice
    And sought in their entrails my wandering mind.
       Powerless remedies for an incurable love!   295

257 *driven by love:* Venus was responsible for Pasiphae's love of the bull.
279 *fated voyage:* the trip of Phaedra and Oenone to Troezen.
290 *the family she pursues:* Venus con-tinues to punish Phaedra's family because it was Apollo who had revealed the secret of the love between the goddess and Mars.

In vain on the altars my hand burned the incense.
While to the name of the goddess my lips formed prayers,
I adored Hippolytus. And seeing him always,
Even at the foot of the altars that I caused to smoke,
I offered all to this god I dared not name.   300
    I avoided him everywhere; then, height of misery!
I found him again in the face of his father.
Against myself at last I dared revolt:
I inflamed my heart that I might persecute him.
To banish the enemy whom I worshiped   305
I assumed the ill-will of an unjust stepmother;
I urged his exile, and by my constant cries
Tore him from his father's arms and heart.
    I breathed at last, Oenone, and since his going,
My calmer days have flowed in innocence.   310
Submissive to my husband, and hiding my torment,
I nursed the fruit of this ill-fated marriage.
    Vain precautions against a cruel destiny!
Brought to Troezen by my husband himself,
I saw again the enemy I had banished.   315
My wound, still too fresh, bled again.
It is no longer an ardor hidden in my veins;
It is Venus clutching tight her prey.
    I have conceived a just terror of my crime
And held my life in hate, my love in horror.   320
I wanted in death to preserve my honor
And to rob the day of so criminal a love.
    I could not withstand your tears and your arguments;
I have confessed all to you, nor do I repent it,
If only, respecting the nearness of my death,   325
You no longer afflict me with unjust reproaches
And if you cease to preserve to no avail
The last bit of warmth on the point of vanishing.

[*Enter* PANOPE.]

PANOPE. I wish that I could hide this tragic news,
    Madam, but to you I must reveal it.   330
    Death has robbed you of your invincible husband,
    And this calamity is known to all but you.
OENONE. Panope, what did you say?
PANOPE. That the Queen, deluded,
    In vain prays heaven for Theseus' return,   335
    And that from the ships just arrived in port
    Hippolytus, his son, has learned of his death.
PHAEDRA. Heaven!

312 *fruit of this ill-fated marriage:* i.e., her
    two sons by Theseus.

PANOPE. For the choice of a master, Athens is divided.
　　Some give their vote to your son, Madam;　　　　　　340
　　Others, forgetting the law of the state,
　　Dare give their voice to the son of the foreigner.
　　It is even said that one insolent group
　　Wants to put Aricia on the throne.
　　　　I felt that I should warn you of this peril.　　　345
　　Hippolytus is about to leave, and it is feared
　　That if he should go to Athens in this unforeseen storm
　　He might carry with him a whole inconstant people.
OENONE. Panope, that is enough. The Queen, who hears you,
　　Will not neglect this important news.　　　　[*Exit* PANOPE.]　　350
　　　　Madam, I had ceased urging you to live;
　　Already I expected to follow you to the tomb
　　And had no voice left to change your mind,
　　But this new misfortune prescribes new obligations.
　　Your situation changes and takes another face.　　　355
　　The King is no more, Madam. You must take his place.
　　His death leaves you a son to whom you owe yourself:
　　A slave if he loses you, a king if you live.
　　On whom, in his grief, do you want him to lean?
　　His tears will have no hand to wipe them away;　　　360
　　And his innocent cries, rising to the gods,
　　Will turn his ancestors against his mother.
　　　　Live. You need reproach yourself no more.
　　Your love has become an ordinary love.
　　Theseus in dying has just undone the knots　　　365
　　Which made all the crime and horror of your passion.
　　Hippolytus becomes for you less dangerous,
　　And you can see him now with no trace of guilt.
　　　　Perhaps, convinced of your aversion,
　　He plans to serve as leader to seditio.　　　370
　　Correct his error. Change his heart and mind.
　　As king of these happy shores, Troezen is his portion,
　　But he knows that the laws give to your son
　　The proud ramparts which Minerva built.
　　You have, both of you, a legitimate enemy:　　　375
　　Unite, both of you, to fight Aricia.
PHAEDRA. Very well, by your counsel I will let myself be led.
　　Let us live, if I can be brought to life,
　　And if the love of a son at this dismal time
　　Can awaken my feeble spirits once again.　　　380

374 *ramparts which Minerva built:* i.e.,
　　Athens.

ACT II

[*Enter* ARICIA *and* ISMENE.]

ARICIA. Hippolytus asks to see me in this place?
    Hippolytus seeks me and wants to say farewell?
    Ismene, is this true? You are not mistaken?
ISMENE. This is the first effect of Theseus' death.
    Prepare yourself, Madam, to see on every side   5
    Men turn to you who were held off by Theseus.
    Aricia at last is mistress of her days.
    And soon at her feet she will see all Greece.
ARICIA. This is not, Ismene, an unfounded tale?
    I am no more a slave and have no enemies?   10
ISMENE. No, Madam, the gods no longer are opposed to you,
    And Theseus has joined the ghosts of your brothers.
ARICIA. Do they say what accident has ended his days?
ISMENE. Unbelievable stories are told of his death.
    They say that as the ravisher of his newest love,   15
    This faithless husband was swallowed by the seas.
    They say too—and this account is widely spread—
    That with Pirithous he descended into hell,
    Where he saw the Cocytus and its shadowy banks
    And showed himself alive among the infernal shades,   20
    But that he could not return from those gloomy parts
    And recross the border that can be crossed but once.
ARICIA. Shall I believe that a mortal, before his final hour,
    Can descend early to the abode of the dead?
    What spell drew him to those fearful shores?   25
ISMENE. Theseus is dead, Madam, and you alone still doubt.
    Athens already mourns, Troezen has heard the news
    And recognizes Hippolytus for king.
    Phaedra in this palace, fearful for her son,
    Asks counsel of her troubled friends.   30
ARICIA. And you think that Hippolytus, more human than his
    father,
    Will lighten the burden of my chains,
    That he will have pity on my misfortune?
ISMENE. Madam, I do believe it.
ARICIA. Do you really know the insensitive Hippolytus?   35
    By what foolish hope do you believe he pities me
    And respects in me alone a sex which he disdains?
    You can see for how long he has avoided our path
    And has sought only those places where we cannot be found.

II.18 *Pirithous:* king of the Lapithae, who was thought to have gone to Hades with his friend Theseus to abduct Persephone.

ISMENE. I know all that has been said of his coldness.   40
    But I have seen this proud Hippolytus beside you,
    And even as I looked, the fame of his aloofness
    Redoubled my curiosity. And yet his aspect
    Agreed in no way with the stories that they tell.
    At your first glance upon him, I saw he was troubled.   45
    His eyes, already languishing, tried to avoid you,
    But in vain; they could not turn away.
    The name of lover perhaps wounds his pride;
    But he has a lover's eyes, though he lack the words.
ARICIA. How my heart, dear Ismene, listens eagerly   50
    To a tale that may have little base!
    You who know me, can you believe
    That this sad plaything of a pitiless fate,
    This heart ever nourished on bitterness and tears,
    Should know love and all its foolish pain?   55
        Descendant of a king, noble son of the Earth,
    I alone escaped from the fury of war.
    I lost, in the flower of their youth, six brothers—
    They were the hope of an illustrious house.
    The sword reaped all, and the dampened ground   60
    Drank with regret the blood of Erechtheus' heirs.
        You know, since their death, by what stern laws
    All Greeks are forbidden to show pity for me.
    It is feared that the sister's rash flame of love
    May bring to life the ashes of her brothers.   65
    But you know too with what disdainful eye
    I looked on the concern of the distrustful King.
    You know that, always contemptuous of love,
    I often forgave the unjust Theseus,
    Whose harshness seconded my scorn.   70
        At that time my eyes had not yet seen his son.
    Not that by my eyes alone, shamefully bewitched,
    Do I love his beauty and his much-praised grace,
    Gifts that nature has freely accorded him,
    Which he scorns and of which he seems unaware.   75
    I love, I prize in him, more noble wealth:
    The virtues of his father, but not the weaknesses.
    I love, I will confess, that splendid pride
    Which never has submitted to the yoke of love.
        Phaedra thinks herself honored by the sighs of Theseus.   80
    As for me, I am more proud and flee the easy glory
    Of winning an homage offered to a thousand more
    And of entering a heart open on every side.

---

19 *Cocytus:* a river of Hades.   his son Erechtheus.
56 *son of the Earth:* Aricia is a descendant   61 *Drank with regret:* because the Pal-
    in a direct line from the Earth, through   lantides were descended from the Earth.

But to sway a will till then inflexible,
To bring pain to an insensitive soul,   85
To enchain a captive, amazed to be in irons,
Revolting in vain against a pleasing yoke:
That is what I want; that is what excites me.
   Hercules was easier to disarm than Hippolytus
And, vanquished more often and sooner overcome,   90
Brought less renown to those who subdued him.
   But, dear Ismene, alas, what rash hope is mine!
I can meet with nothing but his too great resistance.
You may someday hear me, humble in my pain,
Bemoaning the same pride which I admire today.   95
Can Hippolytus love? By what good fortune
Could I have swayed . . .
ISMENE. You will hear him speak himself.
   He comes to you.

[*Enter* HIPPOLYTUS.]

HIPPOLYTUS. Madam, before I leave,   100
   I felt that I should speak of what awaits you.
My father no longer lives. My well-founded fears
Foretold the reason for his too-long absence:
Death alone, putting an end to his brilliant deeds,
Could hide him from the universe so long.   105
At last the gods surrender to the deadly Fates
The friend, the companion, the successor to Alcides.
(Surely even your hate, admitting his virtues,
Listens without distaste to these names that are his due.)
   One hope lightens my deathly grief: 110
I can free you from a strict surveillance;
I revoke the laws whose harshness I deplored;
You are mistress of yourself and of your heart.
And in this Troezen, which now belongs to me,
Once the heritage of my forefather Pittheus,   115
And which, without debate, has named me king,
I leave you free, and more free than I.
ARICIA. Restrain your goodness, whose excess confounds me.
   To honor my misfortune with such generous care
Is to place me, my lord, more than you think,   120
Under as severe laws as those from which you free me.
HIPPOLYTUS. In the choice of a successor, uncertain Athens
   Speaks of you, of me, of the son of the Queen.
ARICIA. Of me, my lord?

---

90 *vanquished more often:* i.e., by love.
106 *Fates:* the three goddesses of destiny and death.
115 *Pittheus:* the maternal grandfather of Theseus, founder of Troezen.

HIPPOLYTUS. I know, without wishing to deceive myself,   125
   That an insolent law appears to reject me:
   Greece reproaches me my foreign mother.
   But if as a rival I had only my brother,
   I could well save from capricious laws
   Certain genuine rights that I have over him.   130
     A more legitimate brake puts a stop to my daring:
   I cede to you, or rather I return, a place
   And sceptre received of old by your forebears
   From that famous mortal conceived by the Earth.
   Adoption put them in Aegeus' hands.   135
   Later Athens, enhanced and protected by my father,
   Recognized with joy so noble a king
   And left your unhappy brothers to forgetfulness.
     Now Athens calls you back within her walls.
   She has suffered enough from a lengthy quarrel,   140
   And long enough has the blood of your family
   Made the fields smoke from which they came.
     Troezen obeys me. The countryside of Crete
   Offers a rich retreat to the son of Phaedra.
   Attica is yours. I go and will unite for you   145
   All the voices now divided between us.
ARICIA. Of all that I hear, astonished and confused,
   I almost fear, I do fear a dream deceives me.
   Am I awake? Can I believe that such a plan is true?
   What god, my lord, has put it in your heart?   150
   How right that your fame is spread afar,
   And yet the truth surpasses reputation!
     In my favor do you really give over your claim?
   Was it not enough that you should not hate me
   And that for so long you could preserve your soul   155
   From that enmity . . .
HIPPOLYTUS. I hate you, Madam?
   In whatever light my pride may have been painted,
   Can one believe a monster gave me birth?
   What savage ways, what hardened hate   160
   Could not be softened merely by seeing you?
   Could I resist the delusive charm . . .
ARICIA. What, my lord?
HIPPOLYTUS. I have gone too far.
   I see that reason yields to the violence of love.   165
     But since I have now begun to break my silence,
   Madam, I must go on. I must inform you

134 *famous mortal:* Erechtheus.
135 *Adoption put them in Aegeus' hands:*
   Aegeus, the father of Theseus, and
   Pallas, the father of Aricia, were both
   sons of Pandion, king of Athens. But
Aegeus was only an adopted son,
whereas Pallas was legitimate. Thus
Aricia's claim to the throne of Athens
is valid.

Of a secret my heart no longer can contain.
  You see before you a pitiful prince,
An enduring example of a presumptuous pride.   170
I have been haughtily rebellious against love,
Have long jeered at the irons of her captives,
And, deploring the shipwreck of weaker men,
Hoped always to watch the storms from shore.
  But now, enslaved by the common law,   175
By what passion I see myself carried away!
One moment has vanquished my rash audacity;
My arrogant soul is at last dependent.
For nearly six months, ashamed and in despair,
Bearing everywhere the arrow by which I am torn,   180
I have contended in vain against you, against myself.
With you present, I flee; absent, I find you.
In the depths of the forest your image follows me.
The light of the day, the shades of the night,
Everything retraces for my eyes the charms that I avoid.   185
Everything vies to deliver the rebel Hippolytus to you.
And as the only fruit of all my useless efforts,
I search now for myself but can no longer find me.
My bow, my javelins, my chariot, all annoy me;
I no longer remember the lessons of Neptune;   190
Only my groans re-echo in the woods,
And my idle coursers have forgotten my voice.
  Perhaps the tale of a love so unrestrained
Makes you blush in shame at the work you have done.
And what uncouth speech to offer you a heart!   195
What a strange captive for so fair a bond!
Yet the offer, to your eyes, should be the more precious.
Remember that I speak a language strange to me;
So do not reject these vows, badly expressed,
Which Hippolytus without you would never have made.   200

[*Enter* THERAMENES.]

THERAMENES. My lord, the Queen comes, and I have come ahead.
  She seeks you.
HIPPOLYTUS. Me?
THERAMENES. I do not know her thought,
  But you are being asked for in her behalf.   205
  Phaedra wants to speak to you before your leaving.
HIPPOLYTUS. Phaedra? What can I say to her? And what can she
  expect?
ARICIA. My lord, you cannot refuse to hear her.
  Though you are too convinced of her ill feeling,
  You owe to her tears some shadow of pity.   210

190 *lessons of Neptune:* i.e., horsemanship.

HIPPOLYTUS [*to* ARICIA.] Meanwhile you go. And I am leaving. And
  I do not know
    If I offend the charms which I adore!
    I do not know if the heart I leave in your hands...
ARICIA. Go, Prince, and follow your generous designs.   215
    Make Athens submissive to my power.
    I accept all the gifts that you offer me.
    But this empire, after all so great, so glorious,
    Is not of your gifts the dearest to my eyes.
[*Exeunt* ARICIA *and* ISMENE.]
HIPPOLYTUS. Friend, are you ready?
    But the Queen comes near.   220
    Go, that all for our departure be prepared in haste.
    Have the signal given—run, order, and return
    To deliver me soon from this unwelcome talk.

[*Exit* THERAMENES *as* PHAEDRA *and* OENONE *enter.*]

PHAEDRA. Here he is. All my blood flows back to my heart.
    I forget, in seeing him, what I came to say.   225
OENONE. Remember a son who has hope but in you.
PHAEDRA [*to* HIPPOLYTUS]. They say a quick departure takes you
  from us,
    My lord. To your grief I come to join my tears.
      And I come to expose my fears for a son.
    My son has now no father, and the day is not far   230
    That will make him witness to my death besides.
    Already a thousand enemies attack him in his youth.
    You alone can take up his defense against them.
    But a secret remorse troubles my spirit.   234
    I fear I have closed your ear to his cries.
    I tremble lest your rightful anger
    Against his hateful mother should fall on him.
HIPPOLYTUS. Madam, I have no thoughts so base as that.
PHAEDRA. If you should hate me, I would not complain,
    My lord. You have seen me striving to hurt you,   240
    And could not read in the depths of my heart.
    I have taken pains to expose myself to your enmity.
    I could not permit you on the shores where I lived.
    Declaring myself against you in public and alone,
    I tried to put the seas between us.   245
    I even forbade, by a special law,
    That anyone utter your name before me.
      If, however, the pain be measured by the offense,
    If only hate can bring about your hate,
    Then never was woman more deserving of pity,   250
    And less deserving, my lord, of your enmity.
HIPPOLYTUS. For the rights of her children a jealous mother

Rarely forgives the son of another wife.
Madam, I know this. Harassing suspicions
Are the most common fruits of a second marriage.   255
Anyone else would have taken the same offense.
And I might have suffered more outrages yet.
PHAEDRA. Ah, my lord, here I dare attest that heaven
    Has excepted me from that common law,
    That a very different care troubles and consumes me!   260
HIPPOLYTUS. Madam, this is not the time still to torment yourself.
    Perhaps your husband yet sees the light of day.
    Heaven may answer our tears and accord his return.
    Neptune protects him, and this guardian god
    Will not be implored in vain by my father.   265
PHAEDRA. No one sees twice the shores of the dead,
    My lord. Since Theseus has seen that somber place,
    You hope in vain a god will send him back to you.
    And the miserly Acheron does not loose its prey.   269
        What am I saying? He is not dead, for he breathes in you.
    Still before my eyes I think I see my husband.
    I see him, I speak to him, and my heart . . . I wander.
    My lord, my insane passion declares itself despite me.
HIPPOLYTUS. I see the marvelous effect of your love.
    Dead though he is, Theseus is present to your eyes;   275
    Your soul is still afire with love of him.
PHAEDRA. Yes, Prince, I languish, I burn for Theseus.
    I love him, but not as he is seen in hell—
    Inconstant lover of a thousand women,
    Gone to dishonor the couch of the god of the dead—   280
    But faithful, but proud, and even a little shy,
    Charming, young, trailing all hearts behind him,
    Such as our gods are painted—or such as I see you.
    He had your bearing, your eyes, your speech;
    The same noble modesty colored his face   285
    When he crossed the waters of our Crete,
    Well deserving the love of the daughters of Minos.
        What were you doing then? Why, without Hippolytus,
    Did he assemble the elite of the heroes of Greece?
    Why could you not then, though still too young,   290
    Board the ship which put him on our shores?
    Through you, the monster of Crete would have perished,
    Despite all the turnings of his endless lair.
    To lead you in safety through the bewildering maze
    My sister would have armed you with the fateful thread.   295

---

280 *god of the dead:* Theseus was said to
    have gone to Hades with Pirithous to
    abduct Persephone, wife of Pluto.
287 *daughters of Minos:* Ariadne and
    Phaedra.

292 *monster of Crete:* the Minotaur.
295 *fateful thread:* Ariadne had given
    Theseus a thread to enable him to
    find his way out of the labyrinth after
    killing the Minotaur.

But no, I would have acted before her in this plan;
Love would first have given the thought to me.
It is I, Prince, it is I whose useful aid
Would have taught you the turnings of the Labyrinth.
What care that charming head would then have cost me!   300
A thread would not have made your lover sure enough.
Companion in the peril which you had to seek,
I myself before you would have wished to walk;
And Phaedra, gone down with you into the Labyrinth,
With you would have been saved or lost.   305

HIPPOLYTUS. Gods! What do I hear? Madam, do you forget
    That Theseus is my father, and that he is your husband?

PHAEDRA. And what makes you think that I have lost this memory,
    Prince? Have I abandoned all concern for my name?

HIPPOLYTUS. Madam, pardon me. I admit, blushing,   310
    That I misunderstood an innocent speech.
    My shame forbids me to look upon you;
    And I go . . .

PHAEDRA. Oh, cruel one, you understood me too well.
    I have told you enough for you to see the truth.   315
    So now you know Phaedra and all of her passion.
    I love. Think not that at the moment when I love you,
    I approve of myself, innocent in my own eyes,
    Nor that an easy complaisance has strengthened the poison
    Of the mad love that troubles my reason.   320
    The ill-fated object of a heavenly vengeance,
    I abhor myself more even than you detest me.
    The gods are my witness, those gods who in my breast
    Kindled the fatal fire of all my line,
    Those gods who have taken a cruel pride   325
    In leading astray the heart of a feeble woman.
       You, in your own mind, recall the past.
    To shun you was not enough; I drove you away.
    I wanted to seem odious to you, inhuman;
    The better to resist you, I sought your hate.   330
    But how did my vain efforts bring me any gain?
    You hated me more; I loved you no less.
    Your misfortunes but lent you more and newer charms.
    I languished and was consumed, by flames and by tears.
    You need only your eyes to be convinced,   335
    If for a moment your eyes could look at me.
       What am I saying? This avowal I have made,
    This so shameful avowal, do you think that I willed it?
    Trembling for a son whom I dared not fail,
    I came to beg you not to hate him.   340
    Futile hope of a heart too full of what it loves!
    Alas, I could speak to you only of yourself.
       Avenge yourself, punish me for an odious love.

Worthy son of the hero who gave you life,
Deliver the universe from a monster that offends you.   345
The widow of Theseus dares to love his son!
  Believe me, this awful monster must not escape you.
Here is my heart. Here your hand must strike.
Impatient already to expiate its offense,
I feel it advance as if to meet your arm.   350
Strike! Or if you think it unworthy of your blows,
If your hate refuse me so mild a punishment,
Or if your hand would be dipped in blood too vile,
Stay your arm, but lend me your sword.
Give me it! [*She pulls his sword from its scabbard.*]   355
OENONE [*rushing to* PHAEDRA *and seizing the sword*]. What are you
  doing, Madam? Merciful gods!
  But someone comes. Avoid a hateful witness.
  Come, go in, flee certain shame.

[*Exeunt* PHAEDRA *and* OENONE *as* THERAMENES *enters.*]

THERAMENES. Is that Phaedra who flees, or rather is dragged away?
  Why, my lord, why these marks of grief?   360
  I see you without your sword, abashed and pale.
HIPPOLYTUS. Theramenes, let us escape.
  My surprise has overwhelmed me.
  I cannot without horror look upon myself.
  Phaedra . . . But, no, may this horrible secret
  Lie buried forever in deep forgetfulness.   365
THERAMENES. If you wish to leave, the ship is set to sail.
  But Athens, my lord, has already declared itself.
  Its chiefs have heard the votes of all its tribes.
  Your brother has won, and Phaedra has the upper hand.
HIPPOLYTUS. Phaedra?   370
THERAMENES. A herald, charged with the will of Athens,
  Has just put in her hands the reins of the State.
  Her son is king, my lord.
HIPPOLYTUS. Gods, you who know her,
  Is it then her virtue you are rewarding?   375
THERAMENES. However, a secret rumor says the King still lives.
  They claim that Theseus has appeared in Epirus.
  But I, who searched for him, my lord, I know too well . . .
HIPPOLYTUS. No matter, let us hear all and neglect nothing.
  Let us examine this rumor; let us go to the source   380
  If it does not deserve to delay my going,
  Then let us leave and at whatever price
  Place the scepter in hands that are worthy of holding it.

383 *hands that are worthy of holding it:*
    i.e., in the hands of Aricia.

ACT III

[*Enter* PHAEDRA *and* OENONE.]

PHAEDRA. Oh, take away these honors that are sent me!
    How can you hope that I should show myself?
    Why do you try to calm my tormented mind?
    Hide me well, instead, for I have spoken but too much.
    The transports of my madness have been spread abroad;   5
    I have said what one should never hear.
    Heaven, how he listened to me! And by what detours
    He tried, unfeeling, to elude my words!
    How he hoptd for nothing but a quick escape,
    And how his shame did but increase my own!   10
    Why did you turn me from my fatal plan?
    Alas, when I held his sword against my breast,
    Did he pale for me? Did he snatch it away?
    It was enough that I should touch it once
    To make it horrible to his inhuman eyes;   15
    That steel thereafter would profane his hands.
OENONE. Thus in your misery, thinking only of your woes,
    You nourish a flame that you had best put out.
    Is it not better, worthy daughter of Minos,
    To seek your repose in more noble concerns   20
    And, in place of the ingrate who resorts to flight,
    To reign and to direct the affairs of state?
PHAEDRA. I, reign! I, bring a state under my law,
    Whes my feeble reason rules me no more!
    When I have abandoned control of my senses!   25
    When under a yoke of shame I barely breathe!
    When I am dying!
OENONE. Then flee!
PHAEDRA. I cannot leave him.
OENONE. You dared to banish him, yet dare not go away!   30
PHAEDRA. It is too late. He knows of my mad love.
    The limits of strict modesty are passed;
    I have revealed my shame to the eyes of my conqueror,
    And hope, despite me, has crept into my heart.
    You yourself, calling back my waning strength   35
    And my breath, already hovering on my lips,
    By your deceiving counsel made me live again.
    You made me glimpse the truth that I could love him.
OENONE. Alas, whether innocent or guilty of your misfortune,
    What would I not have done to save you?   40
    But if ever an offense angered your spirit,

III.1 *take away these honors:* sent by
  Athens to the mother of the new king.

Can you forget the scorn of an arrogant man?
With what cruel eyes his stubborn indifference
Left you nearly prostrate at his feet.
How odious he was in his savage pride!   45
Why, at that moment, could Phaedra not have my eyes?
PHAEDRA. Oenone, he may abandon this pride that hurts you.
He was reared in the forests, and so he is uncouth,
And, hardened by savage ways, Hippolytus   49
Hears talk of love for the first time.
Perhaps his silence was due to his surprise,
And perhaps our complaints have been too severe.
OENONE. Remember that a barbarian formed him in her womb.
PHAEDRA. Though a barbarian and a Scythian, still she loved.
OENONE. He has for all the sex a hate that is his destiny.   55
PHAEDRA. I shall then see no rival preferred to me.
So all of your counsels are now out of place.
Serve my madness, Oenone, and not my reason.
   Since to love he shows an inaccessible heart,
Let us hunt a more sensitive spot to attack.   60
The charms of an empire seemed to affect him.
Athens attracted him; he could not hide the fact.
Already his ships had turned their prows that way,
And the sails floated free in the wind.
   Go find for me this young ambitious man,   65
Oenone; make the crown shine before his eyes.
On his brow must be placed the sacred diadem;
I want only the honor of fixing it there myself.
Let us give him this power that I can hold no more.
He will instruct my son in the art of command   70
And may perhaps be willing to play a father's role.
In his power I place both son and mother.
   Try any means, indeed, to sway him.
Your words will be received more readily than mine.
Press him, weep, wail; bemoan a dying Phaedra.   75
Do not be ashamed to take a pleading voice.
I will approve all you do; in you lies my only hope.
Go. I await your return, that I may live or die. [*Exit* OENONE.]
   Oh you, who see the shame to which I have come,
Implacable Venus, am I humbled enough?   80
You cannot further push your cruelty.
Your triumph is complete; your every shaft has carried.
Cruel goddess, if you wish more glory yet,
Attack an enemy who is more rebellious to you.
Hippolytus flees from you, and, braving your wrath,   85
Never has bent his knee before your altars.
Your name seems to offend his proud ears.
Goddess, avenge yourself. Our cause is the same
May he love . . .

[*Enter* OENONE.]

But already you return, Oenone?   90
He hates me; he will not listen.
OENONE. You must give up all thought of this fruitless love,
Madam. Remember your past virtue.
The King, thought dead, will appear before your eyes.
Theseus has arrived. Theseus is in this place.   95
To see him, the people rush headlong.
I was going, at your command, to seek Hippolytus,
When a thousand cries burst forth toward heaven . . .
PHAEDRA. My husband lives, Oenone; that is enough.
I have confessed in shame a love that wrongs him.   100
He lives. I want to know no more.
OENONE. What?
PHAEDRA. I had foretold it; but you would not believe.
Your tears prevailed over my rightful remorse.
I might have died this morning, worthy to be mourned.   105
I followed your counsel; and I die dishonored.
OENONE. You die?
PHAEDRA. Just heaven! What have I done today?
My husband will appear, and with him his son.
I will see the witness of my adulterous love   110
Watch in what fashion I dare approach his father,
My heart full of sighs which he would not hear,
My eyes wet with tears which he cruelly rebuffed.
Do you think, sensitive as he is to the honor of Theseus,
That he will hide from him the love which enflames me?   115
Will he let his father be betrayed, and his king?
Can he restrain the horror he feels for me?
    Even his silence would be in vain. I know my guilt,
Oenone, and am not of those brazen women
Who, enjoying calm peace even in their crime,   120
Can prepare a brow which never shows a blush.
I know my passions; I recall them, every one.
Even now I feel these walls and these arches
Are about to speak and, ready to accuse me,
Wait only for my husband, that they may tell him all.   125
Let me die, that death deliver me from so much horror.
Is the end of life so great a calamity?
Death holds no terror for those who are wretched.
I fear only the name that I shall leave behind—
What a frightful heritage for my unhappy sons!   130
The blood of Jupiter must strengthen their hearts;
But whatever just pride this lineage inspires,
The crime of a mother is a heavy load.

131 *Jupiter:* through Minos, her two sons
are descended from Jupiter.

I tremble lest talk, alas too true,
May someday reproach them for a guilty mother.   135
I tremble lest, weighted down by this hateful burden,
Neither will dare to raise his eyes again.
OENONE. You must not doubt that I pity them both;
And never was fear better founded than yours.
But why must you expose them to such affronts?   140
Why must you stand as witness against yourself?
If you do this, they will say that the guilty Phaedra
Flees the fearful sight of a husband she has wronged.
Hippolytus is happy that, at the cost of your life,
You support, by dying, the charges that he makes.   145
    What then could I answer to him who accuses you?
Too easily before him would I be rendered silent.
In his awful triumph I can see him rejoice
And tell of your shame to whomever wants to hear.
Ah, may rather the fire of heaven consume me!   150
    But do not deceive me. Is he still dear to you?
With what eye do you look upon that audacious prince?
PHAEDRA. I see him as a monster, frightful to my eyes.
OENONE. Why then concede to him a full victory?
You fear him. Dare to accuse him first   155
On the crime with which he may charge you today.
What will belie you? Everything speaks against him:
His sword, happily left in your own hands,
Your present agitation, your anger in the past,
His father warned against him by your cries,   160
And his exile, which you yourself obtained.
PHAEDRA. Am I then to crush and blacken innocence?
OENONE. My zeal needs nothing but your silence,
Though, trembling like you, I too feel some remorse.
You would see me meet more readily a thousand deaths.   165
But since I would lose you, without this painful cure,
Everything yields before the value of your life.
I will speak.
    Theseus, embittered by what I tell him,
Will limit his vengeance to the exile of his son.   170
A punishing father, Madam, is still a father;
A light penalty is all his wrath demands.
But even should innocent blood be spilled,
What is too much when your honor is at stake?
It is too dear a treasure to risk a compromise.   175
Whatever law it imposes, you must submit,
Madam, and to save your embattled honor,
You must sacrifice all, even virtue itself.
    Someone comes. I see Theseus.
PHAEDRA. Ah, I see Hippolytus.   180
In his insolent eyes, I can see my ruin written.

[*To* OENONE] Do what you wish; I surrender to your will.
In my present turmoil, I can do nothing for myself.

[*Enter* THESEUS *and* HIPPOLYTUS, *separately.*]

THESEUS. Fortune no longer runs counter to my hopes,
    Madam, and puts within your arms . . .   185
PHAEDRA. Stop, Theseus,
    And do not profane such pleasing raptures,
    For I deserve no more this tender show of feeling.
    You have been wronged. In your absence
    Jealous fortune has not spared your wife.   190
    Unworthy to please you or even to come near,
    I must henceforth think only of hiding myself. [*Exit* PHAEDRA.]
THESEUS. What is this strange welcome given to your father,
    My son?
HIPPOLYTUS. Phaedra alone can explain this mystery.
    But if my earnest wishes can move you,   195
    Allow me, my lord, to see her no more.
    Permit this shaken Hippolytus forever
    To quit those regions where Phaedra lives.
THESEUS. You will leave me, my son?
HIPPOLYTUS. I did not seek her out;   200
    It is you who led her to these shores.
    It was your wish, my lord, in the land of Troezen
    To leave in trust Aricia and the Queen,
    And I was given the duty of guarding them.
    But what duty now can hold me here?   205
      Long enough in the forests has my idle youth
    Shown its skill against lowly enemies.
    May I not flee this unworthy repose
    And color my lance in more noble blood?
      You had not yet reached my present age   210
    When your arm had already felt the weight
    Of more than one tyrant, one ferocious beast.
    Already the favored persecutor of oppression,
    You had made safe the shores of the two seas;
    The free voyager feared no further outrage.   215
    Already Hercules, hearing the fame of your blows,
    Could rest from his labors and put his faith in you.
      And I, the unknown son of a glorious father,
    I am still far from even my mother's steps.
    Allow my courage at last to find a goal,   220
    And if ever some monster was able to escape you,
    Let me lay at your feet his worthy hide.
    Or let the lasting memory of a beautiful death,

214 *two seas:* the Ionian and the Aegean
    seas.

Immortalizing my days so nobly ended,
Prove to the universe that I was your son.   225
THESEUS. What do I see? What horror, spread about this place,
Makes my distracted family flee before my eyes?
If I return so feared, so little wanted,
Why, heaven, did you free me from my prison?
I had but one friend. His unwise passion   230
Ravished the wife of the tyrant of Epirus.
To my sorrow I served his amorous designs;
But angered fate blinded the two of us.
The tyrant surprised me without defense, without arms;
I saw Pirithous, unhappy object of my tears,   235
Thrown by the barbarian to cruel monsters
Which feed on the blood of unlucky mortals.
As for me, he shut me in somber caves,
Deep regions near the kingdom of the dead.
The gods, six months after, at last remembered me,   240
And I deceived the eyes by which I was guarded.
I purged nature of a perfidious enemy;
To his own monsters he served as fodder.
And when with joy I think I am returning
To what the gods have left that was dearest to me—   245
When my soul, delivered to itself again,
Comes to feast upon so dear a sight,
I meet only trembling by way of welcome.
All flee; all refuse my embrace.
And I myself, feeling the terror I inspire,   250
Could wish to be again in the prisons of Epirus.
Speak. Phaedra complains that I am wronged.
Who has betrayed me? Why am I not avenged?
Has Greece, to whom my arm has so often been of aid,
Accorded some asylum to the criminal?   255
You do not answer me. My son, my own son,
Is he in collusion with my enemies?
I will go in. It is clinging to a doubt that crushes me.
I will learn at one time both the crime and the guilty one;
Let Phaedra explain at last the distress I see in her.   260

[*Exit* THESEUS.]

HIPPOLYTUS. What did those words mean, which chilled me with
fear?
Does Phaedra, still a prey to her wild madness,
Want to accuse herself and bring herself to ruin?
Gods, what will the King say? What mortal poison

230 *I had but one friend:* Pirithous.
231 *tyrant of Epirus:* As Racine points out
in his preface. Theseus accompanied

Pirithous to Epirus, not to Hades.
261 *What did those words mean:* i.e., Phaedra's last speech.

Love has spread throughout his house!   265
　　Myself, full of a fire which he condemns—
How he looked upon me once, and how he finds me now!
　　Black forebodings come to frighten me.
But innocence, after all, has nothing to fear.
Come, let us seek elsewhere by what happy means   270
I can move my father to tenderness
And tell him of a love he may wish to change
But which he, with all his power, can never shake.

ACT IV

[*Enter* THESEUS *and* OENONE.]

THESEUS. Ah, what is this I hear? A brazen traitor
　　Planned this outrage against the honor of his father?
With what harshness you pursue me, destiny!
I know not where I am going, I know not where I am.
Oh, tenderness and goodness too ill rewarded!   5
Audacious scheme! Detestable thought!
　　To achieve the goal of his black love
The shameless wretch made use of force.
I recognized the sword, the weapon of his fury,
That steel with which I armed him for a nobler cause.   10
Could no ties of blood hold him in check?
And did Phaedra defer his punishment?
Did Phaedra's silence spare the guilty one?
OENONE. Phaedra spared instead a pitiful father.
　　Shamed by the scheme of a lover lost to passion   15
And by the criminal fire that burned within him,
Phaedra was about to die, and her murderous hand
Would have extinguished the innocent light in her eyes.
I saw her lifted arm. I ran to save her.
I alone preserved her for your love,   20
And bemoaning at once her trouble and your alarm,
I came, despite me, to interpret her tears.
THESEUS. False-hearted son! He could not keep from paling.
　　I saw him shudder from fear at meeting me
And was amazed to see his lack of joy;   25
His cold embrace froze my tenderness.
　　But this guilty love by which he is devoured,
Had it already been declared in Athens?
OENONE. My lord, remember the complaint of the Queen.
　　A criminal love was cause of all her hate.   30
THESEUS. And this passion then began anew in Troezen?
OENONE. I have told you, my lord, all that has occurred.
　　But the Queen is left too long in her mortal grief;

Allow me to leave you, to be nearer to her.   [*Exit* OENONE.]
THESEUS [*alone, seeing* HIPPOLYTUS *approach*]. Ah, here he is. Great
    gods, at this noble bearing,   35
      What eye would not have been deceived like mine?
      Must it be that the sacred mark of virtue
      Can shine on the brow of a profane adulterer?
      Should one not be able, by positive signs,
      To recognize the heart of perfidious mortals?   40

[*Enter* HIPPOLYTUS.]

HIPPOLYTUS. May I ask what gloomy cloud, my lord,
      Has come to trouble your august brow?
      Dare you not confide in me the secret?
THESEUS. Traitor! Can you really show yourself before me?
      Monster, whom the thunderbolts too long have spared,   45
      Foul remnant of the bigands of whom I purged the earth!
      After the transports of horror-tainted love
      Have brought their madness to your father's bed,
      You dare to show your hateful self to me;
      You appear in a place you have filled with infamy,   50
      And you do not seek, under an unknown sky,
      Some land where my name has not yet reached!
    Fly, traitor. Do not come here to defy my hate
      And tempt a wrath that I can scarcely hold.
      It is enough for me to earn the eternal disgrace   55
      Of having given life to so treacherous a son,
      Without having your death, shameful blot on my name,
      Defile the glory of my noble deeds.
    Fly; and if you do not wish a sudden punishment
      To add your name to those my hand has scourged,   60
      Take care that the sun which gives us light
      May never see you set your rash foot here.
      Fly, I say, with speed and no return.
      Let none of my States see your countenance again.
    And Neptune, remember—when through my courage   65
      Your shores were cleansed of foul assassins—
      Remember that to reward my successful efforts
      You promised to grant the first of my wishes.
      Through all the long hardship of a cruel prison
      I did not ask aid of your immortal power.   70
      Miserly of the help that I await from you,
      I have saved my wishes for some greater need.
      I implore you today. Avenge an unhappy father.
      Now I abandon this traitor to your wrath.
      Smother in his blood his shameless desires.   75
    By your fury will Theseus know your goodness.
HIPPOLYTUS. Phaedra accuses me of a criminal love!

Such an excess of horror strikes my soul dumb;
So many unforeseen blows crush me at one time
That they steal my speech and choke my voice.   80
THESEUS. Traitor, you assumed that in cowardly silence
    Phaedra would bury your brutal insolence,
    But in fleeing, you should not have abandoned
    The sword that in her hands helps to condemn you.
    Or rather, at one blow, adding to your treachery,   85
    You should have robbed her of both speech and life.
HIPPOLYTUS. Justly angered by so black a lie,
    I should here let truth speak out, my lord,
    But I suppress a secret touching you.
    Be pleased with the respect which seals my lips,   90
    And without seeking to add to your own grief,
    Examine my life, and think of what I am.
       Crimes must always come before great crimes.
    Whoever has crossed the borders fixed by law
    May in the end violate the most sacred rights.   95
    But like virtue itself, crime has its degrees,
    And never has timid innocence been seen
    To pass abruptly to the extremes of license.
    A single day does not turn a virtuous mortal
    Into a false-hearted murderer, an incestuous coward.   100
       Reared at the bosom of a virtuous woman,
    I have not been untrue to her divine origin;
    And Pittheus, considered a sage among all men,
    Deigned to instruct me when I left her care.
       I do not wish to paint myself with vanity;   105
    But if some virtue has fallen to my share,
    I believe I have above all displayed
    The hate of those crimes imputed to me.
    It is thus that I am known in Greece.
    I have pushed virtue to the point of bluntness.   110
    You know the inflexible rigor of my mind,
    Nor is the day more pure than the depths of my heart.
    And yet they claim Hippolytus, lost in a profane love . . .
THESEUS. Yes, it is this same pride, wretch, that condemns you.
    I see the hateful nature of your coldness: 115
    Phaedra alone has charmed your shameless eyes,
    And for all other women your indifferent soul
    Has disdained to burn with an innocent flame.
HIPPOLYTUS. No, I cannot hide from you that my heart
    Has not disdained to burn with a chaste love.   120
    At your feet I confess my true offense:
    I love. I love, it is true, despite your prohibition,

102 *her divine origin:* his mother Antiope   up both his grandson Theseus and his
    was the daughter of Mars.   great-grandson Hippolytus.
103 *Pittheus:* king of Troezen, who brought

For Aricia holds my hopes in slavery to her law.
The daughter of Pallas has conquered your son.
I adore her, and my soul, rebellious to your command,   125
Can neither sigh nor burn but for her alone.
THESEUS. You love her? Heaven! But no, the stratagem is gross.
You pretend to be a criminal, to justify yourself.
HIPPOLYTUS. My lord, six months I have shunned her, and I love.
Tremblingly I came to tell you this yourself.   130
And now, can nothing show you your mistake?
By what awful oath can you be reassured?
May the earth, may heaven, may all nature . . .
THESEUS. Villains must always have recourse to perjury.
Cease, cease, and spare me an unwelcome speech,   135
If your false virtue can do nothisg else.
HIPPOLYTUS. To you it seems false and full of artifice.
Phaedra, in her heart, does me greater justice.
THESEUS. Oh, how your impudence arouses my wrath!
HIPPOLYTUS [after a pause]. What time do you prescribe for my   140
exile, and what place?
THESEUS. If you were beyond the columns of Alcides,
I would still think myself too near a traitor.
HIPPOLYTUS. What friends will pity when you abandon me
And charge me with this awful crime which you suspect?
THESEUS. Go seek some friends whose perverse esteem   145
Honors adultery and applauds incest—
Traitors, wretches without honor and without law,
Worthy of protecting an evil one like you.
HIPPOLYTUS. You speak to me still of adultery and incest?
I say no more. Yet Phaedra had a mother,   150
Phaedra is of a blood, as you well know,
More tainted with these horrors than is mine.
THESEUS. What! Your madness now loses all restraint.
For the last time, take yourself from my sight.
Leave, traitor. Do not wait for a furious father   155
To have you dragged from here in disgrace.

[*Exit* HIPPOLYTUS.]

Wretch, you go to your certain death.
Neptune, by the river terrible to the gods themselves,
Gave me his word and now will execute it.
A vengeful god follows you; you cannot avoid him.   160
I loved you; and I feel, despite your offense,
My heart already troubled at your fate.
But you have obliged me to condemn you.

141 *columns of Alcides:* the Straits of Gib-   158 *river terrible to the gods themselves:*
raltar, the farthest limit of Hercules'   the Styx, by which the gods swore ir-
voyages.   revocable oaths.

Has ever a father, indeed, been more wronged?
Just gods, who see the grief that overwhelms me,   165
How could I have bred so guilty a son?

[*Enter* PHAEDRA.]

PHAEDRA. My lord, I come to you, filled with a just fear,
    For your redoubtable voice reached to where I stood.
    I am afraid a prompt result may have followed your threat,
    But if there still is time, then spare your son.   170
    Respect your own blood, I come to beg of you.
    Save me from the horror of hearing it cry out;
    Do not prepare for me the eternal grief
    Of letting it be shed by a father's hand.
THESEUS. No, Madam, my hand has not dipped into my blood,   175
    But nonetheless, the wretch has not escaped me.
    An immortal hand is charged with his destruction;
    Neptune owes me this, and you will be avenged.
PHAEDRA. Neptune owes it to you! So then your angry prayers . . .
THESEUS. What! Do you already fear they may be heard?   180
    Rather, join me in my lawful prayers.
    Retrace his crimes for me in all their blackness;
    Arouse my anger, still too slow, too restrained.
        All of his crimes are still unknown to you.
    His fury against you pours out in abuse: 185
    Your mouth, he says, is full of deception.
    He claims that Aricia has his heart and pledge,
    That he loves her.
PHAEDRA. What, my lord?
THESEUS. He said it before me.   190
    But I know how to pass off an empty artifice.
    Let us hope for prompt justice from Neptune;
    I myself go again to the foot of his altars
    To press him to fulfill his immortal oath.

[*Exit* THESEUS.]

PHAEDRA. He leaves. What is this news that has struck my ear?   195
    What fire, scarcely out, awakens in my heart?
    What bolt of thunder, oh heaven, what fatal tidings!
        I flew with all speed to the aid of his son,
    And, tearing myself from the arms of Oenone,
    I gave in to the remorse which tortured me.   200
    Who knows where this repentance might have led?
    Perhaps I would have ended by accusing myself.
    Perhaps, if my voice had not been stopped,
    The awful truth would have escaped me.
        Hippolytus feels, yet feels nothing for me!   205

Aricia has his heart! Aricia has his pledge!
Oh gods! When at my pleas the unrelenting ingrate
Showed so proud an eye, so austere a brow,
I thought his heart, still shut against love,
Was armed against all my sex alike.   210
Another, however, has broken his indifference;
Before his cruel eyes, another has found compassion.
Perhaps he has a heart easy to be moved,
And I am the only one he cannot endure.
Should I then undertake to defend him?   215

[*Enter* OENONE.]

Dear Oenone, do you know what I have learned?
OENONE. No, but in truth I come to you in trembling,
    Pale at the intention which made you leave;
    I feared a frenzy that might be fatal to you.
PHAEDRA. Oenone, who would believe it? I had a rival.   220
OENONE. What?
PHAEDRA. Hippolytus loves, and I cannot doubt it.
    This proud enemy whom none could subdue,
    Whom respect offended, whom pleas importuned,
    This tiger, whom I could never meet without fear,   225
    Submissive, tamed, admits a conqueror:
    Aricia has found the way into his heart.
OENONE. Aricia?
PHAEDRA. Oh, pain never before felt!
    For what new torment have I saved myself?   230
    All that I have suffered—my fears, my transports,
    The fury of my fires, the horror of my remorse,
    And the unbearable hurt of a cruel refusal—
    Was but a pale foretaste of my torment now.
    They love. By what spell did they deceive my eyes?   235
    How have they seen each other? Since when? And where?
        [*To* OENONE] You knew. Why did you leave me in ignorance?
    Could you not tell me of their furtive love?
    Have they been often seen speaking, searching for one another?
    In the depths of the forest did they go to hide?   240
        Alas, they saw each other with full liberty.
    As heaven approved the innocence of their sighs,
    They followed without remorse their lovers' inclination.
    For them the days dawned serene and clear,
    And I, sad reject of all nature,   245
    I hid from the day; I fled the light.
        Death was the only god I dared to implore,
    And I awaited the moment when I should expire.
    Nourished with gall and with my tears,
    Still too closely observed in my misfortune,   250

I dared not drown myself in weeping.
Trembling, I tasted this deathly pleasure,
And, disguising my sorrow behind a serene brow,
I had often to deny myself my tears.
OENONE. What fruit will they receive from their vain love?   255
They will not meet again.
PHAEDRA. They will always love.
At the moment that I speak—oh, awful thought—
They defy the fury of my insane passion.
Despite the very exile which is to separate them,   260
They take a thousand oaths never to be parted.
No, I cannot bear a happiness that so offends me,
Oenone. Have pity of my jealous rage.
Aricia must die. Against a hateful line
I must arouse the anger of my husband.   265
Let him not be content to punish lightly,
For the crime of the sister surpasses that of her brothers.
In my jealous transport, I want to beg this of him.
What am I doing? Where does my reason wander?
I, jealous? And is Theseus the one whom I implore?   270
My husband lives, and I still burn with love.
For whom? To whose heart does my love aspire?
Each word I utter stands my hair upright.
My crimes now have overflowed the measure;
I exhale a scent of incest and deception;   275
My murderous hands, ready for revenge,
Burn to plunge themselves in innocent blood.
And yet I live, and I can stand the sight
Of that sacred sun from whom I am descended?
My ancestor is the father and master of the gods;   280
The heavens, the whole universe, are full of my forebears.
Where can I hide? Let me fly into the infernal night.
But what do I say? My father Minos holds the fatal urn;
Destiny, they say, placed it in his stern hands,
And there in hell he judges all the palid mortals .   285
Ah, how his shade, appalled, will tremble
When he sees his daughter before his eyes,
Obliged to admit so many varied crimes,
And crimes perhaps as yet unknown in hell!
What will you say, my father, at this fearful sight?   290
I think I see the urn fall from your hand;
I think I see you, seeking some new torture,
Become the tormentor of your own blood.
Pardon! A cruel goddess has destroyed your family;
See her vengeance in the madness of your daughter.   295

280 *My ancestor is the father and master*   294 *A cruel goddess:* Venus.
of the gods: on her father's side, Phae-
dra is descended from Jupiter.

Alas, of the awful crime whose shame follows me,
My unhappy heart has never reaped the fruit.
Pursued by misfortune unto my last breath,
I end in torment a life of pain.

OENONE. Thrust aside, Madam, a terror that has no base,   300
And look with another eye upon an excusable mistake.
You love. One cannot vanquish his destiny;
You were carried along by a spell of fate.
Is this, then, an unheard-of marvel among us?
Has love triumphed over none but you?   305
Weakness is but too natural to human beings;
Mortal, you must suffer the fate of a mortal.
You complain of a yoke imposed long ago.
The very gods, the gods who live on Olympus,
Those who strike terror into criminals,   310
Have themselves sometimes burned with illicit fire.

PHAEDRA. What do I hear? What counsel dare you give?
So till the end you wish to poison me,
Wretch? That is how you have ruined me.
You gave me back the light that I tried to flee;   315
Your prayers made me forget my duty;
I was avoiding Hippolytus, and you made me see him.
How was this your affair? Why has your blasphemous mouth,
By accusing him, dared to blacken his life?
He now may die, and the sacrilegious prayer   320
Of a maddened father will be fulfilled.
   I listen to you no more. Go, hateful beast!
Go. Leave to me the care of my pitiful fate.
May a just heaven repay you worthily,
And may your punishment forever frighten   325
All those who, like you, by cowardly guile,
Nourish the weakness of the unhappy great,
Push them to the brink toward which their heart inclines,
And smooth for them the road to crime—
Detestable flatterers, the most deadly gift   330
That heavenly anger can make to those who rule!

[*Exit* PHAEDRA.]

OENONE [*alone*]. Oh, gods! To serve her I have done all, left all;
And I am thus repaid. [*Long pause.*] I have well deserved it.

ACT V

[*Enter* ARICIA *and* HIPPLYTUS.]

ARICIA. What, you can keep silent in this extreme peril
And leave in error a father who loves you?

Cruel one, if, disdaining the power of my tears,
You consent so easily to see me no more,
Then go. Leave behind a sad Aricia.   5
But at least in leaving, safeguard your life,
Defend your honor from a shameful reproach,
And force your father to revoke his prayers.
There still is time. Why, by what caprice,
Do you leave the field free to your accuser?   10
Enlighten Theseus.
HIPPOLYTUS. Ah, what have I not said?
Should I have brought to light his bed's disgrace?
Should I, in telling too truthful a story,
Have made my father blush with unworthy shame?   15
You alone have pierced this hateful mystery;
To pour out my heart, I have but you and the gods.
I could not hide from you—judge whether I love—
All that I wanted to hide from myself.
    But remember that I revealed it under seal of secrecy.   20
Forget, if you can, that I have spoken to you,
Madam, and never may so pure a mouth
Open to tell of this horrible adventure.
Let us place our trust in the fairness of the gods,
For they have every reason to vindicate me,   25
And Phaedra, soon or late punished for her crime,
Will not avoid her merited disgrace.
This is as much as I require of you;
All the rest I leave to my free wrath.
    Quit the slavery to which you are reduced;   30
Dare to follow me; dare to join me in flight;
Tear yourself from a baleful and ungodly place,
Where virtue breathes a poisoned air.
To hide your quick departure, take advantage
Of the confusion that my disgrace creates.   35
I can assure you of the means of flight,
For as yet you have no guards but mine.
Powerful defenders will take up our quarrel;
Argos extends its arms, and Sparta calls to us.
To our common friends let us carry our just complaints.   40
Let us not allow Phaedra, profiting by our disgrace,
To drive the two of us from my father's throne
And promise to her son both my heritage and yours.
    The opportunity is good; we must embrace it.
What fear withholds you? You balance undecided?   45
It is your interest alone that inspires my daring.
When I am all fire, whence comes your ice?
Are you afraid to follow in the steps of an exile?
ARACIA. Alas, how such banishment would be dear to me!
In what joyful transports, tied to your fate,   50

Would I live forgotten by all other mortals,
But not being united by so sweet a bond,
Can I with honor flee with you?
I know, without wounding the most exacting honor,
I can deliver myself from the hands of your father;   55
I am not tearing myself from my parents' bosom,
And flight is allowed him who flees his tyrants.
But you love me, my lord, and my threatened name . . .
HIPPOLYTUS. No, no, I have too much regard for your reputation.
A nobler plan brings me before you: 60
Flee from your enemies, and follow your husband.
Free in our misfortune, since so heaven decrees,
The pledging of our faith depends on no one else.
Not always must a wedding be lit by torches.
At the gates of Troezen, and among the tombs,   65
Ancient sepulchre of the princes of my people,
Is a sacred temple, fearful to perjurers.
It is there that mortals dare not swear in vain.
The perfidious receive a sudden punishment,
And no greater barrier to a lie exists   70
Than fear of finding inevitable death.
There, if you believe me, with an eternal love,
We will go to confirm our solemn troth.
We will take as witness the god we worship there,
And we both will pray him to serve as father to us.   75
I will call upon the most sacred of our gods.
Both chaste Diana and august Juno
And all gods, indeed, in witness to my love,
Will guarantee the worth of my holy promises.
ARICIA. The King comes. Flee, Prince, and leave at once.   80
To hide my departure, I will stay a while.
Go. And leave me some faithful guide
To lead my timid steps toward you.

[*Exit* HIPPOLYTUS *as* THESEUS *enters.*]

THESEUS. Gods, shed light on my trouble, and deign
To show me the truth I come here to seek.   85
ARICIA [*to* ISMENE]. Think of everything, dear Ismene, and be ready
for flight.   [*Exit* ISMENE.]
THESEUS. You change color and seen abashed, Madam.
What was Hippolytus doing in this place?
ARICIA. My lord, he was bidding me an eternal farewell.
THESEUS. Your eyes were able to subdue that rebellious heart,   90
And his first sighs are your triumphant work.
ARICIA. My lord, I cannot deny the truth to you.
He has not inherited your unjust hate;
He did not treat me as a criminal.

THESEUS. I understand. He swore eternal love to you.   95
     But do not feel assured of that inconstant heart,
     For he has sworn as much to others.
ARICIA. He, my lord?
THESEUS. You should have rendered him less flighty.
     How could you bear this horrible sharing?   100
ARICIA. And how can you bear that this horrible slander
     Should blacken the course of so fine a life?
     Have you so little knowledge of his heart?
     Do you so ill distinguish crime from innocence?
     Must it be that to your eyes alone a hateful cloud   105
     Conceals his virtue that shines to other eyes?
     Oh, this is giving him up to perfidious tongues.
     Stop. Repent of your murderous prayers.
     Fear, my lord, fear lest a stern heaven
     Should hate you enough to fulfil your wish.   110
     Often in its anger it accepts our sacrifice;
     Its gifts are often the punishment of our crimes.
THESEUS. No, you wish in vain to excuse his outrage;
     Your love blinds you in favor of the wretch.
     But I believe positive, irreproachable witnesses.   115
     I have seen tears, I have seen true tears flow.
ARICIA. Take care, my lord. Your invincible hands
     Have freed men from monsters without number,
     But all are not destroyed, and you let one
     Still live ... Your son, my lord, forbids me to go on.   120
     Aware of the respect for you he wishes to preserve,
     I would afflict him too much if I dared to finish.
     I imitate his reserve and flee from your presence
     That I may not be forced to break my silence.

[*Exit* ARICIA.]

THESEUS [*alone*]. What is her thought? What do her words hide,   125
     Begun so many times, and always interrupted?
     Do they seek to disturb me through a vain pretense?
     Are the two of them agreed to put me to the torture?
        And as for me, despite my harsh severity.
     What plaintive voice cries in the depths of my heart?   130
     A secret pity afflicts and moves me.
     A second time I will question Oenone.
     I wish to be better informed of all the crime.
     Guards, have Oenone come out and approach alone.

[*Enter* PANOPE.]

PANOPE. I do not know the project that the Queen debates,   135
     My lord, but from the emotion that stirs her I fear the worst.

A mortal despair is painted on her face.
And the pallor of death already is upon her.
   Already, sent away in shame from her presence,
Oenone has thrown herself into the sea.   140
No one knows from whence came this mad intent,
And the waves evermore will hide her from our view.
THESEUS. What do I hear?
PANOPE. Her death has not relieved the Queen;
   The trouble seems to grow in her uncertain soul.   145
Sometimes, to soften her secret pain,
She takes her children and bathes them in tears,
And suddenly, renouncing maternal love,
Her hand with horror pushes them away.
Her irresolute steps lead her at random;   150
Her distracted eye no longer recognizes us.
Three times she has written, and changing her mind,
Three times she has torn the letter she had begun.
Deign to set her, my lord; deign to give her aid.
THESEUS. Oh, heaven, Oenone is dead, and Phaedra wants to die?   155
Have my son recalled; let him come to his defense!
Let him come to speak to me. I am ready to listen.
Do not hasten, Neptune. your deadly godsend,
For I prefer my wishes never to be granted.
I perhaps believed too soon unfaithful witnesses,   160
And too soon I lifted my cruel hands to you.
   Ah, what anguish may follow that prayer!

[*Enter* THERAMENES.]

   Theramenes, is that you? What have you done with my son?
I entrusted him to you from the tenderest age.
But whence come these tears I see you shed?   165
What is my son doing?
THERAMENES. Oh, tardy and superfluous care!
   Futile tenderness! Hippolytus is no more.
THESEUS. Gods!
THERAMENES. I have seen perish the most gracious of mortals,   170
   And, I dare to say again, my lord, the least guilty.
THESEUS. My son is no more? When I hold out to him my arms
The impatient gods have hastened his end?
What blow stole him from me? What sudden thunderbolt?
THERAMENES. Scarcely had we left the gates of Troezen,   175
   Than he was in his chariot. His grieving guards,
Ranged all about him, were silent as he.
Pensively he followed the road to Mycena,
Letting the reins float free above his horses.
His proud coursers, which one used to see   180
Full of noble zeal, obedient to his voice,

Now with saddened eye and lowered head
Seemed to conform to his sad thoughts.
   A terrible cry, come from the depths of the sea,
At that moment troubled the quiet of the air;   185
And from the bosom of the earth a formidable voice
Answered with a moan this dreadful sound.
In our very hearts our blood was frozen,
And on the alerted horses the mane stood up.
   Meanwhile on the face of the liquid plain   190
There rises, boiling, a watery mountain.
The wave comes near, breaks, and vomits before our eyes.
Amid a flood of foam, a furious monster.
His wide brow is armed with menacing horns,
His whole body covered with yellowing scales;   195
Untamable bull, hot-headed dragon—
His crupper curls in tortuous folds.
His long bellowing makes the shore tremble.
With horror heaven looks on this savage shape.
The earth is aroused, the air infected;   200
The sea, which brought him, withdraws in terror.
All flee. Without making show of fruitless courage,
In the nearby temple they seek safety.
   Hippolytus alone, worthy son of a hero,
Stops his coursers, seizes his javelins,   205
Rushes upon the beast, and with well-thrown spear
Makes a great wound in his side.
In rage and in pain the leaping monster
Falls moaning at the feet of the horses,
Rolls and turns on them a flaming mouth,   210
Which covers them with smoke, with blood and fire.
Fear carries them off, and deaf this one time,
They no longer know either rein or voice.
In useless effort their master exhausts himself.
They redden the bit with a bloody foam.   215
It is said that in this awful confusion there was even seen
A god who pressed their dusty flanks with goads.
Across the rocks, fright rushes them.
The axle cries and breaks. The intrepid Hippolytus
Sees his shattered chariot fly in splinters;   220
He himself falls, entangled in the reins.
   Excuse my grief. This cruel scene
Will be for me an eternal source of tears.
I saw, my lord, I saw your unhappy son
Dragged by the horses whom his hand had fed.   225
He wants to call them back, and his voice frightens them.
They run. His whole body is soon but one wound.
The plain re-echoes to our grievous cries.
   At last their impetuous dash is slowed;

They stop, not far from those ancient tombs   230
Where lie the cold remains of the kings his ancestors.
I run, panting, and his guard follows me.
The trail of his noble blood shows us the way;
The rocks are stained; the dripping brambles
Carry the bloody strands of his hair.   235
I arrive, I call him. Then, giving me his hand,
He opens his dying eyes, and closes them at once.
"Heaven," he says, "takes an innocent life.
After my death, care well for sad Aricia.
Dear friend, if my father, one day disabused,   240
Regrets the misfortune of a son falsely blamed,
To appease my blood and my plaintive shade,
Tell him to treat his captive with gentleness,
To give her back . . ." At this word, the hero, dead,
Left in my arms but his disfigured body,   245
A sad thing, in which triumphed the anger of the gods,
And which the eye of his very father would not know.
THESEUS. Oh, my son! Dear hope of which I have robbed myself!
Inexorable gods who have served me too well!
To what mortal regrets my life is now given over!   250
THERAMENES. Timid Aricia then arrived.
She was coming, my lord, flying from your wrath,
To take him as husband before the gods.
She approaches. She sees the grass, red and smoking;
She sees (what a sight for the eyes of a lover!)   255
Hippolytus outstretched. without form, without color.
She tries for a time to doubt her misfortune,
And, no longer knowing this hero she adores,
She sees Hippolytus and yet asks for him.
But too sure at last that he is before her eyes,   260
By a sorrowing look she accuses the gods;
And cold, moaning, and almost inanimate,
She falls in a swoon at the feet of her lover.
Ismene is beside her; Ismene, all in tears,
Calls her back to life, or rather back to grief.   265
    And as for me, I have come, cursing life,
To tell you the last wish of a hero
And to fulfill, my lord, the unhappy duty
Which his dying heart placed upon me.
But I see his mortal enemy approach.   270

[*Enter* PHAEDRA.]

THESEUS [*to* PHAEDRA]. Well, you triumph, and my son is without
life.

230 *those ancient tombs:* where Aricia was
    to meet Hippolytus.

Ah, what I have cause to fear, and what cruel suspicion,
Excusing him in my heart, alarms me with reason!
But, Madam, he is dead. Take your victim.
Enjoy his death, unjust or legitimate. 275
I consent that my eyes may always be deluded.
I believe him a criminal, since you accuse him.
His death offers reason enough for my tears
Without my going to seek hateful enlightenment,
Which, unable to return him to my just grief, 280
Might only serve to increase my misery.
　　Let me, far from you and far from these shores,
Flee the bloody image of my torn son.
Bewildered, pursued by this memory of death,
I would banish myself from the entire universe. 285
　　Everything seems to rise against my injustice.
The glory of my name even increases my torture.
Less known to mortals, I could hide myself the better.
I hate the very care with which the gods honor me,
And I leave to bewail their murdering favors, 290
Without bothering them more with futile prayers.
Whatever they do for me, their deadly goodness
Can never repay me for what they have taken.
PHAEDRA. No, Theseus, I must break an unjust silence.
I must give back his innocence to your son. 295
He was not guilty.
THESEUS. Ah, unhappy father!
And it was on your word that I condemned him!
Cruel one, do you believe yourself sufficiently excused . . .
PHAEDRA. Moments are dear to me. Listen to me, Theseus. 300
It is I who on this chaste and respectful son
Dared to cast an impure and incestuous eye.
Heaven placed in my breast a deadly flame;
The detestable Oenone did all the rest.
She feared that Hippolytus, learning of my madness, 305
Might reveal the love that horrified him;
So the treacherous woman, imposing on my weakness,
Hastened to accuse him first before you.
She has punished herself and, fleeing my wrath,
Has sought in the waves too easy a penalty. 310
The sword would already have cut short my destiny,
But I allowed Virtue, compromised, to moan.
Exposing my remorse before you, I wanted
To go down among the dead by a slower route.
I have poured into my burning veins 315
A poison which Medea brought to Athens.

---

303 *Heaven:* more specifically, Venus.　　316 *Medea:* wife of Jason, famous for her
　　　　　　　　　　　　　　　　　　　　　　　magic philters.

Already the venom, having reached my dying heart,
Casts upon it a cold it has never known.
Already I see but through a cloud
Both the sky and the husband that my presence offends;   320
And death, hiding from my eyes the light,
Gives back to the day, which they defiled, all its purity.
PANOPE. She dies, my lord!
THESEUS. Of so black an act
Would that the memory might die with her.   325
Let us go, too well aware, alas, of my error,
To mix our tears with the blood of my unhappy son.
Let us go to embrace what remains of him,
To expiate the madness of a prayer I curse.
Let us render him the honors he has deserved,   300
And the better to appease his angered shade,
Despite the plotting of an unjust family,
Let his loved one be for me a daughter, from today.

332 *an unjust family:* the Pallantides.

Biographical Note

MILTON

JOHN MILTON (1608–1674) was born in London a few blocks from the Mermaid Tavern where Shakespeare and Ben Jonson were supposed to test one another's wit and drinking prowess. Milton's father, a well-to-do dealer in real estate, provided him with an excellent education, first at St. Paul's School where he began to demonstrate his remarkable capacities as a student of languages and later at Christ's College, Cambridge, where he took the B.A. in 1629 and the M.A. in 1632. Instead of entering a religious order after graduation, Milton retired to his father's country estate at Horton in Buckinghamshire where for the next five years he read exhaustively in such languages as English, Greek, Hebrew, Latin, and Italian. At Cambridge he had been too busy with his studies to write more than an occasional poem, though it was while there that he wrote his Nativity Ode. At Horton he wrote the companion pieces "L' Allegro" and "Il Penseroso"; *Comus*, a masque written at the request of some neighbors; and *Lycidas*, a pastoral elegy in honor of a classmate who drowned. In 1938 he went abroad, traveling about the Continent visiting famous personages before rumors of the impending civil war brought him back to England in 1639.

For the next twenty years Milton devoted himself largely to public duty as a propagandist for Cromwell's government, publishing only a small volume of sonnets in 1645. In 1642 he married Mary Powell, the daughter of a Royalist family from Buckinghamshire. After a few weeks she left him, and not long thereafter Milton wrote several tracts arguing that incompatibility be considered adequate grounds for divorce. In 1645 his wife returned to him accompanied by her family. She bore him three daughters before dying in 1652. Four years later Milton married Katherine Woodcock, who died in childbirth in 1658. His last marriage was to Elizabeth Minshull in 1662. During this period 1640 to 1660 Milton's work was almost entirely in prose, notably

Areopagitica, his famous essay in defense of freedom of the press, various tracts denouncing the role of bishops in church government, a series of Latin essays defending Cromwell's government, especially for its execution of Charles I in 1649, and many diplomatic papers associated with his position as Secretary of Foreign Tongues to Cromwell's Council of State.

Milton's eyesight had been fading for several years. In 1652 he became almost totally blind, managing to continue his duties for the government with the aid of readers and secretaries. All that came to an end in 1660 with the defeat of the Puritan political cause and the restoration to the throne of Charles II. Milton was imprisoned by the Royalists but soon released after the intervention of friends. He now set about writing his greatest works. *Paradise Lost*, "justifying the ways of God to men," was published in 1667; *Paradise Regained*, describing Christ's temptation by Satan in the wilderness, in 1671; and *Samson Agonistes* in the same year.

Samson Agonistes:
A Dramatic Poem

john milton

OF THAT SORT OF DRAMATIC
POEM CALLED TRAGEDY

Tragedy, as it was anciently composed, hath been ever held the gravest, moralest, and most profitable of all other poems, therefore said by Aristotle to be of power, by raising pity and fear, or terror, to purge the mind of those and such-like passions—that is, to temper and reduce them to just measure with a kind of delight, stirred up by reading or seeing those passions well imitated. Nor is Nature wanting in her own effects to make good his assertion; for so, in physic,[1] things of melancholic hue and quality are used against melancholy, sour against sour, salt to remove salt humours. Hence philosophers and other gravest writers, as Cicero, Plutarch, and others, frequently cite out of tragic poets, both to adorn and illustrate their discourse. The Apostle Paul himself thought it not unworthy to insert a verse of Euripides[2] into the text of Holy Scripture, I Cor. xv. 33; and Paræus,[3] commenting on the *Revelation*, divides the whole book, as a tragedy, into acts, distinguished each by a Chorus of heavenly harpings and song between. Heretofore men in highest dignity have laboured not a little to be thought able to compose a tragedy. Of that honour Dionysius the elder[4] was no less ambitious than before of his attaining to the tyranny. Augustus Cæsar also had begun his *Ajax*, but, unable to please his own judgment with what he had begun, left it unfinished. Seneca, the philosopher, is by some thought the author of

1 *physic:* medicine.
2 The verse is "Evil communications corrupt good manners."
3 David Paraeus was a German Calvin who wrote about the Book of Revelation.

4 Dionysius (431–367 B.C.), a Syracusan tyrant, wrote *The Ransom of Hector*, which won first prize at the Greater Dionysia in Athens.

those tragedies (at least the best of them) that go under that
name. Gregory Nazianzen, a Father of the Church, thought it
not unbeseeming the sanctity of his person to write a tragedy,
which he entitled *Christ Suffering*.[5] This is mentioned to vindicate
Tragedy from the small esteem, or rather infamy, which in the
account of many it undergoes at this day, with other common inter-
ludes; happening through the poet's error of intermixing comic
stuff with tragic sadness and gravity, or introducing trivial and
vulgar persons: which by all judicious hath been counted absurd,
and brought in without discretion, corruptly to gratify the people.
And, though ancient Tragedy use no Prologue, yet using sometimes, in case of self-defence or explanation, that which Martial
calls an Epistle, in behalf of this tragedy, coming forth after the
ancient manner, much different from what among us passes for
best, thus much beforehand may be *epistled*—that Chorus is here
introduced after the Greek manner, not ancient only, but modern,
and still in use among the Italians. In the modelling therefore of
this poem, with good reason, the Ancients and Italians are rather
followed, as of much more authority and fame. The measure of
verse used in the Chorus is of all sorts, called by the Greeks
Monostrophic, or rather *Apolelymenon*,[6] without regard had to
Strophe, Antistrophe, or Epode—which were a kind of stanzas
framed only for the music, then used with the Chorus that sung;
not essential to the poem, and therefore not material; or, being
divided into stanzas or pauses, they may be called *Allæostropha*.[7]
Division into act and scene, referring chiefly to the stage (to which
this work never was intended), is here omitted.

It suffices if the whole drama be found not produced beyond
the fifth act. Of the style and uniformity, and that commonly called
the plot, whether intricate or explicit—which is nothing indeed
but such economy, or disposition of the fable, as may stand best
with verisimilitude and decorum—they only will best judge who
are not unacquainted with Æschylus, Sophocles, and Euripides, the
three tragic poets unequalled yet by any, and the best rule to all
who endeavour to write Tragedy. The circumscription of time,
wherein the whole drama begins and ends, is, according to ancient
rule and best example, within the space of twenty-four hours.

THE ARGUMENT

Samson, made captive, blind, and now in the prison at Gaza,[8]
there to labour as in a common workhouse, on a festival day, in

5 *Christ Suffering* was popularly thought
  the work of Gregory Nazianzen, a fourth
  century A.D. bishop of Constantinople,
  but now appears to have been written
  by a twelfth century Greek.

6 *Apolelymenno:* free; not bound by the
  usual stanzaic patterns of choral songs.
7 *Allæostropra:* irregular strophes or stanzas.
8 *Gaza:* one of the five major cities of the
  Philistines.

the general cessation from labour, comes forth into the open air, to a place nigh, somewhat retired, there to sit a while and bemoan his condition. When he happens at length to be visited by certain friends and equals of his tribe, which make the Chorus, who seek to comfort him what they can; then by his old father, Manoa, who endeavours the like, and withal tells him his purpose to procure his liberty by ransom; lastly, that this feast was proclaimed by the Philistines as a day of thanksgiving for their deliverance from the hands of Samson—which yet more troubles him. Manoa then departs to prosecute his endeavour with the Philistian lords for Samson's redemption: who, in the meanwhile, is visited by other persons, and, lastly, by a public officer to require his coming to the feast before the lords and people, to play or show his strength in their presence. He at first refuses, dismissing the public officer with absolute denial to come; at length, persuaded inwardly that this was from God, he yields to go along with him, who came now the second time with great threatenings to fetch him. The Chorus yet remaining on the place, Manoa returns full of joyful hope to procure ere long his son's deliverance; in the midst of which discourse an Ebrew comes in haste, confusedly at first, and afterwards more distinctly, relating the catastrophe—what Samson had done to the Philistines and by accident to himself; wherewith the Tragedy ends.

CHARACTERS

SAMSON
MANOA, *the father of* SAMSON
DALILA, *his wife*
HARAPHA *of Gath*

PUBLIC OFFICER
MESSENGER
CHORUS *of Danites*[1]

[*The Scene, before the Prison in Gaza.*:

SAMSON. A little onward lend thy guiding hand
    To these dark steps, a little further on;
    For yonder bank hath choice of sun or shade.
    There I am wont to sit, when any chance
    Relieves me from my task of servile toil,   5
    Daily in the common prison else enjoined me,
    Where I, a prisoner chained, scarce freely draw
    The air, imprisoned also, close and damp,
    Unwholesome draught. But here I feel amends—
    The breath of heaven fresh blowing, pure and sweet,   10
    With day-spring born; here leave me to respire.

1 *Danites:* members of the tribe of Dan, to which Manoa belongs.   11 *day-spring:* daybreak.

This day a solemn feast the people hold
To Dagon, their sea-idol, and forbid
Laborious works. Unwillingly this rest
Their superstition yields me; hence, with leave   15
Retiring from the popular noise, I seek
This unfrequented place to find some ease—
Ease to the body some, none to the mind
From restless thoughts, that, like a deadly swarm
Of hornets armed, no sooner found alone   20
But rush upon me thronging, and present
Times past, what once I was, and what am now.
Oh, wherefore was my birth from Heaven foretold
Twice by an angel, who at last, in sight
Of both my parents, all in flames ascended   25
From off the altar where an offering burned,
As in a fiery column charioting
His godlike presence, and from some great act
Or benefit revealed to Abraham's race?
Why was my breeding ordered and prescribed   30
As of a person separate to God,
Designed for great exploits, if I must die
Betrayed, captived, and both my eyes put out,
Made of my enemies the scorn and gaze,
To grind in brazen fetters under task   35
With this heaven-gifted strength? O glorious strength,
Put to the labour of a beast, debased
Lower than bond-slave! Promise was that I
Should Israel from Philistian yoke deliver!
Ask for this great deliverer now, and find him   40
Eyeless in Gaze, at the mill with slaves,
Himself in bonds under Philistian yoke.
Yet stay; let me not rashly call in doubt
Divine prediction. What if all foretold
Had been fulfilled but through mine own default?   45
Whom have I to complain of but myself,
Who this high gift of strength committed to me,
In what part lodged, how easily bereft me,
Under the seal of silence could not keep,
But weakly to a woman must reveal it,   50
O'ercome with importunity and tears?
O impotence of mind in body strong!
But what is strength without a double share
Of wisdom? Vast, unwieldy, burdensome,

13 *Dagon:* the Philistines' god, "upward Man and downward Fish" as Milton says in *Paradise Lost.*
16 *popular noise:* noise of the people.
24 *Twice:* Samson's birth was foretold first to his mother and again to both his parents.
30 *breeding:* training.
31 *separate to:* set apart for.

Proudly secure, yet liable to fall   55
By weakest subtleties; not made to rule,
But to subserve where wisdom bears command.
God, when he gave me strength, to show withal
How slight the gift was, hung it in my hair.
But peace! I must not quarrel with the will   60
Of highest dispensation, which herein
Haply had ends above my reach to know.
Suffices that to me strength is my bane,
And proves the source of all my miseries—
So many, and so huge, that each apart   65
Would ask a life to wail. But, chief of all,
O loss of sight, of thee I most complain!
Blind among enemies! O worse than chains,
Dungeon, or beggary, or decrepit age!
Light, the prime work of God, to me is extinct,   70
And all her various objects of delight
Annulled, which might in part my grief have eased.
Inferior to the vilest now become
Of man or worm, the vilest here excel me:
They creep, yet see; I, dark in light, exposed   75
To daily fraud, contempt, abuse, and wrong,
Within doors, or without, still as a fool,
In power of others, never in my own—
Scarce half seem to live, dead more than half.
O dark, dark, dark, amid the blaze of noon,   80
Irrecoverably dark, total eclipse
Without all hope of day!
O first-created beam, and thou great Word,
"Let there be light, and light was over all,"
Why am I thus bereaved thy prime decree?   85
The Sun to me is dark
And silent as the Moon,
When she deserts the night,
Hid in her vacant interlunar cave.
Since light so necessary is to life,   90
And almost life itself, if it be true
That light is in the soul,
She all in every part, why was the sight
To such a tender ball as the eye confined,
So obvious and so easy to be quenched,   95

55 *proudly secure:* reckless of danger.
66 *ask:* require.
70 *extinct:* extinguished.
77 *Still:* always.
87 *silent:* nonfunctioning, hence dark.
89 *interlunar:* The period of darkness when the moon supposedly retreated within a cave beneath the earth,

91–93 *if it be true . . . part:* Saint Augustine claimed that the soul was diffused through all parts of the body, in contrast to Descartes, for instance, who argued that it was situated in the pineal gland.
95 *obvious:* openly vulnerable.

And not, as feeling, through all parts diffused,
That she might look at will through every pore?
Then had I not been thus exiled from light,
As in the land of darkness, yet in light
To live a life half dead, a living death,   100
And buried; but, O yet more miserable!
Myself my sepulchre, a moving grave;
Buried, yet not exempt,
By privilege of death and burial,
From worst of other evils, pains, and wrongs;   105
But made hereby obnoxious more
To all the miseries of life,
Life in captivity
Among inhuman foes.
But who are these? for with joint pace I hear   110
The tread of many feet steering this way;
Perhaps my enemies, who come to stare
At my affliction, and perhaps to insult—
Their daily practice to afflict me more.
CHORUS. This, this is he; softly a while;   115
Let us not break in upon him.
O change beyond report, thought, or belief!
See how he lies at random, carelessly diffused,
With languished head unprop,
As one past hope abandoned,   120
And by himself given over,
In slavish habit, ill-fitted weeds
O'er-worn and soiled.
Or do my eyes misrepresent? Can this be he,
That heroic, that renowned,   125
Irresistible Samson? whom, unarmed,
No strength of man, or fiercest wild beast, could withstand;
Who tore the lion as the lion tears the kid;
Ran on embattled armies clad in iron,
And, weaponless himself,   130
Made arms ridiculous, useless the forgery
Of brazen shield and spear, the hammered cuirass,
Chalybean-tempered steel, and frock of mail
Adamantean proof:
But safest he who stood aloof,   135
When insupportably his foot advanced,

106 *obnoxious:* the Latin meaning is "exposed to".
118 *diffused:* Latin "poured out"=stretched out.
119 *languished:* relaxed.
122 *habit:* dress; *weeds:* clothes.
131 *forgery:* as in blacksmiths' forging.

133 *Chalybean-tempered:* the Calybes on the shores of the Black Sea were famous iron-forgers.
134 *Adamantean proof:* proof against the hardest steel.
136 *insupportably:* irresistibly.

In scorn of their proud arms and warlike tools,
Spurned them to death by troops. The bold Ascalonite
Fled from his lion ramp; old warriors turned
Their plated backs under his heel,   140
Or grovelling soiled their crested helmets in the dust.
Then with what trivial weapon came to hand,
The jaw of a dead ass, his sword of bone,
A thousand foreskins fell, the flower of Palestine,
In Ramath-lechi, famous to this day: 145
Then by main force pulled up, and on his shoulders bore,
The gates of Azza, post and massy bar,
Up to the hill by Hebron, seat of giants old—
No journey of a sabbath-day, and loaded so—
Like whom the Gentiles feign to bear up Heaven.   150
Which shall I first bewail—
Thy bondage or lost sight.
Prison within prison
Inseparably dark?
Thou art become (O worst imprisonment!)   155
The dungeon of thyself; thy soul
(Which men enjoying sight oft without cause complain)
Imprisoned now indeed,
In real darkness of the body dwells,
Shut up from outward light   160
To incorporate with gloomy night;
For inward light, alas!
Puts forth no visual beam.
O mirror of our fickle state,
Since man on earth, unparalleled,   165
The rarer thy example stands,
By how much from the top of wondrous glory,
Strongest of mortal men,
To lowest pitch of abject fortune thou art fallen.
For him I reckon not in high estate   170
Whom long descent of birth,
Or the sphere of fortune, raises;
But thee, whose strength, while virtue was her mate,
Might have subdued the Earth,
Universally crowned with highest praises.   175

137 *tools:* weapons.
138 *Ascalonite:* the people of Ascalon, one of the five Philistine cities, who fled from Samson.
139 *ramp:* leap.
140 *plated:* armored.
144 *foreskins:* i.e., the uncircumcised Philistines; *Palestine:* Philistia.
145 *Ramath-lechi:* the name Samson gave the place, meaning "the casting away of the jawbone".
147 *Azza:* Gaza.
148 *Hebron:* city east of Gaza about forty miles.
149 *journey ... sabbath-day:* no one was supposed to travel farther than about 3000 feet on the Sabbath.
150 *Like whom ... Heaven:* i.e., Atlas.
172 *Sphere of fortune:* Fortune's wheel by which men rose and fell.

SAMSON. I hear the sound of words; their sense the air
    Dissolves unjointed ere it reach my ear.
CHORUS. He speaks; let us draw nigh. Matchless in might,
    The glory late of Israel, now the grief!
    We come, thy friends and neighbors not unknown,   180
    From Eshtaol and Zora's fruitful vale,
    To visit or bewail thee; or, if better,
    Counsel or consolation we may bring,
    Salve to thy sores; apt words have power to swage
    The tumours of a troubled mind,   185
    And are as balm to festered wounds.
SAMSON. Your coming, friends, revives me; for I learn
    Now of my own experience, not by talk,
    How counterfeit a coin they are who 'friends'
    Bear in their superscription (of the most   190
    I would be understood). In prosperous days
    They swarm, but in adverse withdraw their head,
    Not to be found, though sought. Ye see, O friends,
    How many evils have enclosed me round;
    Yet that which was the worst now least afflicts me,   195
    Blindness; for, had I sight, confused with shame,
    How could I once look up, or heave the head,
    Who, like a foolish pilot, have shipwracked
    My vessel trusted to me from above,
    Gloriously rigged, and for a word, a tear,   200
    Fool! have divulged the secret gift of God
    To a deceitful woman? Tell me, friends,
    Am I not sung and proverbed for a fool
    In every street? Do they not say, 'How well
    Are come upon him his deserts'? Yet why?   205
    Immeasurable strength they might behold
    In me; of wisdom nothing more than mean.
    This with the other should at least have paired;
    These two, proportioned ill, drove me transverse.
CHORUS. Tax not divine disposal. Wisest men   210
    Have erred, and by bad women been deceived;
    And shall again, pretend they ne'er so wise.
    Deject not, then, so overmuch thyself,
    Who hast of sorrow thy full load besides.
    Yet, truth to say, I oft have heard men wonder   215
    Why thou should'st wed Philistian women rather

---

181 *Eshtaol and Zora:* Israelite towns.
184 *swage:* assuage.
185 *tumours:* term sometimes used to mean swellings of strong feeling.
190 *superscription:* the stamp of value on a coin.
207 *mean:* ordinary.

208 *paired:* equalled.
209 *transverse:* off course from his pre-charted journey of life.
210 *tax:* blame.
212 *pretend ... wise:* no matter how wise their intentions.

Than of thine own tribe fairer, or as fair,
At least of thy own nation, and as noble.
SAMSON. The first I saw at Timna, and she pleased
    Me, not my parents, that I sought to wed   220
    The daughter of an infidel. They knew not
    That what I motioned was of God; I knew
    From intimate impulse, and therefore urged
    The marriage on, that, by occasion hence,
    I might begin Israel's deliverance—   225
    The work to which I was divinely called.
    She proving false, the next I took to wife
    (O that I never had! fond wish too late!)
    Was in the vale of Sorec, Dalila,
    That specious monster, my accomplished snare.   230
    I thought it lawful from my former act,
    And the same end, still watching to oppress
    Israel's oppressors. Of what now I suffer
    She was not the prime cause, but I myself,
    Who, vanquished with a peal of words (O weakness!),   235
    Gave up my fort of silence to a woman.
CHORUS. In seeking just occasion to provoke
    The Philistine, thy country's enemy,
    Thou never wast remiss, I bear thee witness:
    Yet Israel still serves with all his sons.   240
SAMSON. That fault I take not on me, but transfer
    On Israel's governors and heads of tribes,
    Who, seeing those great acts which God had done
    Singly by me against their conquerors,
    Acknowledged not, or not at all considered,   245
    Deliverance offered. I, in the other side,
    Used no ambition to commend my deeds;
    The deeds themselves, though mute, spoke loud the doer.
    But they persisted deaf, and would not seem
    To count them things worth notice, till at length   250
    Their lords, the Philistines, with gathered powers,
    Entered Judea, seeking me, who then
    Safe to the rock of Etham was retired—
    Not flying, but forecasting in what place
    To set upon them, what advantaged best.   255

219 *Timna:* Philistian town.
222 *motioned ... God:* felt was inspired by God.
223 *intimate:* private, inward.
228 *fond:* foolish.
231 *thought ... act:* i.e., Samson generalized from the earlier occasion, thinking that if God had inspired him to marry the woman of Timna in order to benefit Israel He must feel similarly in the case of Dalila a fatal assumption.
240 *serves:* suffers bondage; *sons:* tribes.
245 *considered:* recognized, appreciated.
247 *ambition:* attempt to round up public support.
251 *Powers:* military forces.
253 *Etham:* a hill town where Samson had gone to consider how next to deal with the Philistines.

Meanwhile the men of Judah, to prevent
The harass of their land, beset me round;
I willingly on some conditions came
Into their hands, and they as gladly yield me
To the Uncircumcised a welcome prey,   260
Bound with two cords. But cords to me were threads
Touched with the flame: on their whole host I flew
Unarmed, and with a trivial weapon felled
Their choicest youth; they only lived who fled.
Had Judah that day joined, or one whole tribe,   265
They had by this possessed the towers of Gath,
And lorded over them whom now they serve.
But what more oft, in nations grown corrupt,
And by their vices brought to servitude,
Than to love bondage more than liberty—   270
Bondage with ease than strenuous liberty—
And to despise, or envy, or suspect,
Whom God hath of his special favour raised
As their deliverer? If he aught begin,
How frequent to desert him, and at last   275
To heap ingratitude on worthiest deeds!
CHORUS. Thy words to my remembrance bring
How Succoth and the fort of Penuel
Their great deliverer contemned,
The matchless Gideon, in pursuit   280
Of Madian, and her vanquished kings;
And how ingrateful Ephraim
Had dealt with Jephtha, who by argument,
Not worse than by his shield and spear,
Defended Israel from the Ammonite,   285
Had not his prowess quelled their pride
In that sore battle when so many died
Without reprieve, adjudged to death
For want of well pronouncing *Shibboleth.*
SAMSON. Of such examples add me to the roll.   290
Me easily indeed mine may neglect,
But God's proposed deliverance not so.
CHORUS. Just are the ways of God,
And justifiable to men,

---

263 *trivial weapon:* the jawbone of an ass.
266 *towers of Gath:* i.e., all of Philistia.
281 *vanquished kings:* of Midian; the Hebrew cities of Succoth and Penuel refused to help Gideon chase the vanquished kings.
289 *Shibboleth:* Jephtha's forces (Gileadites) had defeated the Ammonites without help from the Ephraimites.

Later the two tribes quarreled; the Gileadites seized a crucial part of the Jordan river and when the Ephraimites, pretending to be Gileadites, tried to cross the river the Gileadites demanded that they pronounce the word "Shibboleth." If they said "Sibboleth," they were killed on the spot.
291 *mine:* my people.

Unless there be who think not God at all.   295
If any be, they walk obscure;
For of such doctrine never was there school,
But the heart of the fool,
And no man therein doctor but himself.
 Yet more there be who doubt his ways not just,   300
As to his own edicts found contradicting;
Then give the reins to wandering thought,
Regardless of his glory's diminution,
Till, by their own perplexities involved,
They ravel more, still less resolved,   305
But never find self-satisfying solution.
 As if they would confine the Interminable,
And tie him to his own prescript,
Who made our laws to bind us, not himself,
And hath full right to exempt   310
Whomso it please him by choice
From national obstriction, without taint
Of sin, or legal debt.
For with his own laws he can best dispense.
 He would not else, who never wanted means,   315
Nor in respect of the enemy just cause,
To set his people free,
Have prompted this heroic Nazarite,
Against his vow of strictest purity,
To seek in marriage that fallacious bride,   320
Unclean, unchaste.
Down, Reason, then; at least, vain reasonings down;
Though Reason here aver
That moral verdit quits her of unclean:
Unchaste was subsequent; her stain, not his.   325
 But see! here comes thy reverend sire,
With careful step, locks white as down,
Old Manoa: advise
Forthwith how thou ought'st to receive him.
SAMSON. Ay me! another inward grief, awaked   330
 With mention of that name, renews the assault.
MANOA. Brethren and men of Dan (for such ye seem,
 Though in this uncouth place), if old respect,
 As I suppise, towards your once gloried friend,
 My son, now captive, hither hath informed   335

296 *obscure:* in darkness.
305 *ravel:* tangle.
307 *Interminable:* Infinite (God).
312 *obstriction:* obligation.
318 *Nazarite:* one who (Samson here) is dedicated to God and abstains from alcohol, unsanctified food, etc.
320 *fallacious:* deceitful.

321 *Unclean:* as a gentile Dalila is by definition "unclean."
324 *quits:* acquits.
327 *careful:* full of concern.
328 *advise:* think, consider.
333 *uncouth:* unknown, unfamiliar.
335 *informed:* directed.

Your younger feet, while mine, cast back with age,
Came lagging after, say if he be here.
CHORUS. As signal now in low dejected state
    As erst in highest, behold him where he lies.
MANOA. O miserable change! Is this the man,   340
    That invincible Samson, far renowned,
    The dread of Israel's foes, who with a strength
    Equivalent to Angels' walked their streets,
    None offering fight; who, single combatant,
    Duelled their armies ranked in proud array,   345
    Himself an army—now unequal match
    To save himself against a coward armed
    At one spear's length? O ever-failing trust
    In mortal strength! and, oh, what not in man
    Deceivable and vain? Nay, what thing good   350
    Prayed for, but often proves our woe, our bane?
    I prayed for children, and thought barrenness
    In wedlock a reproach; I gained a son,
    And such a son as all men hailed me happy:
    Who would be now a father in my stead?   355
    Oh, wherefore did God grant me my request,
    And as a blessing with such pomp adorned?
    Why are his gifts desirable, to tempt
    Our earnest prayers, then, given with solemn hand
    As graces, draw a scorpion's tail behind?   360
    For this did the Angel twice descend? for this
    Ordained thy nurture holy, as of a plant
    Select and sacred? glorious for a while,
    The miracle of men; then in an hour
    Ensnared, assaulted, overcome, led bound,   365
    Thy foes' derision, captive, poor and blind,
    Into a dungeon thrust, to work with slaves!
    Alas! methinks whom God hath chosen once
    To worthiest deeds, if he through frailty err,
    He should not so o'erwhelm, and as a thrall   370
    Subject him to so foul indignities,
    Be it but for honour's sake of former deeds.
SAMSON. Appoint not heavenly disposition, father
    Nothing of all these evils hath befallen me
    But justly; I myself have brought them on;   375
    Sole author I, sole cause. If aught seem vile,
    As vile hath been my folly, who have profaned
    The mystery of God, given me under pledge
    Of vow, and have betrayed it to a woman,
    A Canaanite, my faithless enemy.   380

338 *As signal:* As distinctive.   373 *Appoint not:* do not prescribe (what
361 *twice descend:* i.e. to foretell Samson's   God should do).
    birth.

This well I knew, nor was at all surprised,
But warned by oft experience. Did not she
Of Timna first betray me, and reveal
The secret wrested from me in her highth
Of nuptial love professed, carrying it straight   385
To them who had corrupted her, my spies
And rivals? In this other was there found
More faith, who, also in her prime of love,
Spousal embraces, vitiated with gold,
Though offered only, by the scent conceived,   390
Her spurious first-born, Treason against me?
Thrice she assayed, with flattering prayers and sighs,
And amorous reproaches, to win from me
My capital secret, in what part my strength
Lay stored, in what part summed, that she might know;   395
Thrice I deluded her, and turned to sport
Her importunity, each time perceiving
How openly and with what impudence
She purposed to betray me, and (which was worse
Than undissembled hate) with what contempt   400
She sought to make me traitor to myself.
Yet, the fourth time, when, mustering all her wiles,
With blandished parleys, feminine assaults,
Tongue-batteries, she surceased not day nor night
To storm me, over-watched and wearied out,   405
At times when men seek most repose and rest,
I yielded, and unlocked her all my heart,
Who, with a grain of manhood well resolved,
Might easily have shook off all her snares;
But foul effeminacy held me yoked   410
Her bond-slave. O indignity, O blot
To honour and religion! servile mind
Rewarded well with servile punishment!
The base degree to which I now am fallen,
These rags, this grinding, is not yet so base   415
As was my former servitude, ignoble,
Unmanly, ignominious, infamous,
True slavery; and that blindness worse than this,
That saw not how degenerately I served.
MANOA. I cannot praise thy marriage-choices, son—   420
　　Rather approved them not; but thou didst plead
　　Divine impulsion prompting how thou might'st
　　Find some occasion to infest our foes.

382–87 *Did not she...And rivals:* Samson
　　had propounded to the Philistines a
　　riddle the answer to which he revealed
　　to the woman of Timna, who then
　　passed it on to the Philistines.

394 *capital:* a pun on the Latin meaning
　　"referring to the head" (i.e., to Sam-
　　son's hair).
405 *over-watched:* weary from lack of sleep.

I state not that; this I am sure—our foes
Found soon occasion thereby to make thee   425
Their captive, and their triumph; thou the sooner
Temptation found'st, or over-potent charms,
To violate the sacred trust of silence
Deposited within thee—which to have kept
Tacit was in thy power. True; and thou bear'st   430
Enough, and more, the burden of that fault;
Bitterly hast thou paid, and still art paying,
That rigid score. A worse thing yet remains:—
This day the Philistines a popular feast
Here celebrate in Gaza, and proclaim   435
Great pomp, and sacrifice, and praises loud,
To Dagon, as their god who hath delivered
Thee, Samson, bound and blind, into their hands—
Them out of thine, who slew'st them many a slain.
So Dagon shall be magnified, and God,   440
Besides whom is no god, compared with idols,
Disglorified, blasphemed, and had in scorn
By the idolatrous rout amidst their wine;
Which to have come to pass by means of thee,
Samson, of all thy sufferings think the heaviest,   445
Of all reproach the most with shame that ever
Could have befallen thee and thy father's house.
SAMSON. Father, I do acknowledge and confess
That I this honour, I this pomp, have brought
To Dagon, and advanced his praises high   450
Among the Heathen round—to God have brought
Dishonour, obloquy, and oped the mouths
Of idolists and atheists; have brought scandal
To Israel, diffidence of God, and doubt
In feeble hearts, propense enough before   455
To waver, or fall off and join with idols:
Which is my chief affliction, shame and sorrow,
The anguish of my soul, that suffers not
Mine eye to harbour sleep, or thoughts to rest.
This only hope relieves me, that the strife   460
With me hath end. All the contest is now
'Twixt God and Dagon. Dagon hath presumed,
Me overthrown, to enter lists with God,
His deity comparing and preferring
Before the God of Abraham. He, be sure,   465
Will not connive, or linger, thus provoked,
But will arise, and his great name assert.
Dagon must stoop, and shall ere long receive

433 *score:* record of debt, I.O.U.   463 *Me overthrown:* now that I have been
454 *diffidence:* distrust.   overthrown.
455 *propense:* inclined.   466 *connive:* ignore.

Such a discomfit as shall quite despoil him
Of all these boasted trophies won on me,   470
And with confusion blank his worshipers.
MANOA. With cause this hope relieves thee; and these words
    I as a prophecy receive; for God
    (Nothing more certain) will not long defer
    To vindicate the glory of his name   475
    Against all competition, nor will long
    Endure it doubtful whether God be Lord
    Or Dagon. But for thee what shall be done?
    Thou must not in the meanwhile, here forgot,
    Lie in this miserable loathsome plight   480
    Neglected. I already have made way
    To some Philistian lords, with whom to treat
    About thy ransom. Well they may by this
    Have satisfied their utmost of revenge,
    By pains and slaveries, worse than death, inflicted   485
    On thee, who now no more canst do them harm.
SAMSON. Spare that proposal, father; spare the trouble
    Of that solicitation. Let me here,
    As I deserve, pay on my punishment,
    And expiate, if possible, my crime,   490
    Shameful garrulity. To have revealed
    Secrets of *men*, the secrets of a friend,
    How heinous had the fact been, how deserving
    Contempt and scorn of all—to be excluded
    All friendship, and avoided as a blab,   495
    The mark of fool set on his front! But I
    God's counsel have not kept, his holy secret
    Presumptuously have published, impiously,
    Weakly at least and shamefully—a sin
    That Gentiles in their parables condemn   500
    To their Abyss and horrid pains confined.
MANOA. Be penitent, and for thy fault contrite;
    But act not in thy own affliction, son.
    Repent the sin; but, if the punishment
    Thou canst avoid, self-preservation bids;   505
    Or the execution leave to high disposal,
    And let another hand, not thine, exact
    Thy penal forfeit from thyself. Perhaps
    God will relent, and quit thee all his debt;
    Who ever more approves and more accepts   510
    (Best pleased with humble and filial submission)
    Him who, imploring mercy, sues for life,
    Than who, self-rigorous, chooses death as due;

471 *blank:* confound.   493 *fact:* deed.
489 *pay on:* continue to pay.   509 *quit ... debt:* cancel your debt to him.

Which argues over-just, and self-displeased
For self-offence more than for God offended.   515
Reject not, then, what offered means who knows
But God hath set before us to return thee
Home to thy country and his sacred house,
Where thou may'st bring thy offerings, to avert
His further ire, with prayers and vows renewed.   520

SAMSON. His pardon I implore; but, as for life,
    To what end should I seek it? When in strength
All mortals I excelled and great in hopes,
With youthful courage, and magnanimous thoughts
Of birth from Heaven foretold and high exploits,   525
Full of divine instinct, after some proof
Of acts indeed heroic, far beyond
The sons of Anak, famous now and blazed,
Fearless of danger, like a petty god
I walked about, admired of all, and dreaded   530
On hostile ground, none daring my affront—
Then, swollen with pride, into the snare I fell
Of fair fallacious looks, venereal trains,
Softened with pleasure and voluptuous life,
At length to lay my head and hallowed pledge   535
Of all my strength in the lascivious lap
Of a deceitful concubine, who shore me,
Like a tame wether, all my precious fleece,
Then turned me out ridiculous, despoiled,
Shaven, and disarmed among my enemies.   540

CHORUS. Desire of wine and alll delicious drinks,
Which many a famous warrior overturns,
Thou could'st repress; nor did the dancing ruby,
Sparkling out-poured, the flavour or the smell,
Or taste, that cheers the heart of gods and men,   545
Allure thee from the cool crystalline stream.

SAMSON. Wherever fountain or fresh current flowed
Against the eastern ray, translucent, pure
With touch ethereal of Heaven's fiery rod,
I drank, from the clear milky juice allaying   550
Thirst, and refreshed; nor envied them the grape
Whose heads that turbulent liquor fills with fumes.

CHORUS. O madness! to think use of strongest wines
And strongest drinks our chief support of health,
When God with these forbidden made choice to rear   555
His mighty champion,, strong above compare,
Whose drink was only from the liquid brook!

SAMSON. But what availed this temperance, not complete

528 *sons of Anak:* Biblical giants.   seductive tricks.
533 *fallacious:* beguiling; *venereal trains:* 548 *Against:* toward.

Against another object more enticing?
What boots it at one gate to make defence,   560
And at another to let in the foe,
Effeminately vanquished? by which means,
Now blind, disheartened, shamed, dishonoured, quelled,
To what can I be useful? wherein serve
My nation, and the work from Heaven imposed?   565
A burdenous drone; to visitants a gaze,
But to sit idle on the household hearth,
Or pitied object; these redundant locks,
Robustious to no purpose, clustering down,,
Vain monument of strength; till length of years   570
And sedentary numbness craze my limbs
To a contemptible old age obscure.
Here rather let me drudge, and earn my bread,
Till vermin, or the draff of servile food,
Consume me, and oft-invocated death   575
Hasten the welcome end of all my pains.
MANOA. Wilt thou then serve the Philistines with that gift
Which was expressly given thee to annoy them?
Better at home lie bed-rid, not only idle,
Inglorious, unemployed, with age outworn.   580
But God, who caused a fountain at thy prayer
From the dry ground to spring, thy thirst to allay
After the brunt of battle, can as easy
Cause light again within thy eyes to spring,
Wherewith to serve him better than thou hast.   585
And I persuade me so. Why else this strength
Miraculous yet remaining in those locks?
His might continues in thee not for naught.
Nor shall his wondrous gifts be frustrate thus.
SAMSON. All otherwise to me my thoughts portend—   590
That these dark orbs no more shall treat with light,
Nor the other light of life continue long,
But yield to double darkness nigh at hand;
So much I feel my genial spirits droop,
My hopes all flat: Nature within me seems   595
In all her functions weary of herself;
My race of glory run, and race of shame,
And I shall shortly be with them that rest.
MANOA. Believe not these suggestions, which proceed

560 *what boots it:* what good does it do.
568 *redundant:* flowing.
571 *craze:* debilitate.
574 *draff:* offal.
581-83 *But God ... battle:* after the battle
at Ramath-lechi (cf. 145 above) Samson's appeals to God for water were
answered by a fountain jetting from a
rock.
593 *double darkness:* of death and blindness.
594 *genial:* distinctive, arising from his
unique nature.

From anguish of the mind, and humours black   600
That mingle with thy fancy. I, however,
Must not omit a father's timely care
To prosecute the means of thy deliverance
By ransom or how else: meanwhile be calm,
And healing words from these thy friends admit.   605
SAMSON. Oh, that torment should not be confined
    To the body's wounds and sores,
    With maladies innumerable
    In heart, head, breast, and reins,
    But must secret passage find   610
    To the inmost mind,
    There exercise all his fierce accidents,
    And on her purest spirits prey,
    As on entrails, joints, and limbs,
    With answerable pains, but more intense,   615
    Though void of corporal sense!
      My griefs not only pain me
    As a lingering disease,
    But, finding no redress, ferment and rage;
    Nor less than wounds immedicable   620
    Rankle, and fester, and gangrene,
    To black mortification.
    Thoughts, my tormentors, armed with deadly stings,
    Mangle my apprehensive tenderest parts,
    Exasperate, exulcerate, and raise   625
    Dire inflammation, which no cooling herb
    Or medicinal liquor can assuage,
    Nor breath of vernal air from snowy Alp.
    Sleep hath forsook and given me o'er
    To death's benumbing opium as my only cure;   630
    Thence faintings, swoonings, of despair,
    And sense of Heaven's desertion.
      I was his nursling once and choice delight,
    His destined from the womb,
    Promised by heavenly message twice descending.   635
    Under his special eye
    Abstemious I grew up and thrived amain;
    He led me on to mightiest deeds,
    Above the nerve of mortal arm,
    Against the Uncircumcised, our enemies: 640
    But now hath cast me off as never known,

600 *humours:* bodily fluids (blood, choler, bile, phlegm) affecting moods and feelings—black humor refers to melancholy.
609 *reins:* kidneys.
612 *accidents:* symptoms of disease.

615 *answerable:* corresponding.
624 *apprehensive:* sensitive.
628 *Alp:* any high mountain.
635 *message:* messenger.
639 *nerve:* muscle, strength.

And to those cruel enemies,
Whom I by his appointment had provoked,
Left me all helpless, with the irreparable loss
Of sight, reserved alive to be repeated   645
The subject of their cruelty or scorn.
Nor am I in the list of them that hope;
Hopeless are all my evils, all remediless.
This one prayer yet remains, might I be heard,
No long petition—speedy death,   650
The close of all my miseries and the balm.
CHORUS. Many are the sayings of the wise,
  In ancient and in modern books enrolled,
  Extolling patience as the truest fortitude,
  And to the bearing well of all calamities,   655
  All chances incident to man's frail life,
  Consolatories writ
  With studied argument, and much persuasion sought,
  Lenient of grief and anxious thought.
  But with the afflicted in his pangs their sound   660
  Little prevails, or rather seems a time
  Harsh, and of dissonant mood from his complaint,
  Unless he feel within
  Some source of consolation from above,
  Secret refreshings that repair his strength   665
  And fainting spirits uphold.
    God of our fathers! what is Man,
  That thou towards him with hand so various—
  Or might I say contrarious?—
  Temper'st thy providence through his short course: 670
  Not evenly, as thou rul'st
  The angelic orders, and inferior creatures mute,
  Irrational and brute?
  Nor do I name of men the common rout,
  That, wandering loose about,   675
  Grow up and perish as the summer fly,
  Heads without name, no more remembered;
  But such as thou hast solemnly elected,
  With gifts and graces eminently adorned,
  To some great work, thy glory,   680
  And people's safety, which in part they effect.
  Yet toward these, thus dignified, thou oft,
  Amidst their highth of noon,
  Changest thy countenance and thy hand, with no regard
  Of highest favours past   685
  From thee on them, or them to thee of service.

659 *Lenient:* ameliorative.   687 *remit:* send back.
677 *Heads:* people.   688 *obscured:* disgraced.

    Nor only dost degrade them, or remit
To life obscured, which were a fair dismission,
But throw'st them lower than thou didst exalt them high—
Unseemly falls in human eye,   690
Too grievous for the trespass or omission;
Oft leav'st them to the hostile sword
Of heathen and profane, their carcasses
To dogs and fowls a prey, or else captived,
Or to the unjust tribunals, under change of times,   695
And condemnation of the ungrateful multitude.
If these they scape, perhaps in povery
With sickness and disease thou bow'st them down,
Painful diseases and deformed,
In crude old age;   700
Though not disordinate, yet causeless suffering
The punishment of dissolute days. In fine,
Just or unjust alike seem miserable,
For oft alike both come to evil end.
    So deal not with this once thy glorious champion,   705
The image of thy strength, and mighty minister.
What do I beg? how hast thou dealt already!
Behold him in this state calamitous, and turn
His labours, for thou canst, to peaceful end.
    But who is this? what thing of sea or land—   710
Female of sex it seems—
That, so bedecked, ornate, and gay,
Comes this way sailing,
Like a stately ship
Of Tarsus, bound for the isles   715
Of Javan or Gadier,
With all her bravery on, and tackle trim,
Sails filled, and streamers waving,
Courted by all the winds that hold them play;
An amber scent of odorous perfume   720
Her harbinger, a damsel train behind?
Some rich Philistian matron she may seem;
And now, at nearer view, no other certain
Than Dalila thy wife.
SAMSON. My wife! my traitress! let her not come near me.   725
CHORUS. Yet on she moves; now stands and eyes thee fixed,
    About to have spoke; but now, with head declined,

700 *crude:* premature.
701 *disordinate:* intemperate.
701 *Though not ... dissolute days:* i.e., though not themselves intemperate some men suffer, without apparent reason, as though they were being punished for living dissolute lives.

715 *Tarsus:* eastern seaport referred to in Old Testament.
716 *Javan or Gadier:* Mediterranean islands near Greece and Phoenicia.
717 *bravery:* finery.
720 *amber:* ambergris.

Like a fair flower surcharged with dew, she weeps,
And words addressed seem into tears dissolved,
Wetting the borders of her silken veil.   730
But now again she makes address to speak.
DALILA. With doubtful feet and wavering resolution
    I came, still dreading thy displeasure, Samson;
    Which to have merited, without excuse,
    I cannot but acknowledge. Yet, if tears   735
    May expiate (though the fact more evil drew
    In the perverse event than I foresaw),
    My penance hath not slackened, though my pardon
    No way assured. But conjugal affection,
    Prevailing over fear and timorous doubt,   740
    Hath led me on, desirous to behold
    Once more thy face, and know of thy estate,
    If aught in my ability may serve
    To lighten what thou suffer'st, and appease
    Thy mind with what amends is in my power—   745
    Though late, yet in some part to recompense
    My rash but more unfortunate misdeed.
SAMSON. Out, out hyæna! These are thy wonted arts,
    And arts of every woman false like thee—
    To break all faith, all vows, deceive, betray;   750
    Then, as repentant, to submit, beseech,
    And reconcilement move with feigned remorse,
    Confess, and promise wonders in her change—
    Not truly penitent, but chief to try
    Her husband, how far urged his patience bears,   755
    His virtue or weakness which way to assail:
    Then, with more cautious and instructed skill,
    Again transgresses, and again submits;
    That wisest and best men, full oft beguiled,
    With goodness principled not to reject   760
    The penitent, but ever to forgive,
    Are drawn to wear out miserable days,
    Entangled with a poisonous bosom-snake,
    If not by quick destruction soon cut off,
    As I by thee, to ages an example.   765
DALILA. Yet hear me, Samson; not that I endeavour
    To lessen or extenuate my offence,
    But that, on the other side, if it be weighed
    By itself, with aggravations not surcharged,

731 *words addressed:* words about to be
    spoken.
736 *fact:* act of betrayal.
737 *event:* outcome.
738 *penance:* penitence.
742 *estate:* state of being, condition.

748 *hyæna:* the hyena was thought to
    mimic human speech in order to lure
    men out of their houses where it could
    devour them.
752 *move:* offer.

Or else with just allowance counterpoised,   770
I may, if possible, thy pardon find
The easier towards me, or thy hatred less.
First granting, as I do, it was a weakness
In me, but incident to all our sex,
Curiosity, inquisitive, importune   775
Of secrets, then with like infirmity
To publish them—both common female faults—
Was it not weakness also to make known
For importunity, that is for naught,
Wherein consisted all thy strength and safety?   780
To what I did thou show'dst me first the way.
But I to enemies revealed, and should not!
Nor should'st thou have trusted that to woman's frailty:
Ere I to thee, thou to thyself wast cruel.
Let weakness, then, with weakness come to parle,   785
So near related, or the same of kind;
Thine forgive mine, that men may censure thine
The gentler, if severely thou exact not
More strength from me than in thyself was found.
And what if love, which thou interpret'st hate,   790
The jealousy of love, powerful of sway
In human hearts, nor less in mine towards thee,
Caused what I did? I saw thee mutable
Of fancy; feared lest one day thou would'st leave me
As her at Timna; sought by all means, therefore,   795
How to endear, and hold thee to me firmest:
No better way I saw than by importuning
To learn thy secrets, get into my power
Thy key of strength and safety. Thou wilt say,
'Why, then, revealed?' I was assured by those   800
Who tempted me that nothing was designed
Against thee but safe custody and hold.
That made for me; I knew that liberty
Would draw thee forth to perilous enterprises,
While I at home sat full of cares and fears,   805
Wailing thy absence in my widowed bed;
Here I should still enjoy thee, day and night,
Mine and love's prisoner, not the Philistines',
Whole to myself, unhazarded abroad,
Fearless at home of partners in my love.   810
These reasons in Love's law have passed for good,

775 *importune:* insistently curious and pry-
   ing.
777 *publish:* make known.
778–79 *Was it not ... For importunity:*
   weren't you equally weak to reveal
   your secret to me when importuned?

785 *parle:* parley.
786 *kind:* nature.
794 *fancy:* love.
803 *That made for me:* that served my
   purposes.

Though fond and reasonless to some perhaps;
And love hath oft, well meaning, wrought much woe,
Yet always pity or pardon hath obtained.
Be not unlike all others, not austere   815
As thou art strong, inflexible as steel.
If thou in strength all mortals dost exceed,
In uncompassionate anger do not so.
SAMSON. How cunningly the sorceress displays
  Her own transgressions, to upbraid me mine!   820
That malice, not repentance, brought thee hither,
By this appears. I gave, thou say'st, the example,
I led the way—bitter reproach, but true;
I to myself was false ere thou to me.
Such pardon, therefore, as I give my folly   825
Take to thy wicked deed; which when thou seest
Impartial, self-severe, inexorable,
Thou wilt renounce thy seeking, and much rather
Confess it feigned. Weakness is thy excuse,
And I believe it—weakness to resist   830
Philistian gold. If weakness may excuse,
What murtherer, what traitor, parricide,
Incestuous, sacrilegious, but may plead it?
All wickedness is weakness; that plea, therefore,
With God or man will gain thee no remission.   835
But love constrained thee? Call it furious rage
To satisfy thy lust! Love seeks to have love;
My love how could'st thou hope, who took'st the way
To raise in me inexpiable hate,
Knowing, as needs I must, by thee betrayed?   840
In vain thou striv'st to cover shame with shame,
Or by evasions thy crime uncover'st more.
DALILA. Since thou determin'st weakness for no plea
  In man or woman, though to thy own condemning,
Hear what assaults I had, what snares besides,   845
What sieges girt me round, ere I consented;
Which might have awed the best-resolved of men,
The constantest, to have yielded without blame.
It was not gold, as to my charge thou lay'st,
That wrought with me. Thou know'st the magistrates   850
And princes of my country came in person,
Solicited, commanded, threatened, urged,
Adjured by all the bonds of civil duty
And of religion—pressed how just it was,
How honourable, how glorious, to entrap   855
A common enemy, who had destroyed
Such numbers of our nation: and the priest

---

812 *fond:* foolish.   835 *remission:* forgiveness.

Was not behind, but ever at my ear,
Preaching how meritorious with the gods
It would be to ensnare an irreligous   860
Dishonourer of Dagon. What had I
To oppose against such powerful arguments?
Only my love of thee held long debate,
And combated in silence all these reasons
With hard contest. At length, that grounded maxim,   865
So rife and celebrated in the mouths
Of wisest men, that to the public good
Private respects must yield, with grave authority
Took full possession of me, and prevailed;
Virtue, as I thought, truth, duty, so enjoining.   870
SAMSON. I thought where all thy circling wiles would end—
In feigned religion, smooth hypocrisy!
But, had thy love, still odiously pretended,
Been, as it ought, sincere, it would have taught thee
Far other reasonings, brought forth other deeds.   875
I, before all the daughters of my tribe
And of my nation, chose thee from among
My enemies, loved thee, as too well thou knew'st;
Too well; unbosomed all my secrets to thee,
Not out of levity, but overpowered   880
By thy request, who could deny thee nothing;
Yet now am judged an enemy. Why, then,
Didst thou at first receive me for thy husband—
Then, as since then, thy country's foe professed?
Being once a wife, for me thou wast to leave   885
Parents and country; nor was I their subject,
Nor under their protection, but my own;
Thou mine, not theirs. If aught against my life
Thy country sought of thee, it sought unjustly,
Against the law of nature, law of nations;   890
No more thy country, but an impious crew
Of men conspiring to uphold their state
By worse than hostile deeds, violating the ends
For which our country is a name so dear;
Not therefore to be obeyed. But zeal moved thee;   895
To please thy gods thou didst it! Gods unable
To acquit themselves and prosecute their foes
But by ungodly deeds, the contradiction
Of their own deity, Gods cannot be—
Less therefore to be pleased, obeyed, or feared.   900
These false pretexts and varnished colours failing,
Bare in thy guilt, how foul must thou appear!

866 *rife:* widespread.   871 *circling:* devious.
868 *respects:* concerns.   897 *acquit:* here, revenge.

DALILA. In argument with men a woman ever
    Goes by the worse, whatever be her cause.
SAMSON. For want of words, no doubt, or lack of breath!   905
    Witness when I was worried with thy peals.
DALILA. I was a fool, too rash, and quite mistaken
    In what I thought would have succeeded best.
    Let me obtain forgiveness of thee, Samson;
    Afford me place to show what recompense   910
    Towards thee I intend for what I have misdone,
    Misguided. Only what remains past cure
    Bear not too sensibly, nor still insist
    To afflict thyself in vain. Though sight be lost,
    Life yet hath many solaces, enjoyed   915
    Where other senses want not their delights—
    At home, in leisure and domestic ease,
    Exempt from many a care and chance to which
    Eyesight exposes, daily, men abroad.
    I to the lords will intercede, not doubting   920
    Their favourable ear, that I may fetch thee
    From forth this loathsome prison-house, to abide
    With me, where my redoubled love and care,
    With nursing diligence, to me glad office,
    May ever tend about thee to old age,   925
    With all things grateful cheered, and so supplied
    That what by me thou hast lost thou least shall miss.
SAMSON. No, no; of my condition take no care,
    It fits not; thou and I long since are twain;
    Nor think me so unwary or accursed   930
    To bring my feet again into the snare
    Where once I have been caught. I know thy trains,
    Though dearly to my cost, thy gins, and toils.
    Thy fair enchanted cup, and warbling charms,
    No more on me have power; their force is nulled;   935
    So much of adder's wisdom I have learned,
    To fence my ear against thy sorceries.
    If in my flower of youth and strength, when all men
    Loved, honoured, feared me, thou alone could hate me,
    Thy husband, slight me, sell me, and forgo me,   940
    How would'st thou use me now, blind and thereby
    Deceivable, in most things as a child

904 *Goes by:* fares.
906 *worried:* harried; *peals:* importunings (to tell his secret).
913 *sensibly:* feelingly.
916 *want:* lack.
924 *office:* service, duty.
926 *grateful:* gratifying.

932 *trains:* tricks.
933 *gins:* devices, traps; *toils:* nets.
934 *charms:* songs.
935 *nulled:* anulled.
936–37 *So much ... fence my ear:* adders were thought to be deaf to charms.

And last neglected! How would'st thou insult,
When I must live uxorious to thy will   945
In perfect thraldom! how again betray me,
Bearing my words and doings to the lords
To gloss upon, and, censuring, frown or smile!
This jail I count the house of liberty
To thine, whose doors my feet shall never enter.   950
DALILA. Let me approach at least, and touch thy hand.
SAMSON. Not for thy life, lest fierce remembrance wake
My sudden rage to tear thee joint by joint.
At distance I forgive thee; go with that;
Bewail thy falsehood, and the pious works   955
It hath brought forth to make thee memorable
Among illustrious women, faithful wives;
Cherish thy hastened widowhood with the gold
Of matrimonial treason: so farewell.
DALILA. I see thou art implacable, more deaf   960
To prayers than winds and seas. Yet winds to seas
Are reconciled at length, and sea to shore:
Thy anger, unappeasable, still rages,
Eternal tempest never to be calmed.
Why do I humble thus myself, and suing   965
For peace, reap nothing but repulse and hate,
Bid go with evil omen, and the brand
Of infamy upon my name denounced?
To mix with thy concernments I desist
Henceforth, nor too much disapprove my own.   970
Fame, if not double-faced, is double-mouthed,
And with contrary blast proclaims most deeds;
On both his wings, one black, the other white,
Bears greatest names in his wild aery flight.
My name, perhaps, among the Circumcised   975
In Dan, in Judah, and the bordering tribes,
To all posterity may stand defamed,
With malediction mentioned, and the blot
Of fasehood most unconjugal traduced.
But in my country, where I most desire,   980
In Ecron, Gaza, Asdod, and in Gath,
I shall be named among the famousest
Of women, sung at solemn festivals,
Living and dead recorded, who, to save
Her country from a fierce destroyer, chose   985
Above the faith of wedlock bands; my tomb
With odours visited and annual flowers;

937 *fence:* shut.
948 *gloss:* comment; *censuring:* judging.
969 *Tomix...concernments:* to involve myself in your affairs.

975 *Circumcised:* the Jews.
976 *Dan:* Samson's tribe.
987 *odours:* spices.

Not less renowned than in Mount Ephraim
Jael, who, with inhospitable guile,
Smote Sisera sleeping, through the temples nailed.   990
Nor shall I count it heinous to enjoy
The public marks of honour and reward
Conferred upon me for the piety
Which to my country I was judged to have shown.
At this whoever envies or repines,   995
I leave him to his lot, and like my own.
CHORUS. She's gone—a manifest serpent by her sting
    Discovered in the end, till now concealed.
SAMSON. So let her go. God sent her to debase me,
    And aggravate my folly, who committed   1000
    To such a viper his most sacred trust
    Of secrecy, my safety, and my life.
CHORUS. Yet beauty, though injurious, hath strange power,
    After offence returning, to regain
    Love once possessed, nor can be easily   1005
    Repulsed, without much inward passion felt,
    And secret sting of amorous remorse.
SAMSON. Love-quarrels oft in pleasing concord end;
    Not wedlock-treachery endangering life.
CHORUS. It is not virtue, wisdom, valour, wit,   1010
    Strength, comeliness of shape, or amplest merit,
    That woman's love can win, or long inherit;
    But what it is, hard is to say,
    Harder to hit,
    Which way soever men refer it,   1015
    (Much like thy riddle, Samson) in one day
    Or seven though one should musing sit.
      If any of these, or all, the Timnian bride
    Had not so soon preferred
    Thy paranymph, worthless to thee compared,   1020
    Successor in thy bed,
    Nor both so loosely disallied
    Their nuptials, nor this last so treacherously
    Had shorn the fatal harvest of thy head.
    Is it for that such outward ornament   1025
    Was lavished on their sex, that inward gifts
    Were left for haste unfinished, judgment scant,
    Capacity not raised to apprehend
    Or value what is best
    In choice, but oftest to affect the wrong?   1030

989–90 *Jael . . . nailed:* Judges 4–5.   1020 *paranymph:* best man, groomsman
1006 *passion:* emotion.   (see *Judges* 14:20).
1007 *remorse:* pity.   1025 *for that:* because.
1012 *inherit:* possess.   1030 *affect:* desire.
1016 *riddle:* See lines 382–87 above.

Or was too much of self-love mixed,
Of constancy no root infixed,
That either they love nothing, or not long?
    Whate'er it be, to wisest men and best
Seeming at first all heavenly under virgin veil,   1035
Soft, modest, meek, demure,
Once joined, the contrary she proves—a thorn
Intestine, far within defensive arms
A cleaving mischief, in his way to virtue
Adverse and turbulent; or by her charms   1040
Draws him awry, enslaved
With dotage, and his sense depraved
To folly and shameful deeds, which ruin ends.
What pilot so expert but needs must wreck,
Embarked with such a steers-mate at the helm?   1045
    Favoured of Heaven who finds
One virtuous, rarely found,
That in domestic good combines!
Happy that house! his way to peace is smooth:
But virtue which breaks through all opposition,   1050
And all temptation can remove,
Most shines and most is acceptable above.
    Therefore God's universal law
Gave to the man despotic power
Over his female in due awe,   1055
Nor from that right to part an hour,
Smile she or lour:
So shall he least confusion draw
On his whole life, not swayed
By female usurpation, nor dismayed.   1060
    But had we best retire? I see a storm.
SAMSON. Fair days have oft contracted wind and rain.
CHORUS. But this another kind of tempest brings.
SAMSON. Be less abstruse; my riddling days are past.
CHORUS. Look now for no enchanting voice, nor fear   1065
The bait of honeyed words; a rougher tongue
Draws hitherward; I know him by his stride,
The giant Harapha of Gath, his look
Haughty, as in his pile high-built and proud.
Comes he in peace? What wind hath blown him hither   1070
I less conjecture than when first I saw
The sumptuous Dalila floating this way:
His habit carries peace, his brow defiance.

1038 *Intestine:* domestic.
1039 *cleaving:* clinging.
1048 *That . . . combines:* that in the interests of domestic happiness unites herself with her husband completely.
1054 *despotic:* absolute.
1062 *contracted:* brought together.
1069 *pile:* body.

SAMSON. Or peace or not, alike to me he comes.
CHORUS. His fraught we soon shall know: he now arrives.   1075
HARAPHA. I come not, Samson, to condole thy chance,
    As these perhaps, yet wish it had not been,
    Though for no friendly intent. I am of Gath;
    Men call me Harapha, of stock renowned
    As Og, or Anak, and the Emims old   1080
    That Kiriathaim held. Thou know'st me now,
    If thou at all art known. Much I have heard
    Of thy prodigious might and feats performed,
    Incredible to me, in this displeased,
    That I was never present on the place   1085
    Of those encounters, where we might have tried
    Each other's force in camp or listed field;
    And now am come to see of whom such noise
    Hath walked about, and each limb to survey,
    If thy appearance answer loud report.   1090
SAMSON. The way to know were not to see, but taste.
HARAPHA. Dost thou already single me? I thought
    Gyves and the mill had tamed thee. O that fortune
    Had brought me to the field where thou art famed
    To have wrought such wonders with an ass's jaw!   1095
    I should have forced thee soon wish other arms,
    Or left thy carcass where the ass lay thrown;
    So had the glory of prowess been recovered
    To Palestine, won by a Philistine
    From the unforeskinned race, of whom thou bear'st   1100
    The highest name for valiant acts. That honour,
    Certain to have won by mortal duel from thee,
    I lose, prevented by thy eyes put out.
SAMSON. Boast not of what thou would'st have done, but do
    What then thou would'st; thou seest it in thy hand.   1105
HARAPHA. To combat with a blind man I disdain,
    And thou hast need much washing to be touched.
SAMSON. Such usage as your honourable lords
    Afford me, assassinated and betrayed;
    Who durst not with their whole united powers   1110
    In fight withstand me single and unarmed,
    Nor in the house with chamber-ambushes
    Close-banded durst attack me, no, not sleeping,
    Till they had hired a woman with their gold,

1074 *Or:* either, whether.
1075 *fraught:* freight (intentions).
1076 *chance:* mischance.
1077 *these:* i.e., the Chorus.
1080 *Og, Anak, Emims:* giants mentioned
    in the Bible.
1087 *camp:* field of battle; *listed field:*
tournament field with lists or lanes
in which combatants met.
1090 *report:* rumor.
1092 *single:* challenge.
1093 *Gyves:* shackles.
1109 *assassinated:* attacked treacherously.
1113 *Close-banded:* secretly united.

Breaking her marriage-faith, to circumvent me.   1115
Therefore, without feign'd shifts, let be assigned
Some narrow place enclosed, where sight may give thee,
Or rather flight, no great advantage on me;
Then put on all thy gorgeous arms, thy helmet
And brigandine of brass, thy broad habergeon,   1120
Vant-brace and greaves and gauntlet; add thy spear,
A weaver's beam, and seven-times-folded shield:
I only with an oaken staff will meet thee,
And raise such outcries on thy clattered iron,
Which long shall not withhold me from thy head,   1125
That in a little time, while breath remains thee,
Thou oft shalt wish thyself at Gath, to boast
Again in safety what thou would'st have done
To Samson, but shalt never see Gath more
HARAPHA. Thou durst not thus disparage glorious arms   1130
Which greatest heroes have in battle worn,
Their ornament and safety, had not spells
And black enchantments, some magician's art,
Armed thee or charmed thee strong, which thou from Heaven
Feign'dst at thy birth was given thee in thy hair,   1135
Where strength can least abide, though all thy hairs
Were bristles ranged like those that ridge the back
Of chafed wild boars or ruffled porcupines.
SAMSON. I know no spells, use no forbidden arts;
My trust is in the Living God, who gave me,   1140
At my nativity, this strength, diffused
No less through all my sinews, joints, and bones,
Than thine, while I preserved these locks unshorn,
The pledge of my unviolated vow.
For proof hereof, if Dagon be thy god,   1145
Go to his temple, invocate his aid
With solemnest devotion, spread before him
How highly it concerns his glory now
To frustrate and dissolve these magic spells,
Which I to be the power of Israel's God   1150
Avow, and challenge Dagon to the test,
Offering to combat thee, his champion bold,
With the utmost of his godhead seconded:
Then thou shalt see, or rather to thy sorrow
Soon feel, whose God is strongest, thine or mine..   1155
HARAPHA. Presume not on thy God. Whate'er he be,
Thee he regards not, owns not, hath cut off
Quite from his people, and delivered up
Into thy enemies' hand; permitted them

1116 *shifts:* tricks.   1121 *Vant-brace:* armor for the forearm;
1120 *brigandine:* armor; *habergeon:* mail   *greaves:* shin armor.
vest.

To put out both thine eyes, and fettered send thee   1160
Into the common prison, there to grind
Among the slaves and asses, thy comrades,
As good for nothing else, no better service
With those thy boisterous locks; no worthy match
For valour to assail, nor by the sword   1165
Of noble warrior, so to stain his honour,
But by the barber's razor best subdued.
SAMSON. All these indignities, for such they are
From thine, these evils I deserve and more,
Acknowledge them from God inflicted on me   1170
Justly, yet despair not of his final pardon,
Whose ear is ever open, and his eye
Gracious to re-admit the suppliant;
In confidence whereof I once again
Defy thee to the trial of mortal fight,   1175
By combat to decide whose god is God,
Thine, or whom I with Israel's sons adore.
HARAPHA. Fair honour that thou dost thy God, in trusting
He will accept thee to defend his cause,
A murtherer, a revolter, and a robber!   1180
SAMSON. Tongue-doughty giant, how dost thou prove me these?
HARAPHA. Is not thy nation subject to our lords?
Their magistrates confessed it when they took thee
As a league-breaker, and delivered bound
Into our hands; for hadst thou not committed   1185
Notorious murder on those thirty men
At Ascalon, who never did thee harm,
Then, like a robber, stripp'dst them of their robes?
The Philistines, when thou hadst broke the league,
Went up with armed powers thee only seeking,   1190
To others did no violence nor spoil.
SAMSON. Among the daughters of the Philistines
I chose a wife, which argued me no foe,
And in your city held my nuptial feast;
But your ill-meaning politician lords,   1195
Under pretence of bridal friends and guests,
Appointed to await me thirty spies,
Who, threatening cruel death, constrained the bride
To wring from me, and tell to them, my secret,
That solved the riddle which I had proposed.   1200
When I perceived all set on enmity,
As on my enemies, wherever chanced,

1164 *boisterous:* thick-grown.
1169 *thine:* thy people.
1184 *league-breaker:* treaty breaker.
1187 *Ascalon:* after the woman of Timna
betrayed his riddle, Samson went to
Ascalon, killed thirty men, took their
clothes, and gave them to the men
who answered the riddle.
1201 *set:* intent.

I used hostility, and took their spoil,
To pay my underminers in their coin.
My nation was subjected to your lords!   1205
It was the force of conquest; force with force
Is well ejected when the conquered can.
But I, a private person, whom my country
As a league-breaker gave up bound, presumed
Single rebellion, and did hostile acts!   1210
I was no private, but a person raised,
With strength sufficient, and command from Heaven,
To free my country. If their servile minds
Me, their deliverer sent, would not receive,
But to their masters gave me up for nought,   1215
The unworthier they; whence to this day they serve.
I was to do my part from Heaven assigned,
And had performed it if my known offence
Had not disabled me, not all your force.
These shifts refuted, answer thy appellant,   1220
Though by his blindness maimed for high attempts,
Who now defies thee thrice to single fight,
As a petty enterprise of small enforce.
HARAPHA. With thee, a man condemned, a slave enrolled,
Due by the law to capital punishment?   1225
To fight with thee no man of arms will deign.
SAMSON. Cam'st thou for this, vain boaster, to survey me,
To descant on my strength, and give thy verdict?
Come nearer; part not hence so slight informed;
But take good heed my hand survey not thee.   1230
HARAPHA. O Baal-zebub! can my ears unused
Hear these dishonours, and not render death?
SAMSON. No man withholds thee; nothing from thy hand
Fear I incurable; bring up thy van;
My heels are fettered, but my fist is free.   1235
HARAPHA. This insolence other kind of answer fits.
SAMSON. Go, baffled coward, lest I run upon thee,
Though in these chains, bulk without spirit vast,
And with one buffet lay thy structure low,
Or swing thee in the air, then dash thee down,   1240
To the hazard of thy brains and shattered sides.
HARAPHA. By Astaroth, ere long thou shalt lament
These braveries, in irons loaden on thee.

1204 *underminers:* those who had persuaded his wife to tell them the
answer to the riddle.
1220 *shifts:* evasions; *appellant:* challenger.
1222 *thrice:* the medieval custom was to
offer a challenge three times.
1223 *enforce:* effort.

1231 *Baal-zebub:* Baal ("god of the flies")
was the sun god of the Philistines;
unused: unaccustomed.
1234 *van:* vanguard.
1242 *Astaroth:* goddess of love and fertility.
1243 *braveries:* boasts.

CHORUS. His giantship is gone somewhat crest-fallen,
  Stalking with less unconscionable strides,   1245
  And lower looks, but in a sultry chafe.
SAMSON. I dread him not, nor all his giant brood,
  Though fame divulge him father of five sons,
  All of gigantic size, Goliath chief.
CHORUS. He will directly to the lords, I fear,   1250
  And with malicious counsel stir them up
  Some way or other yet further to afflict thee.
SAMSON. He must allege some cause, and offered fight
  Will not dare mention, lest a question rise
  Whether he durst accept the offer or not;   1255
  And that he durst not plain enough appeared.
  Much more affliction than already felt
  They cannot well impose, nor I sustain,
  If they intend advantage of my labours,
  The work of many hands, which earns my keeping,   1260
  With so small profit daily to my owners.
  But come what will; my deadliest foe will prove
  My speediest friend, by death to rid me hence;
  The worst that he can give to me the best.
  Yet so it may fall out, because their end   1265
  Is hate, not help to me, it may with mine
  Draw their own ruin who attempt the deed.
CHORUS. O, how comely it is, and how reviving
  To the spirits of just men long oppressed,
  When God into the hands of their deliverer   1270
  Puts invincible might,
  To quell the mighty of the earth, the oppressor,
  The brute and boisterous force of violent men,
  Hardy and industrious to support
  Tyrannic power, but raging to pursue   1275
  The righteous, and all such as honour truth!
  He all their ammunition
  And feats of war defeats
  With plain heroic magnitude of mind
  And celestial vigour armed;   1280
  Their armouries and magazines contemns,
  Renders them useless, while
  With winged expedition
  Swift as the lightning glance he executes
  His errand on the wicked, who, surprised,   1285
  Lose their defence, distracted and amazed.
   But patience is more oft the exercise
  Of saints, the trial of their fortitude,

1245 *unconscionable:* cocky.   1283 *expedition:* swiftness.
1277 *ammunition:* munitions.

Making them each his own deliverer.
And victor over all   1290
That tyranny or fortune can inflict.
Either of these is in thy lot,
Samson, with might endued
Above the sons of men; but sight bereaved
May chance to number thee with those   1295
Whom patience finally must crown.
    This Idol's day hath been to thee no day of rest,
Labouring thy mind
More than the working day thy hands.
And yet, perhaps, more trouble is behind;   1300
For I descry this way
Some other tending; in his hand
A sceptre or quaint staff he bears,
Comes on amain, speed in his look.
By his habit I discern him now   1305
A public officer, and now at hand.
His message will be short and voluble.
OFFICER. Ebrews, the prisoner Samson here I seek.
CHORUS. His manacles remark him; there he sits.
OFFICER. Samson, to thee our lords thus bid me say: 1310
    This day to Dagon is a solemn feast,
With sacrifices, triumph, pomp, and games;
Thy strength they know surpassing human rate,
And now some public proof thereof require
To honour this great feast, and great assembly.   1315
Rise, therefore, with all speed, and come along,
Where I will see thee heartened and fresh clad,
To appear as fits before the illustrious lords.
SAMSON. Thou know'st I am an Ebrew; therefore tell them
    Our law forbids at their religious rites   1320
My presence; for that cause I cannot come.
OFFICER. This answer, be assured, will not content them.
SAMSON. Have they not sword-players, and every sort
    Of gymnic artists, wrestlers, riders, runners,
Jugglers and dancers, antics, mummers, mimics,   1325
But they must pick me out, with shackles tired,
And over-laboured at their public mill,
To make them sport with blind activity?
Do they not seek occasion of new quarrels,
On my refusal, to distress me more,   1330
Or make a game of my calamities?
Return the way thou cam'st; I will not come.

1303 *quaint:* highly decorated.   1313 *rate:* estimation.
1305 *habit:* outfit.   1325 *mummers:* actors.
1309 *remark:* identify.

OFFICER. Regard thyself; this will offend them highly.
SAMSON. Myself! my conscience, and internal peace.
    Can they think me so broken, so debased   1335
    With corporal servitude, that my mind ever
    Will condescend to such absurd commands?
    Although their drudge, to be their fool or jester,
    And, in my midst of sorrow and heart-grief,
    To show them feats, and play before their god—   1340
    The worst of all indignities, yet on me
    Joined with extreme contempt! I will not come.
OFFICER. My message was imposed on me with speed,
    Brooks no delay: is this thy resolution?
SAMSON. So take it with what speed thy message needs.   1345
OFFICER. I am sorry what this stoutness will produce.
SAMSON. Perhaps thou shalt have cause to sorrow indeed.
CHORUS. Consider, Samson; matters now are strained
    Up to the highth, whether to hold or break.
    He's gone, and who knows how he may report   1350
    Thy words by adding fuel to the flame?
    Expect another message, more imperious,
    More lordly thundering than thou well wilt bear.
SAMSON. Shall I abuse this consecrated gift
    Of strength, again returning with my hair   1355
    After my great transgression—so requite
    Favour renewed, and add a greater sin
    By prostituting holy things to idols,
    A Nazarite, in place abominable,
    Vaunting my strength in honour to their Dagon?   1360
    Besides how vile, contemptible, ridiculous,
    What act more execrably unclean, profane?
CHORUS. Yet with this strength thou serv'st the Philistines,
    Idolatrous, uncircumcised, unclean.
SAMSON. Not in their idol-worship, but by labour   1365
    Honest and lawful to deserve my food
    Of those who have me in their civil power.
CHORUS. Where the heart joins not, outward acts defile not.
SAMSON. Where outward force constrains, the sentence holds:
    But who constrains me to the temple of Dagon,   1370
    Not dragging? The Philistian lords command:
    Commands are no constraints. If I obey them,
    I do it freely, venturing to displease
    God for the fear of man, and man prefer,
    Set God behind; which, in his jealousy,   1375
    Shall never, unrepented, find forgiveness.
    Yet that he may dispense with me, or thee,

1333 *Regard thyself:* consider your best in-
    terests.
1342 *Joined:* enjoined, demanded.

1369 *sentence holds:* maxim applies.
1377 *despense with:* provide despensation
    for.

Present in temples at idolatrous rites
For some important cause, thou need'st not doubt.
CHORUS. How thou wilt here come off surmounts my reach.   1380
SAMSON. Be of good courage; I begin to feel
    Some rousing motions in me, which dispose
    To something extraordinary my thoughts.
    I with this messenger will go along—
    Nothing to do, be sure, that may dishonour   1385
    Our Law, or stain my vow of Nazarite.
    If there be aught of presage in the mind,
    This day will be remarkable in my life
    By some great act, or of my days the last.
CHORUS. In time thou hast resolved: the man returns.   1390
OFFICER. Samson, this second message from our lords
    To thee I am bid say: Art thou our slave,
    Our captive, at the public mill our drudge,
    And dar'st thou, at our sending and command,
    Dispute thy coming? Come without delay;   1395
    Or we shall find such engines to assail
    And hamper thee, as thou shalt come of force,
    Though thou wert firmlier fastened than a rock.
SAMSON. I could be well content to try their art,
    Which to no few of them would prove pernicious,   1400
    Yet, knowing their advantages too many,
    Because they shall not trail me through their streets
    Like a wild beast, I am content to go.
    Masters' commands come with a power resistless
    To such as owe them absolute subjection;   1405
    And for a life who will not change his purpose?
    (So mutable are all the ways of men!)
    Yet this be sure, in nothing to comply
    Scandalous or forbidden in our Law.
OFFICER. I praise thy resolution. Doff these links: 1410
    By this compliance thou wilt win the lords
    To favour, and perhaps to set thee free.
SAMSON. Brethren, farewell. Your company along
    I will not wish, lest it perhaps offend them
    To see me girt with friends; and how the sight   1415
    Of me, as of a common enemy,
    So dreaded once, may now exasperate them
    I know not. Lords are lordliest in their wine;
    And the well-feasted priest then soonest fired
    With zeal, if aught religion seem concerned;   1420
    No less the people, on their holy-days,
    Impetuous, insolent, unquenchable.

1382 *motions:* feelings.   1400 *pernicious:* deadly.
1396 *engines:* torture devices.   1402 *Because:* In order that.

Happen what may, of me expect to hear
Nothing dishonourable, impure, unworthy
Our God, our Law, my nation, or myself;   1425
The last of me or no I cannot warrant.
CHORUS. Go, and the Holy One
Of Israel be thy guide
To what may serve his glory best, and spread his name
Great among the Heathen round;   1430
Send thee the Angel of thy birth, to stand
Fast by thy side, who from thy father's field
Rode up in flames after his message told
Of thy conception, and be now a shield
Of fire; that Spirit that first rushed on thee   1435
In the camp of Dan,
Be efficacious in thee now at need!
For never was from Heaven imparted
Measure of strength so great to mortal seed,
As in thy wondrous actions hath been seen.   1440
But wherefore comes old Manoa in such haste
With youthful steps? Much livelier than erewhile
He seems; supposing here to find his son,
Or of him bringing to us some glad news?
MANOA. Peace with you, brethren! My inducement hither   1445
Was not at present here to find my son,
By order of the lords new parted hence
To come and play before them at their feast.
I heard all as I came; the city rings,
And numbers thither flock: I had no will,   1450
Lest I should see him forced to things unseemly.
But that which moved my coming now was chiefly
To give ye part with me what hope I have
With good success to work his liberty.
CHORUS. That hope would much rejoice us to partake   1455
With thee. Say, reverend sire; we thirst to hear.
MANOA. I have attempted, one by one, the lords,
Either at home, or through the high street passing,
With supplication prone and father's tears,
To accept of ransom for my son, their prisoner.   1460
Some much averse I found, and wondrous harsh,
Contemptuous, proud, set on revenge and spite;
That part most reverenced Dagon and his priests:
Others more moderate seeming, but their aim
Private reward, for which both God and State   1465
They easily would set to sale: a third
More generous far and civil, who confessed
They had enough revenged, having reduced

1447 *new parted:* newly departed.   1457 *attempted:* appealed to.

Their foe to misery beneath their fears;
The rest was magnanimity to remit,   1470
If some convenient ransom were proposed.
What noise or shout was that? It tore the sky.
CHORUS. Doubtless the people shouting to behold
   Their once great dread, captive and blind before them,
   Or at some proof of strength before them shown.   1475
MANOA. His ransom, if my whole inheritance
   May compass it, shall willingly be paid
   And numbered down. Much rather I shall choose
   To live the poorest in my tribe, than richest
   And he in that calamitous prison left.   1480
   No, I am fixed not to part hence without him.
   For his redemption all my patrimony,
   If need be, I am ready to forgo
   And quit. Not wanting him, I shall want nothing.
CHORUS. Fathers are wont to lay up for their sons;   1485
   Thou for thy son are bent to lay out all:
   Sons wont to nurse their parents in old age;
   Thou in old age car'st how to nurse thy son,
   Made older than thy age through eye-sight lost.
MANOA. It shall be my delight to tend his eyes,   1490
   And view him sitting in his house, ennobled
   With all those high exploits by him achieved,
   And on his shoulders waving down those locks
   That of a nation armed the strength contained.
   And I persuade me God hath not permitted   1495
   His strength again to grow up with his hair
   Garrisoned round about him like a camp
   Of faithful soldiery, were not his purpose
   To use him further yet in some great service—
   Not to sit idle with so great a gift   1500
   Useless, and thence ridiculous, about him.
   And, since his strength with eye-sight was not lost,
   God will restore him eye-sight to his strength.
CHORUS. Thy hopes are not ill founded, nor seem vain,
   Of his delivery, and thy joy thereon   1505
   Conceived, agreeable to a father's love;
   In both which we, as next, participate.
MANOA. I know your friendly minds, and . . . O, what noise!
   Mercy of Heaven! What hideous noise was that?
   Horribly loud, unlike the former shout.   1510
CHORUS. Noise call you it, or universal groan,
   As if the whole inhabitation perished?
   Blood, death, and deathful deeds, are in that noise,

1469 *beneath their fears:* so that he no   1484 *quit:* release; *wanting:* lacking.
   longer frightened.   1506 *agreeable:* suitable.
1470 *rest:* rest of their revenge.   1507 *as next:* as next of kin.

Ruin, destruction at the utmost point.
MANOA. Of ruin indeed methought I heard the noise.   1515
    Oh! it continues; they have slain my son.
CHORUS. Thy son is rather slaying them: that outcry
    From slaughter of one foe could not ascend.
MANOA. Some dismal accident it needs must be.
    What shall we do—stay here, or run and see?   1520
CHORUS. Best keep together here, lest, running thither,
    We unawares run into danger's mouth.
    This evil on the Philistines is fallen:
    From whom could else a general cry be heard?
    The sufferers, then, will scarce molest us here;   1525
    From other hands we need not much to fear.
    What if, his eye-sight (for to Israel's God
    Nothing is hard) by miracle restored,
    He now be dealing dole among his foes,
    And over heaps of slaughtered walk his way?   1530
MANOA. That were a joy presumptuous to be thought.
CHORUS. Yet God hath wrought things as incredible
    For his people of old; what hinders now?
MANOA. He can, I know, but doubt to think he will;
    Yet hope would fain subscribe, and tempts belief.   1535
    A little stay will bring some notice hither.
CHORUS. Of good or bad so great, of bad the sooner;
    For evil news rides post, while good news baits.
    And to our wish I see one hither speeding—
    An Ebrew, as I guess, and of our tribe.   1540
MESSENGER. O, whither shall I run, or which way fly
    The sight of this so horrid spectacle,
    Which erst my eyes beheld, and yet behold?
    For dire imagination still pursues me.
    But providence or instinct of nature seems,   1545
    Or reason, though disturbed and scarce consulted,
    To have guided me aright, I know not how,
    To thee first, reverend Manoa, and to these
    My countrymen, whom here I knew remaining,
    As at some distance from the place of horror,   1550
    So in the sad event too much concerned.
MANOA. The accident was loud, and here before thee
    With rueful cry; yet what it was we hear not.
    No preface needs; thou seest we long to know.
MESSENGER. It would burst forth; but I recover breath,   1555
    And sense distract, to know well what I utter.
MANOA. Tell us the sum; the circumstance defer.
MESSENGER. Gaza yet stands; but all her sons are fallen,

1515 *ruin:* collapse.   1536 *stay:* wait.
1529 *dole:* grief.   1538 *post:* swiftly; *baits:* lags.
1534 *doubt:* fear.   1543 *erst:* awhile ago.

All in a moment overwhelmed and fallen.
MANOA. Sad! but thou know'st to Israelites not saddest   1560
　　The desolation of a hostile city.
MESSENGER. Feed on that first; there may in grief be surfeit.
MANOA. Relate by whom.
MESSENGER.　　　　　　By Samson.
MANOA.　　　　　　　　　　　That still lessens
　　The sorrow, and converts it nigh to joy.
MESSENGER. Ah! Manoa, I refrain too suddenly   1565
　　To utter what will come at last too soon,
　　Lest evil tidings, with too rude irruption
　　Hitting thy aged ear, should pierce too deep.
MANOA. Suspense in news is torture; speak them out.
MESSENGER. Then take the worst in brief: Samson is dead.   1570
MANOA. The worst indeed! O, all my hope's defeated
　　To free him hence! but Death, who sets all free,
　　Hath paid his ransom now and full discharge.
　　What windy joy this day had I conceived,
　　Hopeful of his delivery, which now proves   1575
　　Abortive as the first-born bloom of spring
　　Nipt with the lagging rear of winter's frost!
　　Yet, ere I give the reins to grief, say first
　　How died he; death to life is crown or shame.
　　All by him fell, thou say'st; by whom fell he?   1580
　　What glorious hand gave Samson his death's wound?
MESSENGER. Unwounded of his enemies he fell.
MANOA. Wearied with slaughter, then, or how? explain.
MESSENGER. By his own hands.
MANOA.　　　　　　　Self-violence! What cause
　　Brought him so soon at variance with himself   1585
　　Among his foes?
MESSENGER.　　　　　Inevitable cause—
　　At once both to destroy and be destroyed.
　　The edifice, where all were met to see him,
　　Upon their heads and on his own he pulled.
MANOA. O lastly over-strong against thyself!   1590
　　A dreadful way thou took'st to thy revenge.
　　More than enough we know; but, while things yet
　　Are in confusion, give us, if thou canst,
　　Eye-witness of what first or last was done,
　　Relation more particular and distinct.   1595
MESSENGER. Occasions drew me early to this city;
　　And, as the gates I entered with sun-rise,
　　The morning trumpets festival proclaimed
　　Through each high street. Little I had dispatched,
　　When all abroad was rumored that this day   1600

1574 *windy:* vacant, transient.　　　　　　1596 *Occasions:* affairs.

Samson should be brought forth, to show the people
Proof of his mighty strength in feats and games.
I sorrowed at his captive state, but minded
Not to be absent at that spectacle.
The building was a spacious theatre,   1605
Half round on two main pillars vaulted high,
With seats where all the lords, and each degree
Of sort, might sit in order to behold;
The other side was open, where the throng
On banks and scaffolds under sky might stand: 1610
I among these aloof obscurely stood.
The feast and noon grew high, and sacrifice
Had filled their hearts with mirth, high cheer, and wine,
When to their sports they turned. Immediately
Was Samson as a public servant brought,   1615
In their state livery clad: before him pipes
And timbrels; on each side went armed guards;
Both horse and foot before him and behind,
Archers and slingers, cataphracts and spears.
At sight of him the people with a shout   1620
Rifted the air, clamouring their god with praise,
Who had made their dreadful enemy their thrall.
He patient, but undaunted, where they led him,
Came to the place; and what was set before him,
Which without help of eye might be assayed,   1625
To heave, pull, draw, or break, he still performed
All with incredible, stupendous force,
None daring to appear antagonist.
At length, for intermission sake, they led him
Between the pillars; he his guide requested   1630
(For so from such as nearer stood we heard),
As over-tired, to let him lean a while
With both his arms on those two massy pillars,
That to the arched roof gave main support.
He unsuspicious led him; which when Samson   1635
Felt in his arms, with head a while inclined,
And eyes fast fixed, he stood, as one who prayed,
Or some great matter in his mind revolved:
At last, with head erect, thus cried aloud:—
"Hitherto, Lords, what your commands imposed   1640
I have performed, as reason was, obeying,
Not without wonder or delight beheld;
Now, of my own accord, such other trial

1603 *minded:* intended.
1607 *degree:* social rank.
1610 *banks:* benches.
1616 *livery clad:* in the uniform of a ser-

vant.
1619 *cataphracts:* soldiers on armored
horses.
1621 *Rifted:* tore.

I mean to show you of my strength yet greater
As with amaze shall strike all who behold."   1645
This uttered, straining all his nerves, he bowed;
As with the force of winds and waters pent
When mountains tremble, those two massy pillars
With horrible convulsion to and fro
He tugged, he shook, till down they came, and drew   1650
The whole roof after them with burst of thunder
Upon the heads of all who sat beneath,
Lords, ladies, captains, counsellors, or priests,
Their choice nobility and flower, not only
Of this, but each Philistian city round,   1655
Met from all parts to solemnize this feast.
Samson, with these immixed, inevitably
Pulled down the same destruction on himself;
The vulgar only scaped, who stood without.
Chorus. O dearly bought revenge, yet glorious!   1660
      Living or dying thou hast fulfilled
      The work for which thou wast foretold
      To Israel, and now liest victorious
      Among thy slain self-killed;
      Not willingly, but tangled in the fold   1665
      Of dire Necessity, whose law in death conjoined
      Thee with thy slaughtered foes, in number more
      Than all thy life had slain before.
Semichorus. While their hearts were jocund and sublime,
      Drunk with idolatry, drunk with wine   1670
      And fat regorged of bulls and goats,
      Chaunting their idol, and preferring
      Before our living Dread, who dwells
      In Silo, his bright sanctuary,
      Among them he a spirit of phrenzy sent,   1675
      Who hurt their minds,
      And urged them on with mad desire
      To call in haste for their destroyer.
      They, only set on sport and play,
      Unwittingly importuned   1680
      Their own destruction to come speedy upon them.
      So fond are mortal men,
      Fallen into wrath divine,
      As their own ruin on themselves to invite,
      Insensate left, or to sense reprobate,   1685
      And with blindness internal struck.
Semichorus. But he, though blind of sight,

1659 *vulgar:* lower classes; *without:* outside.
1669 *sublime:* uplifted.
1674 *Silo:* Shiloh, where the Israelites
erected a tabernacle, the "bright sanctuary."
1682 *fond:* foolish.

Despised, and thought extinguished quite,
With inward eyes illuminated,
His fiery virtue roused   1690
From under ashes into sudden flame,
And as an evening dragon came,
Assailant on the perched roosts
And nests in order ranged
Of tame villatic fowl, but as an eagle   1695
His cloudless thunder bolted on their heads.
So Virtue, given for lost,
Depressed and overthrown, as seemed,
Like that self-begotten bird
In the Arabian woods embost,   1700
That no second knows nor third,
And lay erewhile a holocaust,
From out her ashy womb now teemed,
Revives, reflourishes, then vigorous most
When most unactive deemed;   1705
And, though her body die, her fame survives,
A secular bird, ages of lives.
MANOA. Come, come, no time for lamentation now,
Nor much more cause. Somson hath quit himself
Like Samson, and heroicly hath finished   1710
A life heroic, on his enemies
Fully revenged—hath left them years of mourning,
And lamentation to the sons of Caphtor
Through all Philistian bounds; to Israel
Honour hath left and freedom, let but them   1715
Find courage to lay hold on this occasion;
To himself and father's houses eternal fame;
And, which is best and happiest yet, all this
With God not parted from him, as was feared,
But favouring and assisting to the end.   1720
Nothing is here for tears, nothing to wail
Or knock the breast; no weakness, no contempt,
Dispraise, or blame; nothing but well and fair,
And what may quiet us in a death so noble.
Let us go find the body where it lies   1725
Soaked in his enemies' blood, and from the stream
With lavers pure, and cleansing herbs, wash off
The clotted gore. I, with what speed the while
(Gaza is not in plight to say us nay),

1692 *dragon:* serpent.
1695 *villatic:* farmyard.
1699 *self-begotten bird:* the Phoenix which, destroyed by fire, rises from its own ashes every 500 years.
1707 *secular:* existing centuries (*secle=* century).
1709 *quit:* acquitted.
1713 *sons of Caphtor:* the Phillistines.
1728 *with what speed the while:* as quickly as I can.

Will send for all my kindred, all my friends, 1730
To fetch him hence, and solemnly attend,
With silent obsequy and funeral train,
Home to his father's house.   There will I build him
A monument, and plant it round with shade
Of laurel ever green and branching palm, 1735
With all his trophies hung, and acts enrolled
In copious legend, or sweet lyric song
Thither shall all the valiant youth resort,
And from his memory inflame their breasts
To matchless valour and adventures high; 1740
The virgins also shall, on feastful days,
Visit his tomb with flowers, only bewailing
His lot unfortunate in nuptial choice,
From whence captivity and loss of eyes.
CHORUS. All is best, though we oft doubt 1745
What the unsearchable dispose
Of Highest Wisdom brings about,
And ever best found in the close.
Oft He seems to hide his face,
But unexpectedly returns, 1750
And to his faithful champion hath in place
Bore witness gloriously; whence Gaza mourns,
And all that band them to resist
His uncontrollable intent.
His servants He, with new acquist 1755
Of true experience from this great event,
With peace and consolation hath dismissed,
And calm of mind, all passion spent.

1746 *dispose:* dispensation.   1751 *in place:* in this place.
1748 *close:* end.   1755 *acquist:* acquisition.

Biographical Note

SYNGE

JOHN MILLINGTON SYNGE (1871–1909) was born in Dublin, the son of a lawyer who died a year later, leaving Synge to be raised by his mother. Educated partly at home, partly in private schools, Synge entered Trinity College, Dublin, in 1888 where he studied languages and music. After graduating with honors he left for Germany to study music but instead spent the period from 1893 to 1898 primarily in Paris, studying languages at the Sorbonne, writing verse imitative of continental styles, and doing some free-lance journalism for English newspapers. There he met the vacationing Irish poet W. B. Yeats, who urged Synge to set his literary sights on Irish subjects and spoke enthusiastically of the Irish Literary Theatre which he and Lady Gregory were founding. From 1898 to 1902 Synge spent his summers in the Aran Islands off the west coast of Ireland absorbing the distinctive rhythms and phrasings of the Aran fisher folk and recording his impressions of their hard, simple life (these were published in 1907 as *The Aran Islands*). In 1902 he wrote *Riders to the Sea* and *The Shadow of the Glen,* which greatly offended Irish womanhood by depicting a lonely young woman abandoning her unpleasant older husband in favor of a passing tramp. In 1907 he wrote his comic masterpiece *The Playboy of the Western World* and *The Tinker's Wedding.* When he died in 1909 of Hodgkins Disease he was working on a romantic tragedy called *Deirdre of the Sorrows.*

Riders to the Sea

john millington synge

CHARACTERS

MAURYA, *an old woman.*
BARTLEY, *her son.*

CATHLEEN, *her daughter.*
NORA, *a younger daughter.*
MEN *and* WOMEN.

SCENE: *An island of the West of Ireland. Cottage kitchen, with nets, oilskins spinning-wheel, some new boards standing by the wall, etc.* CATHLEEN, *a girl of about twenty, finishes kneading cake, and puts it down in the pot-oven by the fire; then wipes her hands, and begins to spin at the wheel.* NORA, *a young girl, puts her head in at the door.*

NORA. [*In a low voice.*] Where is she?
CATHLEEN. She's lying down, God help her, and may be sleeping, if she's able.
[NORA *comes in softly, and takes a bundle from under her shawl.*]
CATHLEEN. [*Spinning the wheel rapidly.*]
What is it you have?
NORA. The young priest is after bringing them. It's a shirt and a plain stocking were got off a drowned man in Donegal.
[CATHLEEN. *stops her wheel with a sudden movement, and leans out to listen.*]
NORA. We're to find out if it's Michael's they are, some time herself will be down looking by the sea.
CATHLEEN. How would they be Michael's, Nora? How would he go the length of that way to the far north?
NORA. The young priest says he's known the like of it. "If it's Michael's they are," says he, "you can tell herself he's got a clean burial by the grace of God, and if they're not his let no one say a word about them, for she'll be getting her death,"
[*The door which* NORA *half closed is blown open by a gust of wind.*]
CATHLEEN. [*Looking out anxiously.*] Did you ask him would he

213

stop Bartley going this day with the horses to the Galway fair?

NORA. "I won't stop him," says he, "but let you not be afraid. Herself does be saying prayers half through the night, and the Almighty God won't leave her destitute," says he, "with no son living."

CATHLEEN. Is the sea bad by the white rocks, Nora?

NORA. Middling bad, God help us. There's a great roaring in the west, and it is worse it'll be getting when the tide's turned to the wind. [*She goes over to the table with the bundle.*] Shall I open it now?

CATHLEEN. Maybe she'd wake up on us, and come in before we'd done. [*Coming to the table.*] It is a long time we'll be and the two of us crying.

NORA. [*Goes to the inner door and listens.*] She's moving about on the bed. She'll be coming in a minute.

CATHLEEN. Give me the ladder, and I'll put them up in the turf-loft, the way she won't know of them at all, and maybe when the tide turns she'll be going down to see would he be floating from the east.

[*They put the ladder against the gable of the chimney;* CATHLEEN *goes up few steps and hides the bundle in the turf-loft.* MAURYA *comes in from the inner room.*]

MAURYA. [*Looking up at* CATHLEEN *and speaking querulously.*] Isn't it turf enough you have for this day and evening?

CATHLEEN. There's a cake baking at the fire for a short space [*Throwing the down the turf.*] and Bartley will want it when the tide turns if he goes to Connemara.

[NORA *picks up the turf and puts it round the pot-oven.*]

MAURYA. [*Sitting down on a stool at the fire.*] He won't go this day with the wind rising from the south and west. He won't go this day, for the young priest will stop him surely.

NORA. He'll not stop him. Mother, and I heard Eamon Simon and Stephen Pheety and Colum Shawn saying he would go.

MAURYA. Where is he itself?

NORA. He went down to see would there be another boat sailing in the week and I'm thinking it won't be long till he's here now for the tide's turning at the green head, and the hooker's tacking from the east.

CATHLEEN. I hear some one passing the big stones.

NORA. [*Looking out.*] He's coming now, and he in a hurry.

BARTLEY [*Comes in and looks round the room. Speaking sadly and quietly.*] Where is the bit of new rope, Cathleen, was bought in Connemara?

CATHLEEN. [*Coming down.*] Give it to him, Nora; it's on a nail by the white boards. I hung it up this morning, for the pig with the black feet was eating it.

NORA. [*Giving him a rope.*] Is that it, Bartley?

MAURYA. You'd do right to leave that rope, Bartley, hanging by the boards. [BARTLEY *takes the rope.*] It will be wanting in this place, I'm telling you, if Michael is washed up tomorrow morning, or the next morning, or any morning in the week, for it's a deep grave we'll make him by the grace of God.

BARTLEY. [*Beginning to work with the rope.*] I've no halter the way I can ride down on the mare, and I must go now quickly. This is the one boat going for two weeks or beyond it, and the fair will be a good fair for horses. I heard them saying below.

MAURYA. It's a hard thing they'll be saying below if the body is washed up and there's no man in it to make the coffin, and I after giving a big price for the finest white boards you'd find in Connemara.

[*She looks around at the boards.*]

BARTLEY. How would it be washed up, and we after looking each day for nine days, and a strong wind blowing a while back from the west and south?

MAURYA. If it wasn't found itself, that wind is raising the sea, and there was a star up against the moon, and it rising in the night. If it was a hundred horses, or a thousand horses you had itself, what is the price of a thousand horses against a son where there is one son only?

BARTLEY. [*Working at the halter, to* CATHLEEN.] Let you go down each day, and see the sheep aren't jumping in on the rye, and it the jobber comes you can sell the pig with the black feet if there is a good price going.

MAURYA. How would the like of her get a good price for a pig?

BARTLEY. [*To* CATHLEEN.] If the west wind holds with the last bit of the moon let you and Nora get up weed enough for another cock for the kelp. It's hard set we'll be from this day with no one in it but one man to work.

MAURYA. It's hard set we'll be surely the day you're drownd'd with the rest. What way will I live and the girls with me, and I an old woman looking for the grave?

[BARTLEY *lays down the halter, takes off his old coat, and puts on a newer one of the same flannel.*]

BARTLEY. [*To* NORA.] Is she coming to the pier?

NORA. [*Looking out.*] She's passing the green head and letting fall her sails.

BARTLEY. [*Getting his purse and tobacco.*] I'll have half an hour to go down, and you'll see me coming again in two days, or in three days, or maybe in four days if the wind is bad.

MAURYA. [*Turning around to the fire, and putting her shawl over her head.*] Isn't it a hard and cruel man won't hear a word from an old woman, and she holding him from the sea?

CATHLEEN. It's the life of a young man to be going on the sea, and who would listen to an old woman with one thing and she saying it over?

BARTLEY. [*Taking the halter.*] I must go now quickly. I'll ride down on the red mare, and the gray pony'll run behind me . . . The blessing of God on you.

[*He goes out.*]

MAURYA. [*Crying out as he is in the door.*] He's gone now, God spare us, and we'll not see him again. He's gone now, and when the black night is falling I'll have no son left me in the world.

CATHLEEN. Why wouldn't you give him your blessing and he looking round in the door? Isn't it sorrow enough is on every one in this house without your sending him out with an unlucky word behind him, and a hard word in his ear?

[MAURYA *takes up the tongs and begins raking the fire aimlessly without looking around.*]

NORA. [*Turning toward her.*] You're taking away the turf from the cake.

CATHLEEN. [*Crying out.*] The Son of God forgive us, Nora, we're after forgetting his bit of bread. [*She comes over to the fire.*]

NORA. And it's destroyed he'll be going till dark night, and he after eating nothing since the sun went up.

CATHLEEN. [*Turning the cake out of the oven.*] It's destroyed he'll be, surely. There's no sense left in any person in a house where an old woman will be talking forever.

[MAURYA *sways herself on her stool.*]

CATHLEEN. [*Cutting off some of the bread and rolling it in a cloth; to* MAURYA.] Let you go down now to the spring well and give him this and he passing. You'll see him then and the dark word will be broken, and you can say "God speed you," the way he'll be easy in his mind.

MAURYA. [*Taking the bread.*] Will I be in it as soon as himself?

CATHLEEN. If you go now quickly.

MAURYA. [*Standing up unsteadily.*] It's hard set I am to walk.

CATHLEEN. [*Looking at her anxiously.*] Give her the stick, Nora, or maybe she'll slip on the big stones.

NORA. What stick?

CATHLEEN. The stick Michael brought from Connemara.

MAURYA. [*Taking a stick* NORA *gives her.*] In the big world the old people do be leaving things after them for their sons and children, but in this place it is the young men do be leaving things behind for them that do be old.

[*She goes out slowly.* NORA *goes over to the ladder.*]

CATHLEEN. Wait, Nora, maybe she'd turn back quickly. She's that sorry, God help her, you wouldn't know the thing she'd do.

NORA. Is she gone round by the bush?

CATHLEEN. [*Looking out.*] She's gone now. Throw it down quickly, for the Lord knows when she'll be out of it again.

NORA. [*Getting the bundle from the left.*] The young priest said
   he'd be passing tomorrow, and we might go down and speak
   to him below if it's Michael's they are surely.
CATHLEEN. [*Taking the bundle.*] Did he say what way they were
   found?
NORA. [*Coming down.*] "There were two men," says he, "and they
   rowing round with poteen before the cocks crowed, and the
   oar of one of them caught the body, and they passing the black
   cliffs of the north."
CATHLEEN. [*Trying to open the bundle.*] Give me a knife, Nora,
   the string's perished with the salt water, and here's a black
   knot on it you wouldn't loosen in a week.
NORA. [*Giving her a knife.*] I've heard tell it was a long way to
   Donegal.
CATHLEEN. [*Cutting the string.*] It is surely. There was a man in
   here a while ago—the man sold us that knife—and he said
   if you set off walking from the rocks beyond, it would be seven
   days you'd be in Donegal.
NORA. And what time would a man take, and he floating?
[CATHLEEN *opens the bundle and takes out a bit of stocking. They
look at them eagerly.*]
CATHLEEN. [*In a low voice.*] The Lord spare us, Nora! Isn't it a
   queer hard thing to say if it's his they are surely?
NORA. I'll get his shirt off the hook the way we can put the one
   flannel on the other [*She looks through some clothes hanging
   in the corner.*] It's not with them, Cathleen, and where will
   it be?
CATHLEEN. I'm thinking Bartley put it on him in the morning, for
   his own shirt was heavy with the salt in it. [*Pointing to the
   corner.*] There's a bit of a sleeve was of the same stuff. Give
   me that and it will do.
[NORA *brings it to her and they compare the flannel.*]
CATHLEEN. It's the same stuff, Nora; but if it is itself aren't there
   great rolls of it in the shops of Galway, and isn't it many
   another man may have a shirt of it as well as Michael himself?
NORA. [*Who has taken up the stocking and counted the stitches,
   crying out.*] It's Michael, Cathleen, it's Michael; God spare his
   soul, and what will herself say when she hears this story, and
   Bartley on the sea?
CATHLEEN. [*Taking the stocking.*] It's a plain stocking.
NORA. It's the second one of the third pair I knitted, and I put up
   three score stitches, and I dropped four of them.
CATHLEEN. [*Counts the stitches.*] It's that number is in it. [*Crying
   out.*] Ah, Nora, isn't it a bitter thing to think of him floating
   that way to the far north, and no one to keen him but the
   black hags that do be flying on the sea?
NORA. [*Swinging herself around, and throwing out her arms on the*

clothes.] And isn't it a pitiful thing when there is nothing left of a man who was a great rower and fisher, but a bit of an old shirt and a plain stocking?

CATHLEEN. [*After an instant.*] Tell me, is herself coming, Nora? I hear a little sound on the path.

NORA. [*Looking out.*] She is, Cathleen. She's coming up to the door.

CATHLEEN. Put these things away before she'll come in. Maybe it's easier she'll be after giving her blessing to Bartley, and we won't let on we've heard anything the time he's on the sea.

NORA. [*Helping* CATHLEEN *to close the bundle.*] We'll put them here in the corner.

[*They put them into a hole in the chimney corner.* CATHLEEN *goes back to the spinning-wheel.*]

NORA. Will she see it was crying I was?

CATHLEEN. Keep your back to the door the way the light'll not be on you.

[NORA *sits down at the chimney corner, with her back to the door.* MAURYA *comes in very slowly, without looking at the girls, and goes over to her stool at the other side of the fire. The cloth with the bread is still in her hand. The girls look at each other, and* NORA *points to the bundle of bread.*]

CATHLEEN. [*After spinning for a moment.*] You didn't give him his bit of bread?

[MAURYA *begins to keen softly, without turning around.*]

CATHLEEN. Did you see him riding down?

[MAURYA *goes on keening.*]

CATHLEEN. [*A little impatiently.*] God forgive you; isn't it a better thing to raise your voice and tell what you seen, than to be making lamentation for a thing that's done? Did you see Bartley, I'm saying to you.

MAURYA. [*With a weak voice.*] My heart's broken from this day.

CATHLEEN. [*As before.*] Did you see Bartley?

MAURYA. I seen the fearfulest thing.

CATHLEEN. [*Leaves her wheel and looks out.*] God forgive you; he's riding the mare now over the green head, and the gray pony behind him.

MAURYA. [*Starts, so that her shawl falls back from her head and shows her white tossed hair. With a frightened voice.*] The gray pony behind him.

CATHLEEN. [*Coming to the fire.*] What is it ails you, at all?

MAURYA. [*Speaking very slowly.*] I've seen the fearfulest thing any person has seen, since the day Bride Dara seen the dead man with the child in his arms.

CATHLEEN and NORA. Uah.

[*They crouch down in front of the old woman at the fire.*]

NORA. Tell us what it is you seen.

MAURYA. I went down to the spring well, and I stood there saying a prayer to myself. Then Bartley came along, and he riding on the red mare with the gray pony behind him. [*She puts up her hands, as if to hide something from her eyes.*] The Son of God spare us, Nora!

CATHLEEN. What is it you seen?

MAURYA. I seen Michael himself.

CATHLEEN. [*Speaking softly.*] You did not, Mother. It wasn't Michael you seen, for his body is after being found in the far north, and he's got a clean burial by the grace of God.

MAURYA. [*A little defiantly.*] I'm after seeing him this day, and he riding and galloping. Bartley came first on the red mare; and I tried to say "God speed you," but something choked the words in my throat. He went by quickly; and "the blessing of God on you," says he, and could say nothing. I looked up then, and I crying, at the gray pony, and there was Michael upon it—with fine clothes on him, and new shoes on his feet.

CATHLEEN. [*Begins to keen.*] It's destroyed we are from this day. It's destroyed, surely.

NORA. Didn't the young priest say the Almighty God wouldn't leave her destitute with no son living?

MAURYA. [*In a low voice, but clearly.*] It's little the like of him knows of the sea.... Bartley will be lost now, and let you call in Eamon and make me a good coffin out of the white boards, for I won't live after them. I've had a husband, and a husband's father, and six sons in this house—six fine men, though it was a hard birth I had with every one of them and they coming to the world—and some of them were found and some of them were not found, but they're gone now, the lot of them.... There were Stephen, and Shawn, were lost in the great wind, and found after in the Bay of Gregory of the Golden Mouth, and carried up the two of them on the one plank, and in by that door.

[*She pauses for a moment. The girls start as if they heard something through the door that is half open behind them.*]

NORA. [*In a whisper.*] Did you hear that, Cathleen? Did you hear a noise in the northeast?

CATHLEEN. [*In a whisper.*] There's some one after crying out by the seashore.

MAURYA. [*Continues without hearing anything.*] There was Sheamus and his father, and his own father again, were lost in a dark night, and not a stick or sign was seen of them when the sun went up. There was Patch after was drowned out of a curagh that turned over. I was sitting here with Bartley, and he a baby, lying on my two knees, and I seen two women, and three women, and four women coming in, and they crossing themselves, and not saying a word. I looked out then, and there were men coming after them, and they holding a thing in the half of a red sail, and water dripping out of it—it was a dry day, Nora—and leaving a track to the door.

[*She pause again with her hand stretched out toward the door. It opens softly and* OLD WOMEN *begin to come in, crossing themselves on the threshold, and kneeling down in front of the stage with red petticoats over their heads.*]

MAURYA. [*Half in a dream, to* CATHLEEN.] Is it Patch, or Michael, or what is it at all?

CATHLEEN. Michael is after being found in the far north, and when he is found there how could he be here in this place?

MAURYA. There does be a power of young men floating round in the sea, and what way would they know if it was Michael they had, or another man like him, for when a man is nine days in the sea, and the wind blowing, it's hard set his own mother would be to say what man was it.

CATHLEEN. It's Michael, God spare him, for they're after sending us a bit of clothes from the far north.

[*She reaches out and hands* MAURYA *the clothes that belong to* MICHAEL. MAURYA *stands up slowly, and takes them in her hands.* NORA *looks out.*]

NORA. They're carrying a thing among them and there's water dripping out of it and leaving a track by the big stones.

CATHLEEN. [*In a whisper to the* WOMEN *who have come in.*] Is it Bartley it is?

ONE OF THE WOMEN. It is surely, God rest his soul.

[*Two* YOUNGER WOMEN *come in and pull out the table. Then* MEN *carry in the body of* BARTLEY, *laid on a plank, with a bit of a sail over it, and lay it on the table.*]

CATHLEEN. [*To the* WOMEN, *as they are doing so.*] What way was he drowned?

ONE OF THE WOMEN. The gray pony knocked him into the sea, and he was washed out where there is a great surf on the white rocks.

[MAURYA *has gone over and knelt down at the head of the table. The* WOMEN *are keening softly and swaying themselves with a slow movement.* CATHLEEN *and* NORA *kneel at the other end of the table. The* MEN *kneel near the door.*]

MAURYA. [*Raising her head and speaking as if she did not see the people around her.*] They're all gone now, and there isn't anything more the sea can do to me. . . . I'll have no call now to be up crying and praying when the wind breaks from the south, and you can hear the surf is in the east, and the surf is in the west, making a great stir with the two noises, and they hitting one on the other. I'll have no call now to be going down and getting Holy Water in the dark nights after Samhain, and I won't care what way the sea is when the other women will be keening. [*To* NORA.] Give me the Holy Water, Nora, there's a small sup still on the dresser. [NORA *gives it to her.*]

MAURYA. [*Drops* MICHAEL's *clothes across* BARTLEY's *feet, and sprinkles the Holy Water over him.*] It isn't that I haven't prayed for you, Bartley, to the Almighty God. It isn't that I haven't said prayers in the dark night till you wouldn't know what I'd be saying; but it's a great rest I'll have now, and it's time surely. It's a great rest I'll have now, and great sleeping in the long nights after Samhain, if it's only a bit of wet flour we do have to eat, and maybe a fish that would be stinking.

[*She kneels down again, crossing herself, and saying prayers under her breath.*]

CATHLEEN. [*To an* OLD MAN.] Maybe yourself and Eamon would make a coffin when the sun rises. We have fine white boards herself bought, God help her, thinking Michael would be found, and I have a new cake you can eat while you'll be working.

THE OLD MAN. [*Looking at the boards.*] Are there nails with them?

CATHLEEN. There are not, Colum; we didn't think of the nails.

ANOTHER MAN. It's a great wonder she wouldn't think of the nails, and all the coffins she's seen made already.

CATHLEEN. It's getting old she is, and broken.

[MAURYA *stands up again very slowly and spreads out the pieces of* MICHAEL's *clothes beside the body, sprinkling them with the last of the Holy Water.*]

NORA. [*In a whisper to* CATHLEEN.] She's quiet now, and easy; but the day Michael was drowned you could hear her crying out from this to the spring well. It's fonder she was of Michael, and would any one have thought that?

CATHLEEN. [*Slowly and clearly.*] An old woman will be soon tired with anything she will do, and isn't it nine days herself is after crying and keening, and making great sorrow in the house?

MAURYA. [*Puts the empty cup mouth downwards on the table, and lays her hands together on* BARTLEY's *feet.*] They're all together this time, and the end is come. May the Almighty God have mercy on Bartley's soul, and on Michael's soul, and on the souls of Sheamus and Patch, and Stephen and Shawn. [*Bending her head.*] And may He have mercy on my soul, Nora, and on the soul of every one is left living in the world.

[*She pauses, and the keen rises a little more loudly from the* WOMEN, *then sinks away.*]

MAURYA. [*Continuing.*] Michael has a clean burial in the far north, by the grace of the Almighty God. Bartley will have a fine coffin out of the white boards, and a deep grave surely. What more can we want than that? No man at all can be living forever, and we must be satisfied.

[*She kneels down again and the* CURTAIN *falls slowly.*]

Biographical Note

YEATS

WILLIAM BUTLER YEATS (1865–1939), son of the distinguished artist John Butler Yeats, was born in Dublin and educated in London and Dublin. His early interest in art shifted while he was in his twenties from painting to writing. Yeats is best known for his lyric poetry; T. S. Eliot once called him the finest lyric poet of our time, perhaps of all time. Nevertheless Yeats wrote more than thirty plays during his life, plays in which he, like Eliot himself, helped bring about a reconciliation between poetry and drama after their long theatrical estrangement. Most of his plays were written for the Irish Literary Theater (the Abbey Theater, as it was called) which he and Lady Gregory founded in the hope that it would become the center of the Irish literary renaissance. Though the Abbey Theater became both famous and notorious as the vehicle for the plays of Yeats and John Millington Synge, the poetic drama that Yeats longed for never got firmly established. His own plays reflect his interests in magic and the occult, his belief in a spiritual reality accessible in part through dream, reverie, and the artistic imagination; and his urge to unite the myths and legends of pagan Ireland to the technical resources and forms of the oriental theater.

Some of Yeats' early plays, based largely on Irish legends, are *The Countess Kathleen* (1889–92), *The Land of Heart's Desire* (1894), and *On Baile's Strand* (1903). Some of his later plays based on the Noh drama are *At the Hawk's Well* (1916), *The Only Jealousy of Emer* (1918), and *The Dreaming of the Bones* (1918).

Purgatory

william butler yeats

CHARACTERS

A BOY   AN OLD MAN

SCENE: *A ruined house and a bare tree in the background.*

BOY. Half door, hall door,
    Hither and thither day and night,
    Hill or hollow, shouldering this pack,
    Hearing you talk.
OLD MAN.   Study that house.
    I think about its jokes and stories;   5
    I try to remember what the butler
    Said to a drunken gamekeeper
    In mid-October, but I cannot.
    If I cannot, none living can.
    Where are the jokes and stories of a house,   10
    Its threshold gone to patch a pigsty?
BOY. So you have come this path before?
OLD MAN. The moonlight falls upon the path,
    The shadow of a cloud upon the house,
    And that's symbolical; study that tree,   15
    What is it like?
BOY.   A silly old man.
OLD MAN. It's like—no matter what it's like.
    I saw it a year ago stripped bare as now,
    So I chose a better trade.
    I saw it fifty years ago   20

Before the thunderbolt had riven it,
Green leaves, ripe leaves, leaves thick as butter,
Fat, greasy life. Stand there and look,
Because there is somebody in that house.

[*The* BOY *puts down pack and stands in the doorway.*]

BOY. There's nobody here.   25
OLD MAN. There's somebody there.
BOY. The floor is gone, the windows gone,
    And where there should be roof there's sky,
    And here's a bit of an egg shell thrown
    Out of a jackdaw's nest.
OLD MAN.   But there are some   30
    That do not care what's gone, what's left:
    The souls in Purgatory that come back
    To habitations and familiar spots.
BOY. Your wits are out again.
OLD MAN.   Relive
    Their transgressions, and that not once   35
    But many times; they know at last
    The consequence of those transgressions
    Whether upon others or upon themselves;
    Upon others, others may bring help,
    For when the consequence is at an end   40
    The dream must end; if upon themselves,
    There is no help but in themselves
    And in the mercy of God.
BOY.   I have had enough!
    Talk to the jackdaws, if talk you must.
OLD MAN. Stop! Sit there upon that stone.   45
    That is the house where I was born.
BOY. The big old house that was burnt down?
OLD MAN. My mother that was your grand-dam owned it,
    This scenery and this countryside,
    Kennel and stable, horse and hound—   50
    She had a horse at the Curragh, and there met
    My father, a groom in a training stable,
    Looked at him and married him.
    Her mother never spoke to her again,
    And she did right.
BOY.   What's right and wrong?   55
    My granddad got the girl and the money.
OLD MAN. Looked at him and married him,
    And he squandered everything she had.
    She never knew the worst, because
    She died in giving birth to me,   60
    But now she knows it all, being dead.

Great people lived and died in this house;
Magistrates, colonels, members of Parliament,
Captains and Governors, and long ago
Men that had fought at Aughrim and the Boyne.   65
Some that had gone on Government work
To London or to India came home to die,
Or came from London every spring
To look at the mayblossom in the park.
They had loved the trees that he cut down   70
To pay what he had lost at cards
Or spent on horses, drink and women;
Had loved the house, had loved all
The intricate passages of the house,
But he killed the house; to kill a house   75
Where great men grew up, married, died,
I here declare a capital offence.
BOY. My God, but you had luck! Grand clothes,
And maybe a grand horse to ride.
OLD MAN. That he might keep me upon his level   80
He never sent me to school, but some
Half-loved me for my half of her:
A gamekeeper's wife taught me to read,
A Catholic curate taught me Latin.
There were old books and books made fine   85
By eighteenth-century French binding, books
Modern and ancient, books by the ton.
BOY. What education have you given me?
OLD MAN. I gave the education that befits
A bastard that a pedlar got   90
Upon a tinker's daughter in a ditch.
When I had come to sixteen years old
My father burned down the house when drunk.
BOY. But that is my age, sixteen years old,
At the Puck Fair.
OLD MAN.   And everything was burnt;   95
Books, library, all were burnt;
BOY. Is what I have heard upon the road the truth,
That you killed him in the burning house?
OLD MAN. There's nobody here but our two selves?
BOY. Nobody, Father.
OLD MAN.   I stuck him with a knife,   100
That knife that cuts my dinner now,
And after that I left him in the fire.
They dragged him out, somebody saw
The knife-wound but could not be certain
Because the body was all black and charred.   105
Then some that were his drunken friends
Swore they would put me upon trial,

    Spoke of quarrels, a threat I had made.
    The gamekeeper gave me some old clothes,
    I ran away, worked here and there   110
    Till I became a pedlar on the roads,
    No good trade, but good enough
    Because I am my father's son,
    Because of what I did or may do.
    Listen to the hoof beats; Listen, listen!   115
BOY. I cannot hear a sound.
OLD MAN.   Beat! Beat!
    This night is the anniversary
    Of my mother's wedding night,
    Or of the night wherein I was begotten.
    My father is riding from the public house,   120
    A whiskey-bottle under his arm.

[A window is lit showing a young girl.]

    Look at the window; she stands there
    Listening, the servants are all in bed,
    She is alone, he has stayed late
    Bragging and drinking in the public house   125
BOY. There's nothing but an empty gap in the wall.
    You have made it up. No, you are mad!
    You are getting madder every day.
OLD MAN. It's louder now because he rides
    Upon a gravelled avenue   130
    All grass to-day. The hoof-beat stops,
    He has gone to the other side of the house,
    Gone to the stable, put the horse up.
    She has gone down to open the door.
    This night she is no better than her man   135
    And does not mind that he is half drunk,
    She is mad about him. They mount the stairs,
    She brings him into her own chamber.
    And that is the marriage-chamber now.
    The window is dimly lit again.   140
    Do not let him touch you! It is not true
    That drunken men cannot beget,
    And if he touch he must beget
    And you must bear his murderer.
    Deaf! Both deaf! If I should throw   145
    A stick or a stone they would not hear;
    And that's a proof my wits are out.
    But there's a problem: she must live
    Through everything in exact detail,
    Driven to it by remorse, and yet   150
    Can she renew the sexual act

And find no pleasure in it, and if not,
If pleasure and remorse must both be there,
Which is the greater? I lack schooling.
Go fetch Tertullian; he and I   155
Will ravel all that problem out
Whilst those two lie upon the mattress
Begetting me.   Come back! Come back!
And so you thought to slip away,
My bag of money between your fingers,   160
And that I could not talk and see!
You have been rummaging in the pack.

[*The light in the window has faded out.*]

BOY. You never gave me my right share.
OLD MAN. And had I given it, young as you are,
      You would have spent it upon drink.   165
BOY. What if I did? I had a right
      To get it and spend it as I chose.
OLD MAN. Give me that bag and no more words.
BOY. I will not.
OLD MAN.   I will break your fingers.

[*They struggle for the bag. In the struggle it drops, scattering the
money. The* OLD MAN *staggers but does not fall. They stand looking at each other. The window is lit up. A man is seen pouring
whiskey into a glass.*]

BOY. What if I killed you? You killed my grand-dad,   170
      Because you were young and he was old.
      Now I am young and you are old.
OLD MAN [*staring at window.*] Better looking, those sixteen years—
BOY. What are you muttering?
OLD MAN.   Younger—and yet
      She should have known he was not her kind.   175
BOY. What are you saying? Out with it! [OLD MAN *points to
      window.*]
      My God! The window is lit up
      And somebody stands there, although
      The floorboards are all burnt away.
OLD MAN. The window is lit up because my father   180
      Has come to find a glass for his whiskey.
      He leans there like some tired beast.
BOY. A dead, living, murdered man!
OLD MAN. "Then the bride-sleep fell upon Adam":
      Where did I read those words?
                              And yet   185
      There's nothing leaning in the window

But the impression upon my mother's mind;
Being dead she is alone in her remorse.
Boy. A body that was a bundle of old bones
Before I was born. Horrible! Horrible! [*He covers his eyes.*]   190
Old Man. That beast there would know nothing, being nothing,
If I should kill a man under the window
He would not even turn his head.

[*He stabs the* Boy.]

My father and my son on the same jack-knife!
That finishes—there—there—there—

[*He stabs again and again. The window grows dark.*]

"Hush-a-bye baby, thy father's a knight,   195
Thy mother a lady, lovely and bright."
No, that is something that I read in a book,
And if I sing it must be to my mother,
And I lack rhyme.

[*The stage has grown dark except where the tree stands in white
light.*]

Study that tree.   200
It stands there like a purified soul,
All old, sweet, glistening light.
Dear mother, the window is dark again,
But you are in the light because
I finished all that consequence.   205
I killed that lad because had he grown up
He would have struck a woman's fancy,
Begot, and passed pollution on.
I am a wretched foul old man
And therefore harmless. When I have stuck   210
This old jack-knife into a sod
And pulled it out all bright again,
And picked up all the money that he dropped,
I'll to a distant place, and there
Tell my old jokes among new men.   215

[*He cleans the knife and begins to pick up money.*]

Hoof beats! Dear God,
How quickly it returns—beat—beat—!
Her mind cannot hold up that dream.
Twice a murderer and all for nothing,

And she must animate that dead night   220
Not once but many times! O God,
Release my mother's soul from its dream!
Mankind can do no more. Appease
The misery of the living and the remorse of the dead.

Biographical Note

O'NEILL

EUGENE O'NEILL (1888–1953) was fittingly born on Broadway in New York City, the son of a well known actor, James O'Neill. His early years were spent in various boarding schools and with his theatrical family on tour. After a year at Princeton, from which he was suspended in 1907, he took various office jobs, got married, and took ship for Central America to prospect for gold. He worked for a time on freighters, spent awhile in Brazil, then returned to the United States where he was taken into his father's acting company to do bit parts and office work. In 1912, after working as a reporter for the New London *Telegraph,* he was hospitalized for tuberculosis. While recuperating, he wrote his first play, *The Web,* and in the following year, at his father's expense, he published a collection of one-act plays, *Thirst and Other One-Act Plays.* He enrolled in a drama workshop course at Harvard, where he was encouraged by Professor George Pierce Baker; nevertheless he soon left the workshop to become associated with the Provincetown Players, who produced several of his plays. *Beyond the Horizon,* his first Broadway production, received the Pulitzer Prize in 1920, as did *Anna Christie* the following year.

O'Neill's earliest plays were realistic, but he quickly revolted against conventional dramatic techniques. In the 1920s and 1930s he was America's leading dramatist, turning out an uninterrupted stream of plays in which he constantly experimented with realism, expressionism, naturalism, and impressionism. In 1936 he was awarded the Nobel Prize in Literature. For the next ten years he disappeared from the theatrical scene, busying himself with a cycle of nine plays in which he hoped to dramatize American life and society. This project was abandoned because of illness. In 1946 *The Iceman Cometh,* written in 1929, was produced and well-received, but *A Moon for the Misbegotten,* written in 1943, closed after only a few performances in 1947. No more plays were produced in his lifetime. After his death the autobiographical *Long Day's Journey into Night,* written in 1941, generated an O'Neill revival when it was performed in Stockholm and New York in 1956.

Desire Under the Elms

eugene o'neill

CHARACTERS

EPHRAIM CABOT.
SIMON
PETER } *his sons.*
EBEN

ABBIE PUTNAM.
a SHERIFF, *and other folk from the neighboring farms.*
Young GIRL, *two* FARMERS, *the* FIDDLER,

The action of the entire play takes place in, and immediately outside of, the Cabot farmhouse in New England, in the year 1850. The south end of the house faces front to a stone wall with a wooden gate at center opening on a country road. The house is in good condition but in need of paint. Its walls are a sickly grayish, the green of the shutters faded. Two enormous elms are on each side of the house. They bend their trailing branches down over the roof. They appear to protect and at the same time subdue. There is a sinister maternity in their aspect, a crushing, jealous absorption. They have developed from their intimate contact with the life of man in the house an appalling humaneness. They brood oppressively over the house. They are like exhausted women resting their sagging breasts and hands and hair on its roof, and when it rains their tears trickle down monotonously and rot on the shingles.

There is a path running from the gate around the right corner of the house to the front door. A narrow porch is on this side. The end wall facing us has two windows in its upper story, two larger ones on the floor below. The two upper are those of the father's bedroom and that of the brothers. On the left, ground floors, is the kitchen—on the right, the parlor, the shades of which are always drawn down.

PART I

SCENE I

Exterior of the farmhouse. It is sunset of a day at the beginning of summer in the year 1850. There is no wind and everything is still. The sky above the roof is suffused with deep colors, the green of the elms glows, but the house is in shadow, seeming pale and washed out by contrast.

A door opens and Eben Cabot *comes to the end of the porch and stands looking down the road to the right. He has a large bell in his hand and this he swings mechanically, awakening a deafening clangor. Then he puts his hands on his hips and stares up at the sky. He sighs with a puzzled awe and blurts out with halting appreciation.*

Eben. God! Purty! [*His eyes fall and he stares about him frowningly. He is twenty-five, tall and sinewy. His face is well formed, good-looking, but its expression it resentful and defensive. His defiant, dark eyes remind one of a wild animal's in captivity. Each day is a cage in which he finds himself trapped but inwardly unsubdued. There is a fierce repressed vitality about him. He has black hair, mustache, a thin curly trace of beard. He is dressed in rough farm clothes.*
He spits on the ground with intense disgust, turns and goes back into the house.]

Simeon *and* Peter *come in from their work in the fields. They are tall men, much older than their half-brother (*Simeon *is thirty-nine and* Peter *thirty-seven), built on a squarer, simpler model, fleshier in body, more bovine and homelier in face, shrewder and more practical. Their shoulders stoop a bit from years of farm work. They clump heavily along in their clumsy thick-soled boots caked with earth. Their clothes, their face, hands, bare arms and throats are earth-stained. They smell of earth. They stand together for a moment in front of the houst and, as if with the one impulse, stare dumbly up at the sky, leaning on their hoes. Their faces have a compressed, unresigned expression. As they look upward, this softens.*

Simeon [*Grudgingly.*] Purty.
Peter. Ay-eh.
Simeon [*Suddenly.*] Eighteen year ago.
Peter. What?
Simeon. Jenn. My woman. She died.
Peter. I'd fergot.
Simeon. I rec'lect—now an' agin. Makes it lonesome. She'd hair long's a hoss' tail—an yaller like gold!

PETER. Waa!—she's gone. [*This with indifferent finality—then after a pause.*] They's gold in the West, Sim.

SIMEON [*Still under the influence of sunset—vaguely.*] In the sky?

PETER. Waal—in a manner o' speakin'—that's the promise. [*Growing excited*] Gold in the sky—in the West—Golden Gate—Californi-a!—Goldest West!—fields o' gold!

SIMEON [*Excited in his turn.*] Fortunes layin' just atop o' the ground waitin' t' be picked! Solomon's mines, they says! [*For a moment they continue looking up at the sky—then their eyes drop.*]

PETER [*With sardonic bitterness.*] Here—it's stones atop o' the ground—stones atop o' stones—makin' stone walls—year atop o' year—him 'n' yew 'n' me 'n' then Eben—makin' stone walls fur him to fence us in!

SIMEON. We've wuked. Give our strength. Give our years. Plowed 'em under in the ground—[*he stamps rebelliously.*]—rottin'—makin' soil for his crops! [*A pause.*] Waal—the farm pays good for hereabouts.

PETER. If we plowed in Californi-a, they'd be lumps o' gold in the furrow!

SIMEON. Californi-a's t'other side o' earth, a'most. We got t' calc'late—

PETER [*After a pause.*] 'Twould be hard fur me, too, to give up what we've 'arned here by our sweat. [*A pause, EBEN sticks his head out of the dining-room window, listening.*]

SIMEON. Ay-eh. [*A pause.*] Mebbe—he'll die soon.

PETER [*Doubtfully.*] Mebbe.

SIMEON. Mebbe—fur all we knows—he's dead now.

PETER. Ye'd need proof.

SIMEON. He's been gone two months—with no word.

PETER. Left us in the fields an' evenin' like this. Hitched up an' druv off into the West. That's plum onnateral. He hain't never been off this farm 'ceptin' t' the village in thirty year or more, not since he married Eben's maw. [*A pause. Shrewdly.*] I calc'late we might git him declared crazy by the court.

SIMEON. He skinned 'em too slick. He got the best o' all on 'em. They'd never b'lieve him crazy. [*A pause.*] We got t' wait—till he's under ground.

EBEN [*With a sardonic chuckle*]. Honor thy father! [*They turn, startled, and stare at him. He grins, then scowls.*] I pray he's died. [*They stare at him. He continues matter-of-factly.*] Supper's ready.

SIMEON *and* PETER [*together.*] Ay-eh.

EBEN [*Gazing up at the sky.*] Sun's downin' purty.

SIMEON *and* PETER [*Together.*] Ay-eh. They's gold in the West.

EBEN. Ay-eh. [*Pointing.*] Yonder atop o' the hill pasture, ye mean?

SIMEON *and* PETER [*Together.*] In Californi-a!

EBEN. Hunh? [*Stares at them indifferently for a second, then drawls.*] Waal—supper's gittin' cold. [*He turns back into kitchen.*]

SIMEON [*Startled—smacks his lips.*] I air hungry!

PETER [*Sniffing.*] I smells bacon!

SIMEON [*With hungry appreciation.*] Bacon's good!

PETER [*In same tone.*] Bacon's bacon! [*They turn, shouldering each other, their bodies bumping and rubbing together as they hurry clumsily to their food, like two friendly oxen toward their evening meal. They disappear around the right corner of house and can be heard entering the door.*]

SCENE II

The color fades from the sky. Twilight begins. The interior of the kitchen is now visible. A pine table is at center, a cook-stove in the right rear corner, four rough wooden chairs, a tallow candle on the table. In the middle of the rear wall is fastened a big advertising poster with a ship in full sail and the word "California" in big letters. Kitchen utensils hang from nails. Everything is neat and in order but the atmosphere is of a men's camp kitchen rather than that of a home.

Places for three are laid. EBEN *takes boiled potatoes and bacon from the stove and puts them on the table, also a loaf of bread and a crock of water.* SIMEON *and* PETER *shoulder in, slump down in their chairs without a word.* EBEN *joins them. The three eat in silence for a moment, the two elder as naturally unrestrained as beasts of the field,* EBEN *picking at his food without appetite, glancing at them with a tolerant dislike.*

SIMEON [*Suddenly turns to* EBEN.] Looky here! Ye'd oughtn't t' said that, Eben.

PETER. 'Twa'n't righteous.

EBEN. What?

SIMEON. Ye prayed he'd died.

EBEN. Waal—don't yew pray it? [*A pause.*].

PETER. He's our Paw.

EBEN. [*Violently.*] Not mine!

SIMEON [*Dryly.*] Ye'd not let no one else say that about yer Maw! Ha! [*He gives one abrupt sardonic guffaw.* PETER *grins.*]

EBEN [*Very pale.*] I meant—I hain't his'n—I hain't like him—he hain't me!

PETER [*Dryly.*] Wait till ye've growed his age!

EBEN [*Intensely.*] I'm Maw—every drop o' blood! [*A pause. They stare at him with indifferent curiosity.*]

PETER [*Reminiscently.*] She was good t' Sim 'n' me. A good Step-maw's scurse.

SIMEON. She was good t' everyone.

EBEN [*Greatly moved, gets to his feet and makes an awkward bow

to each of them—stammering.] I be thankful t'ye. I'm her—
    her heir. [*He sits down in confusion.*]

PETER [*After a pause—judicially.*] She was good even t' him.

EBEN [*Fiercely.*] An' fur thanks he killed her!

SIMEON [*After a pause.*] No one never kills nobody. It's allus some-
    thin'. That's the murderer.

EBEN. Didn't he slave Maw t' death?

PETER. He slaved himself t' death. He's slaved Sim 'n' me 'n' yew
    t' death—on'y none o' us hain't died—yit.

SIMEON. It's somethin'—drivin' him—t' drive us!

EBEN [*Vengefully.*] Waal—I hold him t' jedgment! [*Then scorn-
    fully*] Somethin'! What's somethin'?

SIMEON. Dunno.

EBEN [*Sardonically.*] What's drivin' yew to Californi-a, mebbe?
    [*They look at him in surprise.*] Oh, I've heerd ye! [*Then, after
    a pause.*] But ye'll never go t' the gold fields!

PETER [*Assertively.*] Mebbe!

EBEN. Whar'll ye git the money?

PETER. We kin walk. It's an a'mighty ways—Californi-a—but if
    yew was t' put all the steps we've walked on this farm end t'
    end we'd be in the moon!

EBEN. The injuns'll skulp ye on the plains.

SIMEON [*With grim humor.*] We'll mebbe make 'em pay a hair fur
    a hair!

EBEN [*Decisively.*] But t'ain't that. Ye won't never go because ye'll
    wait here fur yer share o' the farm, thinkin' allus he'll die soon.

SIMEON [*After a pause.*] We've a right.

PETER. Two-thirds belongs t' us.

EBEN [*Jumping to his feet.*] Ye've no right! She wa'n't yewr Maw!
    It was her farm! Didn't he steal it from her? She's dead. It's
    my farm.

SIMEON [*Sardonically.*] Tell that t' Paw—when he comes! I'll bet
    ye a dollar he'll laugh—fur once in his life. Ha! [*He laughs
    himself in one single mirthless bark.*]

PETER [*Amused in turn, echoes his brother.*] Ha!

SIMEON [*After a pause.*] What've ye got held agin us. Eben? Year
    after year it's skulked in yer eye—somethin'.

PETER. Ay-eh.

EBEN. Ay-eh. They's somethin'. [*Suddenly exploding*] Why didn't
    ye never stand between him 'n' my Maw when he was slavin'
    her to her grave—t' pay her back fur the kindness she done t'
    yew? [*There is a long pause. They stare at him in surprise.*]

SIMEON. Waal—the stock'd got t' be watered.

PETER. 'R they was woodin' t' do.

SIMEON. 'R plowin'.

PETER. 'R hayin'.

SIMEON. 'R spreadin' manure.

PETER. 'R weedin'.

SIMEON. 'R prunin'.

PETER. 'R milkin'.

EBEN [*Breaking in harshly.*] An' makin' walls—stone atop o' stone —makin' walls till yer heart's a stone ye heft up out o' the way o' growth onto a stone wall t' wall in yer heart!

SIMEON [*matter-of-factly.*] We never had no time t' meddle.

PETER [*To* EBEN.] Yew was fifteen afore yer Maw died—an' big fur yer age. Why didn't ye never do nothin'?

EBEN [*harshly.*] They was chores t' do, wa'n't they? [*A pause— then slowly*] It was on'y arter she died I come to think o' it. Me cookin'—doin' her work—that made me know her, suffer her sufferin'—she'd come back t' help—come back t' bile potatoes—come back t' fry bacon—come back t' bake biscuits —come back all cramped up t' shake the fire, an' carry ashes, her eyes weepin' an' bloody with smoke an' cinders same's they used t' be. She still comes back—stands by the stove thar in the evenin'—she can't find it nateral sleepin' an' testin' in peace. She can't git used t' bein' free—even in her grave.

SIMEON. She never complained none.

EBEN. She'd got too tired. She'd got too used t' bein' too tired. That was what he done. [*With vengeful passion*] An' sooner 'r later, I'll meddle. I'll say the thin's I didn't say then t' him! I'll yell 'em at the top o' my lungs. I'll see t' it my Maw gits some rest an' sleep in her grave! [*He sits down again, relapsing into a brooding silence. They look at him with a queer in- different curiosity.*]

PETER [*After a pause.*] Whar in tarnation d'ye s'pose he went, Sim?

SIMEON. Dunno. He druv off in the buggy, all spick an' span, with the mare all breshed an' shiny, druv off clackin' his tongue an' wavin' his whip. I remember it right well. I was finishin' plowin', it was spring an' May an' sunset, an' gold in the West, an' he druv off into it. I yells "Whar ye goin', Paw?" an' he hauls up by the stone wall a jiffy. His old snake's eyes was glitterin' in the sun like he'd been drinkin' a jugful an' he says with a mule's grin: "Don't ye run away till I come back!"

PETER. Wonder if he knowed we was wantin' fur Californi-a?

SIMEON. Mebbe. I didn't say nothin' and he says, lookin' kinder queer an' sick: "I been hearin' the hens cluckin' an' the roost- ers crowin' all the durn day. I been listenin' t' the cows lowin' an' everythin else kickin' up till I can't stand it no more. It's spring an' I'm feelin' damned," he says. "Damned like an old bare hickory tree fit on'y fur burnin'," he says. An' then I calc'late I must've looked a mite hopeful, fur he adds real spry and vicious: "But don't git no fool idee I'm dead. I've sworn t' live a hundred an' I'll do it, if on'y t' spite yer sinful greed! An' now I'm ridin' out t' learn God's message t' me in the spring, like the prophets done. An' yew git back t' yer plowin'," he says. An' he druv off singin' a hymn. I thought he was drunk

—'r I'd stopped him goin'.

EBEN [*Scornfully.*] No, ye wouldn't! Ye're scared o' him He's stronger—inside—than both o' ye put together!

PETER [*Sardonically.*] An' yew—be yew Samson?

EBEN. I'm gittin' stronger. I kin feel it growin' in me—growin' an' growin'—till it'll bust out—! [*He gets up and puts on his coat and a hat. They watch him, gradually breaking into grins. EBEN avoids their eyes sheepishly.*] I'm goin' out fur a spell —up the road.

PETER. T' the village?

SIMEON. T' see Minnie?

EBEN [*Defiantly.*] Ay-eh!

PETER [*Jeeringly.*] The Scarlet Woman!

SIMEON. Lust—that's what's growin' in ye!

EBEN. Waal—she's purty!

PETER. She's been purty fur twenty year!

SIMEON. A new coat o' paint'll make a heifer out of forty.

EBEN. She hain't forty!

PETER. If she hain't, she's teeterin' on the edge.

EBEN [*Desperately*] What d'yew know—

PETER. All they is . . . Sim knew her—an' then me arter—

SIMEON. An' Paw kin tell yew somethin' too! He was fust!

EBEN. D'ye mean t 'say he . . . ?

SIMEON [*With a grin.*] Ay-eh! We air his heirs in everythin'!

EBEN [*Intensely.*] That's more to it! That grows on it! It'll bust soon! [*Then violently*] I'll go smash my fist in her face! [*He pulls open the door in rear violently.*]

SIMEON [*With a wink at PETER—drawlingly.*] Mebbe—but the night's wa'm—purty—by the time ye get thar mebbe ye'll kiss her instead!

PETER. Sart'n he will [*They both roar with coarse laughter. EBEN rushes out and slams the door—then the outside front door—comes around the corner of the house and stands still by the gate, staring up at the sky.*]

SIMEON [*Looking after him.*] Like his Paw.

PETFR. Dead spit an' image!

SIMEON. Dog'll eat dog!

PETER. Ay-eh. [*Pause. With yearning*] Mebbe a year from now we'll be in Californi-a.

SIMEON. Ay-eh. [*A pause. Both yawn.*] Let's git t'bed. [*He blows out the candle. They go out door in rear. EBEN stretches his arms up to the sky—rebelliously.*]

EBEN. Waal—thar's a star, an' somewhar's they's him, an' here's me, an' thar's Min up the road—in the same night. What if I does kiss her? She's like t'night, she's soft 'n' wa'm, her eyes kin wink like a star, her mouth's wa'm, her arms're wa'm, she smells like a wa'm plowed field, she's purty . . . Ay-eh! By God A'mighty she's purty, an' I don't give a damn how many sins

she's sinned afore mine or who she's sinned 'em with, my sin's
as purty as any one on 'em! [*He strides off down the road to
the left.*]

SCENE III

It is the pitch darkness just before dawn. EBEN *comes in from
the left and goes around to the porch, feeling his way, chuckling
bitterly and cursing half-aloud to himself.*]

EBEN. The cussed old miser! [*He can be heard going in the front
door. There is a pause as he goes upstairs, then a loud knock
on the bedroom door of the brothers.*] Wake up!
SIMEON [*Startledly.*] Who's thar?
EBEN [*Pushing open the door and coming in, a lighted candle in
his hand. The bedroom of the brothers is revealed. Its ceiling
is the sloping roof. They can stand upright only close to the
center dividing wall of the upstairs.* SIMEON *and* PETER *are in
a double bed, front.* EBEN's *cot is to the rear.* EBEN *has a mix-
ture of silly grin and vicious scowl on his face.*] I be!
PETER [*Angrily.*] What in hell's-fire . . . ?
EBEN. I got news fur ye! Ha! [*He gives one abrupt sardonic guffaw.*]
SIMEON. [*Angrily.*] Couldn't ye hold it til we'd got our sleep?
EBEN. It's nigh sunup. [*Then explosively*] He's gone an' married
agen!
SIMEON *and* PETER [*Explosively.*] Paw?
EBEN. Got himself hitched to a female 'bout thirty-five—an' purty,
they says . . .
SIMEON [*Aghast.*] It's a durn lie!
PETER. Who says?
SIMEON. They been stringin' ye!
EBEN. Think I'm a dunce, do ye? The hull village says. The
preacher from New Dover, he brung the news—told it t'our
preacher—New Dover, that's whar the old loon got himself
hitched—that's whar the woman lived—
PETER [*No longer doubting—stunned.*] Waal . . . ?
SIMEON. [*The same.*] Waal . . . !
EBEN [*Sitting down on a bed—with vicious hatred.*] Ain't he a
devil out o' hell? It's jest t' spite us—the damned old mule!
PETER [*After a pause.*] Everythin'll go t' her now.
SIMEON. Ay-eh [*A pause—dully*] Waal—if it's done—
PETER. It's done us. [*Pause—then persuasively*] They's gold in the
fields o' Californi-a, Sim. No good a-stayin' here now.
SIMEON. Jest what I was a-thinkin'. [*Then with decision*] S'well
fust's last! Let's light out and git this mornin'.
PETER. Suits me.
EBEN. Ye must like walkin'.
SIMEON [*Sardonically.*] If ye'd grow wings on us we'd fly thar!

EBEN. Ye'd like ridin' better—on a boat, wouldn't ye? [*Fumbles in his pocket and takes out a crumpled sheet of foolscap.*] Waal, if ye sign this ye kin ride on a boat. I've had it writ out an' ready in case ye'd ever go. It says fur three hundred dollars t' each ye agree yewr shares o' the farm is sold t' me. [*They look supiciously at the paper. A pause.*]

SIMEON [*Wonderingly.*] But if he's hitched agen—

PETER. An' whar'd yew git that sum o' money, anyways?

EBEN [*Cunningly*]. I know whar it's hid. I been writin'—Maw told me. She knew whar it lay fur years, but she was waitin' ... It's her'n—the money he hoarded from her farm an' hid from Maw. It's my money by rights now.

PETER. Whar's it hid?

EBEN [*Cunningly.*] Whar yew won't never find it without me. Maw spied on him—'r she'd never knowed. [*A pause. They look at him suspiciously, and he at them.*] Waal, is it fa'r trade?

SIMEON. Dunno.

PETER. Dunno.

SIMEON [*Looking at window.*] Sky's grayin'.

PETER. Ye better start the fire, Eben.

SIMEON. An' fix some vittles.

EBEN. Ay-eh. [*Then with a forced jocular heartiness*] I'll git ye a good one. If ye're startin' t' hoof it 't Californi-a ye'll need somethin' that'll stick t' yer ribs. [*He turns to the door, adding meaningly.*] But ye kin ride on a boat if ye'll swap. [*He stops at the door and pauses. They stare at him.*]

SIMEON [*Suspiciously.*] Whar was ye all night?

EBEN [*defiantly*]. Up t' Min's. [*Then slowly.*] Walkin' thar, fust I felt 's if I'd kiss her; then I got a-thinkin' o' what ye'd said o' him an' her an' I says, I'll bust her nose fur that! Then I got t' the village an' heerd the news an' I got madder'n hell an' run all the way t' Min's not knowin' what I'd do—[*He pauses then sheepishly but more defiantly*] Waal—when I seen her, I didn't hit her—nor I didn't kiss her nuther—I begun t' beller like a calf an' cuss at the same time, I was so durn mad—an' she got scared—an' I jest grabbed holt an' tuk her! [*Proudly*] Yes, sirree! I tuk her. She may've been his'n—an' your'n, too—but she's mine now!

SIMEON [*Dryly.*] In love, air yew?

EBEN [*With lofty scorn.*] Love! I don't take no stock in sech slop!

PETER [*Winking at SIMEON.*] Mebbe Eben's aimin' t' marry, too.

SIMEON. Min'd make a true faithful he'pmeet! [*They snicker.*]

EBEN. What do I care fur her—'ceptin' she's round an' wa'm? The p'int is she was his'n—an' now she belongs t' me! [*He goes to the door—then turns—rebelliously.*] An' Min hain't sech a bad un. They's worse'n Min in the world, I'll bet ye! Wait'll we see this cow the Old Man's hitched t'! She'll beat Min, I got a notion! [*He starts to go out.*]

SIMEON [*Suddenly.*] Mebbe ye'll try t' make her your'n, too?

PETER. Ha! [*He gives a sardonic laugh of relish at this idea.*]

EBEN [*Spitting with disgust.*] Her—here—sleepin' with him—stealin' my Maw's farm! I'd as soon pet a skunk 'r kiss a snake! [*He goes out. The two stare after him suspiciously. A pause. They listen to his steps receding.*]

PETER. He's startin' the fire.

SIMEON. I'd like t' ride t' Californi-a—but—

PETER. Min might o' put some scheme in his head.

SIMEON. Mebbe it's all a lie 'bout Paw marryin'. We'd best wait an' see the bride.

PETER. An' don't sign nothin' till we does!

SIMEON. Nor till we've tested it's good money! [*Then with a grin*] But if Paw's hitched we'd be sellin' Eben somethin' we'd never git nohow!

PETER. We'll wait an' see. [*Then with sudden vindictive anger*] An' till he comes, let's yew 'n' me not wuk a lick, let Eben tend to thin's if he's a mind t', let's us jest sleep an' eat an' drink likker, an' let the hull damned farm go t' blazes!

SIMEON [*Excitedly.*] By God, we've 'arned a rest! We'll play rich fur a change. I hain't a-goin' to stir outa bed till breakfast's ready.

PETER. An' on the table!

SIMEON [*After a pause—thoughtfully.*] What d' ye calc'late she'll be like—our new Maw? Like Eben thinks?

PETER. More'n likely.

SIMEON [*Vindictively*]. Waal—I hope she's a she-devil that'll make him wish he was dead an' living in the pit o' hell fur comfort!

PETER [*Fervently.*] Amen!

SIMEON [*Imitating his father's voice.*] "I'm ridin' out t' learn God's message t' me in the spring like the prophets done," he says. I'll bet right then an' thar he knew plumb well he was goin' whorin', the stinkin' old hypocrite!

SCENE IV

Same as Scene II—shows the interior of the kitchen with a lighted candle on table. It is gray dawn outside. SIMEON *and* PETER *are just finishing their breakfast.* EBEN *sits before his plate of untouched food, brooding frowningly.*

PETER [*Glancing at him rather irritably.*] Lookin' glum don't help none.

SIMEON [*Sarcastically.*] Sorrowin' over his lust o' the flesh!

PETER [*With a grin.*] Was she yer fust?

EBEN [*Angrily.*] None o' yer business. [*A pause.*] I was thinkin' o' him. I got a notion he's gittin' near—I kin feel him comin' on like yew kin feel malaria chill afore it takes ye.

PETER. It's too early yet.

SIMEON. Dunno. He'd like t' catch us nappin'—jest t' have somethin' t' hoss us 'round over.

PETER [*Mechanically gets to his feet.* SIMEON *does the same.*] Waal —let's git t' wuk. [*They both plod mechanically toward the door before they realize. Then they stop short.*]

SIMEON [*Grinning.*] Ye're a cussed fool, Pete—and I be wuss! Let him see we hain't wukin'! We don't give a durn!

PETER [*As they go back to the table.*] Not a dumned durn! It'll serve t' show him we're done with him. [*They sit down again.* EBEN *stares from one to the other with surprise.*]

SIMEON [*Grins at him.*] We're aimin' t' start bein' lilies o' the field.

PETER. Nary a toil 'r spin 'r lick o' wuk do we put in!

SIMEON. Ye're sole owner—till he comes—that's what ye wanted. Waal, ye got t' be sole hand, too.

PETER. The cows air bellerin'. Ye better hustle at the milkin'.

EBEN [*With excited joy.*] Ye mean ye'll sign the paper?

SIMEON [*Dryly.*] Mebbe.

PETER. Mebbe.

SIMEON. We're considerin'. [*Peremptorily*] Ye better git t' wuk.

EBEN [*With queer excitement.*] It's Maw's farm agen! It's my farm! Them's my cows! I'll milk my durn fingers off fur cows o' mine! [*He goes out door in rear, they stare after him indifferently.*]

SIMEON. Like his Paw.

PETER. Dead spile 'n' image!

SIMEON. Waal—let dog eat dog! [EBEN *comes out of front door and around the corner of the house. The sky is beginning to grow flushed with sunrise.* EBEN *stops by the gate and stares around him with glowing, possessive eyes. He takes in the whole farm with his embracing glance of desire.*]

EBEN. It's purty! It's damned purty! It's mine! [*He suddenly throws his head back boldly and glares with hard, defiant eye at the sky.*] Mine, d'ye hear? Mine! [*He turns and walks quickly off left, rear, toward the barn. The two brothers light their pipes.*]

SIMEON [*Putting his muddy boots up on the table, tilting back his chair, and puffing defiantly.*] Waal—this air solid comfort— fur once.

PETER. Ay-eh. [*He follows suit. A pause. Unconsciously they both sigh.*]

SIMEON [*Suddenly.*] He never was much o' a hand at milkin', Eben wa'n't.

PETER [*With a snort.*] His hands air like hoofs! [*A pause.*]

SIMEON. Reach down the jug thar! Let's take a swaller. I'm feelin' kind o' low.

PETER. Good idee! [*He does so—gets two glasses—they pour out drinks of whisky*]. Here's t' the gold in Californi-a!

SIMEON. An' luck t' find it! [*They drink—puff resolutely—sigh— take their feet down from the table.*]

PETER. Likker don't 'pear t' sot right.

SIMEON. We hain't used t' it this early. [*A pause. They become very restless.*]

PETER. Gittin' close in this kitchen.

SIMEON [*With immense relief.*] Let's git a breath o' air. [*They arise briskly and go out rear—appear around house and stop by the gate. They stare up at the sky with a numbed appreciation.*]

PETER. Purty!

SIMEON. Ay-eh. Gold's t' the East now.

PETER. Sun's startin' with us fur the Golden West.

SIMEON [*Staring around the farm, his compressed face tightened, unable to conceal his emotion.*] Waal—it's our last mornin'—mebbe.

PETER [*The same.*] Ay-eh.

SIMEON [*Stamps his foot on the earth and addresses it desperately.*] Waal—ye've thirty year o' me buried in ye—spread out over ye—blood an' bone an' sweat—rotted away—fertilizin' ye—richin' yer soul—prime manure, by God, that's what I been t' ye!

PETER. Ay-eh! An' me!

SIMEON. An yew, Peter. [*He sighs—then spits.*] Waal—no use'n cryin' over spilt milk.

PETER. They's gold in the West—an' freedom, mebbe. We been slaves t' stone walls here.

SIMEON [*Defiantly.*] We hain't nobody's slaves from this out—nor no thin's slaves nuther. [*A pause—restlessly.*] Speakin' o' milk, wonder how Eben's managin'?

PETER. I spose he's managin'.

SIMEON. Mebbe we'd ought t' help—this once.

PETER. Mebbe. The cows knows us.

SIMEON. An likes us. They don't know him much.

PETER. An' the hosses, an' pigs, an' chickens. They don't know him much.

SIMEON. They knows us like brothers—an' likes us! [*Proudly*] Hain't we raised 'em t' be fust-rate, number one prize stock?

PETER. We hain't—not no more.

SIMEON [*Dully.*] I was fergittin'. [*Then resignedly.*] Waal, le's go help Eben a spell an' git waked up.

PETER. Suits me. [*They are starting off down left, rear, for the barn when EBEN appears from there hurrying toward them, his face excited.*]

EBEN [*Breathlessly.*] Waal—har they be! The old mule an' the bride! I seen 'em from the barn down below at the turnin'.

PETER. How could ye tell that far?

EBEN. Hain't I as far-sight as he's near-sight? Don't I know the mare 'n' buggy, an' two people settin' in it? Who else . . . ? An' I tell ye I kin feel 'em a-comin', too! [*He squirms as if he had the itch.*]

PETER [*Beginning to be angry*]. Waal—let him do his own unhitchin'!

SIMEON [*Angry in his turn.*] Let's hustle in an' git our bundles an' be a-goin' as he's a-comin'. I don't want never t' step inside the door agen arter he's back. [*They both start back around the corner of the house.* EBEN *follows them.*]

EBEN [*Anxiously.*] Will ye sign it afore ye go?

PETER. Let's see the color o' the old skinflint's money an' we'll sign. [*They disappear left. The two brothers clump upstairs to get their bundles.* EBEN *appears in the kitchen, runs to the window, peers out, comes back and pulls up a strip of flooring in under stove, takes out a canvas bag and puts it on table, then sets the floorboard back in place. The two brothers appear a moment after. They carry old carpet bags.*]

EBEN [*Puts his hand on bag guardingly.*] Have ye signed?

SIMEON [*Shows paper in his hand.*] Ay-eh [*Greedily*] Be that the money?

EBEN [*Opens bag and pours out pile of twenty-dollar gold pieces.*] Twenty-dollar pieces—thirty on 'em. Count 'em. [PETER *does so, arranging them in stacks of five, biting one or two to test them.*]

PETER. Six hundred. [*He puts them in bag and puts inside it his shirt, carefully.*]

SIMEON [*Handing paper to* EBEN.] Har ye be.

EBEN [*after a glance, folds it carefully and hides it under his shirt —gratefully.*] Thank yew.

PETER. Thank yew fur the ride.

SIMEON. We'll send ye a lump o' gold fur Christmas. [*A pause.* EBEN *stares at them and they at him.*]

PETER [*Awkwardly.*] Waal—we're a-goin'.

SIMEON. Comin' out t' the yard?

EBEN. No. I'm waitin' in here a spell. [*Another silence. The brothers edge awkwardly to the door in rear—then turn and stand.*]

SIMEON. Waal—good-by.

PETER. Good-by.

EBEN. Good-by. [*They go out. He sits down at the table, faces the stove and pulls out the paper. He looks from it to the stove. His face, lighted up by the shaft of sunlight from the windows, has an expression of trance. His lips move. The two brothers come out to the gate.*]

PETER [*Looking off toward barn.*] Thar he be—unhitchin'.

SIMEON [*With a chuckle.*] I'll bet ye he's riled!

PETER. An' thar she be.

SIMEON. Let's wait 'n' see what our new Maw looks like.

PETER [*With a grin.*] An' give him our partin' cuss!

SIMEON [*Grinning.*] I feel like raisin' fun. I feel light in my head an' feet.

PETER. Me, too. I feel like laffin' till I'd split up the middle.

SIMEON. Reckon it's the likker?

PETER. No. My feet feel itchin' t' walk an' walk—an' jump high over thin's—an'. . . .

SIMEON. Dance? [*A pause.*]

PETER [*Puzzled.*] It's plumb onnateral.

SIMEON [*A light coming over his face.*] I calc'late it's 'cause school's out. It's holiday. Fur once we're free!

PETER [*Dazedly.*] Free?

SIMEON. The halter's broke—the harness is busted—the fence bars is down—the stone walls air crumblin' an' tumblin'! We'll be kickin' up an' tearin' away down the road!

PETER [*Drawing a deep breath—oratorically.*] Anybody that wants this stinkin' old rock-pile of a farm kin hev it. 'Tain't our'n, no sirree!

SIMEON [*Takes the gate off its hinges and puts it under his arm.*] We harby 'bolishes shet gates an' open gates, an' all gates, by thunder!

PETER. We'll take it with us fur luck an' let 'er sail free down some river.

SIMEON [*As a sound of voices comes from left, rear.*] Har they comes! [*The two brothers congeal into two stiff, grim-visaged statues.* EPHRAIM CABOT *and* ABBIE PUTNAM *come in.* CABOT *is seventy-five, tall and gaunt, with great wiry, concentrated power, but stoop-shouldered from toil. His face is as hard as if it were hewn out of a boulder, yet there is a weakness in it, a petty pride in its own narrow strength. His eyes are small, close together, and extremely near-sighted, blinking continually in the effort to focus on objects, their stare having a straining, ingrowing quality. He is dressed in his dismal black Sunday suit.* ABBIE *is thirty-five, buxom, full of vitality. Her round face is pretty but marred by its rather gross sensuality. There is strength and obstinacy in her jaw, a hard determination in her eyes, and about her whole personality the same unsettled, untamed, desperate quality which is so apparent in* EBEN.]

CABOT [*As they enter—a queer strangled emotion in his dry cracking voice.*] Har we be t' hum, Abbie.

ABBIE [*With lust for the word.*] Hum! [*Her eyes gloating on the house without seeming to see the two stiff figures at the gate.*) It's purty—purty! I can't b'lieve it's r'ally mine.

CABOT [*Sharply.*] Yewr'n? Mine! [*He stares at her penetratingly. She stares back. He adds relentingly.*] Our'n—mebbe! It was lonesome too long. I was growin' old in the spring. A hum's got t' hev a woman.

ABBIE [*Her voice taking possession.*] A woman's got t' hev a hum!

CABOT [*Nodding uncertainly.*] Ay-eh. [*Then irritably*] Whar be they? Ain't thar nobody about—'r wukin'—'r nothin'?

ABBIE [*Sees the brothers. She returns their stare of cold appraising*

contempt with interest—slowly.] Thar's two men loafin' at the
gate an' starin' at me like a couple o' strayed hogs.

CABOT [*Straining his eyes.*] I kin see 'em—but I can't make out. . . .

SIMEON. It's Simeon.

PETER. It's Peter.

CABOT [*Exploding.*] Why hain't ye wukin'?

SIMEON [*Druly.*] We're waitin' t' welcome ye hum—yew an' the
bride?

CABOT [*Confusedly.*] Huh? Waal—this be yer new Maw, boys. [*She
stares at them and they at her.*]

SIMEON [*Turns away and spit contemptuously.*] I see her!

PETER [*Spits also.*] An' I see her!

ABBIE [*With the conqueror's conscious superiority.*] I'll go in an'
look at *my* house. [*She goes slowly around to porch.*]

SIMEON [*With a snort.*] Her house!

PETER [*Calls after her.*] Ye'll find Eben inside. Ye better not tell
him it's *yewr* house.

ABBIE [*Mouthing the name.*] Eben. [*Then quietly*] I'll tell Eben.

CABOT [*With a contemptuous sneer.*] Ye needn't heed Eben. Eben's
dumb fool—like his Maw—soft an' simple!

SIMEON [*With his sardonic burst of laughter.*] Ha! Eben's a chip
o' yew—spit 'n' image—hard 'n' bitter's a hickory tree! Dog'll
ear dog. He'll eat ye yet, old man!

CABOT [*Commandingly.*] Ye git t' wuk!

SIMEON [*As* ABBIE *disappears in house—winks at* PETER *and says
tauntingly.*] So that thar's our new Maw, be it? Whar in hell
did ye dig her up? [*He and* PETER *laugh.*]

PETER. Ha? Ye'd better turn her in the pen with the other sows.
[*They laugh uproariously, slapping their thighs.*]

CABOT [*So amazed at their effrontery that he stutters in confusion.*]
Simeon! Peter! What's come over ye? Air ye drunk?

SIMEON. We're free, old man—free o' yew an' the hull damned
farm! [*They grow more and more hilarious and excited.*]

PETER. An' we're startin' out fur the gold fields o' Californi-a!

SIMEON. Ye kin take this place an' burn it!

PETER. An' bury it—fur all we cares!

SIMEON. We're free, old man! [*He cuts a caper.*]

PETER. Free! [*He gives a kick in the air.*]

SIMEON [*In a frenzy.*] Whoop!

PETER. Whoop! [*They do an absurd Indian war dance about the
old man, who is petrified between rage and the fear that they
are insane.*]

SIMEON. We're free as Injuns! Lucky we don't skulp ye!

PETER. An' burn yer barn an' kill the stock!

SIMEON. An' rape yer new woman! Whoop! [*He and* PETER *stop
their dance, holding their sides, rocking with wild laughter.*]

CABOT [*Edging away.*] Lust fur gold—fur the sinful, easy gold o'
Californi-a! It's made ye mad!

SIMEON [*Tauntingly.*] Wouldn't ye like us to send ye back some sinful gold, ye old sinner?

PETER. They's gold besides what's in Californi-a! [*He retreats back beyond the vision of the old man and takes the bag of money and flaunts it in the air above his head, laughing.*]

SIMEON. And sinfuller, too!

PETER. We'll be voyagin' on the sea! Whoop! [*He leaps up and down.*]

SIMEON. Livin' free! Whoop! [*He leaps in turn.*]

CABOT [*Suddenly roaring with rage.*] My cuss on ye!

SIMEON. Take our'n in trade fur it! Whoop!

CABOT. I'll hev ye both chained up in the asylum!

PETER. Ye old skinflint! Good-by!

SIMEON. Ye old blood sucker! Good-by!

CABOT. Go afore I . . . !

PETER. Whoop! [*He picks a stone from the road.* SIMEON *does the same.*]

SIMEON. Maw'll be in the parlor.

PETER. Ay-eh! One! Two!

CABOT [*Frightened.*] What air ye . . . ?

PETER. Three! [*They both throw, the stones hitting the parlor window with a crash of glass, tearing the shade.*]

SIMEON. Whoop!

PETER. Whoop!

CABOT [*In a fury now, rushing toward them.*] If I kin lay hands on ye—I'll break yer bones fur ye! [*But they beat a capering retreat before him,* SIMEON *with the gate still under his arm.* CABOT *comes back, panting with impotent rage. Their voices as they go off take up the song of the gold-seekers to the old tune of* "Oh, Susannah!"]

"I jumped aboard the Liza ship,
And traveled on the sea,
And every time I thought of home
I wished it wasn't me!
Oh! Californi-a,
That's the land fur me!
I'm off to Californi-a!
With my wash bowl on my knee."

[*In the meantime, the window of the upper bedroom on right is raised and* ABBIE *sticks her head out. She looks down at* CABOT—*with a sigh of relief.*]

ABBIE. Waal—that's the last o' them two, hain't it? (*He doesn't answer. Then in possessive tones*] This here's a nice bedroom, Ephraim. It's a r'al nice bed. Is it my room, Ephraim?

CABOT [*Grimly*]—*without looking up.*] Our'n! [*She cannot control a grimace of aversion and pulls back her head slowly and shuts the window. A sudden horrible thought seems to enter* CABOT's

head.] They been up to somethin'! Mebbe—mebbe they're
pizened the stock—'r somethin'! [*He almost runs off down
toward the barn. A moment later the kitchen door is slowly
pushed open and* ABBIE *enters. For a moment she stands looking at* EBEN. *He does not notice her at first. Her eyes take him
in penetratingly with a calculating appraisal of his strength as
against hers. But under this her desire is dimly awakened by
his youth and good looks. Suddenly he becomes conscious of
her presence and looks up. Their eyes meet. He leaps to his
feet, glowering at her speechlessly.*]

ABBIE [*In her most seductive tones, which she uses all through this
scene.*] Be you—Eben? I'm Abbie—[*She laughs.*] I mean, I'm
yer new Maw.

EBEN [*Viciously.*] No, damn ye!

ABBIE [*As if she hadn't heard—with a queer smile.*] Yer Paw's
spoke a lot o' yew. . . .

EBEN. Ha!

ABBIE. Ye mustn't mind him. He's an old man. [*A long pause.
They stare at each other.*] I don't want t' pretend playin'
Maw t' ye, Eben. [*Admiringly*] Ye're too big an' strong fur
that. I want t' be frens with ye. Mebbe with me fur a fren ye'd
find ye'd like livin' here better. I kin make it easy fur ye with
him, mebbe. [*With a scornful sense of power*] I calc'late I
kin git him t' do most anythin' fur me.

EBEN [*With bitter scorn.*] Ha! [*They stare again,* EBEN *obscurely
moved, physically attracted to her—in forced stilted tones*]
Yew kin go t' the devil!

ABBIE [*Calmly.*] If cussin' me does ye good, cuss all ye've a mind
t'. I'm all prepared t' have ye agin me—at fust. I don't blame
ye nuther. I'd feel the same at any stranger comin' t' take my
Maw's place. [*He shudders. She is watching him carefully.*]
Yew must've cared a lot fur yewr Maw, didn't ye? My Maw
died afore I'd growed. I don't remember her none. [*A pause.*]
But yew won't hate me long, Eben. I'm not the wust in the
world—an' yew an' me've got a lot in common. I kin tell that
by lookin' at ye. Waal—I've had a hard life, too—oceans o'
trouble an' nuthin' but wuk fur reward. I was a orphan early
an had t' wuk fur others in other folks hums. Then I married
an' he turned out a drunken spreer an' so he had to wuk fur
others an' me too agen in other folks' hums, an' the baby died,
an' my husband got sick an' died too, an' I was glad, sayin'
now I'm free fur once, on'y I diskivered right away all I was
free fur was t' wuk agen in other folks' hums, doin' other
folks' wuk till I'd most give up hope o' ever doin' my own wuk
in my own hum, an' then your Paw come. . . . [CABOT *appears
returning from the barn. He comes to the gate and looks
down the road the brothers have gone. A faint strain of their*

retreating voices is heard:] "Oh, Californi-a! That's the place for me." *He stands glowering, his fist clenched, his face grim with rage.*]

EBEN [*Fighting against his growing attraction and sympathy— harshly.*] An' bought yew—like a harlot! [*She is stung and flushes angrily. She has been sincerely moved by the recital of her troubles. He adds furiously:*] An' the price he's payin' ye— this farm—was my Maw's, damn ye!—an' mine now!

ABBIE [*With a cool laugh of confidence.*] Yewr'n? We'll see 'bout that! [*Then strongly*] Waal—what if I did need a hum? What else'd I marry an old man like him fur?

EBEN [*Maliciously.*] I'll tell him ye said that!

ABBIE [*Smiling.*] I'll say ye're lyin' a-purpose—an' he'll drive ye off the place!

EBEN. Ye devil!

ABBIE [*Defying him.*] This be my farm—this be my hum—this be my kitchen—!

EBEN [*Furiously, as if he were going to attack her.*] Shut up, damn ye!

ABBIE [*Walks up to him—a queer coarse expression of desire in her face and body—slowly.*] An' upstairs—that be my bedroom an' my bed! [*He stares into her eyes, terribly confused and torn. She adds softly:*] I hain't bad nor mean—'ceptin' fur an enemy—but I got t' fight fur what's due me out o' life, if I ever 'spect t' git it. [*Then putting her hand on his arm— seductively*] Let's yew 'n' me be frens, Eben.

EBEN [*Stupidly—as if hypnotized.*] Ay-eh. [*Then furiously flinging off her arm*] No, ye durned old witch! I hate ye! [*He rushes out the door.*]

ABBIE [*Looks after him smiling satisfiedly—then half to herself, mouthing the word.*] Eben's nice. [*She looks at the table, proudly.*] I'll wash up *my* dishes now. [EBEN *appears outside, slamming the door behind him. He comes around corner, stops on seeing his father, and stands staring at him with hate.*]

CABOT [*Raising his arms to heaven in the fury he can no longer control.*] Lord God o' Hosts, smite the undutiful sons with Thy wust cuss!

EBEN [*Breaking in violently.*] Yew 'n' yewr God! Allus cussin' folks allus naggin' 'em!

CABOT [*Oblivious to him—summoningly.*] God o' the old! God o' the lonesome!

EBEN [*Mockingly.*] Naggin' His sheep t' sin! T' hell with yewr God! [CABOT *turns. He and* EBEN *glower at each other.*]

CABOT [*Harshly.*] So it's yew. I might've knowed it. [*Shaking his finger threateningly at him*] Blasphemin' fool! [*Then quickly*] Why hain't ye t' wuk?

EBEN. Why hain't yew? They've went. I can't wuk it all alone.

CABOT [*Contemptuously.*] Nor noways! I'm wuth ten o' ye yi, old's

I be! Ye'll never be more'n half a man! [*Then, matter-of-factly*] Waal—let's git t' the barn. [*They go. A last faint note of the "Californi-a" song is heard from the distance.* ABBIE *is washing her dishes.*]

PART II

SCENE I

The exterior of the farmhouse, as in Part I—a hot Sunday afternoon two months later. ABBIE, *dressed in her best, is discovered sitting in a rocker at the end of the porch. She rocks listlessly, enervated by the heat, staring in front of her with bored, half-closed eyes.*

EBEN *sticks his head out of his bedroom window. He looks around furtively and tries to see—or hear—if anyone is on the porch, but although be has been careful to make no noise,* ABBIE *has sensed his movement. She stops rocking, her face grows animated and eager, she waits attentively.* EBEN *seems to feel her presence, he scowls back his thoughts of her and spits with exaggerated disdain—then withdraws back into the room.* ABBIE *waits, holding her breath as she listens with passionate eagerness for every sound within the house.*

EBEN *comes out. Their eyes meet. His falter, he is confused, he turns away and slams the door resentfully. At this gesture,* ABBIE *laughs tantalizingly, amused but at the same time piqued and irritated. He scowls, strides off the porch to the path and starts to walk past her to the road with a grand swagger of ignoring her existence. He is dressed in his store suit, spruced up, his face shines from soap and water.* ABBIE *leans forward on her chair, her eyes hard and angry now, and, as he passes her, gives a sneering, taunting chuckle.*

EBEN [*Stung—turns on her furiously.*] What air yew cacklin' 'bout?
ABBIE [*Triumphant.*] Yew!
EBEN. What about me?
ABBIE. Ye look all slicked up like a prize bull.
EBEN [*With a sneer.*] Waal—ye hain't so durned purty yerself, be ye? [*They stare into each other's eyes, his held by hers in spite of himself, hers glowingly possessive. Their physical attraction becomes a palpable force quivering in the hot air.*]
ABBIE [*Softly.*] Ye don't mean that, Eben. Ye may think ye mean it, mebbe, but ye don't. Ye can't. It's agin nature, Eben. Ye been fightin' yer nature ever since the day I come—tryin' t' tell yerself I hain't purty t'ye. [*She laughs a low humid laugh without taking her eyes from his. A pause—her body squirms desirously—she murmurs languorously.*] Hain't the sun strong

an' hot? Ye kin feel it burnin' into the earth—Nature—makin'
thin's grow—bigger 'n' bigger—burnin' inside ye—makin' ye
want t' grow—into somethin' else—till ye're jined with it—
an' it's your'n—but it owns ye, too—an' makes ye grow bigger
—like a tree—like them elums—[*She laughs again softly, holding his eyes. He takes a step toward her, compelled against his
will.*] Nature'll beat ye, Eben. Ye might's well own up t' it
fust's last.

EBEN [*Trying to break from her spell—confusedly.*] If Paw'd hear
ye goin' on. . . . [*Resentfully*] But ye've made such a damned
idjit our o' the old devil . . . ! [ABBIE *laughs.*]

ABBIE. Waal—hain't it easier fur yew with him changed softer?

EBEN [*Defiantly.*] No. I'm fightin' him—fightin' yew—fightn' fur
Maw's rights t' her hum! [*This breaks her spell for him. He
glowers at her.*] An' I'm onto ye. Ye hain't foolin' me a mite.
Ye're aimin' t' swaller up everythin'· an' make it your'n. Waal,
you'll find I'm a heap sight bigger hunk nor yew kin chew!
[*He turns from her with a sneer.*]

ABBIE [*Trying to regain her ascendancy—seductively.*] Eben!

EBEN. Leave me be! [*He starts to walk away.*]

ABBIE [*More commandingly.*] Eben!

EBEN [*Stops—resentfully.*] What d'ye want?

ABBIE [*Trying to conceal a growing excitement.*] Whar air ye goin?

EBEN [*With malicious nonchalance.*] Oh—up the road a spell.

ABBIE. T' the village?

EBEN [*Airily.*] Mebbe.

ABBIE [*Excitedly.*] T' see that Min, I s'pose?

EBEN. Mebbe.

ABBIE [*Weakly.*] What d'ye want t' waste time on her fur?

EBEN [*Revenging himself now—grinning at her.*] Ye can't beat
Nature, didn't ye say? [*He laughs and again starts to walk
away.*]

ABBIE [*Bursting out.*] An ugly old hake!

EBEN [*With a tantalizing sneer.*] She's purtier'n yew be!

ABBIE. That every wuthless drunk in the county has. . . .

EBEN [*Tauntingly.*] Mebbe—but she's better'n yew. She owns up
fa'r 'n' squar' t' her doin's.

ABBIE [*Furiously.*] Don't ye dare compare. . . .

EBEN. She don't go sneakin' an' stealin'—what's mine.

ABBIE [*Savagely seizing on his weak point.*] Your'n? Yew mean—
my farm?

EBEN. I mean the farm yew sold yerself fur like any other old
whore—my farm!

ABBIE [*Stung—fiercely.*] Ye'll never live t' see the day when even a
stinkin' weed on it'll belong t' ye! [*Then in a scream*] Git out
o' my sight! Go on t' yer slut—disgracin' yer Paw 'n' me! I'll
git yer Paw t' horsewhip ye off the place if I want t'! Ye're

only livin' here 'cause I tolerate ye! Git along! I hate the sight
o' ye! [*She stops, panting and glaring at him.*]

EBEN [*Returning her glance in kind.*] An' I hate the sight o' yew!
[*He turns and strides off up the road. She follows his retreating
figure with concentrated hate. Old* CABOT *appears coming up
from the barn. The hard, grim expression of his face has
changed. He seems in some queer way softened, mellowed. His
eyes have taken on a strange, incongruous dreamy quality. Yet
there is no hint of physical weakness about him—rather he
looks more robust and younger.* ABBIE *sees him and turns away
quickly with unconcealed aversion. He comes slowly up to
her.*]

CABOT [*Mildly.*] War yew an' Eben quarrelin' agen?

ABBIE [*Shortly.*] No.

CABOT. Ye was talkin' a'mighty loud. [*He sits down on the edge
of porch.*]

ABBIE. [*Snappishly.*] If ye heerd us they hain't no need askin'
questions.

CABOT. I didn't hear what ye said.

ABBIE [*Releaved.*] Waal—it wa'n't nothin' t' speak on.

CABOT [*After a pause.*] Eben's queer.

ABBIE [*Bitterly.*] He's the dead spit 'n' image o' yew!

CABOT [*Queerly interested.*] D'ye think so, Abbie? [*After a pause,
ruminatingly*] Me 'n' Eben's allus fit 'n' fit. I never could b'ar
him noways. He's so thunderin' soft—like his Maw.

ABBIE [*Scornfully.*] Ay-eh! 'Bout as soft as yew be!

CABOT [*As if he hadn't heard.*] Mebbe I been too hard on him.

ABBIE [*Jeeringly.*] Waal— ye're gettin' soft now—soft as slop!
That's what Eben was sayin'.

CABOT [*his face instantly grim and ominous.*] Eben was sayin'?
Waal, he'd best not do nothin' t' try me 'r he'll soon diskiver. . . .
[*A pause. She keeps her face turned away. His gradually softens.
He stares up at the sky.*] Purty, hain't it?

ABBIE [*Crossly.*] I don't see nothin' purty.

CABOT. The sky. Feels like a wa'm field up thar.

ABBIE [*Sarcastically.*] Air yew aimin' t' buy up over the farm too?
[*She snickers contemptuously.*]

CABOT [*Strangely.*] I'd like t' own my place up thar. [*A pause.*] I'm
gittin' old Abbie, I'm gittin' ripe on the bough. [*A pause. She
stares at him mystified. He goes on.*] It's allus lonesome cold
in the house—even when it's bilin' hot outside. Hain't yew
noticed?

ABBIE. No.

CABOT. It's wa'm down t' the barn—nice smellin' an' warm—with
the cows. [*A pause.*] Cows is queer.

ABBIE. Like yew?

CABOT. Like Eben. [*A pause.*] I'm gittin' t' feel resigned t' Eben—

jest as I got t' feel 'bout his Maw. I'm gittin' t' learn to b'ar his softness—jest like her'n. I calc'late I c'd a'most take t' him —if he wa'n't sech a dumb fool! [*A pause.*] I s'pose it's old age a-creepin' in my bones.

ABBIE [*Indifferently.*] Waal—ye hain't dead yet.

CABOT [*Roused.*] No, I hain't, yew bet—not by a hell of a sight— I'm sound 'n' tough as hickory! [*Then moodily*] But arter three score and ten the Lord warns ye t' prepare. [*A pause.*] That's why Eben's come in my head. Now that his cussed sinful brothers is gone their path t' hell, they's no one left but Eben.

ABBIE [*Resentfully.*] They's me, hain't they? [*Agitated*] What's all this sudden likin' ye tuk to Eben? Why don't ye say nothin' 'bout me? Hain't I yer lawful wife?

CABOT [*Simply.*] Ay-eh. Ye be. [*A pause—he stares at her desirously —his eyes grow avid—then with a sudden movement he seizes her hands and squeezes them, declaiming in a queer camp meeting preacher's tempo:*] Yew air my Rose o' Sharon! Behold, yew air fair; yer eyes air doves; yer lips air like scarlet; yer two breasts air like two fawns; yer naval be like a round goblet; yer belly be like a heap o' wheat.... [*He covers her hand with kisses. She does not seem to notice. She stares before her with hard angry eyes.*]

ABBIE [*Jerking her hands away—harshly.*] So ye're plannin' t' leave the farm t' Eben, air ye?

CABOT [*Dazedly.*] Leave...? [*Then with resentful obstinacy*] I hain't a-givin' it t' no one!

ABBIE [*Remorselessly.*] Ye can't take it with ye.

CABOT [*Thinks a moment—then reluctantly.*] No, I calc'late not. [*After a pause—with a strange passion*] But if I could, I would, by the Etarnal! 'R if I could, in my dyin' hour, I'd set it afire an' watch it burn—this house an' every ear o' corn an' every tree down t' the last blade o' hay! I'd sit an' know it was all a-dying with me an' no one else'd ever own what was mine, what I'd made out o' nothin' with my own sweat 'n' blood! [*A pause—then he adds with a queer affection.*] Ceptin' the cows. Then I'd turn free.

ABBIE [*Harshly.*] An' me?

CABOT [*With a queer smile.*] Ye'd be turned free, too.

ABBIE [*Furiously.*] So that's the thanks I git fur marryin' ye—t' have ye change kind to Eben who hates ye, an' talk o' turnin' me out in the road.

CABOT [*Hastily.*] Abbie! Ye know I wa'n't....

ABBIE [*Vengefully.*] Just let me tell ye a thing or two 'bout Eben. Whar's he gone? T' see that harlot, Min! I tried fur t' stop him. Disgracin' yew an' me—on the Sabbath, too!

CABOT [*Rather guiltily.*] He' a sinner—nateral-born. It's lust eatin' his heart.

ABBIE [*Enraged beyond endurance—wildly vindictive.*] An' his lust fur me! Kin ye find excuses fur that?

CABOT [*Stares at her—after a dead pause.*] Lust—fur yew?

ABBIE [*Defiantly.*] He was tryin' t' make love t' me—when ye heerd us quarrelin'.

CABOT [*Stares at her—then a terrible expression of rage comes over his face—he springs to his feet shaking all over.*] By the A'mighty God—I'll end him!

ABBIE [*Frightened now for* EBEN.] No! Don't ye!

CABOT [*Violently.*] I'll git the shotgun an' blow his soft brains t' the top o' them elums!

ABBIE [*Throwing her arms around him.*] No, Ephraim!

CABOT [*Pushing her away violently.*] I will, by God!

ABBIE [*In a quieting tone.*] Listen, Ephraim. 'Twa'n't nothin' bad —on'y a boy's foolin'—'twa'n't meant serious—jest jokin' and teasin'. . . .

CABOT. Then why did ye say—lust?

ABBIE. It must hev sounded wusser'n I meant. An' I was mad at thinkin'—ye'd leave him the farm.

CABOT [*Quieter but still grim and cruel.*] Waal then, I'll horse-whip him off the place if that much'll content ye.

ABBIE [*Reaching out and taking his hand.*] No. Don't think o' me! Ye mustn't drive him off. 'Tain't sensible. Who'll ye get to help ye on the farm? They's no one hereabouts.

CABOT [*Considers this—then nodding his appreciation.*] Ye got a head on ye. [*Then irritably:*] Waal, let him stay. [*He sits down on the edge of the porch. She sits beside him. He murmurs contemptuously:*] I oughn't git riled so—at that 'ere fool calf. [*A pause.*] But har's the p'int. What son o' mine'll keep on here t' the farm—when the Lord does call me? Simeon an' Peter air gone t' hell—an' Eben's follerin' 'em.

ABBIE. They's me.

CABOT. Ye're on'y a woman.

ABBIE. I'm yewr wife.

CABOT. That hain't me. A son is me—my blood—mine. Mine ought t' git mine. An' then it's still mine—even though I be six foot under. D'ye see?

ABBIE [*Giving him a look of hatred.*] Ay-eh. I see. [*She becomes very thoughtful, her face growing shrewd, her eyes studying* CABOT *craftily.*]

CABOT. I'm gittin' old—ripe on the bough. [*Then with a sudden forced reassurance*] Not but what I hain't a hard nut t' crack even yet—an' fur many a year t' come! By the Eternal, I kin break most o' the young fellars' backs at any kind o' work any day o' the year!

ABBIE [*Suddenly.*] Mebbe the Lord'll give *us* a son.

CABOT [*Turns and stares at her eagerly.*] Ye mean—a son—t' me 'n' yew?

ABBIE [*With a cajoling smile.*] Ye're a strong man yet, hain't ye? 'Tain't noways impossible, be it? We know that. Why d'yt stare so? Hain't ye never thought o' that afore? I been thinkin' o' it all along, Ay-eh—an' I been prayin' it'd happen, too.

CABOT [*His face growing full of joyous pride and a sort of religious ecstasy.*] Ye been prayin', Abbie?—fur a son?—t' us?

ABBIE. Ay-eh. [*With a grim resolution*] I want a son now.

CABOT [*Excitedly clutching both of her hands in his.*] It'd be the blessin' o' God, Abbie—the blessin' o' God A'mighty on me —in my old age—in my lonesomeness! They hain't nothin' I wouldn't do fur ye then, Abbie. Ye'd hev on'y ask it—anythin' ye'd a mind t'!

ABBIE [*Interrupting.*] Would ye will the farm t' me then—t' me an' it . . . ?

CABOT [*Vehemently.*] I'd do anythin' ye axed, I tell ye! I swar it! May I be everlastin' damned t' hell if I wouldn't! [*He sinks to his knees, pulling her down with him. He trembles all over with the fervor of his hopes.*] Pray t' the Lord agen, Abbie. It's the Sabbath! I'll jine ye! Two prayers air better nor one. "An' God hearkened unto Rachel"! An' God hearkened unto Abbie! Pray, Abbie! Pray fur him to hearken! [*He bows his head, mumbling. She pretends to do likewise but gives him a side glance of scorn and triumph.*]

SCENE II

About eight in the evening. The interior of the two bedrooms on the top floor is shown—EBEN *is sitting on the side of his bed in the room on the left. On account of the heat he has taken off everything but his undershirt and pants. His feet are bare. He faces front, brooding moodily, his chin propped on his hands, a desperate expression on his face.*

In the other room CABOT *and* ABBIE *are sitting side by side on the edge of their bed, an old four-poster with feather mattress. He is in his night shirt, she in her nightdress. He is still in the queer, excited mood into which the notion of a son has thrown him. Both rooms are lighted dimly and flickeringly by tallow candles.*

CABOT. The farm needs a son.

ABBIE. I need a son.

CABOT. Ay-eh. Sometimes ye air the farm an' sometimes the farm be yew That's why I clove t' ye in my lonesomeness. [*A pause. He pounds his knee with his fist.*] Me an' the farm has got t' beget a son!

ABBIE. Ye'd best go t' sleep Ye're gittin' trin's all mixed.

CABOT [*With an impatient gesture.*] No, I hain't. My mind's clear's a well. Ye don't know me, that's it. [*He stares hopelessly at the floor.*]

ABBIE [*Indifferently.*] Mebbe. [*In the next room* EBEN *gets up and paces up and down distractedly.* ABBIE *hears him. Her eyes fasten on the intervening wall with concentrated attention.* EBEN *stops and stares. Their hot glances seem to meet through the wall. Unconsciously he stretches out his arms for her and she half rises. Then aware, he mutters a curse at himself and flings himself face downward on the bed, his clenched fists above his head, his face buried in the pillow.* ABBIE *relaxes with a faint sigh but her eyes remain fixed on the wall; she listens with all her attention for some movement from* EBEN.]

CABOT [*Suddenly raises his head and looks at her—scornfully.*] Will ye ever know me—'r will any man 'r woman? [*Shaking his head*] No. I calc'late 't wa'n't t' be. [*He turns away.* ABBIE *looks at the wall. Then, evidently unable to keep silent about his thoughts, without looking at his wife, he puts out his hand and clutches her knee. She starts violently, looks at him, sees he is not watching her, concentrates again on the wall and pays no attention to what he says.*] Listen, Abbie. When I come here fifty odd year ago—I was jest twenty an' the strongest an' hardest ye ever seen—ten times as strong an' fifty times as hard as Eben. Waal—this place was nothin' but fields o' stones. Folks laughed when I tuk it. They couldn't know what I knowed. When ye kin make corn sprout out o' stones, God's livin' in yew! They wa'n't strong enuf fur that! They reckoned God was easy. They laughed. They don't laugh no more. Some died hereabouts. Some went West an' died. They're all under ground—fur follerin' arter an easy God. God hain't easy. [*He shakes his head slowly.*] An' I growed hard. Folks kept allus sayin' he's a hard man like 'twas sinful t' be hard, so's at last I said back at 'em: Waal then, by thunder, ye'll git me hard an' see how ye like it! [*Then suddenly*] But I give in t' weakness once. 'Twas arter I'd been here two year. I got weak—despairful—they was so many stones. They was a party leavin', givin' up, goin' West. I jined 'em. We tracked on 'n on. We come t' broad medders, plains, whar the soil was black an' rich as gold. Nary a stone. Easy. Ye'd on'y to plow an' sow an' then set an' smoke yer pipe an' watch thin's grow. I could o' been a rich man—but somethin' in me fit me an' fit me—the voice o' God sayin': "This hain't wuth nothin' t' Me. Get ye back t' hum!" I got afeerd o' that voice an' I lit out back t' hum here, leavin' my claim an crops t' whoever'd a mind t' take 'em. Ay-eh. I actoolly give up what was rightful mine! God's hard, not easy! God's in the stones! Build my church on a rock—out o' stones an' I'll be in them! That's what He meant t' Peter! [*He sighs heavily—a pause.*] Stones. I picked 'em up an' piled 'em into walls. Ye kin read the years o' my life in them walls, every day a hefted stone, climbin' over the hills up and down, fencin' in the

fields that was mine, whar I'd made thin's grow out o' nothin'
—like the will o' God, like the servant o' His hand. It wa'n't
easy. It was hard an' He made me hard fur it. [*He pauses.*]
All the time I kept gittin' lonesomer. I tuk a wife. She bore
Simeon an' Peter. She was a good woman. She wuked hard.
We was married twenty year. She never knowed me. She helped
but she never knowed what she was helpin'. I was allus lonesome. She died. After that it wa'n't so lonesome fur a spell.
[*A pause.*] I lost count o' the years. I had no time t' fool away
countin' 'em. Sim an' Peter helped. The farm growed. It was
all mine! When I thought o' that I didn't feel lonesome. [*A
pause.*] But ye can't hitch yer mind t' one thin' day an' night.
I tuk another wife—Eben's Maw. Her folks was contestin' me
at law over my deeds t' the farm—my farm! That's why Eben
keeps a-talkin' his fool talk o' this bein' his Maw's farm. She
bore Eben. She was purty—but soft. She tried t' be hard. She
couldn't. She never knowed me nor nothin'. It was lonesomer
'n hell with her. After a matter o' sixteen odd years, she died.
[*A pause.*] I lived with the boys. They hated me 'cause I was
hard. I hated them 'cause they was soft. They coveted the farm
without knowin' what it meant. It made me bitter 'n worm-
wood. It aged me—them coveting what I'd made fur mine.
Then this spring the call come—the voice o' God cryin' in
my wilderness, is my lonesomeness—t' go out an' seek an' find!
[*Turning to her with strange passion*] I sought ye an' I found
ye! Yew air my Rose o' Sharon! Yer eyes air like.... [*She has
turned a blank face, resentful eyes to his. He stares at her for a
moment—then harshly*] Air ye any the wiser fur all I've told
ye?

ABBIE [*Confusedly.*] Mebbe.

CABOT [*Pushing her away from him—angrily.*] Ye don't know
nothin'—nor never will. If ye don't hev a son t' redeem ye ...
[*This in a tone of cold threat.*]

ABBIE [*Resentfully.*] I've prayed, hain't I?

CABOT [*Bitterly.*] Pray agen—fur understandin'!

ABBIE [*A veiled threat in her tone.*] Ye'll have a son out o' me, I
promise ye.

CABOT. How kin ye promise?

ABBIE. I got second-sight mebbe. I kin foretell. [*She gives a queer
smile.*]

CABOT. I believe ye have. Ye give me the chills sometimes. [*He
shivers.*] It's cold in this house. It's oneasy. They's thin's pokin'
about in the dark—in the corners. [*He pulls on his trousers,
tucking in his night shirt, and pulls on his boots.*]

ABBIE [*Surprised.*] What air ye goin'?

CABOT [*Queerly.*] Down whar it's restful—what it's warm—down t'
the barn. [*Bitterly*] I kin talk t' the cows. They know. They

know the farm an' me. They'll give me peace. [*He turns to go out the door.*]

ABBIE [*A bit frightenedly.*] Air ye ailin' tonight, Ephraim?

CABOT. Growin'. Growin' ripe on the bough. [*He turns and goes, his boots clumping down the stairs.* EBEN *sits up with a start, listening.* ABBIE *is conscious of his movement and stares at the wall.* CABOT *comes out of the house around the corner and stands by the gate, blinking at the sky. He stretches up his hands in a tortured gesture*] God A'mighty, call from the dark! [*He listens as if expecting an answer. Then his arms drop, he shakes his head and plods off toward the barn.* EBEN *and* ABBIE *stare at each other through the wall.* EBEN *sighs heavily and* ABBIE *echoes it. Both become terribly nervous, uneasy. Finally* ABBIE *gets up and listens, her ear to the wall. He acts as if he saw every move she was making, he becomes resolutely still. She seems driven into a decision—goes out the door in rear determinedly. His eyes follow her. Then as the door of his room is opened softly, he turns away, waits in an attitude of strained fixity.* ABBIE *stands for a second staring at him, her eyes burning with desire. Then with a little cry she runs over and throws her arms about his neck, she pulls his head back and covers his mouth with kisses. At first, he submits dumbly; then he puts his arms about her neck and returns her kisses, but finally, suddenly aware of his hatred, he hurls her away from him, springing to his feet. They stand speechless and breathless, panting like two animals.*]

ABBIE [*At last—painfully.*] Ye shouldn't, Eben—ye shouldn't—I'd make ye happy!

EBEN [*Harshly.*] I don't want t' be happy—from yew!

ABBIE [*Helplessly.*] Ye do, Eben! Ye do! Why d'ye lie?

EBEN [*Viciously.*] I don't take t' ye, I tell ye! I hate the sight o' ye!

ABBIE [*With an uncertain troubled laugh.*] Waal, I kissed ye anyways—an' ye kissed back—yer lips was burnin'—ye can't lie 'bout that! [*Intensely*] If ye don't care, why did ye kiss me back—why was yer lips burnin'?

EBEN [*Wiping his mouth.*] It was like pizen on 'em [*Then tauntingly*] When I kissed ye back, mebbe I thought 'twas someone else.

ABBIE [*Wildly.*] Min?

EBEN. Mebbe.

ABBIE [*Torturedly.*] Did ye go t' see her? Did ye r'ally go? I thought ye mightn't. Is that why ye throwed me off jest now?

EBEN [*Sneeringly.*] What if it be?

ABBIE [*Raging.*] Then ye're a dog, Eben Cabot!

EBEN [*Threateningly.*] Ye can't talk that way t' me!

ABBIE [*With a shrill laugh.*] Can't I? Did ye think I was in love with ye—a weak thin' like yew? Not much! I on'y wanted ye fur a purpose o' my own—an' I'll hev ye fur it yet 'cause I'm stronger'n yew be!

EBEN [*Resentfully.*] I knowed well it was on'y part o' yer plan t' swaller everythin'!

ABBIE [*Tauntingly.*] Mebbe!

EBEN [*Furious.*] Git out o' my room!

ABBIE. This air my room an' ye're on'y hired help!

EBEN [*Threateningly.*] Git out afore I murder ye!

ABBIE [*Quite confident now.*] I hain't a mite afeerd. Ye want me, don't ye? Yes, ye do! An' yer Paw's son'll never kill what he wants! Look at yer eyes! They's lust fur me in 'em, burnin' 'em up! Look at yer lips now! They're tremblin' an' longin' t' kiss me, an' yer teeth t' bite [*He is watching her now with a horrible fascination. She laughs a crazy triumphant laugh.*] I'm a-goin' t' make all o' this hum my hum! They's one room hain't mine yet, but it's a-goin' t' be tonight. I'm a-goin' down now an light up! [*She makes him a mocking bow.*] Won't ye come courtin' me in the best parlor, Mister Cabot?

EBEN [*Staring at her—horribly confused—dully.*] Don't ye dare! It hain't been opened since Maw died an' was laid out thar! Don't ye . . . ! [*But her eyes are fixed on his so burningly that his will seems to wither before hers. He stands swaying toward her helplessly.*]

ABBIE [*Holding his eyes and putting all her will into her words as she backs out the door.*] I'll expect ye afore long, Eben.

EBEN [*Stares after her for a while, walking toward the door. A light appears in the parlor window. He murmurs.*] In the parlor? [*This seems to arouse connotations for he comes back and puts on his white shirt, collar, half ties the tie mechanically, puts on coat, takes his hat, stands barefooted looking about him in bewilderment, mutters wonderingly:*] Maw! Whar air yew? [*Then goes slowly toward the door in rear.*]

SCENE III

A few minutes later. The interior of the parlor is shown. A grim, repressed room like a tomb in which the family has been interred alive. ABBIE *sits on the edge of the horsehair sofa. She has lighted all the candles and the room is revealed in all its preserved ugliness. A change has come over the woman. She looks awed and frightened now, ready to run away.*

The door is opened and EBEN *appears. His face wears an expression of obsessed confusion. He stands staring at her, his arms hanging disjointedly from his shoulders, his feet bare, his hat in his hand.*

ABBIE [*After a pause—with a nervous, formal politeness.*] Won't ye set?

EBEN [*Dully.*] Ay-eh. [*Mechanically be places his hat carefully on the floor near the door and sits stiffly beside her on the edge of the sofa. A pause. They both remain rigid, looking straight ahead with eyes full of fear.*]

ABBIE. When I fust came in—in the dark—they seemed somethin' here.

EBEN [*Simply.*] Maw.

ABBIE. I kin still feel—somethin'. . . .

EBEN. It's Maw.

ABBIE. At fust I was feerd o' it. I wanted t' yell an' run. Now—since yew come—seems like it's growin' soft an' kind t' me. [*Addressing the air—queerly*] Thank yew.

EBEN. Maw allus loved me.

ABBIE. Mebbe it knows I love yew too. Mebbe that makes it kind t' me.

EBEN [*Dully.*] I dunno. I should think she'd hate ye.

ABBIE [*With certainty.*] No. I kin feel it don't—not no more.

EBEN. Hate ye fur stealin' her place—here in her hum—settin' in her parlor whar she was laid— [*He suddenly stops, staring stupidly before him.*]

ABBIE. What is it, Eben?

EBEN [*In a whisper.*] Seems like Maw didn't want me t' remind ye.

ABBIE [*Excitedly.*] I knowed, Eben! It's kind t' me! It don't b'ar me no grudges fur what I never knowed an' couldn't help!

EBEN. Maw b'ars him a grudge.

ABBIE. Waal, so does all o' us.

EBEN. Ay-eh. [*With passion*] I does, by God!

ABBIE [*Taking one of his hands in hers and patting it.*] Thar! Don't git riled thinkin' o' him. Think o' yer Maw who's kind t' us. Tell me about yer Maw, Eben.

EBEN. They hain't nothin' much. She was kind. She was good.

ABBIE [*Putting one arm over his shoulder. He does not seem to notice—passionately.*] I'll be kind an' good t' ye!

EBEN. Sometimes she used t' sing fur me.

ABBIE. I'll sing fur ye!

EBEN. This was her hum. This was her farm.

ABBIE. This is my hum! This is my farm!

EBEN. He married her t' steal 'em. She was soft an' easy. He couldn't 'preciate her.

ABBIE. He can't 'preciate me!

EBEN. He murdered her with his hardness.

ABBIE. He's murderin' me!

EBEN. She died. [*A pause.*] Sometimes she used to sing fur me. [*He bursts into a fit of sobbing.*]

ABBIE. [*both her arms around him—with wild passion.*] I'll sing fur ye! I'll die fur ye! [*In spite of her overwhelming desire for him, there is a sincere maternal love in her manner and voice—a horribly frank mixture of lust and mother love.*] Don't cry,

Eben! I'll take yer Maw's place! I'll be everythin' she was t' ye!
Let me kiss ye, Eben! [*She pulls his head around. He makes a
bewildered pretense of resistance. She is tender.*] Don't be
afeerd! I'll kiss ye pure, Eben—same 's if I was a Maw t' ye—
an' ye kin kiss me back 's if yew was my son—my boy—sayin'
good-night t' me! Kiss me, Eben. [*They kiss in restrained
fashion. Then suddenly wild passion overcomes her. She kisses
him lustfully again and again and he flings his arms about her
and returns her kisses. Suddenly, as in the bedroom, he frees
himself from her violently and springs to his feet. He is trembling all over, in a strange state of terror.* ABBIE *strains her arms
toward him with fierce pleading.*] Don't ye leave me, Eben!
Can't ye see it hain't enuf—lovin' ye like a Maw—can't ye see
it's got t' be that an' more—much more—a hundred times
more—fur me t' be happy—fur yew t' be happy?

EBEN [*To the presence he feels in the room.*] Maw! Maw! What d'ye
want! What air ye tellin' me?

ABBIE. She's tellin' ye t' love me. She knows I love ye an' I'll be
good t' ye. Can't ye feel it? Don't ye know? She's tellin' ye t'
love me, Eben!

EBEN. Ay-eh. I feel—mebbe she—but—I can't figger out—why—
when ye've stole her place—here in her hum—in the parlor
what she was—

ABBIE [*Fiercely.*] She knows I love ye!

EBEN [*His face suddenly lighting up with a fierce triumphant grin.*]
I see it! I see why. It's her vengeance on him—so's she kin rest
quiet in her grave!

ABBIE [*Wildly.*] Vengeance o' God on the hull o' us. What d'we give
a durn? I love ye, Eben! God knows I love ye! [*She stretches
out her arms for him.*]

EBEN [*Throws himself on his knees beside the sofa and grabs her in
his arms—releasing all his pent-up passion.*] An' I love yew,
Abbie!—now I kin say it! I been dyin' fur want o' ye—every
hour since ye come! I love ye! [*Their lips meet in a fierce,
bruising kiss.*]

SCENE IV

*Exterior of the farmhouse. It is just dawn. The front door at
right is opened and* EBEN *comes out and walks around to the gate.
He is dressed in his working clothes. He seems changed. His face
wears a bold and confident expression, he is grinning to himself
with evident satisfaction. As he gets near the gate, the window of
the parlor is heard opening and the shutters are flung back and*
ABBIE *sticks her head out. Her hair tumbles over her shoulders in
disarray, her face is flushed, she looks at* EBEN *with tender, lan-
guorous eyes and calls softly.*]

ABBIE. Eben. [*As he turns—playfully*] Jest one more kiss afore ye go. I'm goin' to miss ye fearful all day.

EBEN. An' me yew, ye kin bet! [*He goes to her. They kiss several times. He draws away, laughingly.*] Thar. That's enuf, hain't it? Ye won't hev none left fur next time.

ABBIE. I got a million o' 'em left fur yew! [*Then a bit anxiously*] D'ye r'ally love me, Eben?

EBEN [*Emphatically.*] I like ye better'n any gal I ever knowed! That's gospel!

ABBIE. Likin' hain't lovin'.

EBEN. Waal then—I love ye. Now air yew satisfied?

ABBIE. Ay-eh, I be. [*She smiles at him adoringly.*]

EBEN. I better git t' the barn. The old critter's liable t' suspicion an' come sneakin' up.

ABBIE [*With a confident laugh.*] Let him! I kin allus pull the wool over his eyes. I'm goin' t' leave the shutters open and let in the sun 'n' air. This room's been dead long enuf. Now it's goin' t' be my room!

EBEN [*Frowning.*] Ay-eh.

ABBIE [*Hastily.*] I meant—our room.

EBEN. Ay-eh.

ABBIE. We made it our'n last night, didn't we? We give it life—our lovin' did. [*A pause.*]

EBEN [*With a strange look.*] Maw's gone back t' her grave. She kin sleep now.

ABBIE. May she rest in peace! [*Then tenderly rebuking*] Ye oughtn't t' talk o' sad thin's—this mornin'.

EBEN. It jest come up in my mind o' itself.

ABBIE. Don't let it. [*He doesn't answer. She yawns.*] Waal, I'm a-goin' t' steal a wink o' sleep. I'll tell the Old Man I hain't feelin' pert. Let him git his own vittles.

EBEN. I see him comin' from the barn. Ye better look smart an' git upstairs.

ABBIE. Ay-eh. Good-by. Don't fergit me. [*She throws him a kiss. He grins—then squares his shoulders and awaits his father confidently.* CABOT *walks slowly up from the left, staring up at the sky with a vague face.*]

EBEN [*Jovially.*] Mornin', Paw. Stargazin' in daylight?

CABOT. Purty, hain't it?

EBEN [*Looking around him possessively.*] It's a durned purty farm.

CABOT. I mean the sky.

EBEN [*Grinning.*] How d'ye know? Them eyes o' your'n can't see that fur. [*This tickles his humor and he slaps his thigh and laughs.*] Ho-ho! That's a good un!

CABOT [*Grimly sarcastic.*] Ye're feelin' right chipper, hain't ye? Whar'd ye steal the likker?

EBEN [*Good-naturedly.*] 'Tain't likker. Jest life. [*Suddenly holding

out his hand—soberly] Yew 'n' me is quits. Let's shake hands.
CABOT [*Suspiciously.*] What's come over ye?
EBEN. Then don't. Mebbe it's jest as well. [*A moment's pause.*]
   What's come over me? [*Queerly*] Didn't ye feel her passin'—
   Goin' back t' her grave?
CABOT [*Dully.*] Who?
EBEN. Maw. She kin rest now an' sleep content. She's quits with ye.
CABOT [*confusedly.*] I rested. I slept good—down with the cows.
   They know how t' sleep. They're teachin' me.
EBEN [*Suddenly jovial again.*] Good fur the cows! Waal—ye better
   git t' work.
CABOT [*Grimly amused.*] Air ye bossin' me, ye calf?
EBEN [*Beginning to laugh.*] Ay-eh! I'm bossin' yew! Ha-ha-ha! see
   how ye like it! Ha-ha-ha! I'm the prize rooster o' this roost.
   Ha-ha-ha! [*He goes off toward the barn laughing.*]
CABOT [*Looks after him with scornful pity.*] Soft-headed. Like his
   Maw. Dead spit 'n' image. No hope in him! [*He spits with
   contemptuous disgust.*] A born fool! [*Then matter-of-factly*]
   Waal—I'm gittin' peckish. [*He goes toward door.*]

PART III

SCENE I

*A night in late spring the following year. The kitchen and the
two bedrooms upstairs are shown. The two bedrooms are dimly
lighted by a tallow candle in each.* EBEN *is sitting on the side of the
bed in his room, his chin propped on his fists, his face a study of the
struggle he is making to understand his conflicting emotions. The
noisy laughter and music from below where a kitchen dance is in
progress annoy and distract him. He scowls at the floor.*

In the next room a cradle stands beside the double bed.

*In the kitchen all is festivity. The stove has been taken down to
give more room to the dancers. The chairs, with wooden benches
added, have been pushed back against the walls. On these are seated,
squeezed in tight against one another, farmers and their wives and
their young folks of both sexes from the neighboring farms. They
are all chattering and laughing loudly. They evidently have some
secret joke in common. There is no end of winking, of nudging, of
meaning nods of the head toward* CABOT *who, in a state of extreme
hilarious excitement increased by the amount he has drunk, is
standing near the rear door where there is a small keg of whisky
and serving drinks to all the men. In the left corner, front, dividing the attention with her husband,* ABBIE *is sitting in a rocking
chair, a shawl wrapped about her shoulders. She is very pale, her
face is thin and drawn, her eyes are fixed anxiously on the open
door in rear as if waiting for someone.*

The musician is tuning up his fiddle, seated in the far right corner. He is a lanky young fellow with a long, weak face. His pale eyes blink incessantly and he grins about him slyly with a greedy malice.

ABBIE [*Suddenly turning to a young girl on her right.*] Whar's Eben?

YOUNG GIRL [*Eying her scornfully.*] I dunno, Mrs. Cabot. I hain't seen Eben in ages. [*Meaningly*] Seems like he's spent most o' his time t' hum since yew come.

ABBIE [*Vaguely.*] I tuk his Maw's place.

YOUNG GIRL. Ay-eh. So I heerd. [*She turns away to retail this bit of gossip to her mother sitting next to her.* ABBIE *turns to her left to a big stoutish middle-aged man whose flushed face and staring eyes show the amount of "likker" he has consumed.*]

ABBIE. Ye hain't see Eben, hev ye?

MAN. No, I hain't. [*Then he adds with a wink*] If yew hain't, who would?

ABBIE. He's the best dancer in the county. He'd ought t' come an' dance.

MAN [*With a wink.*] Mebbe he's doin' the dutiful an' walkin' the kid t' sleep. It's a boy, hain't it?

ABBIE [*Nodding vaguely.*] Ay-eh—born two weeks back—purty's a picter.

MAN. They all is—t' their Maws. [*Then in a whisper, with a nudge and a leer*] Listen, Abbie—if ye ever git tired o' Eben, remember me! Don't fergit now! [*He looks at her uncomprehending face for a second—then grunts disgustedly.*] Waal—guess I'll likker agin. [*He goes over and joins* CABOT, *who is arguing noisily with an old farmer over cows. They all drink.*]

ABBIE [*This time appealing to nobody in particular.*] Wonder what Eben's a-doin'? [*Her remark is repeated down the line with many a guffaw and titter until it reaches the fiddler. He fastens his blinking eyes on* ABBIE.]

FIDDLER [*Raising his voice.*] Bet I kin tell ye, Abbie, what Eben's doin'! He's down t' the church offerin' up prayers o' thanksgivin'. [*They all titter expectantly.*]

MAN. What fur? [*Another titter.*]

FIDDLER. 'Cause unto him a—[*he hesitates just long enough*]—brother is born! [*A roar of laughter. They all look from* ABBIE *to* CABOT. *She is oblivious, staring at the door.* CABOT, *although he hasn't heard the words, is irritated by the laughter and steps forward, glaring about him. There is an immediate silence.*]

CABOT. What're ye all bleatin' about—like a flock o' goats? Why don't ye dance, damn ye? I axed ye here t' dance—t' eat, drink an' be merry—an' thar ye set cacklin' like a lot o' wet hens with the pip! Ye've swilled my likker an' guzzled my vittles like hogs, hain't ye? Then dance fur me, can't ye? That's fa'r an' squar', hain't it? [*A grumble of resentment goes around but they are all evidently in too much awe of him to express it openly.*]

FIDDLER [*Slyly.*] We're waitin' fur Eben. [*A suppressed laugh.*]

CABOT [*With a fierce exultation.*] T'hell with Eben! Eben's done fur now! I got a new son! [*His mood switching with drunken suddenness*] But ye needn't t' laugh at Eben, none o' ye! He's my blood, if he be a dumb fool. He's better nor any o' yew! He kin do a day's work a'most up t' what I kin—an' that'd put any o' yew pore critters t' shame!

FIDDLER. An' he kin do a good night's work, too! [*A roar of laughter.*]

CABOT. Laugh, ye damn fools! Ye're right jist the same, Fiddler. He kin work day an' night too, like I kin, if need be!

OLD FARMER [*From behind the keg where he is weaving drunkenly back and forth—with great simplicity.*] They hain't many t' touch ye, Ephraim—a son at seventy-six. That's a hard man fur ye! I be on'y sixty-eight an' I couldn't do it. [*A roar of laughter in which* CABOT *joins uproariously.*]

CABOT [*Slapping him on the back.*] I'm sorry fur ye, Hi. I'd never suspicion sech weakness from a boy like yew!

OLD FARMER. An' I never reckoned yew had it in ye nuther, Ephraim. [*There is another laugh.*]

CABOT [*Suddenly grim.*] I got a lot in me—a hell of a lot—folks don't know on. [*Turning to the* FIDDLER] Fiddle 'er up, durn ye! Give 'em somethin' t' dance t'! What air ye, an ornament? Hain't this a celebration? Then grease yer elbow an' go it!

FIDDLER [*Seizes a drink which the* OLD FARMER *holds out to him and downs it.*] Here goes! [*He starts to fiddle "Lady of the Lake." Four young fellows and four girls form in two lines and dance a square dance. The* FIDDLER *shouts directions for the different movements, keeping his words in the rhythm of the music and interspersing them with jocular personal remarks to the dancers themselves. The people seated along the walls stamp their feet and clap their hands in unison.* CABOT *is especially active in this respect. Only* ABBIE *remains apathetic, staring at the door as if she were alone in a silent room.*]

FIDDLER. Swing your partner t' the right! That's it, Jim! Give her a b'ar hug! Her Maw hain't lookin'. [*Laughter.*] Change partners! That suits ye, don't it, Essie, now ye got Reub afore ye? Look at her redden up, will ye! Waal, life is short an' so's love, as the feller says. [*Laughter.*]

CABOT [*Excitedly, stamping his foot.*] Go it, boys! Go it, gals!

FIDDLER [*With a wink at the others.*] Ye're the spryest seventy-six ever I sees, Ephraim! Now if ye'd on'y good eye-sight...! [*Suppressed laughter. He gives* CABOT *no chance to retort but roars.*] Promenade! Ye're walkin' like a bride down the aisle, Sarah! Waal, while they's life they's allus hope, I've heerd tell. Swing your partner to the left! Gosh A'mighty, look at Johnny

Cook high-steppin'! They hain't goin' t' be much strength left
fur hoein' in the corn lot t'morrow. [*Laughter.*]

CABOT. Go it! Go it! [*Then suddenly, unable to restrain himself
any longer, he prances into the midst of the dancers, scattering
them, waving his arms about wildly.*] Ye're all hoofs! Git out
o' my road! Give me room! I'll show ye dancin'. Ye're all too
soft! [*He pushes them roughly away. They crowd back toward
the walls, muttering, looking at him resentfully.*]

FIDDLER [*Jeeringly.*] Go it, Ephraim! Go it! [*He starts "Pop Goes
the Weasel," increasing the tempo with every verse until at the
end he is fiddling crazily as fast as he can go.*]

CABOT [*Starts to dance, which he does very well and with tremen-
dous vigor. Then he begins to improvise, cuts incredibly grotesque capers, leaping up and cracking his heels together,
prancing around in a circle with body bent in an Indian war
dance, then suddenly straightening up and kicking as high as
he can with both legs. He is like a monkey on a string. And all
the while he intersperses his antics with shouts and derisive
comments.*] Whoop! Here's dancin' fur ye! Whoop! See that!
Seventy-six, if I'm a day! Hard as iron yet! Beatin' the young
'uns like I allus done! Look at me! I'd invite ye t' dance on my
hundredth birthday on'y ye'll all be dead by them. Ye're a
sickly generation! Yer hearts air pink, not red! Yer veins is full
o' mud an' water! I be the on'y man in the county! Whoop!
See that! I'm a Injun! I've killed Injuns in the West afore ye
was born—an' skulped 'em too! They's a arrer wound on my
backside I c'd show ye! The hull tribe chased me. I outrun 'em
all—with the arrer stuck in me! An' I tuk vengeance on 'em.
Ten eyes fur an eye, that was my motter! Whoop! Look at me!
I kin kick the ceilin' off the room! Whoop!

FIDDLER [*Stops playing—exhaustedly.*] God A'mighty, I got enuf.
Ye got the devil's strength in ye.

CABOT [*Delightedly.*] Did I beat yew, too? Wa'al, ye played smart.
Hev a swig. [*He pours whisky for himself and* FIDDLER. *They
drink. The others watch* CABOT *silently with cold, hostile eyes.
There is a dead pause. The* FIDDLER *rests.* CABOT *leans against
the keg, panting, glaring around him confusedly. In the room
above,* EBEN *gets to his feet and tiptoes out the door in rear,
appearing a moment later in the other bedroom. He moves
silently, even frightenedly, toward the cradle and stands there
looking down at the baby. His face is as vague as his reactions
are confused, but there is a trace of tenderness, of interested
discovery. At the same moment that he reaches the cradle,*
ABBIE *seems to sense something. She gets up weakly and goes
to* CABOT.]

ABBIE. I'm goin' up t' the baby.

CABOT [*With real solicitude.*] Air ye able fur the stairs? D'ye want
me t' help ye, Abbie?

ABBIE. No. I'm able. I'll be down agen soon.

CABOT. Don't ye git wore out! He needs ye, remember—our son does! [*He grins affectionately, patting her on the back. She shrink from his touch.*]

ABBIE [*Dully.*] Don't—tech me. I'm goin'—up. [*She goes. CABOT looks after her. A whisper goes around the room. CABOT turns. It ceases. He wipes his forehead streaming with sweat. He is breathing pantingly.*]

CABOT. I'm a-goin' out t' git fresh air. I'm feelin' a mite dizzy. Fiddle up thar! Dance, all o' ye! Here's likker fur them as wants it. Enjoy yerselves. I'll be back. [*He goes, closing the door behind him.*]

FIDDLER [*Sarcastically.*] Don't hurry none on our account! [*A suppressed laugh. He imitates ABBIE.*] Whar's Eben? [*More laughter.*]

A WOMAN. [*Loudly.*] What's happened in this house is plain as the nose on yer face! [*ABBIE appears in the doorway upstairs and stands looking in surprise and adoration at EBEN, who does not see her.*]

A MAN. Ssshh! He's li'ble t' be listenin' at the door. That'd be like him. [*Their voices die to an intensive whispering. Their faces are concentrated on this gossip. A noise as of dead leaves in the wind comes from the room. CABOT has come out from the porch and stands by the gate, leaning on it, staring at the sky blinkingly. ABBIE comes across the room silently. EBEN does not notice her until she is quite near.*]

EBEN [*Starting.*] Abbie!

ABBIE. Ssshh! [*She throws her arms around him. They kiss—then bend over the cradle together.*] Ain't he purty?—dead spit 'n' image o' yew!

EBEN [*Pleased.*] Air he? I can't tell none.

ABBIE. E-zactly like!

EBEN [*Frowningly.*] I don't like this. I don't like lettin' on what's mine's his'n. I been doin' that all my life. I'm gittin' t' the end o' b'arin' it!

ABBIE [*Putting her finger on his lips.*] We're doin' the best we kin. We got t' wait. Somethin's bound t' happen. [*She puts her arms around him.*] I got t' go back.

EBEN. I'm goin' out. I can't b'ar it with the fiddle playin' an' the laughin'.

ABBIE. Don't git feelin' low. I love ye, Eben. Kiss me. [*He kisses her. They remain in each other's arms.*]

CABOT [*At the gate, confusedly.*] Even the music can't drive it out— somethin'. Ye kin feel it droppin' off the elums, climbin' up the roof, sneakin' down the chimney, pokin' in the corners! They's no peace in houses, they's no rest livin' with folks. Somethin's always livin' with ye. [*With a deep sigh*] I'll go t' the barn an' rest a spell. [*He goes wearily toward the barn.*]

FIDDLER [*Tuning up.*] Let's celebrate the old skunk gittin' fooled! We kin have some fun now he's went. [*He starts to fiddle "Turkey in the Straw." There is real merriment now. The young folks get up to dance.*]

SCENE II

*A half hour later—exterior—*EBEN *is standing by the gate looking up at the sky, an expression of dumb pain bewildered by itself on his face.* CABOT *appears, returning from the barn, walking wearily, his eyes on the ground. He sees* EBEN *and his whole mood immediately changes. He becomes excited, a cruel, triumphant grin comes to his lips, he strides up and slaps* EBEN *on the back. From within comes the whining of the fiddle and the noise of stamping feet and laughing voices.*

CABOT. So har ye be!

EBEN [*Startled, stares at him with hatred for a moment—then dully.*] Ay-eh.

CABOT [*Surveying him jeeringly.*] Why hain't ye been in t' dance? They was all axin' fur ye.

EBEN. Let 'em ax!

EBEN. They's a hull passel o' purty gals.

EBEN. T' hell with 'em!

CABOT. Ye'd ought t' be marryin' one o' 'em soon.

EBEN. I hain't marryin' no one.

CABOT. Ye might 'arn a share o' a farm that way.

EBEN [*With a sneer.*] Like yew did, ye mean? I hain't that kind.

CABOT [*Stung.*] Ye lie! 'Twas yer Maw's folks aimed t' steal my farm from me.

EBEN. Other folks don't say so. [*After a pause—defiantly*] An' I got a farm, anyways!

CABOT [*Derisively.*] Whar?

CABOT [*Stamps a foot on the ground.*] Har!

CABOT [*Throws his head back and laughs coarsely.*] Ho-ho! Ye hev, hev ye? Waal, that's a good un!

EBEN [*Controlling himself—grimly.*] Ye'll see!

CABOT [*Stares at him suspiciously, trying to make him out—a pause—then with scornful confidence.*] Ay-eh. I'll see. So'll ye. It's ye that's blind—blind as a mole underground [EBEN *suddenly laughs, one short sardonic bark: "Ha." A pause.* CABOT *peers at him with renewed suspicion.*] What air ye hawin' 'bout? [EBEN *turns away without answering.* CABOT *grows angry.*] God A'mighty, yew air a dumb dunce! They's nothin' in that thick skull o' your'n but noise—like a empty keg it be! [EBEN *doesn't seem to hear—*CABOT's *rage grows.*] Yewr farm! God A'mighty! If ye wa'n't a born donkey ye'd know ye'll never own stick nor stone on it, specially now arter him bein' born. It's his'n, I

tell ye—his'n arter I die—but I'll live a hundred jest t' fool
ye all—an' he'll be growed then—yewr age a'most! [EBEN
laughs again his sardonic "Ha." This drives CABOT *into a fury.*]
Ha? Ye think ye kin git 'round that someways, do ye? Waal,
it'll be her'n, too—Abbie's—ye won't git 'round her—she knows
yer tricks—she'll be too much fur ye—she wants the farm her'n
—she was afeerd o' ye—she told me ye was sneakin' 'round
tryin' t' make love t' her t' git her on yer side . . . ye . . . ye mad
fool, ye! [*He raises his clenched fists threateningly.*]

EBEN [*Is confronting him, choking with rage.*] Ye lie, ye old skunk!
Abbie never said no sech thing!

CABOT [*Suddenly triumphant when he sees how shaken* EBEN *is.*]
She did. An' I says, I'll blow his brains t' the top o' them elums
—an' she says no, that hain't sense, who'll ye git t'help ye on
the farm in his place—an' then she says yew'n me ought t' have
a son—I know we kin, she says—an' I says, if we do, ye kin
have anythin' I've got ye've a mind t. An' she says, I wants
Eben cut off so's this farm'll be mine when ye die! [*With terrible gloating.*] An' that's what's happened, hain't it? An' the
farm's her'n! An' the dust o' the road—that's you'rn! Ha! Now
who's hawin'?

EBEN [*Has been listening, petrified with grief and rage—suddenly
laughs wildly and brokenly.*] Ha-ha-ha! So that's her sneakin'
game—all along!—like I suspicioned at fust—t' swaller it all—
an' me, too . . . ! [*Madly.*] I'll murder her! [*He springs toward
the porch but* CABOT *is quicker and gets in between.*]

CABOT. No, ye don't!

EBEN. Git out o' my road! [*He tries to throw* CABOT *aside. They
grapple in what becomes immediately a murderous struggle.
The old man's concentrated strength is too much for* EBEN.
CABOT *gets one hand on his throat and presses him back across
the stone wall. At the same moment,* ABBIE *comes out on the
porch. With a stifled cry she runs toward them.*]

ABBIE. Eben! Ephraim! [*She tugs at the hand on* EBEN's *throat.*]
Let go, Ephraim! Ye're chokin' him!

CABOT [*Removes his hand and flings* EBEN *sideways full length on
the grass, gasping and choking. With a cry,* ABBIE *kneels beside
him, trying to take his head on her lap, but he pushes her away.*
CABOT *stands looking down with fierce triumph.*] Ye needn't
t've fret, Abbie, I wa'n't aimin' t' kill him. He hain't wuth
hangin' fur—not by a hell of a sight! [*More and more tri-
umphantly.*] Seventy-six an' him not thirty yit—an' look whar
he be fur thinkin' his Paw was easy! No, by God, I hain't easy!
An' him upstairs, I'll raise him t' be like me! [*He turns to
leave them.*] I'm goin' in an' dance!—sing an' celebrate! [*He
walks to the porch—then turns with a great grin.*] I don't
calc'late it's left in him, but if he gits pesky, Abbie, ye jest sing
out. I'll come a-runnin' an' by the Etarnal, I'll put him across

my knee an' birch him! Ha-ha-ha! [*He goes into the house laughing. A moment later his loud "whoop" is heard.*]

ABBIE [*Tenderly.*] Eben. Air ye hurt? [*She tries to kiss him but he pushes her violently away and struggles to a sitting position.*]

EBEN [*Gaspingly.*] T'hell—with ye!

ABBIE [*Not believing her ears.*] It's me, Eben—Abbie—don't ye know me?

EBEN [*Glowering at her with hatred.*] Ay-eh—I know ye—now! [*He suddenly breaks down, sobbing weakly.*]

ABBIE [*Fearfully.*] Eben—what's happened t' ye—why did ye look at me 's if ye hated me?

EBEN [*Violently, between sobs and gasps.*] I do hate ye! Ye're a whore—a damn trickin' whore!

ABBIE [*Shrinking back horrified.*] Eben! Ye don't know what ye're sayin'!

EBEN [*Scrambling to his feet and following her—accusingly.*] Ye're nothin' but a stinkin' passel o' lies! Ye've been lyin' t' me every word ye spoke, day an' night, since we fust—done it. Ye've kept sayin' ye loved me. . . .

ABBIE [*Frantically.*] I do love ye! [*She takes his hand but he flings hers away.*]

EBEN [*Unheeding.*] Ye've made a fool o' me—a sick, dumb fool— a-purpose! Ye've been on'y playin' yer sneakin', stealin' game all along—gittin' me t' lie with ye so's ye'd hev a son he'd think was his'n, an' makin' him promise he'd give ye the farm and let me eat dust, if ye did git him a son! [*Staring at her with anguished, bewildered eyes*] They must be a devil livin' in ye! 'Tain't human t' be as bad as that be!

ABBIE [*Stunned—dully.*] He told yew . . . ?

EBEN. Hain't it true? It hain't no good in yew lyin'.

ABBIE [*Pleadingly.*] Eben, listen—ye must listen—it was long ago— afore we done nothin'—yew was scornin' me—goin' t' see Min —when I was lovin' ye—an' I said it t' him t' git vengeance on ye!

EBEN [*Unheedingly. With tortured passion.*] I wish ye was dead! I wish I was dead along with ye afore this come! [*Ragingly*] But I'll git my vengeance too! I'll pray Maw t' come back t' help me—t' put her cuss on yew an' him!

ABBIE [*Brokenly.*] Don't ye, Eben! Don't ye! [*She throws herself on her knees before him, weeping.*] I didn't mean t' do bad t'ye! Fergive me, won't ye?

EBEN [*Not seeming to hear her—fiercely.*] I'll git squar' with the old skunk—an' yew! I'll tell him the truth 'bout the son he's so proud o'! Then I'll leave ye here t' pizen each other—with Maw comin' out o' her grave at nights—an' I'll go t' the gold fields o' Californi-a whar Sim an' Peter be!

ABBIE [*Terrified.*] Ye won't—leave me? Ye can't!

EBEN [*With fierce determination.*] I'm a-goin', I tell ye! I'll git rich thar an' come back an' fight him fur the farm he stole—an' I'll kick ye both out in the road—t' beg an' sleep in the woods—an' yer son along with ye—t' starve an' die! [*He is hysterical at the end.*]

ABBIE [*With a shudder—humbly.*] He's yewr son, too, Eben.

EBEN [*Torturedly.*] I wish he never was born! I wish he'd die this minit! I wish I'd never sot eyes on him! It's him—yew havin' him—a-purpose t' steal—that's changed everythin'!

ABBIE [*Gently.*] Did ye believe I loved ye—afore he come?

EBEN. Ay'eh—like a dumb ox!

ABBIE. An' ye don't believe no more?

EBEN. B'lieve a lyin' thief! Ha!

ABBIE [*Shudders—then humbly.*] An' did ye r'ally love me afore?

EBEN [*Brokenly.*] Ay-eh—an' ye was trickin' me!

ABBIE. An' ye don't love me now!

EBEN [*Violently.*] I hate ye, I tell ye!

ABBIE. An' ye're truly goin' West—goin' t' leave me—all account o' him being born?

EBEN. I'm a-goin' in the mornin'—or may God strike me t' hell!

ABBIE [*After a pause—with a dreadful cold intensity—slowly.*] If that's what his comin's done t' me—killin' yewr love—takin' yew away—my on'y joy—the on'y joy I've ever knowed—like heaven t' me—purtier'n heaven—then I hate him, too, even if I be his Maw!

EBEN [*Bitterly.*] Lies! Ye love him! He'll steal the farm fur ye! [*Brokenly*] But 'tain't the farm so much—not no more—it's yew foolin' me—gittin' me t' love ye—lyin' yew loved me—jest t' git a son t' steal!

ABBIE [*Distractedly.*] He won't steal! I'd kill him fust! I do love ye! I'll prove t' ye . . . !

EBEN [*Harshly.*] 'Tain't no use lyin' no more. I'm deaf t' ye! [*He turns away.*] I hain't seein' ye agen. Good-by!

ABBIE [*Pale with anguish.*] Hain't ye even goin' t' kiss me—not once —arter all we loved?

EBEN [*In a hard voice.*] I hain't wantin' t' kiss ye never agen! I'm wantin' t' forgit I ever sot eyes on ye!

ABBIE. Eben!—ye mustn't—wait a spell—I want t' tell ye. . . .

EBEN. I'm a-goin' in t' git drunk. I'm a-goin' t' dance.

ABBIE [*Clinging to his arm—with passionate earnestness.*] If I could make it—'s if he'd never come up between us—if I could prove t' ye I wa'n't schemin' t' steal from ye—so's everythin' could be jest the same with us, lovin' each other jest the same, kissin' an' happy the same's we've been happy afore he come—if I could do it—ye'd love me agen, wouldn't ye? Ye'd kiss me agen? Ye wouldn't never leave me, would ye?

EBEN [*Moved.*] I calc'late not. [*Then shaking her hand off his arm —with a bitter smile*] But ye hain't God, be ye?

ABBIE [*Exultantly.*] Remember ye've promised! [*Then with strange intensity*] Mebbe I kin take back one thin' God does!

EBEN [*Peering at her.*] Ye're gittin' cracked, hain't ye? [*Then going towards door*] I'm a-goin' t' dance.

ABBIE [*Calls after him intensely.*] I'll prove t' ye! I'll prove I love ye better'n. . . . [*He goes in the door, not seeming to hear. She remains standing where she is, looking after him—then she finishes desperately:*] Better'n everythin' else in the world!

SCENE III

Just before dawn in the morning—shows the kitchen and CABOT'S *bedroom. In the kitchen, by the light of a tallow candle on the table,* EBEN *is sitting, his chin propped on his hands, his drawn face blank and expressionless. His carpet-bag is on the floor beside him. In the bedroom, dimly lighted by a small whale-oil lamp,* CABOT *lies asleep.* ABBIE *is bending over the cradle, listening, her face full of terror yet with an undercurrent of desperate triumph. Suddenly, she breaks down and sobs, appears about to throw herself on her knees beside the cradle; but the old man turns restlessly, groaning in his sleep, and she controls herself, and shrinking away from the cradle with a gesture of horror, backs swiftly toward the door in rear and goes out. A moment later she comes into the kitchen and, running to* EBEN, *flings her arms about his neck and kisses him wildly. He hardens himself, he remains unmoved and cold, he keeps his eyes straight ahead.*

ABBIE [*Hysterically.*] I done it, Eben! I told ye I'd do it! I've proved I love ye—better'n everythin'—so's ye can't never doubt me no more!

EBEN [*Dully.*] Whatever ye done, it hain't no good now.

ABBIE [*Wildly.*] Don't ye say that! Kiss me, Eben, won't ye? I need ye t' kiss me arter what I done! I need ye t' say ye love me!

EBEN [*Kisses her without emotion—dully.*] That's fur good-by. I'm a-goin' soon.

ABBIE. No! No! Ye won't go—not now!

EBEN [*Going on with his own thoughts.*] I been a-thinkin'—an' I hain't goin' t' tell Paw nothin'. I'll leave Maw t' take vengeance on ye. If I told him, the old skunk'd jest be stinkin' mean enuf to take it out on that baby. [*His voice showing emotion in spite of him*] An' I don't want nothin' bad t' happen t' him. He hain't t' blame fur yew. [*He adds with a certain queer pride:*] An' he looks like me! An' by God, he's mine! An' some day I'll be a-comin' back an' . . . !

ABBIE [*Too absorbed in her own thoughts to listen to him—pleadingly.*] They's no cause fur ye t' go now—they's no sense—it's

all the same's it was—they's nothin' come b'tween us now—
arter what I done!

EBEN [*Something in her voice arouses him. He stares at her a bit
frightenedly.*] Ye look mad, Abbie. What did ye do?

ABBIE. I—I killed him, Eben.

EBEN [*Amazed.*] Ye killed him?

ABBIE [*Dully.*] Ay-eh.

EBEN [*Recovering from his astonishment—savagely.*] An' serves him
right! But we got t' do somethin' quick t' make it look s'if the
old skunk'd killed himself when he was drunk. We kin prove
by 'em all how drunk he got.

ABBIE [*Wildly.*] No! No! Not him! [*Laughing distractedly*] But
that's what I ought t' done, hain't it? I oughter killed him
instead! Why didn't ye tell me?

EBEN [*Appalled.*] Instead? What d'ye mean?

ABBIE. Not him.

EBEN [*His face grown ghastly.*] Not—not that baby!

ABBIE [*Dully.*] Ay-eh!

EBEN [*Falls to his knees as if he'd been struck—his voice trembling
with horror.*] Oh, God A'mighty! A'mighty God! Maw, whar
was ye, why didn't ye stop her?

ABBIE [*Simply.*] She went back t' her grave that night we fust done
it, remember? I hain't felt her about since. [*A pause.* EBEN
*hides his head in his hands, trembling all over as if he had the
ague. She goes on dully:*] I left the piller over his little face.
Then he killed himself. He stopped breathin'. [*She begins to
weep softly.*]

EBEN [*Rage beginning to mingle with grief.*] He looked like me. He
was mine, damn ye!

ABBIE [*Slowly and brokenly.*] I didn't want t' do it. I hated myself
fur doin' it. I loved him. He was so purty—dead spit 'n' image
o' yew. But I loved yew more—an' yew was goin' away—far off
whar I'd never see ye agen, never kiss ye, never feel ye pressed
agin me agen—an' ye said ye hated me fur havin' him—ye said
ye hated him an' wished he was dead—ye said if it hadn't been
fur him comin' it'd be the same's afore between us.

EBEN [*Unable to endure this, springs to his feet in a fury, threatening her, his twitching fingers seeming to reach out for her
throat.*] Ye lie! I never said—I never dreamed ye'd—I'd cut off
my head afore I'd hurt his finger!

ABBIE [*Piteously, sinking on her knees.*] Eben, don't ye look at me
like that—hatin' me—not after what I done fur ye—fur us—
so's we could be happy agen—

EBEN [*Furiously now.*] Shut up, or I'll kill ye! I see yer game now—
the same old sneakin' trick—ye're aimin' t' blame me fur the
murder ye done!

ABBIE [*Moaning—putting her hands over her ears.*] Don't ye, Eben!
Don't ye! [*She grasps his legs.*]

EBEN [*His mood suddenly changing to horror, shrinks away from her.*] Don't ye tech me! Ye're pizen! How could ye—t' murder a pore little critter—Ye must've swapped yer soul t' hell! [*Sudden raging*] Ha! I kin see why ye done it! Not the lies ye jest told—but 'cause ye wanted t' steal agen—steal the last thin' ye'd left me—my part o' him—no, the hull o' him—ye saw he looked like me—ye knowed he was all mine—an' ye couldn't b'ar it—I know ye! Ye killed him fur bein' mine! [*All this has driven him almost insane. He makes a rush past her for the door—then turns—shaking both fists at her, violently.*] But I'll take vengeance now! I'll git the Sheriff! I'll tell him everythin'! Then I'll sing "I'm off to Californi-a!" an' go—gold—Golden Gate—gold sun—fields o' gold in the West! [*This last he half shouts, half croons incoherently, suddenly breaking off passionately.*] I'm a-goin' fur the Sheriff t' come an' git ye! I want ye tuk away, locked up from me! I can't stand t' luk at ye! Murderer an' thief 'r not, ye still tempt me! I'll give ye up t' the Sheriff! [*He turns and runs out, around the corner of house, panting and sobbing, and breaks into a swerving sprint down the road.*]

ABBIE [*Struggling to her feet, runs to the door, calling after him.*] I love ye, Eben! I love ye! [*She stops at the door weakly, swaying, about to fall.*] I don't care what ye do—if ye'll on'y love me agen— [*She falls limply to the floor in a faint.*]

SCENE IV

About an hour later. Same as Scene III. Shows the kitchen and CABOT's *bedroom. It is after dawn. The sky is brilliant with the sunrise. In the kitchen,* ABBIE *sits at the table, her body limp and exhausted, her head bowed down over her arms, her face hidden. Upstairs,* CABOT *is still asleep but awakens with a start. He looks toward the window and gives a snort of surprise and irritation—throws back the covers and begins hurriedly pulling on his clothes. Without looking behind him, he begins talking to* ABBIE, *whom he supposes beside him.*

CABOT. Thunder 'n' lightnin', Abbie! I hain't slept this late in fifty year! Looks 's if the sun was full riz a'most. Must've been the dancin' an' likker. Must be gittin' old. I hope Eben's t'wuk. Ye might've tuk the trouble t' rouse me, Abbie. [*He turns—sees no one there—surprised.*] Waal—whar air she? Gittin' vittles, I calc'late. [*He tiptoes to the cradle and peers down—proudly*] Mornin', sonny. Purty's a picter! Sleepin' sound. He don't beller all night like most o' 'em. [*He goes quietly out the door in rear —a few moments later enters kitchen—sees* ABBIE—*with satisfaction*] So thar ye be. Ye got any vittles cooked?

ABBIE [*Without moving.*] No.

CABOT [*Coming to her, almost sympathetically.*] Ye feelin' sick?

ABBIE. No.

CABOT [*Pats her on shoulder. She shudders.*] Ye'd best lie down a spell. [*Half jocularly*] Yer son'll be needin' ye soon. He'd ought t' wake up with a gnashin' appetite, the sound way he's sleepin'.

ABBIE [*Shudders—then in a dead voice.*] He ain't never goin' to wake up.

CABOT [*Jokingly.*] Takes after me this mornin'. I ain't slept so late in . . .

ABBIE. He's dead.

CABOT [*Stares at her—bewilderedly.*] What . . .

ABBIE. I killed him.

CABOT [*Stepping back from her—aghast.*] Air ye drunk—'r crazy—'r . . . !

ABBIE [*Suddenly lifts her head and turns on him—wildly.*] I killed him, I tell ye! I smothered him. Go up an' see if ye don't b'lieve me! [CABOT *stares at her a second, then bolts out the rear door, can be heard bounding up the stairs, and rushes into the bedroom and over to the cradle,* ABBIE *has sunk back lifelessly into her former position.* CABOT *puts his hand down on the body in the crib. An expression of fear and horror comes over his face.*]

CABOT [*Shrinking away—tremblingly.*] God A'mighty! God A'mighty! [*He stumbles out the door—in a short while returns to the kitchen—comes to* ABBIE, *the stunned expression still on his face—hoarsely*] Why did ye do it? Why? [*As she doesn't answer, he grabs her violently by the shoulder and shakes her.*] I ax ye why ye done it! Ye'd better tell me 'r . . . !

ABBIE [*Gives him a furious push which sends him staggering back and springs to her feet—with wild rage and hatred.*] Don't ye dare tech me! What right hev ye t' question me 'bout him? He wa'n't yewr son! Think I'd have a son by yew? I'd die fust! I hate the sight o' ye an' allus did! It's yew I should've murdered, if I'd had good sense! I hate ye! I love Eben. I did from the fust. An' he was Eben's son—mine an' Eben's—not your'n.

CABOT [*Stands looking at her dazedly—a pause—finding his words with an effort—dully.*] That was it—what I felt—pokin' round the corners—while ye lied—holdin' yerself from me—sayin' ye'd a'ready conceived— [*He lapses into crushed silence—then with a strange emotion*] He's dead, sart'n. I felt his heart. Pore little critter! [*He blinks back one tear, wiping his sleeve across his nose.*]

ABBIE [*Hysterically.*] Don't ye! Don't ye! [*She sobs unrestrainedly.*]

CABOT [*With a concentrated effort that stiffens his body into a rigid line and hardens his face into a stony mask—through his teeth to himself.*] I got t' be—like a stone—a rock o' jedgment! [*A pause. He gets complete control over himself—harshly*] If he was Eben's, I be glad he air gone! An' mebbe I suspicioned it all along. I felt they was somethin' onnateral—somewhars—

the house got so lonesome—an' cold—drivin' me down t' the barn—t' the beasts o' the field. . . . Ay'eh. I must've suspicioned —somethin'. Ye didn't fool me—not altogether, leastways—I'm too old a bird—growin' ripe on the bough. . . . [*He becomes aware he is wandering, straightens again, looks at* ABBIE *with a cruel grin.*] So ye'd liked t' hev murdered me 'stead o' him, would ye? Waal, I'll live to a hundred! I'll live t' see ye hung! I'll deliver ye up t' the judgment o' God an' the law! I'll git the Sheriff now. [*Starts for the door.*]

ABBIE [*Dully.*] Ye needn't. Eben's gone fur him.

CABOT [*Amazed.*] Eben—gone fur the Sheriff?

ABBIE. Ay-eh.

CABOT. T' inform agen ye?

ABBIE. Aye-eh.

CABOT [*Considers this—a pause—then in a hard voice.*] Waal, I'm thankful fur him savin' me the trouble. I'll git t' wuk. [*He goes to the door—then turns—in a voice full of strange emotion*] He'd ought t' been my son, Abbie. Ye'd ought t' loved me. I'm a man. If ye'd loved me, I'd never told no Sheriff on ye no matter what ye did, if they was t' brile me alive!

ABBIE [*Defensively.*] They's more to it nor yew know, makes him tell.

CABOT [*Dryly.*] Fur yewr sake, I hope they be. [*He goes out—comes around to the gate—stares up at the sky. His control relaxes. For a moment he is old and weary. He murmurs despairingly:*] God A'mighty, I be lonesomer'n ever! [*He hears running foot-steps from the left, immediately is himself again.* EBEN *runs in, panting exhaustedly, wild-eyed and mad looking. He lurches through the gate.* CABOT *grabs him by the shoulder.* EBEN *stares at him dumbly.*] Did ye tell the Sheriff?

EBEN [*Nodding stupidly.*] Ay-eh.

CABOT [*Gives him a push away that sends him sprawling—laughing with withering contempt.*] Good fur ye! A prime chip o' yer Maw ye be! [*He goes toward the barn, laughing harshly.* EBEN *scrambles to his feet. Suddenly* CABOT *turns—grimly threatening*] Git off this farm when the Sheriff takes her—or, by God, he'll have t' come back an' git me fur murder, too! [*He stalks off.* EBEN *does not appear to have heard him. He runs to the door and comes into the kitchen.* ABBIE *looks up with a cry of anguished joy.* EBEN *stumbles over and throws himself on his knees beside her—sobbing brokenly.*]

EBEN. Fergive me!

ABBIE [*Happily.*] Eben! [*She kisses him and pulls his head over against her breast.*]

EBEN. I love ye! Fergive me!

ABBIE [*Ecstatically.*] I'd fergive ye all the sins in hell fur sayin' that! [*She kisses his head, pressing it to her with a fierce passion of possession.*]

EBEN [*Brokenly.*] But I told the Sheriff. He's comin' fur ye!

ABBIE. I kin b'ar what happens t' me—now!

EBEN. I woke him up. I told him. He says, wait 'til I git dressed. I was waiting. I got to thinkin' o' yew. I got to thinkin' how I'd loved ye. It hurt like somethin' was bustin' in my chest an' head. I got t' cryin'. I knowed sudden I loved ye yet, an' allus would love ye!

ABBIE [*Caressing his hair—tenderly.*] My boy, hain't ye?

EBEN. I begun t' run back. I cut across the fields an' through the woods. I thought ye might have time t' run away—with me— an' . . .

ABBIE [*Shaking her head.*] I got t' take my punishment—t' pay fur my sin.

EBEN. Then I want t' share it with ye.

ABBIE. Ye didn't do nothin'.

EBEN. I put it in yer head. I wisht he was dead! I as much as urged ye t' do it!

ABBIE. No. It was me alone!

EBEN. I'm as guilty as yew be! He was the child o' our sin.

ABBIE [*Lifting her head as if defying God.*] I don't repent that sin! I hain't askin' God t' fergive that!

EBEN. Nor me—but it led up t' the other—an' the murder ye did, ye did 'count o' me—an' it's my murder, too, I'll tell the Sheriff —an' if ye deny it, I'll say we planned it t'gether—an' they'll all b'lieve me, fur they suspicion everythin' we've done, an' it'll seem likely an' true to 'em. An' it is true—way down. I did help ye—somehow.

ABBIE [*Laying her head on his—sobbing.*] No! I dont want yew t' suffer!

EBEN. I got t' pay fur my part o' the sin! An' I'd suffer wuss leavin' ye, goin' West, thinking' o' ye day an' night, bein' out when yew was in—[*lowering his voice*]—'r bein' alive when yew was dead. [*A pause.*] I want t' share with ye, Abbie—prison 'r death 'r hell 'r anythin'! [*He looks into her eyes and forces a trembling smile.*] If I'm sharin' with ye, I won't feel lonesome, leastways.

ABBIE [*Weakly.*] Eben! I won't let ye! I can't let ye!

EBEN [*Kissing her—tenderly.*] Ye can't he'p yerself. I got ye beat fur once!

ABBIE [*Forcing a smile—adoringly.*] I hain't beat—s'long's I got ye!

EBEN [*Hears the sound of feet outside.*] Ssshh! Listen! They're come t' take us!

ABBIE. No, it's him. Don't give him no chance to fight ye, Eben. Don't say nothin'—no matter what he says. An' I won't neither. [*It is* CABOT. *He comes up from the barn in a great state of excitement and strides into the house and then into the kitchen.*

EBEN *is kneeling beside* ABBIE, *his arm around her, hers around him. They stare straight ahead.*]

CABOT [*Stares at them, his face hard. A long pause—vindictively.*] Ye make a slick pair o' murderin' turtle doves! Ye'd ought t' be both hung on the same limb an' left thar t' swing in the breeze an' rot—a warnin' t' old fools like me t' b'ar their lonesomeness alone—an' fur young fools like ye t' hobble their lust. [*A pause. The excitement returns to his face, his eyes snap, he looks a bit crazy.*] I couldn't work today. I couldn't take no interest. T' hell with the farm! I'm leavin' it! I've turned the cows an' other stock loose! I've druv 'em into the woods whar they kin be free! By freein' 'em, I'm freein' myself! I'm quittin' here today! I'll set fire t'house an' barn an' watch 'em burn, an I'll leave yer Maw t' haunt the ashes, an' I'll will the fields back t' God, so that nothin' human kin never touch 'em! I'll be a-goin' to Californi-a—t' jine Simeon an' Peter—true sons o' mine if they be dumb fools—an' the Cabots'll find Solomon's Mines t'gether! [*He suddenly cuts a mad caper*] Whoop! What was the song they sung? "Oh, Californi-a! That's the land fur me." [*He sings this—then gets on his knees by the floorboard under which the money was hid.*] An' I'll sail thar on one o' the finest clippers I kin find! I've got the money! Pity ye didn't know whar this was hidden so's ye could steal... [*He has pulled up the board. He stares—feels—stares again. A pause of dead silence. He slowly turns, slumping into a sitting position on the floor, his eyes like those of a dead fish, his face the sickly green of an attack of nausea. He swallows painfully several times—forces a weak smile at last.*] So—ye did steal it!

EBEN [*Emotionlessly.*] I swapped it t' Sim an' Peter fur their share o' the farm—t' pay their passage t' Californi-a.

CABOT [*With one sardonic*] Ha! [*He begins to recover. Gets slowly to his feet—strangely.*] I calc'late God give it to 'em—not yew! God's hard, not easy! Mebbe they's easy gold in the West but it hain't God's gold. It hain't fur me. I kin hear His voice warnin' me agen t' be hard an' stay on my farm. I kin see his hand usin' Eben t' steal t' keep me from weakness. I kin feel I be in the palm o' His hand, His fingers guidin' me. [*A pause— then he mutters sadly:*] It's a-goin' t' be lonesomer now than ever it war afore—an' I'm gittin' old, Lord—ripe on the bough.... [*Then stiffening*] Waal—what d'ye want? God's lonesome, hain't He? God's hard an' lonesome! [*A pause. The* SHERIFF *with two men comes up the road from the left. They move cautiously to the door. The* SHERIFF *knocks on it with the butt of his pistol.*]

SHERIFF. Open in the name o' the law! [*They start.*]

CABOT. They've come fur ye. [*He goes to the rear door.*] Come in,

Jim! [*The three men enter.* CABOT *meets them in doorway.*] Jest a minit, Jim. I got 'em safe here. [*The* SHERIFF *nods. He and his companions remain in the doorway.*]

EBEN [*Suddenly calls.*] I lied this mornin', Jim. I helped her to do it. Ye kin take me, too.

ABBIE [*Brokenly.*] No!

CABOT. Take 'em both. [*He comes forward—stares at* EBEN *with a trace of grudging admiration*] Purty good—fur yew! Waal, I got t' round up the stock. Good-by.

EBEN. Good-by.

ABBIE. Good-by. [CABOT *turns and strides past the men—comes out and around the corner of the house, his shoulders squared, his face stony, and stalks grimly toward the barn. In the meantime the* SHERIFF *and men have come into the room.*]

SHERIFF [*Embarrassedly.*] Waal—We'd best start.

ABBIE. Wait. [*Turns to* EBEN.] I love ye, Eben.

EBEN. I love ye, Abbie. [*They kiss. The three men grin and shuffle embarrassedly.* EBEN *takes* ABBIE's *hand. They go out the door in rear, the men following, and come from the house, walking hand in hand to the gate.* EBEN *stops there and points to the sunrise sky.*] Sun's a-risin'. Purty, hain't it?

ABBIE. Ay-eh. [*They both stand for a moment looking up raptly in attitudes strangely aloof and devout.*]

SHERIFF [*Looking around at the farm enviously—to his companion.*] It's a jim-dandy farm, no denyin'. Wished I owned it!

Biographical Note

ANOUILH

Jean Anouilh was born in 1910 in Bordeaux. He studied in Paris at the Collège Chaptal and at nineteen became secretary to Louis Jouvet, the famous actor-director at the Théâtres des Champs-Elysees. After a period of military service Anouilh studied law and worked for a short while in an advertising agency. L'Hermine, his first play, was produced in 1932. Since then Anouilh has made his living entirely as a writer, mostly for the theater, occasionally for the movies.

Until about the end of the war Anouilh divided his plays into two categories depending on their tragic or comic leanings. Some of the more popular of the latter category, which he called Pièces roses, are Le Bal des voleurs (produced in 1938), Léocadia (1939), and Le Rendez-vous de Senlis (1941). During the war he did several "black" plays—Pièces noires—based on classic literary subjects: Eurydice (1942), Antigone (1944), and Roméo et Jeannette (1946). Since the war Anouilh has invented two other terms to describe the genre of his plays, Pièces brillantes and Pièces grinçantes, the former emphasizing a kind of hard brilliance given to the comic themes Anouilh had treated more romantically before the war and the latter emphasizing the addition of a grating harshness and bitterness to the tragic themes. Some of the Pièces brillantes are L'Invitation au Château (1947), La Répétition (1950), and Colombe (1951). Some of the Pièces grinçantes are La Valse des toréadors (1952)—later made into a movie starring Peter Sellers—and Pauvre Bitos (1956). Two other plays that lie outside these categories are the well known historical studies L'Alouette (1953), about Joan of Arc, and Becket (1959).

Antigone

jean anouilh

CHARACTERS

CHORUS
ANTIGONE
NURSE
ISMENE
HAEMON
CREON

FIRST GUARD *Jonas*
SECOND GUARD *a Corporal*
THIRD GUARD
MESSENGER
MESSENGER
PAGE
EURYDICE

ANTIGONE, *her hands clasped round her knees, sits on the top step. The* THREE GUARDS *sit on the steps, in a small group, playing cards. The* CHORUS *stands on the top step.* EURYDICE *sits on the top step, just left of center, knitting. The* NURSE *sits on the second step, left of* EURYDICE. ISMENE *stands in front of arch, left, facing* HAEMON, *who stands left of her.* CREON *sits in the chair at right end of the table, his arm over the shoulder of his* PAGE, *who sits on the stool beside his chair. The* MESSENGER *is leaning against the downstage portal of the right arch.*

> *The curtain rises slowly; then the* CHORUS *turns and moves downstage.*

CHORUS. Well, here we are.

These people are about to act out for you the story of Antigone. That thin little creature sitting by herself, staring straight ahead, seeing nothing, is Antigone. She is thinking. She is thinking that the instant I finish telling you who's who and what's what in this play, she will burst forth as the tense, sallow, willful girl whose

---

* *Antigone*, by Jean Anouilh, adapted and translated by Lewis Galantière. Copyright 1946 by Random House, Inc. Reprinted from The Modern Library volume, FOUR CONTEMPORARY FRENCH PLAYS, by permission of the publisher.

family would never take her seriously and who is about to rise up alone against Creon, her uncle, the King.

Another thing that she is thinking is this: she is going to die. Antigone is young. She would much rather live than die. But there is no help for it. When your name is Antigone, there is only one part you can play; and she will have to play hers through to the end.

From the moment the curtain went up, she began to feel that inhuman forces were whirling her out of this world, snatching her away from her sister Ismene, whom you see smiling and chatting with that young man; from all of us who sit or stand here, looking at her, not in the least upset ourselves—for we are not doomed to die to night.

CHORUS *turns and indicates* HAEMON.

The young man talking to Ismene—to the gay and beautiful Ismene—is Haemon. He is the King's son, Creon's son. Antigone and he are engaged to be married. You wouldn't have thought she was his type. He likes dancing, sports, competition; he likes women, too. Now look at Ismene again. She is certainly more beautiful than Antigone. She is the girl you'd think he'd go for. Well . . . There was a ball one night. Ismene wore a new evening frock. She was radiant. Haemon danced every dance with her. And yet, that same night, before the dance was over, suddenly he went in search of Antigone, found her sitting alone—like that, with her arms clasped round her knees—and asked her to marry him. We still don't know how it happened. It didn't seem to surprise Antigone in the least. She looked up at him out of those solemn eyes of hers, smiled sort of sadly and said "yes." That was all. The band struck up another dance. Ismene, surrounded by a group of young men, laughed out loud. And . . . well, here is Haemon expecting to marry Antigone. He won't, of course. He didn't know, when he asked her, that the earth wasn't meant to hold a husband of Antigone, and that this princely distinction was to earn him no more than the right to die sooner than he might otherwise have done.

CHORUS *turns toward* CREON.

That gray-haired, powerfully built man sitting lost in thought, with his little page at his side, is Creon, the King. His face is lined. He is tired. He practices the difficult art of a leader of men. When he was younger, when Oedipus was King and Creon was no more than the King's brother-in-law, he was different. He loved music, bought rare manuscripts, was a kind of art patron. He would while away whole afternoons in the antique shops of this city of Thebes. But Oedipus died. Oedipus' sons died. Creon had to roll up his sleeves and take over the kingdom. Now and then, when he goes to bed weary with the day's work, he wonders whether this business of being a leader of men is worth the trouble. But when he wakes up, the problems are there to be solved; and like a conscientious workman, he does his job.

Creon has a wife, a Queen. Her name is Eurydice. There she sits, the old lady with the knitting, next to the Nurse who brought up the two girls. She will go on knitting all through the play, till the times comes for her to go to her room and die. She is a good woman, a worthy, loving soul. But she is no help to her husband. Creon has to face the music alone. Alone with his Page, who is too young to be of any help.

The others? Well, let's see.

He points toward the MESSENGER.

That pale young man leaning against the wall is the Messenger. Later on he will come running in to announce that Haemon is dead. He has a premonition of catastrophe. That's what he is brooding over. That's why he won't mingle with the others.

As for those three red-faced card players—they are the guards. One smells of garlic, another of beer; but they're not a bad lot. They have wives they are afraid of, kids who are afraid of them; they're bothered by the little day-to-day worries that beset us all. At the same time—they are policemen: eternally innocent, no matter what crimes are committed; eternally indifferent, for nothing that happens can matter to them. They are quite prepared to arrest anybody at all, including Creon himself, should the order be given by a new leader.

That's the lot. Now for the play.

Oedipus, who was the father of the two girls, Antigone and Ismene, had also two sons, Eteocles and Polynices. After Oedipus died, it was agreed that the two sons should share his throne, each to reign over Thebes in alternate years.

Gradually, the lights on the stage have been dimmed.

But when Eteocles, the elder son, had reigned a full year, and time had come for him to step down, he refused to yield up the throne to his younger brother. There was civil war. Polynices brought up allies—six foreign princes; and in the course of the war he and his foreigners were defeated, each in front of one of the seven gates of the city. The two brothers fought, and they killed one another in single combat just outside the city walls. Now Creon is King.

CHORUS *is leaning, at this point, against the left proscenium arch. By now the stage is dark, with only the cyclorama bathed in dark blue. A single spot lights up the face of* CHORUS.

Creon has issued a solemn edict that Eteocles, with whom he had sided, is to be buried with pomp and honours, and that Polynices is to be left to rot. The vultures and the dogs are to bloat themselves on his carcass. Nobody is to go into mourning for him. No gravestone is to be set up in his memory. And above all, any person who attempts to give him religious burial will himself be put to death.

While CHORUS *has been speaking the characters have gone out one by one.* CHORUS *disappears through the left arch.*

It is dawn, gray and ashen, in a house asleep. ANTIGONE *steals in from out-of-doors, through the arch, right. She is carrying her sandals in her hand. She pauses, looking off through the arch, taut, listening, then turns and moves across downstage. As she reaches the table, she sees the* NURSE *approaching through the arch, left. She runs quickly toward the exit. As she reaches the steps, the* NURSE *enters through arch and stands still when she sees* ANTIGONE.

NURSE. Where have you been?
ANTIGONE. Nowhere. It was beautiful. The whole world was gray when I went out. And now—you wouldn't recognize it. It's like a post card: all pink, and green, and yellow. You'll have to get up earlier, Nurse, if you want to see a world without color.
NURSE. It was still pitch black when I got up. I went to your room, for I thought you might have flung off your blanket in the night. You weren't there.
ANTIGONE [*Comes down the steps.*] The garden was lovely. It was still asleep. Have you ever thought how lovely a garden is when it is not yet thinking of men?
NURSE. You hadn't slept in your bed. I couldn't find you. I went to the back door. You'd left it open.
ANTIGONE. The fields were wet. They were waiting for something to happen. The whole world was breathless, waiting. I can't tell you what a roaring noise I seemed to make alone on the road. It bothered me that whatever was waiting wasn't waiting for me. I took off my sandals and slipped into a field. [*She moves down to the stood and sits.*]
NURSE [*Kneels at* ANTIGONE's *feet to chafe them and put on the sandals.*] You'll do well to wash your feet before you go back to bed, Miss.
ANTIGONE. I'm not going back to bed.
NURSE. Don't be a fool! You get some sleep! And me, getting up to see if she hasn't flung off her blanket; and I find her bed cold and nobody in it!
ANTIGONE. Do you think that if a person got up every morning

like this, it would be just as thrilling every morning to be the first girl out-of-doors?

NURSE *puts* ANTIGONE's *left foot down, lifts her other
foot and chafes it.*

NURSE. Morning my grandmother! It was night. It still is. And now, my girl, you'll stop trying to squirm out of this and tell me what you were up to. Where've you been?

ANTIGONE. That's true. It was still night. There wasn't a soul out of doors but me, who thought that it was morning. Don't you think it's marvelous—to be the first person who is aware that it is morning?

NURSE. Oh, my little flibbertigibbet! Just can't imagine what I'm taking about, can she? Go on with you! I know that game. Where have you been, wicked girl?

ANTIGONE [*Soberly.*] No. Not wicked.

NURSE. You went out to meet someone, didn't you? Deny it if you can.

ANTIGONE. Yes. I went out to meet someone.

NURSE. A lover?

ANTIGONE. Yes, Nurse. Yes, the poor dear. I have a lover.

NURSE [*Stands up; bursting out.*] Ah, that's very nice now, isn't it? Such goings-on! You, the daughter of a king, running out to meet lovers. And we work our fingers to the bone for you, we slave to bring you up like young ladies! [*She sits on chair, right of table.*] You're all alike, all of you. Even you—who never used to stop to primp in front of a looking glass, or smear your mouth with rouge, or dindle and dandle to make the boys ogle you, and you ogle back. How many times I'd say to myself, "Now that one, now: I wish she was a little more of a coquette—always wearing the same dress, her hair tumbling round her face. One thing's sure," I'd say to myself, "none of the boys will look at her while Ismene's about, all curled and cute and tidy and trim. I'll have this one on my hands for the rest of my life." And now, you see? Just like your sister, after all. Only worse: a hypocrite. Who is the lad? Some little scamp, eh? Somebody you can't bring home and show to your family, and say, "Well, this is him, and I mean to marry him and no other." That's how it is, is it? Answer me!

ANTIGONE [*Smiling faintly.*] That's how it is. Yes, Nurse.

NURSE. Yes, says she! God save us! I took her when she wasn't that high. I promised her poor mother I'd make a lady of her. And look at her! But don't you go thinking this is the end of this, my young 'un. I'm only your nurse and you can play deaf and dumb with me; I don't count. But your Uncle Creon will hear of this! That, I promise you.

ANTIGONE [*A little weary.*] Yes. Creon will hear of this.

NURSE. And we'll hear what he has to say when he finds out that you go wandering alone o' nights. Not to mention Haemon. For the girl's engaged! Going to be married! Going to be married, and she hops out of bed at four in the morning to meet somebody else in a field. Do you know what I ought to do to you? Take you over my knee the way I used to do when you were little.

ANTIGONE. Please, Nurse, I want to be alone.

NURSE. And if you so much as speak of it, she says she wants to be alone!

ANTIGONE. Nanny, you shouldn't scold, dear. This isn't a day when you should be losing your temper.

NURSE. Not scold, indeed! Along with the rest of it, I'm to like it. Didn't I promise your mother? What would she say if she was here? "Old Stupid!" That's what she'd call me. "Old Stupid. Not to know how to keep my little girl pure! Spend your life making them behave, watching over them like a mother hen, running after them with mufflers and sweaters to keep them warm, and eggnogs to make them strong; and then at four o'clock in the morning, you who always complained you never could sleep a wink, snoring in your bed and letting them slip out into the bushes." That's what she'd say, your mother. And I'd stand there, dying of shame if I wasn't dead already. And all I could do would be not to dare look her in the face; and "That's true," I'd say. "That's all true what you say, Your Majesty."

ANTIGONE. Nanny, dear. Dear Nanny. Don't cry. You'll be able to look Mamma in the face when it's your time to see her. And she'll say, "Good morning, Nanny. Thank you for my little Antigone. You did look after her so well." She knows why I went out this morning.

NURSE. Not to meet a lover?

ANTIGONE. No. Not to meet a lover.

NURSE. Well, you've a queer way of teasing me, I must say! Not to know when she's teasing me! [*Rises to stand behind* ANTIGONE.] I must be getting awfully old, that's what it is. But if you loved me, you'd tell me the truth. You'd tell me why your bed was empty when I went along to tuck you in. Wouldn't you?

ANTIGONE. Please, Nanny, don't cry any more. [ANTIGONE *turns partly toward* NURSE, *puts an arm up to* NURSE's *shoulder. With her other hand,* ANTIGONE *caresses* NURSE's *face.*] There now, my sweet red apple. Do you remember how I used to rub your cheeks to make them shine? My dear, wrinkled red apple! I didn't do anything tonight that was worth sending tears down the little gullies of your dear face. I am pure, and I swear that I have no other lover that Haemon. If you like, I'll swear that I shall never have any other lover than Haemon.

Save your tears, Nanny, save them, Nanny dear; you may still need them. When you cry like that, I become a little girl again; and I mustn't be a little girl today. [ANTIGONE *rises and moves upstage.*]

ISMENE *enters through arch, left. She pauses in front of arch.*

ISMENE. Antigone! What are you doing up at this hour? I've just been to your room.
NURSE. The two of you, now! You're both going mad, to be up before the kitchen fire has been started. Do you like running about without a mouthful of breakfast? Do you think it's decent for the daughters of a king? [*She turns to* ISMENE.] And look at you, with nothing on, and the sun not up! I'll have you both on my hands with colds before I know it.
ANTIGONE. Nanny dear, go away now. It's not chilly, really. Summer's here. Go and make us some coffee. Please, Nanny, I'd love some coffee. It would do me so much good.
NURSE. My poor baby! Her head's swimming, what with nothing on her stomach, and me standing here like an idiot when I could be getting her something hot to drink. [*Exit* NURSE.]

A pause.

ISMENE. Aren't you well?
ANTIGONE. Of course I am. Just a little tired. I got up too early. [ANTIGONE *sits on a chair, suddenly tired.*]
ISMENE. I couldn't sleep, either.
ANTIGONE. Ismene, you ought not to go without your beauty sleep.
ISMENE. Don't make fun of me.
ANTIGONE. I'm not, Ismene, truly. This particular morning, seeing how beautiful you are makes everything easier for me. Wasn't I a miserable little beast when we were small? I used to fling mud at you, and put worms down your neck. I remember tying you to a tree and cutting off your hair. Your beautiful hair! How easy it must be never to be unreasonable with all that smooth silken hair so beautifully set round your head.
ISMENE [*Abruptly.*] Why do you insist upon talking about other things?
ANTIGONE [*Gently.*] I am not talking about other things.
ISMENE. Antigone, I've thought about it a lot.
ANTIGONE. Have you?
ISMENE. I thought about it all night long. Antigone, you're mad.
ANTIGONE. Am I?
ISMENE. We cannot do it.
ANTIGONE. Why not?
ISMENE. Creon will have us put to death.

ANTIGONE. Of course he will. That's what he's here for. He will
do what he has to do, and we will do what we have to do.
He is bound to put us to death. We are bound to go out and
bury our brother. That's the way it is. What do you think we
can do to change it?

ISMENE. [Releases ANTIGONE's hand; draws back a step.] I don't
want to die.

ANTIGONE. I'd prefer not to die, myself.

ISMENE. Listen to me, Antigone. I thought about it all night. I'm
older than you are. I always think things over, and you don't.
You are impulsive. You get a notion in your head and you
jump up and do the thing straight off. And if it's silly, well,
so much the worse for you. Whereas, I think things out.

ANTIGONE. Sometimes it is better not to think too much.

ISMENE. I don't agree with you! [ANTIGONE looks at ISMENE, then
turns and moves to chair behind table. ISMENE leans on end
of table top, toward ANTIGONE.] Oh, I know it's horrible. And
I pity Polynices just as much as you do. But all the same, I
sort of see what Uncle Creon means.

ANTIGONE. I don't want to "sort of see" anything.

ISMENE. Uncle Creon is the king. He has to set an example!

ANTIGONE. But I am not the king; and I don't have to set people
examples. Little Antigone gets a notion in her head—the
nasty brat, the willful, wicked girl; and they put her in a
corner all day, or they lock her up in the cellar. And she
deserves it. She shouldn't have disobeyed!

ISMENE. There you go, frowning, glowering, wanting your own
stubborn way in everything. Listen to me. I'm right oftener
than you are.

ANTIGONE. I don't want to be right!

ISMENE. At least you can try to understand.

ANTIGONE. Understand! The first word I ever heard out of any
of you was that word "understand." Why didn't I "understand" that I must not play with water—cold, black, beautiful
flowing water—because I'd spill it on the palace tiles. Or with
earth, because earth dirties a little girl's frock. Why didn't I
"understand" that nice children don't eat out of every dish at
once; or give everything in their pockets to beggars; or run in
the wind so fast that they fall down; or ask for a drink when
they're perspiring; or want to go swimming when it's either
too early or too late, merely because they happen to feel like
swimming. Understand! I don't want to understand. There'll
be time enough to understand when I'm old . . . If I ever am
old. But not now.

ISMENE. He is stronger than we are, Antigone. He is the king. And
the whole city is with him. Thousands and thousands of them,
swarming through all the streets of Thebes.

ANTIGONE. I am not listening to you.

ISMENE. His mob will come running, howling as it runs. A thousand arms will seize our arms. A thousand breaths will breathe into our faces. Like one single pair of eyes, a thousands eyes will stare at us. We'll be driven in a tumbrel through their hatred, through the smell of them and their cruel, roaring laughter. We'll be dragged to the scaffold for torture, surrounded by guards with their idiot faces all bloated, their animal hands clean-washed for the sacrifice, their beefy eyes squinting as they stare at us. And we'll know that no shrieking and no begging will make them understand that we want to live, for they are like slaves who do exactly as they've been told, without caring about right or wrong. And we shall suffer, we shall feel pain rising in us until it becomes so unbearable that we *know* it must stop. But it won't stop; it will go on rising and rising, like a screaming voice. Oh, I can't, I can't, Antigone!

A pause.

ANTIGONE. How well have you thought it all out.

ISMENE. I thought of it all night long. Didn't you?

ANTIGONE. Oh, yes.

ISMENE. I'm an awful coward, Antigone.

ANTIGONE. So am I. But what has that to do with it?

ISMENE. But, Antigone! Don't you want to go on living?

ANTIGONE. Go on living! Who was it that was always the first out of bed because she loved the touch of the cold morning air on her bare skin? Who was always the last to bed because nothing less than infinite weariness could wean her from the lingering night? Who wept when she was little because there were too many grasses in the meadow, too many creatures in the field, for her to know and touch them all?

ISMENE [*Clasps* ANTIGONE'S *hands, in a sudden rush of tenderness.*] Darling little sister!

ANTIGONE [*Repulsing her.*] No! For heaven's sake! Don't paw me! And don't let us start sniveling! You say you've thought it all out. The howling mob—the torture—the fear of death... They've made up your mind for you. Is that it?

ISMENE. Yes.

ANTIGONE. All right. They're as good excuses as any.

ISMENE. Antigone, be sensible. It's all very well for men to believe in ideas and die for them. But you are a girl!

ANTIGONE. Don't I know I'm a girl? Haven't I spent my life cursing the fact that I was a girl?

ISMENE [*With spirit.*] Antigone! You have everything in the world to make you happy. All you have to do is reach out for it. You are going to be married; you are young; you are beautiful—

ANTIGONE. I am not beautiful.

ISMENE. Yes, you are! Not the way other girls are. But it's always
  you that the little boys turn to look back at when they pass us
  in the street. And when you go by, the little girls stop talking.
  They stare and stare at you, until we've turned a corner.
ANTIGONE [*A faint smile.*] "Little boys—little girls."
ISMENE [*Challengingly.*] And what about Haemon?

                         A pause.

ANTIGONE. I shall see Haemon this morning. I'll take care of
  Haemon. You always said I was mad; and it didn't matter
  how little I was or what I wanted to do. Go back to bed now,
  Ismene. The sun is coming up, and, as you see, there is nothing
  I can do today. Our brother Polynices is as well guarded as
  if he had won the war and were sitting on his throne. Go along.
  You are pale with weariness.
ISMENE. What are you going to do?
NURSE [*Calls from off-stage.*] Come along, my dove. Come to break-
  fast.
ANTIGONE. I don't feel like going to bed. However, if you like, I'll
  promise not to leave the house till you wake up. Nurse is
  getting me breakfast. Go and get some sleep. The sun is just
  up. Look at you: you can't keep your eyes open. Go.
ISMENE. And you will listen to reason, won't you? You'll let me
  talk to you about this again? Promise?
ANTIGONE. I promise. I'll let you talk. I'll let all of you talk. Go
  to bed, now. [ISMENE *goes to arch; exit.*] Poor Ismene!
NURSE [*Enters through arch, speaking as she enters.*] Come along,
  my dove. I've made you some coffee and toast and jam. [*She
  turns towards arch as if to go out.*]
ANTIGONE. I'm not really hungry, Nurse.

  NURSE *stops, looks at* ANTIGONE, *then moves behind her.*

NURSE [*Very tenderly.*] Where is your pain?
ANTIGONE. Nowhere, Nanny dear. But you must keep me warm
  and safe, the way you used to do when I was little. Nanny!
  Stronger than all fever, stronger than any nightmare, stronger
  than the shadow of the cupboard that used to snarl at me and
  turn into a dragon on the bedroom wall. Stronger than the
  thousand insects gnawing and nibbling in the silence of the
  night. Stronger than the night itself, with the weird hooting
  of the night birds that fightened me even when I couldn't hear
  them. Nanny, stronger than death. Give me your hand, Nanny,
  as if I were ill in bed, and you sitting beside me.
NURSE. My sparrow, my lamb! What is it that's eating your heart
  out?

ANTIGONE. Oh, it's just that I'm a little young still for what I have to go through. But nobody but you must know that.

NURSE [*places her other arm around* ANTIGONE's *shoulder*]. A little young for what, my kitten?

ANTIGONE. Nothing in particular, Nanny. Just—all this. Oh, it's so good that you are here. I can hold your callused hand, your hand that is so prompt to ward off evil. You are very powerful, Nanny.

NURSE. What is it you want me to do for you, my baby?

ANTIGONE. There isn't anything to do, except put your hand like this against my cheek. [*She places the* NURSE's *hand against her cheek. A pause, then, as* ANTIGONE *leans back, her eyes shut.*] There! I'm not afraid any more. Not afraid of the wicked ogre, nor of the sandman, nor of the dwarf who steals little children. [*A pause.* ANTIGONE *resumes on another note.*] Nanny . . .

NURSE. Yes?

ANTIGONE. My dog, Puff . . .

NURSE [*Straightens up, draws her hand away*]. Well?

ANTIGONE. Promise me that you will never scold her again.

NURSE. Dogs that dirty up a house with their filthy paws deserve to be scolded.

ANTIGONE. I know. Just the same, promise me.

NURSE. You mean you want me to let her make a mess all over the place and not say a thing?

ANTIGONE. Yes, Nanny.

NURSE. You're asking a lot. The next time she wets my living-room carpet, I'll——

ANTIGONE. Please, Nanny, I beg of you!

NURSE. It isn't fair to take me on my weak side, just because you look a little peaked today. . . . Well, have it your own way. We'll mop up and keep our mouth shut. You're making a fool of me, though.

ANTIGONE. And promise me that you will talk to her. That you will talk to her often.

NURSE [*Turns and looks at* ANTIGONE.] Me, talk to a dog!

ANTIGONE. Yes. But mind you: you are not to talk to her the way people usually talk to dogs. You're to talk to her the way I talk to her.

NURSE. I don't see why both of us have to make fools of ourselves. So long as you're here, one ought to be enough.

ANTIGONE. But if there was a reason why I couldn't go on talking to her——

NURSE [*Interrupting.*] Couldn't go on talking to her! And why couldn't you go on talking to her? What kind of poppycock——?

ANTIGONE. And if she got too unhappy, if she moaned and moaned, waiting for me with her nose under the door as she does when I'm out all day, then the best thing, Nanny, might be to have her mercifully put to sleep.

NURSE. Now what *has* got into you this morning? [HAEMON *enters through arch.*] Running around in the darkness, won't sleep, won't eat—[ANTIGONE *sees* HAEMON.]—and now it's her dog she wants killed. I never.

ANTIGONE [Interrupting.] Nanny! Haemon is here. Go inside, please. And don't forget that you've promised me. [NURSE *goes to arch; exit.* ANTIGONE *rises.*] Haemon, Haemon! Forgive me for quarreling with you last night. [*She crosses quickly to* HAEMON *and they embrace.*] Forgive me for everything. It was all my fault. I beg you to forgive me.

HAEMON. You know that I've forgiven you. You had hardly slammed the door, your perfume still hung in the room, when I had already forgiven you. [*He holds her in his arms and smiles at her. Then draws slightly back.*] You stole that perfume. From whom?

ANTIGONE. Ismene.

HAEMON. And the rouge? and the face powder? and the frock? Whom did you steal them from?

ANTIGONE. Ismene.

HAEMON. And in whose honor did you get yourself up so elegantly?

ANTIGONE. I'll tell you everything. [*She draws him closer.*] Oh, darling, what a fool I was! To waste a whole evening! A whole, beautiful evening!

HAEMON. We'll have other evenings, my sweet.

ANTIGONE. Perhaps we won't.

HAEMON. And other quarrels, too. A happy love is full of quarrels, you know.

ANTIGONE. A happy love, yes. Haemon, listen to me.

HAEMON. Yes?

ANTIGONE. Don't laugh at me this morning. Be serious.

HAEMON. I am serious.

ANTIGONE. And hold me tight. Tighter than you have ever held me. I want all your strength to flow into me.

HAEMON. There! With all my strength.

A pause.

ANTIGONE. [*Breathless.*] That's good. [*They stand for a moment, silent and motionless.*] Haemon! wanted to tell you. You know —the little boy we were going to have when we were married?

HAEMON. Yes?

ANTIGONE. I'd have protected him against everything in the world.

HAEMON. Yes, dearest.

ANTIGONE. Oh, you don't know how I should have held him in my arms and given him my strength. He wouldn't have been afraid of anything, I swear he wouldn't. Not of the falling night, nor of the terrible noonday sun, nor of all the shadows, or all the walls in the world. Our little boy, Haemon! His mother wouldn't have been very imposing: her hair wouldn't always have been brushed; but she would have been strong where he was concerned, so much stronger than all those real mothers with their real bosoms and their aprons around their middle. You believe that, don't you, Haemon?

HAEMON [*Soothingly.*] Yes, yes, my darling.

ANTIGONE. And you believe me when I say that you would have had a real wife?

HAEMON. Darling, you are my real wife.

ANTIGONE. [*Pressing against him and crying out.*] Haemon, you loved me! You did love me that night, didn't you? You're sure of it!

HAEMON [*Rocking her gently.*] What night, my sweet?

ANTIGONE. And you are very sure, aren't you, that that night, at the dance, when you came to the corner where I was sitting, there was no mistake? It was me you were looking for? It wasn't another girl? And you're sure that never, not in your most secret heart of hearts, have you said to yourself that it was Ismene you ought to have asked to marry you?

HAEMON [*Reproachfully.*] Antigone, you are idiotic. You might give me credit for knowing my own mind. It's you I love, and no one else.

ANTIGONE. But you love me as a woman—as a woman wants to be loved, don't you? Your arms around me aren't lying, are they? Your hands, so warm against my back—they're not lying? This warmth that's in me; this confidence, this sense that I am safe, secure, that flows through me as I stand here with my cheek in the hollow of your shoulder: they are not lies, are they?

HAEMON. Antigone, darling, I love you exactly as you love me. With all of myself.

They kiss.

ANTIGONE. I'm sallow, and I'm scrawny. Ismene is pink and golden. She's like a fruit.

HAEMON. Look here, Antigone——

ANTIGONE. Ah, dearest, I am ashamed of myself. But this morning, this special morning, I must know. Tell me the truth! I beg you to tell me the truth! When you think about me, when it strikes you suddenly that I am going to belong to you—do you have the feeling that—that a great empty space is being hollowed out inside you, that there is something inside you that is just—dying?

HAEMON. Yes, I do, I do.

A pause.

ANTIGONE. That's the way I feel. And another thing. I wanted you
to know that I should have been very proud to be your wife—
the woman whose shoulder you would put your hand on as
you sat down to table, absent-mindedly, as upon a thing that
belonged to you. [*After a moment, draws away from him. Her
tone changes.*] There! Now I have two things more to tell
you. And when I have told them to you, you must go away
instantly, without asking any questions. However strange they
may seem to you. However much they may hurt you. Swear
that you will!

HAEMON [*Beginning to be troubled.*] What are these things that
you are going to tell me?

ANTIGONE. Swear, first, that you will go away without one word.
Without so much as looking at me. [*She looks at him, wretched-
ness in her face.*] You hear me, Haemon. Swear it, please.
This is the last mad wish that you will ever have to grant me.

A pause.

HAEMON. I swear it, since you insist. But I must tell you that I
don't like this at all.

ANTIGONE. Please, Haemon. It's very serious. You must listen to
me and do as I ask. First, about last night, when I came to
your house. You asked me a moment ago why I wore Ismene's
dress and rouge. It was because I was stupid. I wasn't very sure
that you loved me as a woman; and I did it—because I wanted
you to want me. I was trying to be more like other girls.

HAEMON. Was *that* the reason? My poor—

ANTIGONE. Yes. And you laughed at me. And we quarreled; and
my awful temper got the better of me and I flung out of the
house. . . . The real reason was that I wanted you to take me;
I wanted to be your wife before—

HAEMON. Oh, my darling——

ANTIGONE [*Shuts him off.*] You swore you wouldn't ask any questions. You swore, Haemon. [*Turns her face away and goes on
in a hard voice.*] As a matter of fact, I'll tell you why. I wanted
to be your wife last night because I love you that way very—
very strongly. And also because—— Oh, my darling, my
darling, forgive me; I'm going to cause you quite a lot of pain.
[*She draws away from him.*] I wanted it also because I shall
never, never be able to marry you, never! [HAEMON *is stupefied
and mute; then he moves a step towards her.*] Haemon! You
took a solemn oath! You swore! Leave me quickly! Tomorrow
the whole thing will be clear to you. Even before tomorrow:
this afternoon. If you please, Haemon, go now. It is the only
thing left that you can do for me if you still love me. [*A pause*

as HAEMON *stares at her. Then he turns and goes out through the arch.* ANTIGONE *stands motionless, then moves to a chair at end of table and lets herself gently down on it. In a mild voice, as of calm after storm.*] Well, it's over for Haemon, Antigone.

ISMENE *enters through arch, pauses for a moment in front of it when she sees* ANTIGONE, *then crosses behind table.*

ISMENE. I can't sleep. I'm terrified. I'm so afraid that, even though it is daylight, you'll still try to bury Polynices. Antigone, little sister, we all want to make you happy—Haemon, and Nurse, and I, and Puff whom you love. We love you, we are alive, we need you. And you remember what Polynices was like. He was our brother, of course. But he's dead; and he never loved you. He was a bad brother. He was like an enemy in the house. He never thought of you. Why should you think of him? What if his soul does have to wander through endless time without rest or peace? Don't try something that is beyond your strength. You are always defying the world, but you're only a girl, after all. Stay at home tonight. Don't try to do it, I beg you. It's Creon's doing not ours.

ANTIGONE. You are too late, Ismene. When you first saw me this morning, I had just come in from burying him. [*Exit* ANTIGONE *through arch.*]

The lighting, which by this time has reached a point of early morning sun, is quickly dimmed out, leaving the stage bathed in a light blue color. ISMENE *runs out after* ANTIGONE. *On* ISMENE's *exit the lights are brought up suddenly to suggest a later period of the day.* CREON *and* PAGE *enter through curtain upstage.* CREON *stands on the top step; his* PAGE *stands at his right side.*

CREON. A private of the guards, you say? One of those standing watch over the body? Show him in.

The PAGE *crosses to arch; exit.* CREON *moves down to end of table.* PAGE *re-enters, preceded by the* FIRST GUARD, *livid with fear.* PAGE *remains on upstage side of arch.* GUARD *salutes.*

GUARD. Private Jonas, Second Battalion.
CREON. What are you doing here?
GUARD. It's like this, sir. Soon as it happened, we said: "Got to tell the chief about this before anybody else spills it. He'll want to know right away." So we tossed a coin to see which one would come up and tell you about it. You see, sir, we thought only one man had better come, because, after all, you don't want to leave the body without a guard. Right? I mean, there's three of us on duty, guarding the body.

CREON. What's wrong about the body?

GUARD. Sir, I've been seventeen years in the service. Volunteer.
Wounded three times. Two mentions. My record's clean. I
know my business and I know my place. I carry out orders.
Sir, ask any officer in the battalion; they'll tell you. "Leave it
to Jonas. Give him an order: he'll carry it out." That's what
they'll tell you, sir. Jonas, that's me—that's my name.

CREON. What's the matter with you, man? What are you shaking
for?

GUARD. By rights it's the corporal's job, sir. I've been recommended for a corporal, but they haven't put it through yet.
June, it was supposed to go through.

CREON. [*Interrupts.*] Stop chattering and tell me why you are here.
If anything has gone wrong, I'll break all three of you.

GUARD. Nobody can say we didn't keep our eye on that body. We
had the two-o'clock watch—the tough one. You know how
it is, sir. It's nearly the end of the night. Your eyes are like
lead. You've got a crick in the back of your neck. There's
shadows, and the fog is beginning to roll in. A fine watch they
give us! And me, seventeen years in the service. But we was
doing our duty all right. On our feet, all of us. Anybody says
we were sleeping is a liar. First place, it was too cold. Second
place—— [CREON *makes a gesture of impatience.*] Yes, sir.
Well, I turned around and looked at the body. We wasn't only
ten feet away from it, but that's how I am. I was keeping my
eye on it. [*Shouts.*] Listen, sir, I was the first man to see it!
Me! They'll tell you. I was the one let out that yell!

CREON. What for? What was the matter?

GUARD. Sir, the body! Somebody had been there and buried it.
[CREON *comes down a step on the stair. The* GUARD *becomes
more frightened.*] It wasn't much, you understand. With us
three there, it couldn't have been. Just covered over with a
little dirt, that's all. But enough to hide it from the buzzards.

CREON. By God, I'll——! [*He looks intently at the* GUARD.] You
are sure that it couldn't have been a dog, scratching up the
earth?

GUARD. Not a chance, sir. That's kind of what we hoped it was.
But the earth was scattered over the body just like the priests
tell you you should do it. Whoever did that job knew what
he was doing, all right.

CREON. Who could have dared? [*He turns and looks at the* GUARD.]
Was there anything to indicate who might have done it?

GUARD. Not a thing, sir. Maybe we heard a footstep—I can't swear
to it. Of course we started right in to search, and the corporal
found a shovel, a kid's shovel no bigger than that, all rusty
and everything. Corporal's got the shovel for you. We thought
maybe a kid did it.

CREON. [*To himself.*] A kid! [*He looks away from the* GUARD.] I
broke the back of the rebellion; but like a snake, it is coming
together again. Polynices' friends, with their gold, blocked by
my orders in the banks of Thebes. The leaders of the mob,
stinking of garlic and allied to envious princes. And the temple
priests, always ready for a bit of fishing in troubled waters. A
kid! I can imagine what he is like, their kid: a baby-faced killer,
creeping in the night with a toy shovel under his jacket. [*He
looks at his* PAGE.] Though why shouldn't they have corrupted
a real child? Very touching! Very useful to the party, an innocent child. A martyr. A real white-faced baby of fourteen who
will spit with contempt at the guards who kill him. A free
gift to their cause: the precious, innocent blood of a child
on my hands. [*He turns to the* GUARD.] They must have
accomplices in the Guard itself. Look here, you. Who knows
about this?

GUARD. Only us three, sir. We flipped a coin, and I came right over.

CREON. Right. Listen, now. You will continue on duty. When the
relief squad comes up, you will tell them to return to barracks.
You will uncover the body. If another attempt is made to bury
it, I shall expect you to make an arrest and bring the person
straight to me. And you will keep your mouths shut. Not one
word of this to a human soul. You are all guilty of neglect of
duty, and you will be punished; but if the rumor spreads
through Thebes that the body received burial, you will be
shot—all three of you.

GUARD [*Excitedly.*] Sir, we never told nobody, I swear we didn't!
Anyhow, I've been up here. Suppose my pals spilled it to the
relief; I couldn't have been with them and here too. That
wouldn't be my fault if they talked. Sir, I've got two kids.
You're my witness, sir, it couldn't have been me. I was here
with you. I've got a witness! If anybody talked, it couldn't
have been me! I was——

CREON. [*Interrupting..*] Clear out! If the story doesn't get around,
you won't be shot. [*The* GUARD *salutes, turns, and exits at the
double.* CREON *turns and paces upstage, then comes down to
end of the table.*] A child! [*He looks at* PAGE.] Come along, my
lad. Since we can't hope to keep this to ourselves, we shall
have to be the first to give out the news. And after that, we
shall have to clean up the mess. [PAGE *crosses to side of* CREON.
CREON *puts his hand on* PAGE's *shoulder.*] Would you be willing to die for me? Would you defy the Guard with your little
shovel? [PAGE *looks up at* CREON.] Of course you would. You
would do it, too. [*A pause.* CREON *looks away from* PAGE *and
murmurs*] A child! [CREON *and* PAGE *go slowly upstage center
to top step.* PAGE *draws aside the curtain, through which exit*
CREON *with* PAGE *behind him.*]

As soon as CREON *and* PAGE *have disappeared,* CHORUS *enters and leans against the upstage portal or arch, left. The lighting is brought up to its brightest point to suggest mid-afternoon.* CHORUS *allows a pause to indicate that a crucial moment has been reached in the play, then moves slowly downstage, center. He stands for a moment silent, reflecting, and then smiles faintly.*

CHORUS. The spring is wound up tight. It will uncoil of itself. That is what is so convenient in tragedy. The least little turn of the wrist will do the job. Anything will set it going: a glance at a girl who happens to be lifting her arms to her hair as you go by; a feeling when you wake up on a fine morning that you'd like a little respect paid to you today, as if it were as easy to order as a second cup of coffee; one question too many, idly thrown out over a friendly drink—and the tragedy is on.

The rest is automatic. You don't need to lift a finger. The machine is in perfect order; it has been oiled ever since time began, and it runs without friction. Death, treason, and sorrow are on the march; and they move in the wake of storm, of tears, of stillness. Every kind of stillness. The hush when the executioner's ax goes up at the end of the last act. The unbreathable silence when, at the beginning of the play, the two lovers, their hearts bared, their bodies naked, stand for the first time face to face in the darkened room, afraid to stir. The silence inside you when the roaring crowd acclaims the winner—so that you think of a film without a sound track, mouths agape and no sound coming out of them, a clamor that is no more than a picture; and you, the victor, already vanquished, alone in the desert of your silence. That is tragedy.

Tragedy is clean, it is restful, it is flawless. It has nothing to do with melodrama—with wicked villains, persecuted maidens, avengers, sudden revelations, and eleventh-hour repentances. Death, in a melodrama, is really horrible because it is never inevitable. The dear old father might so easily have been saved; the honest young man might so easily have brought in the police five minutes earlier.

In a tragedy, nothing is in doubt and everyone's destiny is known. That makes for tranquility. There is a sort of fellow-feeling among characters in a tragedy: he who kills is as innocent as he who gets killed: it's all a matter of what part you are playing. Tragedy is restful; and the reason is that hope, that foul, deceitful thing, has no part in it. There isn't any hope. You're trapped. The whole sky has fallen on you, and all you can do about it is to shout.

Don't mistake me: I said "shout": I did not say groan, whimper, complain. That, you cannot do. But you can shout aloud; you can get all those things said that you never thought you'd be able to say—or never even knew you had it in you to say. And you don't

say these things because it will do any good to say them: you
know better than that. You say them for their own sake; you say
them because you learn a lot from them.

   In melodrama you argue and struggle in the hope of escape.
That is vulgar, it's practical. But tragedy, where there is no temptation to try to escape, argument is gratuitous: it's kingly.

Voices of the GUARDS *and scuffling sound heard through the arch-
way.* CHORUS *looks in that direction; then, in a changed tone:*

   The play is on. Antigone has been caught. For the first time
in her life, little Antigone is going to be able to be herself.

Exit CHORUS *through arch. A pause, while the offstage voices rise
in volume, then the* FIRST GUARD *enters, followed by* SECOND *and*
THIRD GUARDS, *holding the arms of* ANTIGONE *and dragging her
along. The* FIRST GUARD, *speaking as he enters, crosses swiftly to
end of the table.*
   The two GUARDS *and* ANTIGONE *stop downstage.*

FIRST GUARD [*Recovered from his fright.*] Come on, now, Miss,
   give it a rest. The chief will be here in a minute and you can
   tell him about it. All I know is my orders. I don't want to
   know what you were doing there. People always have excuses;
   but I can't afford to listen to them, see. Why, if we had to
   listen to all the people who want to tell us what's the matter
   with this country, we'd never get our work done. [*To the*
   GUARDS.] You keep hold of her and I'll see that she keeps her
   face shut.
ANTIGONE. They are hurting me. Tell them to take their dirty
   hands off me.
FIRST GUARD. Dirty hands, eh? The least you can do is try to be
   polite, Miss. Look at me: I'm polite.
ANTIGONE. Tell them to let me go. I shan't run away. My father
   was King Oedipus. I am Antigone.
FIRST GUARD. King Oedipus' little girl! Well, well, well! Listen,
   Miss, the night watch never picks up a lady but they say, you
   better be careful: I'm sleeping with the police commissioner.

The GUARDS *laugh.*

ANTIGONE. I don't mind being killed, but I don't want them to
   touch me.
FIRST GUARD. And what about stiffs, and dirt, and such like? You
   wasn't afraid to touch them, was you? "Their dirty hands!"
   Take a look at your own hands. [ANTIGONE, *handcuffed, smiles
   despite herself as she looks down at her hands. They are
   grubby.*] You must have lost your shovel, didn't you? Had to

go at it with your fingernails the second time, I'll bet. By God, I never saw such nerve! I turn my back for about five seconds; I ask a pal for a chew; I say "thanks"; I get the tobacco stowed away in my cheek— the whole thing don't take ten seconds; and there she is, clawing away like a hyena. Right out in broad daylight! And did she scratch and kick when I grabbed her! Straight for my eyes with them nails she went. And yelling something fierce about, "I haven't finished yet; let me finish!" She ain't got all her marbles!

SECOND GUARD. I pinched a nut like that the other day. Right on the main square she was, hoisting up her skirts and showing her behind to anybody that wanted to take a look.

FIRST GUARD. Listen, we're going to get a bonus out of this. What do you say we throw a party, the three of us?

SECOND GUARD. At the old woman's? Behind Market Street?

THIRD GUARD. Suits me. Sunday would be a good day. We're off duty Sunday. What do you say we bring our wives?

FIRST GUARD. No. Let's have some fun this time. Bring your wife, there's always something goes wrong. First place, what do you do with the kids? Bring them, they always want to go to the can just when you're right in the middle of a game of cards or cards or something. Listen, who would have thought an hour ago that us three would be talking about throwing a party now? The way I felt when the old man was interrogating me, we'd be lucky if we got off with being docked a month's pay. I want to tell you, I was scared.

SECOND GUARD. You sure we're going to get a bonus?

FIRST GUARD. Yes. Something tells me this is big stuff.

THIRD GUARD. [To SECOND GUARD.] What's-his-name, you know— in the Third Battalion? He got an extra month's pay for catching a firebug.

SECOND GUARD. If we get an extra month's pay, I vote we throw the party at the Arabian's.

FIRST GUARD. You're crazy! He changes twice as much for liquor as anybody else in town. Unless you want to go upstairs, of course. Can't do that at the old woman's.

THIRD GUARD. Well, we can't keep this from our wives, no matter how you work it out. You get an extra month's pay, and what happens? Everybody in the battalion knows it, and your wife knows it too. They might even line up the battalion and give it to you in front of everybody, so how could you keep your wife from finding out?

FIRST GUARD. Well, we'll see about that. If they do the job out in the barrack yard—of course that means women, kids, every-thing.

ANTIGONE. I should like to sit down, if you please.

A pause, as the FIRST GUARD *thinks it over.*

FIRST GUARD. Let her sit down. But keep hold of her. [*The two GUARD start to lead her toward the chair at end of table. The curtain upstage opens, and CREON enters, followed by his PAGE. FIRST GUARD turns and moves upstage a few steps, sees CREON.*] 'Tenshun! [*The three GUARDS salute. CREON, seeing ANTIGONE handcuffed to THIRD, GUARD, stops on the top step, astonished.*]
CREON. Antigone! [*To the FIRST GUARD.*] Take off those handcuffs! [*FIRST GUARD crosses above table to left of ANTIGONE.*] What is this? [*CREON and his PAGE come down off the steps.*]
FIRST GUARD *takes key from his pocket and unlocks the cuff on ANTIGONE's hand. ANTIGONE rubs her wrist as she crosses below table toward chair at end of table. SECOND and THIRD GUARDS step back to front of arch. FIRST GUARD turns upstage toward CREON.*

FIRST GUARD. The watch, sir. We all came this time.
CREON. Who is guarding the body?
FIRST GUARD. We sent for the relief.

CREON *comes down.*

CREON. But I gave orders that the relief was to go back to barracks and stay there! [*ANTIGONE sits on chair at left of table.*] I told you not to open your mouth about this!
FIRST GUARD. Nobody's said anything, sir. We made this arrest, and brought the party in, the way you said we should.
CREON [*to ANTIGONE.*] Where did these men find you?
FIRST GUARD. Right by the body.
CREON. What were you doing near your brother's body? You knew what my orders were.
FIRST GUARD. What was she doing? Sir, that's why we brought her in. She was digging up the dirt with her nails. She was trying to cover up the body all over again.
CREON. Do you realize what you are saying?
FIRST GUARD. Sir, ask these men here. After I reported to you, I went back, and first thing we did, we uncovered the body. The sun was coming up and it was beginning to smell, so we moved it up on a little rise to get him in the wind. Of course, you wouldn't expect any trouble in broad daylight. But just the same, we decided one of us had better keep his eye peeled all the time. About noon, what with the sun and the smell, and as the wind dropped and I wasn't feeling none too good, I went over to my pal to get a chew. I just had time to say "thanks" and stick it in my mouth, when I turned round and there she was, clawing away at the dirt with both hands. Right out in broad daylight! Wouldn't you think when she saw me come running she'd stop and leg it out of there? Not her! She went right on digging as fast as she could, as if I wasn't there at all. And when I grabbed her, she scratched

and bit and yelled to leave her alone, she hadn't finished yet, the body wasn't all covered yet, and the like of that.

CREON [*to* ANTIGONE.] Is this true?

ANTIGONE. Yes, it is true.

FIRST GUARD. We scraped the dirt off as fast as we could, then we sent for the relief and we posted them. But we didn't tell them a thing, sir. And we brought in the party so's you could see her. And that's the truth, so help me God.

CREON [*to* ANTIGONE.] And was it you who covered the body the first time? In the night?

ANTIGONE. Yes, it was. With a toy shovel we used to take to the seashore when we were children. It was Polynices' own shovel; he had cut his name in the handle. That was why I left it with him. But these men took it away; so the next time, I had to do it with my hands.

FIRST GUARD. Sir, she was clawing away like a wild animal. Matter of fact, first minute we saw her, what with the heat haze and everything, my pal says, "That must be a dog," he says. "Dog!" I says, "That's a girl, that is!" And it was.

CREON. Very well. [*Turns to the* PAGE.] Show these men to the anteroom.[*The* PAGE *crosses to the arch, stands there, waiting.* CREON *moves behind the table. To the* FIRST GUARD.] You three men will wait outside. I may want a report from you later.

FIRST GUARD. Do I put the cuffs back on her, sir?

CREON. No. [*The three* GUARDS *salute, do an about-turn, and exeunt through arch, right.* PAGE *follows them out. A pause.*] Had you told anybody what you meant to do?

ANTIGONE. No.

CREON. Did you meet anyone on your way—coming or going?

ANTIGONE. No, nobody.

CREON. Sure of that, are you?

ANTIGONE. Perfectly sure.

CREON. Very well. Now listen to me. You will go straight to your room. When you get there, you will go to bed. You will say that your are not well and that you have not been out since yesterday. Your nurse will tell the same story. [*He looks toward arch, through which the* GUARDS *have gone out.*] And I'll get rid of those three men.

ANTIGONE. Uncle Creon, you are going to a lot of trouble for no good reason. You must know that I'll do it all over again tonight.

A pause. They look one another in the eye.

CREON. Why did you try to bury your brother?

ANTIGONE. I owed it to him.

CREON. I had forbidden it.

ANTIGONE. I owed it to him. Those who are not buried wander eternally and find no rest. If my brother were alive, and he came home weary after a long day's hunting, I should kneel down and unlace his boots, I should fetch him food and drink, I should see that his bed was ready for him. Polynices is home from the hunt. I owe it to him to unlock the house of the dead in which my father and my mother are waiting to welcome him. Polynices has earned his rest.

CREON. Polynices was a rebel and a traitor, and you know it.

ANTIGONE. He was my brother.

CREON. You heard my edict. It was proclaimed throughout Thebes. You read my edict. It was posted up on the city walls.

ANTIGONE. Of course I did.

CREON. You knew the punishment I decreed for any person who attempted to give him burial.

ANTIGONE. Yes, I knew the punishment.

CREON. Did you by any chance act on the assumption that a daughter of Oedipus, a daughter of Oedipus' stubborn pride, was above the law?

ANTIGONE. No, I did not act on that assumption.

CREON. Because if you had acted on that assumption, Antigone, you would have been deeply wrong. Nobody has a more sacred obligation to obey the law than those who make the law. You are a daughter of lawmakers, a daughter of kings, Antigone. You must observe the law.

ANTIGONE. Had I been a scullery maid washing my dishes when that law was read aloud to me, I should have scrubbed the greasy water from my arms and gone out in my apron to bury my brother.

CREON. What nonsense! If you had been a scullery maid, there would have been no doubt in your mind about the seriousness of that edict. You would have known that it meant death; and you would have been satisfied to weep for your brother in your kitchen. But you! You thought that because you come of the royal line, because you were my niece and were going to marry my son, I shouldn't dare have you killed.

ANTIGONE. You are mistaken. Quite the contrary. I never doubted for an instant that you would have me put to death.

A pause, as CREON *stares fixedly at her.*

CREON. The pride of Oedipus! Oedipus and his headstrong pride all over again. I can see your father in you—and I believe you. Of course you thought that I should have you killed! Proud as you are, it seemed to you a natural climax in your existence. Your father was like that. For him as for you human happiness was meaningless; and mere human misery was not enough to satisfy his passion for rorment. [*He sits on stool behind the table.*] You come of people for whom the human vestment is a kind of straitjacket: it cracks at the seams. You spend your lives wriggling to get out of it. Nothing less than a cosy tea party with death and destiny will quench your thirst. The happiest hour of your father's life came when he listened greedily to the story of how, unknown to himself, he had killed his own father and dishonored the bed of his own mother. Drop by drop, word by word, he drank in the dark story that the gods had destined him first to live and then to hear. How avidly men and women drink the brew of such a tale when their names are Oedipus—and Antigone! And it is so simple, afterwards, to do what your father did, to put out one's eyes and take one's daughter begging on the highways.

Let me tell you, Antigone: those days are over for Thebes. Thebes has a right to a king without a past. My name, thank God, is only Creon. I stand here with both feet firm on the grounds; with both hands in my pockets; and I have decided that so long as I am king—being less ambitious than your father was—I shall merely devote myself to introducing a little order into this absurd kingdom; if that is possible.

Don't think that being a king seems to me romantic. It is my trade; a trade a man has to work at every day; and like every other trade, it isn't all beer and skittles. But since it is my trade, I take it seriously. And if, tomorrow, some wild and bearded messenger walks in from some wild and distant valley —which is what happened to your dad—and tells me that he's not quite sure who my parents were, but thinks that my wife Eurydice is actually my mother, I shall ask him to do me the kindness to go back where he came from; and I shan't let a little matter like that persuade me to order my wife to take a blood test and the police to let me know whether or not my birth certificate was forged. Kings, my girl, have other things to do than to surrender themselves to their private feelings. [*He looks at her and, smiles.*] Hand *you* over to be killed! [*He rises, moves to end of table and sits on the top of table.*] I have other plans for you. You're going to marry Haemon; and I want you to fatten up a bit so that you can give him a sturdy boy. Let me assure you that Thebes needs that boy a good deal more than it needs your death. You will go to your room, now, and do as you have been told; and you won't say a word about this to anybody. Don't fret about the guards: I'll see that their mouths are shut. And don't annihilate me with those eyes. I know that you think I am a brute, and I'm sure you must consider me very prosaic. But the fact is, I have always been fond of you, stubborn though you always were. Don't forget that the first doll you ever had came from me. [*A pause.* ANTIGONE *says nothing, rises, and crosses slowly below the table toward the arch.* CREON *turns and watches her; then*] Where are you going?

ANTIGONE. [*Stops downstage. Without any show of rebellion.*] You know very well where I am going.

CREON [*After a pause.*] What sort of game are you playing?

ANTIGONE. I am not playing games.

CREON. Antigone, do you realize that if, apart from those three guards, a single soul finds out what you have tried to do, it will be impossible for me to avoid putting you to death? There is still a chance that I can save you; but only if you keep this to yourself and give up your crazy purpose. Five minutes more, and it will be too late. You understand that?

ANTIGONE. I must go and bury my brother. Those men uncovered him.

CREON. What good will it do? You know that there are other men standing guard over Polynices. And even if you did cover him over with earth again, the earth would again be removed.

ANTIGONE. I know all that. I know it. But that much, at least, I can do. And what a person can do, a person ought to do.

A pause.

CREON. Tell me, Antigone, do you believe all that flummery about religious burial? Do you really believe that a so-called shade of your brother is condemned to wander for ever homeless if a little earth is not flung on his corpse to the accompaniment of some priestly abracadabra? Have you ever listened to the priests of Thebes when they were mumbling their formula? Have you ever watched those dreary bureaucrats while they were preparing the dead for burial—skipping half the gestures required by the ritual, swallowing half their words, hustling the dead into their graves out of fear that they might be late for lunch?

ANTIGONE. Yes, I have seen all that.

CREON. And did you never say to yourself as you watched them, that if someone you really loved lay dead under the shuffling, mumbling ministrations of the priests, you would scream aloud and beg the priests to leave the dead in peace?

ANTIGONE. Yes, I've thought all that.

CREON. And you still insist upon being put to death—merely because I refuse to let your brother go out with that grotesque passport; because I refuse his body the wretched consolation of that mass-production jibber-jabber, which you would have been the first to be embarrassed by if I had allowed it. The whole thing is absurd!

ANTIGONE. Yes, it's absurd.

CREON. Then why, Antigone, why? For whose sake? For the sake of them that believe in it? To raise them against me?

ANTIGONE. No.

CREON. For whom then if not for them and not for Polynices either?

ANTIGONE. For nobody. For myself.

A pause as they stand looking at one another.

CREON. You must want very much to die. You look like a trapped animal.

ANTIGONE. Stop feeling sorry for me. Do as I do. Do your job. But if you are a human being, do it quickly. That is all ask of you. I'm not going to be able to hold out for ever.

CREON [*Takes a step toward her.*] I want to save you, Antigone.

ANTIGONE. You are the king, and you are all-powerful. But that you cannot do.

CREON. You think not?

ANTIGONE. Neither save me nor stop me.

CREON. Prideful Antigone! Little Oedipus!

ANTIGONE. Only this can you do: have me put to death.

CREON. Have you tortured, perhaps?

ANTIGONE. Why would you do that? To see me cry? To hear me beg for mercy? Or swear whatever you wish, and then begin over again?

A pause.

CREON. You listen to me. You have cast me for the villain in this little play of yours, and yourself for the heroine. And you know it, you damned little mischief-maker! But don't you drive me too far! If I were one of your preposterous little tyrants that Greece is full of, you would be lying in a ditch this minute with your tongue pulled out and your body drawn and quartered. But you can see something in my face that makes me hesitate to send for the guards and turn you over to them. Instead, I let you go on arguing; and you taunt me, you take the offensive. [*He grasps her left wrist.*] What are you driving at, you she devil?

ANTIGONE. Let me go. You are hurting my arm.

CREON [*Gripping her tighter.*] I will not let you go.

ANTIGONE. [*Moans.*] Oh!

CREON. I was a fool to waste words. I should have done this from the beginning. [*He looks at her.*] I may be your uncle—but we are not a particularly affectionate family. Are we, eh? [*Through his teeth, as he twists.*] Are we? [CREON *propels* ANTIGONE *round below him to his side.*] What fun for you, eh? To be able to spit in the face of a king who has all the power in the world; a man who has done his own killing in his day; who has killed people just as pitiable as you are—and who is still soft enough to go to all this trouble in order to keep you from being killed.

A pause.

ANTIGONE. Now you are squeezing my arm too tightly. It doesn't hurt any more.

CREON *stares at her, then drops her arm.*

CREON. I shall save you yet. [*He goes below the table to the chair at end of table, takes off his coat, and places it on the chair.*] God knows, I have things enough to do today without wasting my time on an insect like you. There's plenty to do, I assure you, when you've just put down a revolution. But urgent things can wait. I am not going to let politics be the cause of your death. For it is a fact that this whole business is nothing but politics: the mournful shade of Polynices, the decomposing corpse, the sentimental weeping, and the hysteria that you mistake for heroism—nothing but politics.

   Look here. I may not be soft, but I'm fastidious. I like things clean, shipshape, well scrubbed. Don't think that I am not just as offended as you are by the thought of that meat rotting in the sun. In the evening, when the breeze comes in off the sea, you can smell it in the palace, and it nauseates me. But I refuse even to shut my window. It's vile; and I can tell you what I wouldn't tell anybody else: it's stupid, monstrously stupid. But the people of Thebes have got to have their noses rubbed into it a little longer. My God! If it was up to me, I should have had them bury your brother long ago as a mere matter of public hygiene. I admit that what I am doing is childish. But if the featherheaded rabble I govern are to understand what's what, that stench has got to fill the town for a month!

ANTIGONE. [*Turns to him.*] You are a loathsome man!

CREON. I agree. My trade forces me to be. We could argue whether I ought or ought not to follow my trade; but once I take on the job, I must do it properly.

ANTIGONE. Why do you do it at all?

CREON. My dear, I woke up one morning and found myself King of Thebes. God knows, there were other things I loved in life more than power.

ANTIGONE. Then you should have said no.

CREON. Yes, I could have done that. Only, I felt that it would have been cowardly. I should have been like a workman who turns down a job that has to be done. So I said yes.

ANTIGONE. So much the worse for you, then. I didn't say yes. I can say no to anything I think vile, and I don't have to count the

cost. But because you said yes, all that you can do, for all
your crown and your trappings, and your guards—all that you
can do is to have me killed.

CREON. Listen to me.

ANTIGONE. If I want to. I don't have to listen to you if I don't
want to. You've said your *yes*. There is nothing more you can
tell me that I don't know. You stand there, drinking in my
words. [*She moves behind chair.*] Why is it that you don't call
your guards? I'll tell you why? You want to hear me out to
the end; that's why.

CREON. You amuse me.

ANTIGONE. Oh, no, I don't. I frighten you. That is why you talk
about saving me. Everything would be so much easier if you
had a docile, tongue-tied little Antigone living in the palace.
I'll tell you something, Uncle Creon: I'll give you back one
of your own words. You are too fastidious to make a good
tyrant. But you are going to have to put me to death today,
and you know it. And that's what frightens you. God! Is there
anything uglier than a frightened man!

CREON. Very well. I am afraid, then. Does that satisfy you? I am
afraid that if you insist upon it, I shall have to have you killed.
And I don't want to.

ANTIGONE. I don't have to do things that I think are wrong. If it
comes to that, you didn't really want to leave my brother's
body unburied, did you? Say it! Admit that you didn't.

CREON. I have said it already.

ANTIGONE. But you did it just the same. And now, though you
don't want to do it, you are going to have me killed. And you
call that being a king!

CREON. Yes, I call that being a king.

ANTIGONE. Poor Creon! My nails are broken, my fingers are bleeding, my arms are covered with the welts left by the paws of
your guards—but I am a queen!

CREON. Then why not have pity on me, and live? Isn't your
brother's corpse, rotting there under my windows, payment
enough for peace and order in Thebes? My son loves you.
Don't make me add your life to the payment. I've paid enough.

ANTIGONE. No, Creon! You said yes, and made yourself king. Now
you will never stop paying.

CREON. But God in heaven! Won't you try to understand me! I'm
trying hard enough to understand you! There had to be one
man who said yes. Somebody had to agree to captain the ship.
She had sprung a hundred leaks; she was loaded to the water
line with crime, ignorance, poverty. The wheel was swinging
with the wind. The crew refused to work and were looting
the cargo. The officers were building a raft, ready to slip over-
board and desert the ship. The mast was splitting, the wind
was howling, the sails were beginning to rip. Every man jack

on board was about to drown—and only because the only
thing they thought of was their own skins and their cheap
little day-to-day traffic. Was that a time, do you think, for
playing with words like yes and no? Was that a time for a
man to be weighing the pros and cons, wondering if he wasn't
going to pay too dearly later on; if he wasn't going to lose
his life, or his family, or his touch with other men? You grab
the wheel, you right the ship in the face of a mountain of
water. You shout an order, and if one man refuses to obey,
you shoot straight into the mob. Into the mob, I say! The
beast as nameless as the wave that crashes down upon your
deck; as nameless as the whipping wind. The thing that drops
when you shoot may be someone who poured you a drink the
night before; but it has no name. And you, braced at the
wheel, you have no name, either. Nothing has a name—except
the ship, and the storm. [*A pause as he looks at her.*] Now do
you understand?

ANTIGONE. I am not here to understand. That's all very well for
you. I am here to say no to you, and die.

CREON. It is easy to say no.

ANTIGONE. Not always.

CREON. It is easy to say no. To say yes, you have to sweat and roll
up your sleeves and plunge both hands into life up to the
elbows. It is easy to say no, even if saying no means death.
All you have to do is to sit still and wait. Wait to go on living;
wait to be killed. That is the coward's part. *No* is one of your
man-made words. Can you imagine a world in which trees say
no to the sap? In which beasts say *no* to hunger or to propa-
gation? Animals are good, simple, tough. They move in droves,
nudging one another onwards, all traveling the same road.
Some of them keel over, but the rest go on; and no matter
how many may fall by the wayside, there are always those
few left that go on bringing their young into the world, traveling the same road with the same obstinate will, unchanged
from those who went before.

ANTIGONE. Animals, oh, Creon! What a king you could be if only
men were animals!

A pause. CREON *turns and looks at her.*

CREON. You despise me, don't you? [ANTIGONE *is silent.* CREON
goes on, as if to himself.] Strange. Again and again, I have
imagined myself holding this conversation with a pale young
man I have never seen in the flesh. He would have come to
assassinate me, and would have failed. I would be trying to
find out from him why he wanted to kill me. But with all my
logic and all my powers of debate, the only thing I could get
out of him would be that he despised me. Who would have

thought that the white-faced boy would turn out to be you? And that the debate would arise out of something so meaningless as the burial of your brother?

ANTIGONE [*Repeats contemptuously.*] Meaningless!

CREON [*Earnestly, almost desperately.*] And yet, you must hear me out. My part is not an heroic one, but I shall play my part. I shall have you put to death. Only, before I do, I want to make one last appeal. I want to be sure that you know what you are doing as well as I know what I am doing. Antigone, do you know what you are dying for? Do you know the sordid story to which you are going to sign your name in blood, for all time to come?

ANTIGONE. What story?

CREON. The story of Eteocles and Polynices, the story of your brothers. You think you know it, but you don't Nobody in Thebes knows that story but me. And it seems to me, this afternoon, that you have a right to know it too. [*A pause as* ANTIGONE *moves to chair and sits.*] It's not a pretty story. [*He turns, gets stool from behind the table and places it between the table and the chair.*] You'll see. [*He looks at her for a moment.*] Tell me, first. What do you remember about your brothers? They were older than you, so they must have looked down on you. And I imagine that they tormented you— pulled your pigtails, broke your dolls, whispered secrets to each other to put you in a rage.

ANTIGONE. They were big and I was little.

CREON. And later on, when they came home wearing evening clothes, smoking cigarettes, they would have nothing to do with you; and you thought they were wonderful.

ANTIGONE. They were boys and I was a girl.

CREON. You didn't know why, exactly, but you knew that they were making your mother unhappy. You saw her in tears over them; and your father would fly into a rage because of them. You heard them come in, slamming doors, laughing noisily in the corridors—insolent, spineless, unruly, smelling of drink.

ANTIGONE [*Staring outward.*] Once, it was very early and we had just got up. I saw them coming home, and hid behind a door. Polynices was very pale and his eyes were shining. He was so handsome in his evening clothes. He saw me, and said: "Here, this is for you"; and he gave me a big paper flower that he had brought home from his night out.

CREON. And of course you still have that flower. Last night, before you crept out, you opened a drawer and looked at it for a time, to give yourself courage.

ANTIGONE. Who told you so?

CREON. Poor Antigone! With her night club flower. Do you know what your brother was?

ANTIGONE. Whatever he was, I know that you will say vile things about him.

CREON. A cheap, idiotic bounder, that is what he was. A cruel, vicious little voluptuary. A little beast with just wit enough to drive a car faster and throw more money away than any of his pals. I was with your father one day when Polynices, having lost a lot of money gambling, asked him to settle the debt; and when your father refused, the boy raised his hand against him and called him a vile name.

ANTIGONE. That's a lie!

CREON. He struck your father in the face with his fist. It was pitiful. Your father sat at his desk with his head in his hands. His nose was bleeding. He was weeping with anguish. And in a corner of your father's study, Polynices stood sneering and lighting a cigarette.

ANTIGONE. That's a lie.

A pause.

CREON. When did you last see Polynices alive? When you were twelve years old. *That's* true, isn't it?

ANTIGONE. Yes, that's true.

CREON. Now you know why, Oedipus was too chicken-hearted to have the boy locked up. Polynices was allowed to go off and join the Argive army. And as soon as he reached Argos, the attempts upon your father's life began—upon the life of an old man who couldn't make up his mind to die, couldn't bear to be parted from his kingship. One after another, men slipped into Thebes from Argos for the purpose of assassinating him, and every killer we caught always ended by confessing who had put him up to it, who had paid him to try it. And it wasn't only Polynices. That is really what I am trying to tell you. I want you to know what went on in the back room, in the kitchen of politics; I want you to know what took place in the wings of this drama in which you are burning to play a part.

Yesterday, I gave Eteocles a State funeral, with pomp and honors. Today, Eteocles is a saint and a hero in the eyes of all Thebes. The whole city turned out to bury him. The school-children emptied their saving boxes to buy wreaths for him. Old men, orating in quavering, hypocritical voices, glorified the virtues of the greathearted brother, the devoted son, the loyal prince. I made a speech myself; and every temple priest was present with an appropriate show of sorrow and solemnity in his stupid face. And military honors were accorded the dead hero.

Well, what else could I have done? People had taken sides in the civil war. Both sides couldn't be wrong; that would be

too much. I couldn't have made them swallow the truth. Two
gangsters was more of a luxury than I could afford. [*He pauses
for a moment.*] And this is the whole point of my story. Eteocles, that virtuous brother, was just as rotten as Polynices.
That great-hearted son had done his best, too, to procure the
assassination of his father. That loyal prince had also offered
to sell out Thebes to the highest bidder.

Funny, isn't it? Polynices lies rotting in the sun while
Eteocles is given a hero's funeral and will be housed in a marble
vault. Yet I have absolute proof that everything that Polynices
did, Eteocles had plotted to do. They were a pair of black-
guards—both engaged in selling out Thebes, and both engaged
in selling out each other; and they died like the cheap gangsters they were, over a division of the spoils.

But, as I told you a moment ago, I had to make a martyr
of one of them. I sent out to the holocaust for their bodies; they
were found clasped in one another's arms—for the first time
in their lives, I imagine. Each had been spitted on the other's
sword, and the Argive cavalry had trampled them down. They
were mashed to a pulp, Antigone. I had the prettier of the two
carcasses brought in and gave it a State funeral; and I left the
other to rot. I don't know which was which. And I assure you,
I don't care.

Long silence, neither looking at the other.

ANTIGONE [*In a mild voice.*] Why do you tell me all this?
CREON. Would it have been better to let you die a victim to that
    obscene story?
ANTIGONE. It might have been. I had my faith.
CREON. What are you going to do now?
ANTIGONE [*Rises to her feet in a daze.*] I shall go up to my room.
CREON. Don't stay alone. Go and find Haemon. And get married
    quickly.
ANTIGONE [*In a whisper.*] Yes.
CREON. All this is really beside the point. You have your whole life
    ahead of you—and life is a treasure.
ANTIGONE. Yes.
CREON. And you were about to throw it away. Don't think me
    fatuous if I say that I understand you; and that at your age
    I should have done the same thing. A moment ago, when we
    were quarreling, you said I was drinking in your words. I was.
    But it wasn't you I was listening to; it was a lad named Creon
    who lived here in Thebes many years ago. He was thin and
    pale, as you are. His mind, too, was filled with thoughts of self-
    sacrifice. Go and find Haemon. And get married quickly,
    Antigone. Be happy. Life flows like water, and you young
    people let it run away through your fingers. Shut your hands;

hold on to it, Antigone. Life is not what you think it is. Life
is a child playing around your feet, a tool you hold firmly in
your grip, a bench you sit down upon in the evening, in your
garden. People will tell you that that's not life, that life is
something else. They will tell you that because they need your
strength and your fire, and they will want to make use of you.
Don't listen to them. Believe me, the only poor consolation
that we have in our old age is to discover that what I have
just said to you is true. Life is nothing more than the happiness that you get out of it.

ANTIGONE [*Murmurs, lost in thought.*] Happiness . . .

CREON [*Suddenly a little sefl-conscious*] Not much of a word, is it?

ANTIGONE [*Quietly.*] What kind of hapiness do you foresee for me?
Paint me the picture of your happy Antigone. What are the
unimportant little sins that I shall have to commit before I am
allowed to sink my teeth into life and tear happiness from it?
Tell me: to whom shall I have to lie? Upon whom shall I have
to fawn? To whom must I sell myself? Whom do you want me
to leave dying, while I turn away my eyes?

CREON. Antigone, be quiet.

ANTIGONE. Why do you tell me to be quiet when all I want to know
is what I have to do to be happy? This minute; since it is this
very minute that I must make my choice. You tell me that life
is so wonderful. I want to know what I have to do in order to
be able to say that myself.

CREON. Do you love Haemon?

ANTIGONE. Yes, I love Haemon. The Haemon I love is hard and
young, faithful and difficult to satisfy, just as I am. But if what
I love in Haemon is to be worn away like a stone step by the
tread of the thing you call life, the thing you call happiness,
if Haemon reaches the point where he stops growing pale with
fear when I grow pale, stops thinking that I must have been
killed in an accident when I am five minutes late, stops feeling that he is alone on earth when I laugh and he doesn't
know why—if he too has to learn to say yes to everything—
why, no, then, no! I do not love Haemon!

CREON. You don't know what you are talking about!

ANTIGONE. I do know what I am talking about! Now it is you who
have stopped understanding. I am too far away from you now,
talking to you from a kingdom you can't get into, with your
quick tongue and your hollow heart. [*Laughs.*] I laugh, Creon,
because I see you suddenly as you must have been at fifteen:
the same look of impotence in your face and the same inner
conviction that there was nothing you couldn't do. What has
life added to you, except those lines in your face, and that fat
on your stomach?

CREON. Be quiet, I tell you!

ANTIGONE. Why do you want me to be quiet? Because you know

that I am right? Do you think I can't see in your face that what I am saying is true? You can't admit it, of course; you have to go on growling and defending the bone you call happiness.

CREON. It is your happiness, too, you little fool!

ANTIGONE. I spit on your happiness! I spit on your idea of life—that life that must go on, come what may. You are all like dogs that lick everything they smell. You with your promise of hum-drum happiness—provided a person doesn't ask too much of life. I want everything of life, I do; and I want it now! want it total, complete: otherwise I reject it! I will not be moderate. I will not be satisfied with the bit of cake you offer me if I promise to be a good little girl. I want to be sure of everything this very day; sure that everything will be as beautiful as when I was a little girl. If not, I want to die!

CREON. Scream on, daughter of Oedipus! Scream on, in your father's own voice!

ANTIGONE. In my father's own voice, yes! We are of the tribe that asks questions, and we ask them to the bitter end. Until no tiniest chance of hope remains to be strangled by our hands. We are of the tribe that hates your filthy hope, your docile, female hope; hope, your whore——

CREON [*Grasps her by her arms.*] Shut up! If you could see how ugly you are, shrieking those words!

ANTIGONE. Yes, I am ugly! Father was ugly, too. [CREON *releases her arms, turns and moves away. Stands with his back to* ANTIGONE.] But Father became beautiful. And do you know when? [*She follows him to behind the table.*] At the very end. When all his questions had been answered. When he could no longer doubt that he *had* killed his own father; that he *had* gone to bed with his own mother. When all hope was gone, stamped out like a beetle. When it was absolutely certain that nothing, nothing could save him. Then he was at peace; then he could smile, almost; then he became beautiful . . . Whereas you! Ah, those faces of yours, you candidates for elec-tion to happiness! It's you who are the ugly ones, even the handsomest of you—with that ugly glint in the corner of your eyes, that ugly crease at the corner of your mouths. Creon, you spoke the word a moment ago: the kitchen of politics. You look it and you smell of it.

CREON [*Struggles to put his hand over her mouth.*] I order you to shut up! Do you hear me?

ANTIGONE. You order me? Cook! Do you really believe that you can give me orders?

CREON. Antigone! The anteroom is full of people! Do you want them to hear you?

ANTIGONE. Open the doors! Let us make sure that they can hear me!

CREON. By God! You shut up, I tell you!

ISMENE *enters through arch.*

ISMENE [*Distraught.*] Antigone!
ANTIGONE [*Turns to* ISMENE.] You, too? What do you want?
ISMENE. Oh, forgive me, Antigone. I've come back. I'll be brave.
  I'll go with you now.
ANTIGONE. Where will you go with me?
ISMENE [*To* CREON.] Creon! If you kill her, you'll have to kill me
  too.
ANTIGONE. Oh, no, Ismene. Not a bit of it. I die alone. You don't
  think I'm going to let you die with me after what I've been
  through? You don't deserve it.
ISMENE. If you die, I don't want to live. I don't want to be left
  behind, alone.
ANTIGONE. You chose life and I chose death. Now stop blubbering.
  You had your chance to come with me in the black night,
  creeping on your hands and knees. You had your chance to
  claw up the earth with your nails, as I did; to get yourself
  caught like a thief, as I did. And you refused it.
ISMENE. Not any more. I'll do it alone tonight.
ANTIGONE [*Turns round toward* CREON.] You hear that, Creon? The
  thing is catching! Who knows but that lots of people will catch
  the disease from me! What are you waiting for? Call in your
  guards! Come on, Creon! Show a little courage! It only hurts
  for a minute! Come on, cook!
CREON [*Turns toward arch and calls.*] Guard!

GUARDS *enter through arch.*

ANTIGONE [*In a great cry of relief.*] At last, Creon!

CHORUS *enters through left arch.*

CREON [*To the* GUARDS.] Take her away! [CREON *goes up on top
  step.*]

GUARDS *grasp* ANTIGONE *by her arms, turn and hustle her toward
the arch, right, and exeunt.* ISMENE *mimes horror, backs away
toward the arch, left, then turns and runs out through the arch. A
long pause, as* CREON *moves slowly downstage.*

CHORUS [*Behind* CREON. *Speaks in a deliberate voice.*] You are out
  of your mind, Creon. What have you done?
CREON [*His back to* CHORUS.] She had to die.
CHORUS. You must not let Antigone die. We shall carry the scar of
  her death for centuries.
CREON. She insisted. No man on earth was strong enough to dis-
  suade her. Death was her purpose, whether she knew it or not.

Polynices was a mere pretext. When she had to give up that pretext, she found another one—that life and happiness were tawdry things and not worth possessing. She was bent upon only one thing: to reject life and to die.

CHORUS. She is a mere child, Creon.

CREON. What do you want me to do for her? Condemn her to live?

HAEMON [*Calls from offstage.*] Father! [HAEMON *enters through arch, right.* CREON *turns toward him.*]

CREON. Haemon, forget Antigone. Forget her, my dearest boy.

HAEMON. How can you talk like that?

CREON [*Grasps* HAEMON *by the hands.*] I did everything I could to save her, Haemon. I used every argument. I swear I did. The girl doesn't love you. She could have gone on living for you; but she refused. She wanted it this way; she wanted to die.

HAEMON. Father! The guards are dragging Antigone away! You've got to stop them! [*He breaks away from* CREON.]

CREON [*Looks away from* HAEMON.] I can't stop them. It's too late. Antigone has spoken. The story is all over Thebes. I cannot save her now.

CHORUS. Creon, you must find a way. Lock her up. Say that she has gone out of her mind.

CREON. Everybody will know it isn't so. The nation will say that I am making an exception of her because my son loves her. I cannot.

CHORUS. You can still gain time, and get her out of Thebes.

CREON. The mob already knows the truth. It is howling for her blood. I can do nothing.

HAEMON. But, Father, you are master in Thebes!

CREON. I am master under the law. Not above the law.

HAEMON. You cannot let Antigone be taken from me. I am your son!

CREON. I cannot do anything else, my poor boy. She must die and you must live.

HAEMON. Live, you say! Live a life without Antigone? A life in which I am to go on admiring you as you busy yourself about your kingdom, make your persuasive speeches, strike your attitudes? Not without Antigone. I love Antigone. I will not live without Antigone!

CREON. Haemon—you will have to resign yourself to life without Antigone. [*He moves to left of* HAEMON.] Sooner or later there comes a day of sorrow in each man's life when he must cease to be a child and take up the burden of manhood. That day has come for you.

HAEMON [*Backs away a step.*] That giant strength, that courage. That massive god who used to pick me up in his arms and shelter me from shadows and monsters—was that you, Father? Was it of you I stood in awe? Was that man you?

CREON. For God's sake, Haemon, do not judge me! Not you, too!

HAEMON [*Pleading now.*] This is all a bad dream, Father. You are
not yourself. It isn't true that we have been backed up against
a wall, forced to surrender. We don't have to say *yes* to this
terrible thing. You are still king. You are still the father I
revered. You have no right to desert me, to shrink into nothing-
ness. The world will be too bare, I shall be too alone in the
world, if you force me to disown you.
CREON. The world *is* bare, Haemon, and you *are* alone. You must
cease to think your father all-powerful. Look straight at me.
See your father as he is. That is what it means to grow up and
be a man.
HAEMON [*Stares at* CREON *for a moment.*] I tell you that I will not
live without Antigone. [*Turns and goes quickly out through
arch.*]
CHORUS. Creon, the boy will go mad.
CREON. Poor boy! He loves her.
CHORUS. Creon, the boy is wounded to death.
CREON. We are all wounded to death.

FIRST GUARD *enters through arch, right, followed by* SECOND *and*
THIRD GUARDS *pulling* ANTIGONE *along with them.*

FIRST GUARD. Sir, the people are crowding into the palace!
ANTIGONE. Creon, I don't want to see their faces. I don't want to
hear them howl. You are going to kill me; let that be enough.
I want to be alone until it is over.
CREON. Empty the palace! Guards at the gates!

CREON *quickly crosses toward the arch; exit. Two* GUARDS *release*
ANTIGONE; *exeunt behind* CREON. CHORUS *goes out through arch,
left. The lighting dims so that only the area about the table is
lighted. The cyclorama is covered with a dark blue color. The scene
is intended to suggest a prison cell, filled with shadows and dimly
lit.* ANTIGONE *moves to stool and sits. The* FIRST GUARD *stands upstage. He watches* ANTIGONE, *and as she sits, he begins pacing slowly
downstage, then upstage. A pause.*

ANTIGONE [*Turns and looks at the* GUARD.] It's you, is it?
GUARD. What do you mean, me?
ANTIGONE. The last human face that I shall see. [*A pause as they
look at each other, then* GUARD *paces upstage, turns, and crosses
behind table.*] Was it you that arrested me this morning?
GUARD. Yes, that was me.
ANTIGONE. You hurt me. There was no need for you to hurt me.
Did I act as if I was trying to escape?
GUARD. Come on now, Miss. It was my business to bring you in. I
did it. [*A pause. He paces to and fro upstage. Only the sound
of his boots is heard.*]

ANTIGONE. How old are you?

GUARD. Thirty-nine.

ANTIGONE. Have you any children?

GUARD. Yes. Two.

ANTIGONE. Do you love your children?

GUARD. What's that got to do with you? [*A pause. He paces upstage and downstage.*]

ANTIGONE. How long have you been in the Guard?

GUARD. Since the war. I was in the army. Sergeant. Then I joined the Guard.

ANTIGONE. Does one have to have been an army sergeant to get into the Guard?

GUARD. Supposed to be. Either that or on special detail. But when they make you a guard, you lose your stripes.

ANTIGONE [*Murmurs.*] I see.

GUARD. Yes. Of course, if you're a guard, everybody knows you're something special; they know you're an old N.C.O. Take pay, for instance. When you're a guard you get your pay, and on top of that you get six months' extra pay, to make sure you don't lose anything by not being a sergeant any more. And of course you do better than that. You get a house, coal, rations, extras for the wife and kids. If you've got two kids, like me, you draw better than a sergeant.

ANTIGONE [*Barely audible.*] I see.

GUARD. That's why sergeants, now, they don't like guards. Maybe you noticed they try to make out they're better than us? Promotion, that's what it is. In the army, anybody can get promoted. All you need is good conduct. Now in the Guard, it's slow, and you have to know your business—like how to make out a report and the like of that. But when you're an N.C.O. in the Guard, you've got something that even a sergeant-major ain't got. For instance——

ANTIGONE [*Breaking him off.*] Listen.

GUARD. Yes, Miss.

ANTIGONE. I'm going to die soon.

The GUARD *looks at her for a moment, then turns and moves away.*

GUARD. For instance, people have a lot of respect for guards, they have. A guard may be a soldier, but he's kind of in the civil service, too.

ANTIGONE. Do you think it hurts to die?

GUARD. How would I know? Of course, if somebody sticks a saber in your guts and turns it round, it hurts.

ANTIGONE. How are they going to put me to death?

GUARD. Well, I'll tell you. I heard the proclamation all right. Wait a minute. How did it go now? [*He stares into space and recites from memory.*] "In order that our fair city shall not be pol-

luted with her sinful blood, she shall be im-mured—immured."
That means, they shove you in a cave and wall up the cave.
ANTIGONE. Alive?
GUARD. Yes. . . . [*He moves away a few steps.*]
ANTIGONE [*Murmurs.*] O tomb! O bridal bed! Alone! [ANTIGONE *sits
there, a tiny figure in the middle of the stage. You would say
she felt a little chilly. She wraps her arms round herself.*]
GUARD. Yes! Outside the southeast gate of the town. In the Cave
of Hades. In broad daylight. Some detail, eh, for them that's
on the job! First they thought maybe it was a job for the army.
Now it looks like it's going to be the Guard. There's an outfit
for you! Nothing the Guard can't do. No wonder the army's
jealous.
ANTIGONE. A pair of animals.
GUARD. What do you mean, a pair of animals?
ANTIGONE. When the winds blow cold, all they need do is to press
close against one another. I am all alone.
GUARD. Is there anything you want? I can send out for it, you know.
ANTIGONE. You are very kind. [*A pause.* ANTIGONE *looks up at the
GUARD.*] Yes, there is something I want. I want you to give
someone a letter from me, when I am dead.
GUARD. How's that again? A letter?
ANTIGONE. Yes, I want to write a letter; and I want you to give it
to someone for me.
GUARD [*Straightens up.*] Now, wait a minute. Take it easy. It's as
much as my job is worth to go handing out letters from
prisoners.
ANTIGONE. [*Removes a ring from her finger and holds it out toward
him.*] I'll give you this ring if you will do it.
GUARD. Is it gold? [*He takes the ring from her.*]
ANTIGONE. Yes, it is gold.
GUARD [*Shakes his head.*] Uh-uh. No can do. Suppose they go
through my pockets. I might get six months for a thing like
that. [*He stares at the ring, then glances off right to make sure
that he is not being watched.*] Listen, tell you what I'll do. You
tell me what you want to say, and I'll write it down in my
book. Then, afterwards, I'll tear out the pages and give them
to the party, see? If it's in my handwriting, it's all right.
ANTIGONE. [*Winces.*] In your handwriting? [*She shudders slightly.*]
No. That would be awful. The poor darling! In your handwriting.
GUARD [*Offers back the ring.*] O.K. It's no skin off my nose.
ANTIGONE [*Quickly.*] Of course, of course. No, keep the ring. But
hurry. Time is getting short. Where is your notebook? [*The
GUARD pockets the ring, takes his notebook and pencil from
his pocket, puts his foot up on chair, and rests the notebook
on his knee, licks his pencil.*] Ready? [*He nods.*] Write, now.
"My darling . . ."

GUARD. [*Writes as he mutters.*] The boy friend, eh?

ANTIGONE. "My darling. I wanted to die, and perhaps you will not love me any more . . ."

GUARD [*Mutters as he writes*] ". . . will not love me any more."

ANTIGONE. "Creon was right. It is terrible to die."

GUARD [*Repeats as he writes*] ". . . terrible to die."

ANTIGONE. "And I don't even know what I am dying for. I am afraid . . ."

GUARD. [Looks at her.] Wait a minute! How fast do you think I can write?

ANTIGONE [*Takes hold of herself.*] Where are you?

GUARD [*Reads from his notebook.*] "And I don't even know what I am dying for."

ANTIGONE. No. Scratch that out. Nobody must know that. They have no right to know. It's as if they saw me naked and touched me, after I was dead. Scratch it all out. Just write: "Forgive me."

GUARD [*Looks at* ANTIGONE.] I cut out everything you said there at the end, and I put down, "Forgive me"?

ANTIGONE. Yes. "Forgive me, my darling. You would all have been so happy except for Antigone. I love you."

GUARD [*Finishes the letter*] ". . . I love you." [*He looks at her.*] Is that all?

ANTIGONE. That's all.

GUARD [*Straightens up, looks at notebook.*] Damn funny letter.

ANTIGONE. I know.

GUARD. [*Looks at her.*[Who is it to? [*A sudden roll of drums begins and continues until after* ANTIGONE's *exit. The* FIRST GUARD *pockets the notebook and shouts at* ANTIGONE.] O.K. That's enough out of you! Come on!

At the sound of the drum roll, SECOND *and* THIRD GUARDS *enter through the arch.* ANTIGONE *rises.* GUARDS *seize her and exeunt with her. The lighting moves up to suggest late afternoon.* CHORUS *enters.*

CHORUS. And now it is Creon's turn.

MESSENGER *runs through the arch, right.*

MESSENGER. The Queen . . . the Queen! Where is the *Queen?*

CHORUS. What do you want with the Queen? What have you to tell the Queen?

MESSENGER. News to break her heart. Antigone had just been thrust into the cave. They hadn't finished heaving the last block of stone into place when Creon and the rest heard a sudden moaning from the tomb. A hush fell over us all, for it was not the voice of Antigone. It was Haemon's voice that came forth from the tomb. Everybody looked at Creon; and he howled like a man demented: "Take away the stones! Take away the

stones!" The slaves leaped at the wall of stones, and Creon
worked with them, sweating and tearing at the blocks with his
bleeding hands. Finally a narrow opening was forced, and into
it slipped the smallest guard.

Antigone had hanged herself by the cord of her robe, by the
red and golden twisted cord of her robe. The cord was round
her neck like a child's collar. Haemon was on his knees, holding
her in his arms and moaning, his face buried in her robe. More
stones were removed, and Creon went into the tomb. He tried
to raise Haemon to his feet. I could hear him begging Haemon
to rise to his feet. Haemon was deaf to his father's voice, till
suddenly he stood up of his own accord, his eyes dark and
burning. Anguish was in his face, but it was the face of a little
boy. He stared at his father. Then suddenly he struck him—
hard; and he drew his sword. Creon leaped out of range.
Haemon went on staring at him, his eyes full of contempt—a
glance that was like a knife, and that Creon couldn't escape.
The King stood trembling in the far corner of the tomb, and
Haemon went on staring. Then, without a word, he stabbed
himself and lay down beside Antigone, embracing her in a
great pool of blood.

A pause as CREON *and* PAGE *enter through arch on the* MESSENGER'S
last words. CHORUS *and the* MESSENGER *both turn to look at* CREON;
then exit the MESSENGER *through curtain.*

CREON. I have had them laid out side by side. They are together
   at last, and at peace. Two lovers on the morrow of their bridal.
   Their work is done.
CHORUS. But not yours, Creon. You have still one thing to learn.
   Eurydice, the Queen, your wife——
CREON. A good woman. Always busy with her garden, her preserves,
   her sweaters—those sweaters she never stopped knitting for the
   poor. Strange, how the poor never stop needing sweaters. One
   would almost think that was all they needed.
CHORUS. The poor in Thebes are going to be cold this winter,
   Creon. When the Queen was told of her son's death, she waited
   carefully until she had finished her row, then put down her
   knitting calmly—as she did everything. She went up to her
   room, her lavender-scented room, with its embroidered doilies
   and its pictures framed in plush; and there, Creon, she cut her
   throat. She is laid out now in one of those two old-fashioned
   twin beds, exactly where you went to her one night when she
   was still a maiden. Her smile is still the same, scarcely a shade
   more melancholy. And if it were not for that great red blot on
   the bed linen by her neck, one might think she was asleep.
CREON [*In a dull voice.*] She, too. They are all asleep. [*Pause.*] It
   must be good to sleep.

CHORUS. And now you are alone, Creon.

CREON. Yes, all alone. [*To* PAGE.] My lad.

PAGE. Sir?

CREON. Listen to me. They don't know it, but the truth is the work is there to be done, and a man can't fold his arms and refuse to do it. They say it's dirty work. But if we didn't do it, who would?

PAGE. I don't know, sir.

CREON. Of course you don't. You'll be lucky if you never find out In a hurry to grow up, aren't you?

PAGE. Oh, yes, sir.

CREON. I shouldn't be if I were you. Never grow up if you can help it. [*He is lost in thought as the hour chimes.*] What time is it?

PAGE. Five o'clock, sir.

CREON. What have we on at five o'clock?

PAGE. Cabinet meeting, sir.

CREON. Cabinet meeting. Then we had better go along to it.

> *Exeunt* CREON *and* PAGE *slowly through arch, left, and* CHORUS *moves downstage.*

CHORUS. And there we are. It is quite true that if it had not been for Antigone they would all have been at peace. But that is over now. And they are all at peace. All those who were meant to die have died: those who believed one thing, those who believed the contrary thing, and even those who believed nothing at all, yet were caught up in the web without knowing why. All dead: stiff, useless, rotting. And those who have survived will now begin quietly to forget the dead: they won't remember who was who or which was which. It is all over. Antigone is calm tonight, and we shall never know the name of the fever that consumed her. She has played her part.

> *Three* GUARDS *enter, resume their places on steps as at the rise of the curtain, and begin to play cards.*

A great melancholy wave of peace now settles down upon Thebes, upon the empty palace, upon Creon, who can now begin to wait for his own death.

Only the guards are left, and none of this matters to them. It's no skin off their noses. They go on playing cards.

> CHORUS *walks toward the arch, left, as the curtain falls.*

Commentaries

OEDIPUS TYRANNOS

OEDIPUS TYRANNOS is the most frequently mentioned play in Aristotle's *Poetics*, where it is regarded as a model of tragic composition; but its date is unknown (scholars guess it to have appeared around 429 B.C.) and all we know of its theatrical life is that it was awarded, remarkably enough, only the second prize when first presented in competition. The Oedipus story had existed in myth long before Sophocles chose to dramatize it; in literature it shows up as early as Homer, undergoing various alterations before appearing in dramatic form. Aeschylus wrote a Theban trilogy in which the second play, since lost, was entitled *Oedipus*, and Sophocles had himself written, about ten or twelve years earlier, *Antigone*, which treats the last phase of the Oedipus myth. In the form in which Sophocles used it, the entire myth runs as follows:

> According to a prophecy the son to be born of Laius and Jocastra, the King and Queen of Thebes, would kill his father and marry his mother. To prevent this they "exposed" the child—had him abondoned on Mount Cithairon, feet pinned together, to die. However a compassionate shepherd found the infant and took him to Corinth, where he was adopted by the childless rulers Polybus and Merope, who gave him the name "Oedipus" (swollen foot). Much later, as a young man, Oedipus learned of the prophecy concerning him and fled immediately from Corinth and his supposed parents. At a crossroad near Thebes he quarreled with an old man—actually his father Laius—over the right of way and in the ensuing fight killed him. Continuing on, he found Thebes suffering under the tyranny of the Sphinx, a creature part woman and part animal who destroyed everyone who could not answer her riddle: "What is it that walks on four legs in the morning, two in the afternoon, and three in the evening?" Oedipus gave the right answer, "Man," who crawls on all fours in infancy, walks upright in his maturity, and employs a cane or other support in

old age. The Sphinx destroyed herself; the city was released from its bondage; and, the news of Laius' death having arrived, Oedipus was awarded Jocasta and the rule of Thebes for his victory. He had four children by Jocasta, two girls named Antigone and Ismene and two boys named Polynices and Eteocles, and all was well until a mysterious plague settled over Thebes that, according to an oracle, could be lifted only by the death or banishment of Laius' killer. At this point *Oedipus Tyrannos* begins, continuing on to the banishment of Oedipus. After departing from Thebes Oedipus wanders for some time, a pariah, until he is given sanctuary in Athens by King Theseus, at which point in the story Sophocles' play *Oedipus at Colonus* begins, moving on to the death of Oedipus. After his death the struggle for power in Thebes leads to a civil war in which Oedipus' two sons kill each other in single combat outside the gates. Creon then becomes king and decrees that the body of Polynices, who had opposed him and Eteocles, is to be left unburied and unhallowed. Antigone, the elder daughter of Oedipus, defies this edict, and the remainder of the play *Antigone* explores the tragic consequences of her defiance and Creon's insistence.

From one standpoint, what Sophocles has dramatized in *Oedipus Tyrannos* is a purgation ritual in which the hero, having freed the city from the dragon of death, becomes himself the center of pollution, radiating a plague of sterility and sickness (see the Priest's description of the plague in his opening speech) that only his scapegoat sacrifice can cure. The play thus carries a rich cargo of religious and anthropological significance. But seeing the primary meaning of the play only in an underlying ritual structure is as reductive in its way as trying to make the Freudian Oedipus complex account for Sophocles' complex Oedipus. Though tragedy and other kinds of drama probably developed from ritual and still draw on reservoirs of human feeling also tapped by ritual, the greater sophistication and artistry of drama and the linguistic and scenic power articulating these feelings and generating others must also be accounted for. Thus while we should by no means ignore the ritual dimension of drama, we should no more substitute ritual for drama than we would a moan of grief for an elegy.

For one thing ritual is not especially noted for its irony, but Sophocles' play is freighted with it, the title itself, as Bernard Knox has pointed out, being a network of ironies. The Greek word *tyrannos*, usually translated as either king or tyrant, actually means neither. The term king implies the orderly succession of rule, primarily through lineal descent, and the term tyrant implies despotic rule; but *tyrannos* refers to the ruler who has acquired power on his own hook through force, intrigue, or as in Oedipus' case intelligence—a self-made ruler who may or may not be despotic. The irony lies in the fact that while Oedipus is a *tyrannos* by virtue of his own riddle-answering talents the action of the play leads him to discover that as the son of Laius he is also king. This same sort of irony invades Oedipus' name, which means swollen foot, in reference of course to the injuries caused by the pinning of his feet in infancy. *Oidi* meaning "swell," however is nearly identical to the Greek *oida*, which means "I know," and knowing is the means by which Oedipus became *tyrannos*. His intellectual victory over the Sphinx dominates the consciousness both of Oedipus himself and the citizens of Thebes throughout the play. (The student should glance through the play noting the extraordinary number of times the phrase "I know" finds its way into Oedipus' language.) But if we accept the punning identity of *oida-oidi* the result is a fusion of *oida* and *pous*, or "I know-foot," whereas it is precisely why his foot is mangled that Oedipus does not know.

So too with the celebrated imagery of sight. A play that presents so horrible an image as that of Oedipus emerging from his palace with eyes streaming blood raises the critical question whether this is horror for its own spectacular sake or horror somehow assimilated into dramatic form. Answering that question requires a careful examination of the imagery of seeing and of light and darkness, which of course involves comparing Oedipus and Teiresias. As the man of seeing and knowing ("I see" in the sense of "I know") Oedipus seems to reflect the Greek spirit of self-sufficient rationalism that Protagoras so confidently referred to in saying "Man is the measure of all things." Considered along these lines, the play becomes a critique of rationalism (in modern America no less than in ancient Greece) designed not to reject but to define the limits of reason by distinguishing between knowledge, or intellectual know-how, which may provide answers to the Sphinx, and wisdom, which may include an awareness that knowledge is not always beneficial, that the truth may enslave as well as set free.

Reason, logic, and the causal evolution of action are congenial to tragic plots, but the tragic mode, Oedipus discovers, also specializes in the illogic of paradox. The man who finds himself to be the husband of his mother and the brother of his children, who is both judge and criminal, physician and disease, world-renowned and world-abhorred, has experienced the collapse of the rational surfaces of reality and encountered a chaos within. Harrowing as it is however, that encounter is also an achievement, and the suffering Oedipus undergoes upon seeing the truth is not more pitiable than is his insistence on seeing it ennobling. In a world shaped at least in part by the mysterious forces with which the oracle is in contact Oedipus transcends the role of blind victim by shaping his own form of awareness. Though fated to perform certain acts, he is not, as Sophocles has chosen to dramatize the myth, fated to discover what he has done. His tragedy lies less in killing his father and marrying his mother than in his courageous search for a knowledge that can only bring him suffering. Thus though Yeats' remark about heroism applies to most tragic heroes, it has special significance for Oedipus: "Why should we honor those who die on the field of battle? A man may show as reckless a courage in entering into the abyss of himself?"

MACBETH

Apart from *The Comedy of Errors, Macbeth* is Shakespeare's shortest play. That is appropriate because a major concern of this tragedy is to explore the lock-step inevitability with which consequences follow from a fatal act, and by compressing his dramatic structure Shakespeare intensifies this sense of inevitability. But if the play has linear compression it also has a kind of vertical expansiveness. In the first brief scene we are introduced to the witches. Chanting prophetic verse on a heath tormented by thunder and lightning, they "look not like the inhabitants o' the earth," Banquo says, "And yet are on't" (I.iii.41-2). Though much has been written to explain the witches, explanations are rather beside the point. Whatever our beliefs or those, if we knew them, of Shakespeare and his Jacobean audiences, the dramatic function of the witches is to establish the range of the play's fictional universe, which extends literally from hell to heaven. The witches put us on notice that reality has been released from its usual confines in this play and that a certain imaginative free play on our parts is necessary. Norms of cause and effect, fact, and credibility must be suspended. No instruments of measurement will register Banquo's presence at the banquet, tell us what happened to Lady Macbeth's mysterious children, or account for the presence of the third murderer (III.iii). In short Shakespeare has woven into the fabric of *Macbeth* patterns of mystery and surreality that will not abide our analysis.

The supernatural not only adds imaginative range to *Macbeth* but provides points of moral reference that help up evaluate characters and actions. After the witches have delivered their first prophecy, for instance, Banquo reminds Macbeth that sometimes

> *The instruments of darkness tell us truths,*
> *Win us with honest trifles, to betray's*
> *In deepest consequence.*

> (I. iii. 124–26)

Banquo's remarks accurately forecast Macbeth's experience when, aligning himself with the "instruments of darkness" ("Let not light see my black and deep desires"—I.iv.51), he murders Duncan only to discover ultimately that his own death is an unavoidable consequence of that act. If Macbeth's values are clarified by his association with the instruments of darkness, those of the Scots exiles are too when they gather under the aegis of England's saintly king and become instruments of divine force:

> *Macbeth*
> *Is ripe for shaking, and the powers above*
> *Put on their instruments.*

> (IV. iii. 237–39)

With powers both above and below involved, it is evident that human action in *Macbeth* occurs within a universe of exceeding sensitivity and responsiveness. Nothing takes place quite in isolation. The morning after Duncan's murder Ross glances at the murky sky and says,

> *Thou seest the heavens, as troubled with man's act,*
> *Threatens his bloody stage.*

> (II. iv. 5–6)

This basic moral division in the play between the divine and the demonic is reinforced at every turn by symbols and images; the student would do well to identify and analyze as many of these as he can isolate, beginning perhaps with such examples as light and dark, water and blood, fertility and sterility, growth and decay, natural and unnatural.

This moral division does not mean that *Macbeth* is reducible to a melodramatic confrontation of good and evil in the form of heroes and villains. Macbeth himself is far more deeply dyed in evil than Shakespeare's other tragic heroes; but in a world founded on paradox, where as the witches claim "Fair is foul, and foul is fair," we would not expect the hero to be exempt from complexity. Like most tragic heroes Macbeth combines good and evil, guilt and innocence so thoroughly that a keen sense of moral discrimination is required if we are to assess him justly. By the same token a Lady Macbeth who can callously dismiss the murder of Duncan by saying "what's done is done" (III.ii.12) but whose dreams later on are racked by the thought that "what's done cannot be undone" (V.i.90–91) is hardly a stereotype of evil inviting us to respond with snap moral judgments.

Lady Macbeth's lines just cited illustrate the prominence in this play of the concept of act, deed, thing done. As we pointed out in the "Introduction to Tragedy" at the beginning of this book, tragedy normally proceeds from act to suffering to understanding. *Macbeth* obviously traces this sequence: the act of murdering Duncan produces the profound anxiety that Macbeth seeks to put to rest with subsequent murders that lead him ultimately to realize the full and damning implications of what he has done. In a sense however Macbeth is never more deeply sensitive to moral issues than prior to the murder when he weighs his ambition against the prohibitions of conscience, duty, justice (I.vii.1–28). He is fascinated at this point with the nature of action itself, its timing, its consequences, its irreversibility—

> *If it were done when 'tis done, then 'twere well*
> *It were done quickly.*

The word "done" reverberates through these lines with a kind of ceaselessness, as though giving the lie to his hopes even while he voices them: The deed, generating as it does a sequence of reactions, will never be quite done. The inconclusiveness of action is further underscored by Macbeth's inability to say "Amen" immediately after the murder. Macbeth is responsible for three main acts in the play: the murder of Duncan, of Banquo, and of Lady Macduff and her son. Does the fact that Malcolm and Donalbain, Fleance, and Macduff escape on these three occasions have a bearing on the theme of the inconclusiveness of action?

An act is performed in time and in space. Consider the theme of time in *Macbeth*. At one point prior to the murder Macbeth can think of time as reassuringly transitory: "Come what come may,/Time and the hour runs through the roughest day" (I.iii.146–47). When he responds to the news of his wife's death with his famous "Tomorrow and tomorrow and tomorrow" soliloquy (V.v), however, his conception of time has altered considerably. The student should analyze the many references to time in the play, with special attention to differences between Lady Macbeth and Macbeth and between Banquo and Macbeth. Consider also the act of murder in relation to its spatial scene. Before the murder Macbeth's castle is associated with "heaven's breath" (I.vi.5); as he girds himself to perform the murder Macbeth verbally transforms the castle and even the world into a place of horror (II.i.49–60); and after the murder the Porter associates the castle with Hell (II.iii.1–28). The scene of the murder, though, is not merely Macbeth's castle; it is also Scotland and ultimately the many dimensioned universe of which we spoke earlier. Is there, as with the castle, a coalescence of scene and act at these further ranges? Does the murderous act transform Scotland and the universe also?

But perhaps of greatest interest is the way in which the act and its agent interact. Macbeth is the agent who brings the act into being, but the act also brings Macbeth into being in that it imparts an identity or character to him. When the murder is done (though far from finished, as we know) Macbeth says "To know my deed, 'twere best not know myself" (II.ii.72). What he has done has created an identity that he cannot bear to acknowledge. Thus the immediate effect of the murderous act is to stifle self-awareness, to make life endurable only at the cost of moral and spiritual oblivion. His subsequent murders are accompanied by an increasing numbness of thought and feeling, a willful dehumanization as Macbeth thrusts into deeper and deeper regions of consciousness his awareness of what he is. Action becomes possible only by bypassing the mind and conscience: "The very firstlings of my heart shall be/The firstlings of my hand" (IV.i.147–48). But it is typical of tragic heroes that the courage to see—even though what is seen is appalling—triumphs over the self-protective desires that dominate ordinary men. That this is true of Macbeth helps rescue him from the nontragic category of the hero who, because he cannot recognize values beyond the borders of self, dwindles into demonism or becomes fortified in evil.

PHAEDRA

Like most of Racine's tragedies *Phaedra* derives from classical sources, its main events and characters coming from Euripides' play *Hippolytus*. But as he explains in his preface to *Phaedra* Racine has by no means taken his function to be that of a mere imitator. Thus as the changed title would suggest Phaedra is given a prominence in Racine's play that she did not have in *Hippolytus*, where she appears in only two scenes before dying in midplay. Racine also notes that to bring his play in line with propriety he has lessened the purity of Euripides' Hippolytus by having him betray a weakness in falling in love with Aricia (who did not appear in *Hippolytus*), and he has ennobled Phaedra somewhat by having the idea of accusing Hippolytus come from Oenone rather than herself. Racine has also eliminated the goddesses Aphrodite and Artemis—whose appearances at the beginning and the end of Euripides' play provide a structural frame—and the chorus of Troezenian ladies.

Despite the disappearance of the chorus *Phaedra* is a neoclassic work consciously modeled on the form of Greek tragedy, much as Milton modeled *Samson Agonistes* after Greek tragedy. Hence Racine's employment of the "dramatic unities" of time, place, and action so often ridiculed by critics as arbitrary and unnatural. It is true that many neoclassic dramatists with little talent and much respect for rules turned out absurdly contrived plays, such as Joseph Addison's *Cato*; but Racine manages to conform to the unities with such ease and naturalness that their presence passes almost unnoticed Not merely that; under his control the unities and the neoclassic form in general impart a distinctive character to Racinian tragedy. Perhaps this is best described in contrast to Shakespeare.

Turning from Shakespearean to Racinian tragedy is a bit like turning from epic to lyric. In the Shakespearean form action shifts back and forth from main plot to subplot, scenes change from one country to another, time gaps are frequent, the number of characters is large, and the tone is not exclusively tragic but also comic or satiric on occasion. Tragedy of this sort embraces a great range of human experience; but what it gains in scope, it tends to lose in concentration. Just the reverse is true of Racine's tragedies. The manifold levels and variety of action in Shakespeare gives way in Racine to a simple, highly compressed structure of events, a scaffolding of bare incidents designed to exhibit an inner psychological and emotional intensity. Whereas the whole course of Macbeth's tragic career is presented from the beginning, the action of *Phaedra* commences *in medias res*, well along in the plot, in the approved Aristotelean fashion. Reading *Phaedra* is therefore a bit like reading an expanded last act of a Shakespearean tragedy.

The neoclassic form of *Phaedra* gives the play an air of order and balance, acting as a rational envelope or boundary restraining the play of emotional energy in the characters. The play's form is not however merely an artificial outside container but also an *in*forming element that coalesces with and helps shape Racine's tragic vision. His beginning *in medias res* for example, quite apart from merely curtailing the scope of presentation, contributes certain meanings to Phaedra's experience. By giving the action a momentum it would otherwise have to generate on its own, it augments the sense of inevitability with which the tragedy evolves. Corollary to this, beginning at an advanced point in the action also suggests the inescapable constraints that constrict the range of human freedom. Contrast *Phaedra* with *Macbeth* in this regard. Because Racine begins his play with Phaedra's fatal love for Hippolytus already in full career, whereas Shakespeare begins his play with Macbeth's ambition not yet in evidence and with the murder of Duncan unimagined, Phaedra appears already to have lost a freedom of choice that Macbeth has not yet exercised; he stands on the edge of a cliff from which she has already plunged.

In this respect dramatic form reinforces thematic import, for Racine's play repeatedly sets forth a view of man as victimized by forces from within and without. When Freud said that the poets discovered the unconscious long before he did, he might have been thinking of Racine, who finds men's destinies shaped less by the conscious forces of reason, will, and conscience than by ungovernable passions. Phaedra suffers from a love that is not so much a desire of the mind as a disease that invades the whole person: "She dies in my arms," Oenone says, "of an ill that she conceals" (I. 147). And of Hippolytus' love for Aricia, so contrary to filial duty and political wisdom, Theramenes speaks in similar terms: "You are dying from an ill which you would hide" (1. 137). Even Theseus' six month imprisonment in the earth, which plays a crucial role in the tragic sequence, results directly from the "unwise passion" of his friend Pirithous (III. 230–51).

It would seem then that the motive force in the play is an irrepressible passion that in expressing itself creates a web of incrimination from which no one escapes. Racine's tragic vision appears to suggest that, as George Meredith's sonnet puts it, "We are betrayed by what is false within." But Phaedra is doubly betrayed, from without as well as from within. Though unlike Euripides' *Hippolytus* the play does not directly exhibit the gods, their shadow falls over the action. The hereditary curse on the women of Minos—Pasiphae, Ariadne, and Phaedra—goes back in Cretan myth to Minos' flouting of the will of Poseidon (Neptune), which should remind us that the sea-monster that destroys Hippolytus is also associated with Poseidon. Phaedra's passion, as she well knows, is generated as much by Venus as by herself; and her pathological sense of personal contamination is partly guilt originating within her and partly shame deriving from her awareness of outside ancestral disapproval. In the play's imagery of light and fire, the fiery passion within subjects Phaedra to the flames of Minos' judgment and to the exposing light of Jupiter the sun.

In addition to being dominated by passion and the gods, Phaedra is prey to a malign concatenation of accident, coincidence, and mistakes. Twice she is thrown into the company of Hippolytus by the oblivious Theseus, being brought to Troezen in the first place and then being left there in her husband's absence. The ill-timed report of Theseus' death prompts her to reveal her love, and his equally ill-timed return transforms that indiscretion into catastrophe. Able for awhile to resist Oenone's urgings to accuse Hippolytus unjustly she then misinterprets his expression when he enters with Theseus (III. 180), assuming from his grave looks that he intends to expose her, and so authorizes Oenone to proceed. And finally, when she is prepared to exonerate Hippolytus, her good intentions are perversely intercepted by Theseus' revelation that Hippolytus loves Aricia.

With this stress on internal passions and external gods, on family curses, mistakes, and adverse coincidences, the student may well feel that Racine has loaded the dramatic dice against Phaedra from the start. Is she really a tragic heroine or merely a victim of cosmic persecution? Victimization is incompatible with tragedy emotionally, since it draws only on pity; morally, since it oversimplifies in its focus on the evil outside man; and intellectually, since it specializes in blind suffering. *Phaedra* is more complex. Racine's heroine does not merely suffer a passion inflicted on her by Venus; she commits herself to her passion and acts in terms of it, thus transcending the role of pathetic victim. Nor is evil represented as outside the pale of human responsibility; Phaedra is not just the innocent pawn of evil gods and untoward circumstances but the guilty agent of Hippolytus' destruction, "neither completely guilty nor completely innocent," as Racine says in his preface. If we feel that at the end of the play she fails fully to declare her independence in guilt from Oenone, still in committing suicide she is executing justice on herself.

Phaedra confronts a world in which the range of human freedom is severely limited. Caught between contraries that are mutually exclusive, she can choose and act only with reluctance and sense of loss. This curtailment of action however does not entail a reduction of vision. Her mind is as restive as her passions, constantly exploring, testing, sharpening the issues that engage her. *Anagnorisis* is not limited to any one phase of her experience but is distributed throughout. Action becomes transformed into thought and feeling. Unable freely to do, she suffers. But her suffering is far from the unexpressive helplessness of the persecuted, it is an active encounter, a debate of the spirit in crisis, rendered with the eloquence of an inflamed and brilliant imagination.

SAMSON AGONISTES

In his preface on "that sort of dramatic poem which is called tragedy" Milton makes it clear that his dramatic sympathies lie with the classical Greek playwrights Aeschylus, Sophocles, and Euripides and his critical sympathies with Aristotle. Thus though the play was not designed to be acted on stage it observes many of the conventions of Greek tragedy and disregards most of those of English drama. Most obvious perhaps is the presence of the chorus, an unsinging chorus to be sure but one that serves like those in Greek plays, in *Oedipus Tyrannos* for instance, both to separate and to mediate between us and the tragic hero. Again, Milton maintains a consistently serious tone throughout the play; though the Harapha episode offers a few ironic moments, there are no drunken porters as in *Macbeth* or witty gravediggers as in *Hamlet*. Also as in Greek tragedy, the scene of violent suffering—the murder of Agamemnon, the blinding of Oedipus, the fatal chariot ride of Hippolytus, the destruction of the temple by Samson—occurs offstage. And finally, Milton shapes his play in terms of the "dramatic unities" which neoclassic critics derived (and to some extent invented) from Aristotle's *Poetics*: the unity of action, which is single because there is no subplot; the unity of time, since events occur within one day; and the unity of place, since everything occurs at the prison at Gaza.

It might appear that Milton has deliberately and somewhat unreasonably cramped his artistic freedom by following classical models. Isn't it a foolish form of pedantry, for instance, to have the scene of suffering occur offstage as the Greeks did when, after all, the play is not intended for the stage in the first place? However, before dismissing Milton as a pedant we ought to consider whether he is using the convention conventionally, passively acceding to its authority, or creatively, exploiting it for his own special purposes. Samson's toppling of the pillar is not merely violence but violence that occurs at a specific point, a culminating point in Samson's long and painful spiritual development. There is a sense then in which Samson may be said to have earned the distance that Milton now puts between him and not only the Chorus and Manoa but ourselves too. And that distance, which Milton so expertly manipulates—playing off the foreground of Messenger, Manoa, and Chorus against the background events in the temple, approaching those events by way of the ordinary human perspectives of the Messenger and returning us to ordinariness by way of tragic greatness—serves Milton's tragic purposes perfectly, especially his aim of inducing catharsis. By filtering Samson's final actions through the Messenger's report to Manoa and the Chorus, Milton lets his final focus fall on those whose role is not to act but to react and whose reactions undergo a series of subsiding modulations toward "calm of mind, all passions spent."

Some critics have found the play unsatisfactory even on its own classical terms. Samuel Johnson for instance claimed that although it "has a beginning and an end which Aristotle himself could not have disapproved" the play must "be allowed to have no middle, since nothing passes between the first act and the last, that either hastens or delays the death of Samson." By the "middle" Johnson refers to the scenes featuring Manoa, Dalila, and Harapha, scenes in which he feels there is a lack of significant action. Until the end of course there is very little physical action in the play, especially we might feel in a play whose hero is famed for feats of physical strength.

Milton's reply to the charge of lack of action might begin with an analysis of the word *agonistes*, which originally meant a contestant, as for instance an athlete who participated in the games at Olympia. Gradually however the word acquired "interior" connotations; the agony of body became a metaphor and ultimately a name for agonies of mind and spirit —hence Christ's "agony" in the garden of Gethsemane. In the lexicon of the Church *agonistes* gradually came to mean one who suffered for God and Christ, an athlete of the spirit.

In Samson's blindness and tormented labor at the mill there is more than enough agony of body. But his suffering is clearly less physical than spiritual, as his opening remarks suggest. If we think of *praxis, pathos,* and *anagnorisis* as the key phases of tragic form, *Samson Agonistes* is a play centering in the pathos and anagnorisis phases. Samson begins in suffering and ends in understanding, and the movement from the one to the other, which takes place in those middle scenes that Johnson criticized, constitutes a subtle and sustained action. It is an action conducted on many fronts, most of them internal—psychological, intellectual, moral, spiritual. But the internal action prepares for the final physical act. Each of Samson's encounters in the middle of the play is itself an *agon,* or contest, that tests his inner reserves and builds his understanding of his situation, its causes, and himself.

After the departure of Harapha the Chorus makes a distinction between heroic action, which results in victory over others—"When God into the hands of their deliverer/Puts invincible might" (1270–71)—and heroic patience, which results in victory over self—"But patience is more oft the exercise/Of Saints, the trial of their fortitude" (1287–88). The Chorus at this point is uncertain which of these two ways will be Samson's; but in the final event the way of the saint fuses with the way of the hero—heroic patience leads to and unites with heroic action. The collaboration of patience and action is emblemized by that moment of inwardness when Samson stands with head inclined "as one who prayed/Or some great matter in his mind revolved" (1637–38) before summoning the strength that topples the pillars.

The destruction of the Philistine enemy by Samson's final act lends the ending of the play a triumphant aspect that may not seem in keeping with tragedy. But as we mentioned in the "Introduction to Tragedy" tragic endings are never simple, never merely depressing or pessimistic; there is always a complex tension between the hero's descent into death and his ascent toward truth, and his death itself usually is qualified by a sense of victory-in-defeat. The banishment of Oedipus frees Thebes of its curse; the death of Macbeth liberates Scotland from his tyranny; the death of Samson becomes a national victory for the Israelites. But the national victory does not blot out the individual sacrifice any more than the fact that Samson has fulfilled himself as God's athlete and will no doubt benefit from divine grace blots out the magnificently human ways in which that fulfillment was achieved.

RIDERS TO THE SEA

Coming to *Riders to the Sea* from *Phaedra* and *Samson Agonistes* is a descent from rarefied artistic atmosphere to familiar terrain; it may even seem like a movement from art to life. Part of the difference results from the shift from stylized verse to idiomatic prose. Not that there is anything drab or ordinary about Synge's prose. It is as rhythmic and lyrical itself as most verse, full of arresting images and singing phrases. And yet it manages by means of homespun diction and colloquial expressions to seem as unaffectedly natural to the Irish peasants of the play as the surf on the rocks below Maurya's cottage.

But the realism of the play is more than linguistic. In part it comes from our felt sense of the grain and texture of life in the Aran islands, our sense of entering a world fully furnished with concrete details—of shirts stiffened with salt spray, dripping oilskins, the odor of bread dough, darned stockings, clean white boards against grey walls, and in the distance always the soughing of the surf. In *Phaedra*, on the other hand, this sort of thing is quite absent. We have only the vaguest notion of how the characters are dressed, of where they sleep, of what food they eat, of how the land looks; such matters are almost beneath their dignity. Phaedra works out her destiny within herself, psychologically and spiritually, not by interacting with a world outside.

Just the reverse is true in Synge's play, and appropriately so. We need to experience intimately the coastal life of the Aran Islanders because it is the nature of that life itself, rather than the nature of the characters, that summons disaster. What that implies is that *Riders to the Sea* is not only a realistic but also a naturalistic play. That is, realism as a form of literary presentation is neutral; it holds no brief as to the way things operate in life. But naturalism presents us with a realistic treatment of a world governed by some form of mechanical causality. A simpler way of putting it is to say that in naturalistic works man is essentially a victim of his environment, of life. He is molded by nature, society, economic systems, the family, biological drives, and so forth. In naturalistic "tragedies" the hero is destroyed by some such force. Which is of course the case in *Riders to the Sea,* where the sea combines with a bleak, impoverished way of life to kill, one by one, the husband and sons of Maurya.

A play that stresses man as a victim of external forces will inevitably tend to minimize human action, simply because man is conceived of not as acting but as being acted upon. Thus in *Riders to the Sea* there is a strong choric quality to the main characters. Like the Chorus in *Oedipus Tyrannos,* whose role is not to engage in the action of the play but to respond to it—to feel and comment on it—Maurya and her daughters can only react to the murderous acts of the sea. The characters cannot affect the sea, cannot alter their lives; they can only register the sea's doings and identify their own losses. Thus their only action consists in two discoveries —that the clothes in the bundle are in fact Michael's and that the body carried in at the end is Bartley.

And how, then, are we to respond to such a play of responses? *Samson Agonistes* may make us wonder whether Christianity, with its conception of salvation in heaven, is compatible with the tragic vision. We may feel at the end perhaps that tragedy is shading upward into something like a drama of triumph. *Riders to the Sea* poses a similar question from a different perspective. Does it not become, instead of tragedy, a drama of futility and despair? If we think of the tragic hero's experience as one that culminates with insight, awareness, *anagnorisis,* then we may wonder what sort of *anagnorisis* is available to a character like Maurya who suffers through no fault of her own. There is no doubting her spirit of resignation at the end of the play. "They're all gone now," she says, "and there isn't anything more the sea can do to me." Oedipus and Macbeth, on the other hand, come to a realization not of what the world has done to them but of what they have done to the world and to themselves. Perhaps we may say, then, that Maurya's *anagnorisis* consists, if not in self-awareness, in a recognition of the bleakness of the human condition and an acceptance of it nevertheless. If this is so, then we need to consider how well she understands the human situation. Do her final words, with their stress on the grace and mercy of God, take account of the implicit conflict in the play between the idea of a beneficent deity—"didn't the young priest say the Almighty God wouldn't leave her destitute with no son living?"—and our sense of a malevolent force behind the workings of the sea that does leave Maurya destitute with no son living—a force perhaps more fundamental and irresistible than God? Should we construe Maurya's Christian resignation, then, as a noble transcendance of life's ugliness or as a comforting illusion that shields her from a full recognition of that ugliness?

How one answers these questions may help determine the *kind* of play he thinks *Riders to the Sea* is; it does not necessarily affect the *quality* of the play. Whether tragic or not, Synge's drama is a powerful and moving articulation of human suffering borne with grace, of a doomed family enduring what Gerard Manley Hopkins called "the blight man was born for."

PURGATORY

As a great lyricist Yeats would not seem at first glance to have been well equipped for dramatic art. The great lyric poets of the nineteenth century —Blake, Coleridge, Wordsworth, Byron, Shelley, Keats, Tennyson, Browning, etc.—were undistinguished playwrights, and the major dramatists of the nineteenth century—Ibsen, Strindberg. Chekhov—wrote little or nothing in the way of lyric poetry. Their drama, the tradition most immediately available to Yeats, was naturalistic with the stress on realism of situation, character, and dialogue. For Yeats such drama fell into the category of "unimaginative art," which was "content to set a piece of the world as we know it in a place by itself." The lyric imagination is normally not anxious to restrict anything to "a place by itself" and usually prefers to transcend rather than imitate "the world as we know it." For drama to become imaginative art, Yeats felt, it must purify reality in the interests of artifice, creating a theater in which verse, ritual, music, and dance interdict the ordinary world so that the undistracted mind gains access to its own "inner deeps."

In the Noh theater of Japan Yeats found a dramatic form wonderfully suited to his aims. Designed for an aristocratic audience of initiates, the Noh is a highly ritualized dramatic form in which all the elements of enactment—scenery, stage properties, number of actors—are reduced to a bare minimum. The actors wear masks (they are often gods, ghosts, or demons), speak in formal prose and verse, and perform in ceremonial style. As in neoclassic tragedy—for example *Phaedra* and *Samson Agonistes*— concentration of means and elevation of style are the governing laws. Everything irrelevant having been burned away, what remains is a purified form in which each word and gesture is full of symbolic intensity.

With its two actors starkly outlined between a ruined house and a bare tree *Purgatory* obviously reflects the Noh theater. But it also reflects the lyric predispositions of its author. Its charged emotional atmosphere, dream-

like movement, brevity, and associative verse style make it a kind of dramatic analogue to the lyric poem. The plot of the play is spare, less an
involved sequence of specific incidents and actions than a frame in which
phases of imaginative apprehension may be exhibited. As the play opens,
an old man tells a boy to "study that house," a ruined structure once
owned, he says, by his aristocratic mother but burned down years ago by
her drunken husband, "a groom in a training stable" who wasted her
fortune and degraded her family name. During the fire (the old man tells
the boy) he stabbed and killed his father, ran away, and became a peddler,
fathering his bastard son upon a "tinker's daughter in a ditch." Now on
the anniversary of his mother's wedding the peddler hears the hoofbeats of
the past, his father riding drunkenly home once more, and as a light goes
on in the house he sees images of his parents re-enacting his own conception. His son, seeing nothing and thinking him mad, attempts to make
off with their bag of money, but the old man stops him; as they struggle
for the bag the boy suddenly sees the same images in the house and covers
his eyes in horror. The old man takes this opportunity to stab his son with
the same knife he used to kill his father. Immediately afterward the lighted
window darkens—in acknowledgement, the peddler feels, of the fact that
he has prevented the guilt and degredation of his mother's marriage from
being perpetuated through the boy, who would have "begot, and passed
pollution on." But as he cleans his knife and picks up the money, the hoofbeats commence again. Despite his actions, he realizes, his mother remains
imprisoned in her purgatory of guilt, condemned endlessly to repeat her sin.

  Yeats conceived of *Purgatory* as, in his phrase, "a scene of tragic intensity"—which is probably not the same thing as tragedy proper. Structurally
however the play traces out the tragic sequence of action-suffering-under-
standing as the old peddler murders both his father and his son and suffers
the realization of futility: "Twice a murderer and all for nothing." On
the other hand the old man would seem to lack the tragic stature of such
heroes as Oedipus, Macbeth, and Samson, all of whom dominate their
dramatic worlds in a way that he does not. From kings to peddlers is quite
a falling off. Yet this is no ordinary peddler, though in some regards he
seems less than ordinary. He has none of the social and psychological reality
of salesmen like Willie Loman in Arthur Miller's *Death of a Salesman*.
He lacks even that most basic of individualizing features, a name, and
instead of being defined by his practical relations to such things as the
house and the tree he is metaphorically identified with them: a gutted
mansion with all inner values burned out, a thunderbolt-riven tree once
full of "fat, greasy life" but now "stripped bare." In depriving the old
man of ordinary plausibility as a dramatic character Yeats paradoxically
invests him with something more, an archetypal intensity that stations
him out of time on the fringes of reality, in at least tenuous contact with
the supernatural, as Oedipus, Hamlet, Macbeth, and other more dignified
tragic heroes are. Like Hamlet the old man inherits a polluted world and
seeks through a murderous act to purge the present and the past. Like most
tragic heroes too he is a divided personality, shaped both by the patrician
influences of his mother's family and by the vulgarity of his father. Thus

as the final stage direction indicates he can both clean his knife, a gesture that symbolizes his impulse to purify corruption, *and* pick up the scattered money, a gesture that associates him with his grasping father and with his son, in whom the groom's materialistic grossness has recurred in intensified form. As that recurrence would suggest, the old man and the boy are both victims of the pollution passed on through his mother's marriage—a kind of genetic deterioration analogous to the role of the family curse in Greek tragic cycles like the *Oresteia* of Aeschylus and the Theban plays of Sophocles. Short of killing himself the old man has done what he can to purge the consequences in others of his mother's transgression (see lines 38–39); but the cycle of remorse and sin in his mother's dream continues nevertheless. Like most tragic heroes he comes to acknowledge the limits of human aspiration—"Mankind can do no more"—and in so doing to discover his own identity newly defined in guilt, misery, and remorse.

DESIRE UNDER THE ELMS

With the opening words of O'Neill's play, Eben's "God! Purty!" it is clear that we are no longer in the tragic realms of Sophocles, Shakespeare, Milton, or Racine. It is not just a matter of passing from poetry to prose; we are at some distance from the prose of Ibsen too. In many of his other plays of this time, the mid-twenties, O'Neill's dialogue runs to rhetoric and uncontrolled prolixity; in *Desire* it has been disciplined to a monosyllabic economy that at its best has a naturalistic rightness for its characters and at its worst loads the grunt with an excessive burden of meaning. Though there is some question whether language reduced to this level of crudity can convey the complexity of value and meaning we associate with tragedy, whether it is an instrument capable of presenting more than rudimentary insights and feelings, nevertheless it can generate considerable intensity and a sense of elemental passion.

Using the term grunt above is not merely derogatory; it accords with a pervasive theme of animalism that runs through the play, beginning with the stage direction after Eben's opening words: "His defiant, dark eyes remind one of a wild animal's in captivity." Imagery of animals in captivity is frequent in "naturalistic" literature. As a literary program naturalism attempts, as realism does, to reproduce actual life with documentary accuracy; but naturalism goes beyond the philosophically neutral recordings of realism to invest life with a distinctive character in which the principle of determinism plays a central role. Men's lives, like all of life, are not, as in the medieval metaphor, journeys on an open road but treadmills in a cage. If man once thought he shaped his own fate by the exercise of reason and the observance of moral laws, he is now the victim of environmental forces—the harsh conditions of earthly survival, the economic and social pressures of society—and of inner needs generated by these outside conditions—his appetites for food, sex, and as this play emphasizes, property. Because no radical distinction exists between man and other animals, as was once thought—all of nature being trapped in this deterministic cage—animal imagery becomes a means of defining the human plight.

It is not hard to find evidence of naturalism in *Desire Under the Elms;* in fact the title itself stresses the longings and drives that impel men, sometimes against their will, toward ends that are often irrational. The phrase "dog eat dog," a slang version of Darwin's "survival of the fittest," echoes again and again, not merely to underscore the competitive viciousness of the Cabots' behavior, but to remind us that this is the condition of life in general. Life is a jungle inhabited by predators, such as Cabot, Abbie, and Eben, and by those they prey on, such as Eben's mother and his two half-brothers Simeon and Peter. But in a larger perspective, predator and prey are equally preyed on by life itself. Thus when Eben accuses Cabot of having killed his mother, Simeon replies, "No one ever kills nobody. It's allus somethin'. That's the murderer." If only "life" kills, then men are not responsible; murderer and victim are equally innocent. Eben rejects this view, at least as it would apply to Cabot: "I hold him t' jedgment." In a play whose plot hinges on crime and punishment the issue of justice and human responsibility looms large.

In a deterministic world all men are in bondage. The dehumanizing mechanism of economic slavery has reduced Simeon and Peter to beasts of burden—they are "bovine" and "like two friendly oxen" in the opening scene. Bondage takes many forms. Abbie has moved from one form of domestic enslavement to another. Cabot is enslaved by his conception of an austere and demanding God Who is inseparable, like Cabot himself, from the rocky land. Eben is enslaved by the memory of his mother, by his obsessive desire for vengeance against Cabot, and of course by sexual desire ("Nature'll beat ye, Eben," Abbie says when he takes a step toward her "compelled against his will").

To be enslaved is, in a sense, to be a possession of someone else, to be owned. To become one's own man, acquiring ownership over oneself, is to be free, and most of the characters are striving for freedom. Simeon and Peter appear to escape from slavery, but though they depart capering they have probably only acquired the freedom to enslave themselves in new ways in California. As Abbie says of her supposed freedom after her first husband died, "I diskivered right away all I was free fur was t' wuk agen in other folks' hums." Permanent freedom from slavery, from being merely someone else's possession, can be achieved only by becoming a possessor oneself. So, at least, most of the characters feel to begin with. Thus "desire" in the play initially centers on ownership of the farm. Ownership of property is a sophisticated economic version of the devouring impulse of animals. As he leaves the farm, Simeon taunts Cabot by saying of Eben, "He'll eat ye yet, old man!" And to Eben, Abbie's sexual appeal seems merely another weapon in a dog-eat-dog world: "Ye're aimin' t' swaller up everythin' an' make it your'n. Waal, you'll find I'm a heap sight bigger hunk nor yew kin chew!" Most of the disastrous misunderstandings of the play stem from an underlying fear that human motives can never rise above their animalistic origins—that kill or be killed, own or be owned, are the only laws operative in the world.

Nevertheless, out of slavery, conflict, and misunderstanding certain freedoms are achieved. Eben's Oedipal hatred of Cabot and his obsession with his mother's need to be revenged are at least temporarily surmounted in Part II, Scenes III and IV. The stage direction "mechanical" applied to Eben's behavior stresses the psychological conditioning that has kept him in robotlike bondage, but from which he is released when he transcends incestuous desires by accepting Abbie not merely as a mother-substitute but as a woman in her own right. In his next encounter with Cabot (Part II, Scene IV) Eben is no longer consumed with hatred; his mother's restless spirit and his own impulse to revenge are quieted. Abbie too achieves a transcendance of her acquisitive impulse—the desire to possess the farm which had been her hope of escaping from economic bondage—when she voluntarily sacrifices both her child and her hope for security in order to convince Eben of her love. But the costs of disregarding the survival of the fittest principle run very high indeed. Eben too disregards that principle at the end, rejecting selfishness in favor of "sharing" Abbie's guilt, an act that draws Cabot's grudging comment: "Purty good—fur yew!"

If there is an *anagnorisis* at the end of the play, then, it would seem to center in the notion that men can rise above a strict determinism and in acts of free will like Eben's not merely acknowledge but claim the right to be responsible for their lives and deeds. The price of such a claim here, the claim to be morally free, is paradoxically imprisonment and perhaps death, the usual price of tragic action which not even tragic insight can gainsay.

ANTIGONE

Normally at the opening of a tragedy we expect to find ourselves swept emotionally into a current of action, an absorbing world of rather larger-than-life characters whose destinies compel our imaginative participation. From this standpoint the opening remarks of the Chorus in *Antigone* appear to detract from the tragic character of the play. No attempt is made to present an illusion of life, to persuade us of the at least imaginative "reality" of the experiences before us. Instead Anouilh deliberately disengages our emotions by reminding us that this is not life at all but an artificial imitation, a play. This breaking-of-the-illusion is a standard technique of comedy, where a certain emotional distance is prerequisite to amusement, laughter, affective security. But Anouilh's use of this technique is more complicated. In the first place the technique is made to serve a tragic function by introducing a sense of inevitability to the action. The girl who plays Antigone is already committed to playing Antigone. By the time we see her she is beyond choice. Whatever identity she may have had before making her choice has disappeared; she is now merely that "thin little creature sitting by herself," oppressed by the knowledge of what she is about to be—a tragic heroine. So it is with all the other characters, who as soon as they enter into their roles are fated by the plot of the play to be as they will be and to do as they will do.

In the second place, if the illusion-breaking device calls our attention to the separateness of life and drama, that is necessary. As the Chorus says at its second entrance, "Tragedy is clean, it is restful, it is flawless." That is precisely why tragedy is found only in literature. The dismaying, frightening, agonizing experiences we call "tragic" in real life are never clean or restful and certainly not flawless, because life, as the Irish playwright Samuel Beckett says, is a "mess" in which the grand and the trivial, the absurd and the meaningful, the fatuous and the profound interpenetrate. These experiences are "tragic" only in metaphor; or perhaps we could say that they are "pre-tragic" in that from their welter of chaotic experience a tragic dramatist might through selection and transformation shape a drama that is clean, restful, and flawless.

Finally, Anouilh's Chorus is appropriate because its remarks do define our relations as audience to the tragic events. Paradoxically, we are invited into the play by being excluded from it. That is, though each of the characters is fated to play his particular role in the drama, not all of the characters are pulled into the tragic vortex. Antigone is jealous of her role as tragic heroine. When Ismene wants to join her in dying, Antigone rejects her: "You don't think I'm going to let you die with me after what I've been through? You don't deserve it." She tries to keep even Haemon from participating in her experience, partly from love perhaps but partly also from possessiveness, a desire to hug her role to herself. For the most part, she has no difficulty separating herself from others. The Nurse is absorbed in her own trivial complaints; Ismene is not really interested in dying; the Guard at the prison simply ignores her when she says "I'm going to die soon." The only person who probes her motives and in a sense shares her trial is Creon, who represents all she detests; and at the end, after all that has happened, Creon remains detached, heading for his council meeting. In short, Antigone's tragedy takes place in isolation; she is a tragic actor on a bare stage beyond which are seated the other characters, indifferent spectators of her ordeal. And outside this inner circle of spectator-characters is the audience in the theater, no less detached and indifferent presumably, watching an actress playing Antigone. At the end the audience will depart, like Creon, for its separate versions of his council meeting, a world of minor responsibilities and major compromises. Still, if the audience can depart like Creon, then it too must have played a part in the play. If we do not identify ourselves with the heroine, then we identify ourselves with the nontragic characters in the play who are detached from her too. Thus by being outside, as it were, we are inside the play.

However, we may not want to be inside the play quite as Anouilh has maneuvered us. The Nurse, Ismene, the Guards—the spectator-characters are largely summed up in Creon, whose confrontation with Antigone constitutes the moral and intellectual center of the play. The confrontation provides the means to *anagnorisis* for both of them. Creon, the politician devoted to compromise as a mode of survival, has no time for grand tragic gestures. Moral extremism of Antigone's sort is politically awkward; it must be reduced to the level of manipulable ordinariness where most human conduct takes place. To this end he redefines her defiant act in light of the debasing facts of sham religious rites, of her brothers' worthlessness, and of the unidentifiable body. Antigone, realizing that her death has been rendered meaningless, capitulates. Seeking to persuade her of the value of living, Creon has a tragic moment of his own when he compares himself as a young man—his mind then, like Antigone's, "filled with thoughts of self-sacrifice"—to the shabby person he has since become, an advocate of "happiness"; "Not much of a word, is it?" he adds. His conception of happiness—a life of creature comforts gained at the cost of truth and dignity—revives a sense of tragic purpose in Antigone. If Creon's earlier facts convinced her that dying is pointless, his "happiness" now convinces her that living is equally pointless. With nothing to die for and nothing to live for, she embraces the sheer hopelessness of her plight with something like relief.

Once Creon's "happiness" is introduced the dramatic conflict centers not in the obligations of religion and family as against those of the state and its laws but in Creon's and Antigone's contrasting attitudes toward life. Owing to the extremity of this contrast in attitude, when the play was first performed in wartime Paris it aroused violent disagreement, some people feeling that it glorified the resistance movement, others that it counseled collaboration with the Nazis. Neither view is correct, since the play is hardly a political tract—nor is it an editorial on what in the 1970s is called the "generation gap" (though it is inevitably pertinent to both). For Antigone revolt and rejection have the status of moral law: "I want everything of life, I do; and I want it now! I want it total, complete otherwise I reject it!" A consuming idealism that has its heroic appeal, to be sure. On the other hand:

> I will *not* be moderate. I will *not* be satisfied with the bit of cake you offer me if I promise to be a good little girl. I want to be sure of everything this very day; sure that everything will be as beautiful as when I was a little girl. If not, I want to die!

The almost foot stamping petulance of this may persuade us that there is something after all—not everything but something—to Creon's principle of compromise. If Creon will sacrifice everything to survive, Antigone will sacrifice everything to fail; she has a passion for defeat, setting her sights on an ideal world of impossible purity.

A question that must confront the student of tragedy is whether *Antigone* wins its way through to tragic meaning or lapses into a cry of despair. If Antigone seems to have shrugged off her original motives and come to embrace the concept of romantic revolt in itself, if she is affirmative at least in her commitment to saying "no," has her death then become meaningful? Or must we deny meaning to her because of her words written to Haemon from prison and subsequently scratched out: "And I don't even know what I am dying for"? How does her death differ from that of Eurydice, Creon's wife, whose "smile is still the same" in death as it was in life—the implication being that a life devoted to a garden, preserves, and sweaters cannot really end because it has never really begun? If all the deaths are meaningless, Creon, who survives, seems to have won—Creon and the guards whose view of everything is summed up in the phrase of the Chorus, "It's no skin off their noses." But to win and to survive are not, except in Creon's logic, necessarily identical. Like Antigone, who says "We are of the tribe that ask questions, and we ask them to the bitter end," Anouilh's play raises questions of enduring complexity to the bitter end also, questions that dissolve that artificial barrier that the Chorus sets between the audience and the play and make us full participants in its action.

DATE DUE

MAR 1 5 '75			
FE 1 8 '80			
MR 2 '8			
APR 1 '86			
APR 17 '8			